Experiencing Music – Restoring the Spiritual

Series Editor

JUNE BOYCE-TILLMAN

PETER LANG
Oxford · Bern · Berlin · Bruxelles · Frankfurt am Main · New York · Wien

Experiencing Music – Restoring the Spiritual

Music as Well-being

JUNE BOYCE-TILLMAN

PETER LANG
Oxford · Bern · Berlin · Bruxelles · Frankfurt am Main · New York · Wien

Bibliographic information published by Die Deutsche Nationalbibliothek.
Die Deutsche Nationalbibliothek lists this publication in the Deutsche Nationalbibliografie; detailed bibliographic data is available on the Internet at http://dnb.d-nb.de.

A catalogue record for this book is available from the British Library.

Library of Congress Control Number: 2015951515

ISSN 2296-164X
ISBN 978-3-0343-1952-2 (print)
ISBN 978-3-0353-0801-3 (eBook)

Hochfeldstrasse 32, CH-3012 Bern, Switzerland
info@peterlang.com, www.peterlang.com, www.peterlang.net

This publication has been peer reviewed.

Printed in Germany

This book is dedicated to my good friends
Sir John Tavener and his wife Maryanna

Contents

Acknowledgements

This book has taken at least twenty years to write. It started with a PhD from the Institute of Education, London University; many people, both professional colleagues and personal friends, have helped me along the way. I am extremely grateful to the *Philosophy of Music Education Review* which has published many of my ideas over a period of time in a series of articles; its conferences enabled me to refine these ideas – in particular thanks to my friends Estelle Jorgensen and Iris Yob.

Another place where refining of the ideas has taken place is the Early Childhood Music Education Seminar of the International Society for Music Education with the help of my good friend Carol Scott-Kassner; all of these people encouraged me to write this book. Panos Kanellopoulos also made some very insightful comments on the paper I gave at the Philosophy of Music Education Conference in New York in 2013, which are included here.

A further area of exploration has been writing for liturgical contexts which enabled me to examine the effect of context on spirituality and here I am grateful to many feminist friends who have been prepared to experiment with me (Boyce-Tillman 2014). Collaboration with Kay Norrington and the Southern Sinfonia has enabled me to develop experimental large scale pieces. Stainer and Bell published my collection of hymns (Boyce-Tillman 2006c) and allowed me to use them in this book. Olivier Urbain and the music and peace-making group informed my work on Values. Finally the access to Winchester Cathedral as a performance space is due to the Very Rev James Atwell whose view of the cathedral as a place for everyone has informed not only the access that he gave to so many different groups of people but also the spirit in which that access has been granted. I am grateful to Elizabeth and Stanley Baxter at Holy Rood House, Centre for Health and Pastoral Care, Thirsk, Yorkshire where many of the initial ideas were interrogated.

This book is dedicated to Sir John Tavener and his wife, Lady Tavener. It contains many rich fruits from my friendship with them. It is hoped that at the University of Winchester – from which Sir John held an honorary doctorate – we shall, in association with Winchester Cathedral, launch the Tavener Centre for the Study of Spirituality and Music, with a programme of regular concerts, festivals and conferences.

I am also grateful to Petra Griffiths of the Living Spirituality Network and the forming of the group interested in the Spirituality of Music within that organisation.

In the production of this book I am grateful to Oliver Osman for his proof reading skills, to Hannah Ward for helping me with the index and to my personal assistant, Charlotte Osman. The University of Winchester provided research support; my colleague Dr Malcolm Floyd helped me to develop the earlier ideas in this book and Dr Olu Taiwo contributed a great deal to my understanding of the place of the beat in orate drumming traditions. Dr Sarah Morgan's thesis on the community choir also informed my thinking on orate singing traditions. Professor Elizabeth Stuart, Professor Joy Carter, David Walters (and other colleagues in the Winchester Centre for the Arts as Wellbeing) and Dr Simon Jobson have supported my work in a variety of ways. At North West University, South Africa, I am grateful to Hetta Potgieter, Liesl van der Merwe and Dirkie Nell for their continued encouragement and opportunities to share my work.

Many friends have helped and encouraged me along the way, especially the Rev Wilma Roest, the Rev Bill Scott, the Rev David Page, Sue Lawes, Dr Carol Boulter, Professor Mary Grey, Professor Michael Finnissy, Ianthe Pratt and Myra Poole. I am very grateful to Lucy Melville at Peter Lang for her encouragement in setting up the series *Music and Spirituality*, in which this book sits. I am grateful to my two sons – Matthew and Richard and my granddaughter, Scarlett – some of whose stories appear in this book – for their continued encouragement of my creative enterprises.

The Rev Dr June Boyce-Tillman MBE FRSA FHEA Professor of Applied Music, Artistic Convenor for the Centre for the Arts as Wellbeing, University of Winchester, Extraordinary Professor North-West University, South Africa.

Figures

Introduction

This book represents a journey through experiences in a variety of classrooms and lecture halls, studies of the mystical experience, religious music by women composers, especially Hildegard of Bingen, the philosophy of Michel Foucault, feminism and ecotheology, interfaith dialogue through music-making, the Anglican priesthood, creating and performing one-woman multi-disciplinary performances and composing and conducting large pieces for young people with a variety of other ensembles represents an interdisciplinary weaving together of philosophy, theology, music (as approached by musicology, ethnomusicology and music therapy), hymns, poetry and musical practice in the form of a crystallisation project (Richardson 2000). I have gradually moved towards this methodology and way of presenting; it sees truth as a crystal with different facets acting as lenses to reveal different aspects of it:

> Crystallization combines multiple forms of analysis and multiple genres of representation into a coherent text or series of related texts, building a rich and openly partial account of a phenomenon that problematizes its own construction, highlights researchers' vulnerabilities and positionality, makes claims about socially constructed meanings, and reveals the indeterminacy of knowledge claims even as it makes them. (Ellingson 2009 p. 4)

The structure I have chosen for the book starts with a Prelude, which is complete in its own right and uses Greek mythology and Christianity as the basis of a process of interrogation of the principles and practices that underpin music in Western cultures.[1] This book is essentially a journey into the musical experience drawing on my own musical autobiography. My grandfather was the local dance band pianist in a New Forest village

1 This was originally given as part of a keynote panel at the International Society of Music Education Conference in Thessaloniki, July 2012.

and played mostly by ear; but he wanted his granddaughter to enter the world of classical music (epitomised by his 78rpm recording of Jose Iturbi playing Chopin's *Fantaisie Impromptu* which I listened to with him many times). I was too young when he died to realise what I had missed by not learning his skills.

I moved through experiencing this rural music scene to initiation into the classical tradition via the examination system of the Associated Board of the Royal Schools of Music. From there I entered Oxford University where I had a grounding in the musicology of the 1960s. The degree consisted of history and analysis with written pastiche composition in the style of composers from 1550–1900. This was a place where sexist jokes were the common currency of the lecture hall and, in general, unquestioned by men or women; more significantly it taught a limited range of musical values linked with musical literacy and European traditions I have spent the rest of my life expanding my musical horizons and value-systems. My education was immediately followed by a time spent learning folk guitar at Cecil Sharp House and wandering around London singing Bob Dylan and Malvina Reynolds in an experimental period that represented an embracing of musical freedom not found in my classical instruction. I have spent the rest of my life expanding my musical horizons and value-systems.

I went to work in schools – first primary and then secondary – breaking new ground in initiating composing/improvising in the classroom. All this time, I was observing the children's musical understanding carefully. When my own children were born I observed very young children's musical development. These times led me deeper into the musical experience. My research (which included a PhD at London University's Institute of Education) has enabled me to present a more inclusive model of musicking in parallel with other thinkers such as Christopher Small (1998), George Odam (Paterson and Odam, 2000) and John Paynter (1970).

Meanwhile I was involved in liturgical music at a parish level and was seeing the part that music plays in people's spiritual experience. I was also experiencing musical healing traditions which have a spiritual dimension. This book does not deal with the history of the relationship between religious traditions and music nor the complex relationship between various healing traditions, spirituality and music which I explored in *Constructing*

Musical Healing: The Wounds that Sing (2000a). This is simply a detailed exploration of the way the relationship between a person and musicking functions using ideas from process philosophy. Rowan Williams postulates a relationship between religious and artistic sensibility in its 'affirmation of inaccessible perspectives' (Williams 2012 p. 14), although he states that you cannot quite assimilate aesthetic and spiritual discourses (Williams 2012 p. 17). John Millbank sees humanity as a poetic being. He calls the human capacity for meaning-making poeticity, which aligns human creativity with the divine art of the eternal Word (Milbank 1997 p. 79). This book explores this relationship in more detail including an interlude on Christian theology and music. Certainly music will be linked with the process of meaning-making. However, I leave it to the reader to decide whether what I have called 'spiritual' is, in fact, the aesthetic.

In the last twenty-five years I have attempted to gather together in my songs and hymns insights from theology and musicology (Boyce-Tillman 2006c). Because for most of pre-Enlightenment Europe the majority of 'high art' music was written for the Church, the 'objective' underpin of much musicology can be laid at the door of the notion of God as constructed by mainstream theologians during that period (Boyce-Tillman 2014) – as male, all-powerful, hierarchical, perfect and unchanging. As a Higher Education lecturer I have had more time and pressure to think and reflect on the experience and explore the literature.

This book reflects that journey in various idiosyncratic ways and therefore may not include the literature that others would consider central to such a journey. It is an exploration of the musical experience by means primarily of observation, experience and interview. I build on the philosophy set out by John Dewey in his seminal text *Art as Experience* (1934); in this he sees the aesthetic as residing primarily not in the music itself, but the relationship between the musicker and the music. I draw on disciplines that have often been excluded in musicology such as anthropology, therapy, politics, sociology and liminality. In this way it challenges approaches to music that concentrate exclusively on a set of canonic musical texts and seeks to interrogate the so-called aesthetic principles on which this approach has been based. In this context I will use Christopher Small's (1998) term 'musicking,' a verb that encompasses all musical activity from composing to performing to listening-in-audience to singing in the shower. Using Gregory Bateson's ecology of mind (1972) and a Geertzian (1973) thick description of a typical concert in a typical symphony hall, Small (1998) demonstrates how musicking forms a ritual through which all the participants explore and celebrate multiple relationships.

In this search I have been joined by many other people exploring the entirety of the experience rather than a limited part of it. To that end, a variety of purposes have been fulfilled:

- The valuing of orate traditions including Western community music making
- The inclusion of women's contribution to music-making traditions
- The establishment of a spiritual dimension of music making which is not limited to pieces with sacred text or intention
- The understanding of the potential of the idea of spiritual but not religious in the context of nation states that have banned religion from the public sphere
- Person-centred approaches to music making
- The validation and encouragement of a greater variety of ways of knowing, including those that challenge the Cartesian split in Western society and its concentration on rational ways of knowing

The rest of the book follows the plan of the Prelude unpacking its ideas and working it out in more detail. The chapters start by exploring the journey of the soul in Western culture from ancient Greek thought and practice to contemporary semi-secularised society. It interrogates the common contemporary descriptor – spiritual but not religious. Here I describe the development of a spirituality based on process rather than the dogmas and creeds of the defined world religions. The second chapter concentrates on the development of the idea of creativity as an example of where spiritual concepts still exist in contemporary thought revisiting the ideas in Chapter One from a different perspective. The third chapter starts by looking at models of the musicking experience encompassing the ideas of Chapters One and Two; it leads to the development of the phenomenographic/crystalline map that will be explored for the rest of the book. A First Interlude drawing on Shakespeare's play, *A Midsummer Night's Dream*, forms a bridge to the second section of the book exploring the nature of the Spiritual/ liminal space and its transformative potential.

The next four chapters explore the four domains of the musical experience identified in the model – the environment, the self, the debating of ideas and cultural values. A second interlude looks at Music and Christian theology. This is followed by a chapter exploring the fusion of these domains into the Spiritual/liminal experience. As such, this book explores how musical meaning is constructed in lived experience and sees it as essentially relational, contextual and potentially changing. The musical experience is seen as one of encounter through a variety of musicking activities such as listening-in-audience, performing or composing. The model (phenomenographic map) attempts to show how this might work. Bearing in mind that each model has a purpose and cannot encapsulate every aspect of anything, its intention is to represent an ecology of music:

> Ecology is the study of *the relationships* between organisms and there environments … within the framework of ecology, autonomy is therefore an impossible state: organisms and environments are *always* in a condition of mutual dependence; to isolate either one is to destroy the whole and with it any hope of understanding it *as* a whole. (E Clarke 2005 p. 132)

In two further chapters I use a number of case studies to show how the model might work as a tool for musical understanding, particularly in the domain of Values. The final chapter concentrates on two projects that I have initiated to show how I have used the model to develop my own practice. It shows how values based on a reworking of an ecclesiological model have underpinned my thinking and been worked out in my own musicking. It postulates the possibility of creating radically musically inclusive events. These final chapters may also serve to see music as a potential strategy of resistance to the dehumanising effects of the fragmentation within Western culture. The Postlude revisits the themes of the Prelude and Interludes to examine the spiritual dimension of the musical experience and its potential. I hope that this will enable readers to gain a deeper understanding of their own use of music in their lives and also the potentially transformative nature of the musical experience.

PRELUDE

And Still I Wander ... through Greek Mythology and the Idea of the Soul

The Greek Myths

This Prelude is based on three Greek myths – those of Psyche, Hermes and Orpheus – which I am going to use to illuminate the way we see music in Western culture. The first one is that of Psyche and Eros.

> Psyche was a mortal woman of extraordinary beauty, truth and goodness whom Aphrodite wished to wound; she sent Eros to carry out her wishes by making Psyche fall in love with a monster in a mysterious castle. It did not go according to plan; for the interface between Greek gods and humans often went awry. Eros fell in love with Psyche; but gave her one condition that she would not to discover his identity by looking at his face. Because of this, she was separated from him. However, Psyche could not bear this and found out that it was Eros – the god of love – that she was to marry. In order to re-unite with him, she was set four tasks to complete. The first was to sort a room full of seeds; the second was to obtain a golden fleece from fierce rams. Then she had to fill a glass from the waters of the River Styx. Finally she had to go to Hades to retrieve a beautiful box. In some versions she opens this box and is again forced to wander (although in some she succeeds and becomes divine).

I see her still wandering through Western culture as a symbol of the loss of soul/spiritual values (Grey 1995). Everywhere material values rule – in music education, music marketing, musical performance as in other places – and we search longingly for a heart and a soul. Many people do find these aspects of themselves through experiencing music – often called the last remaining ubiquitous spiritual experience in Western culture and so the fundamental question of this book is: how can we approach music in a way that will empower people to recover the spiritual aspect of musicking with integrity and judgement, and use music as a growing point and source of transformation in their lives?

The Concept of Soul

What can ancient Greek culture teach us about this wandering soul? In ancient Greece the soul was referred to as breath, spirit and mind and associated with the butterfly – a symbol of transformation (Batzoglou 2011). This has continued to be an image that represents the soul right up to the present day. For the early Greek Orphic philosophers (Claus 1981) it was associated with the deepest feelings and imagination. In Plato it became an eternal entity made up of intellect (logos), passion (thymos) and desire or appetitive (epithumia).[1] Aristotle saw it as the form of the living body, the entire organism's active functioning. So it became the totality of experience in which conscious and unconscious elements of the mind are manifest within the body – the totality of being. Olympic religion never spoke of the soul through dogmatic formulae but as a vital force in everything (W. F. Otto 1955 p. 15) – the collective soul of the world – anima mundi. If we could rediscover this notion in contemporary society, it would have huge implications in the area of peace, understanding and reconciliation between cultures.

The polytheism of the ancient Greeks allowed for a more diversely interactive view of the divinities' interaction with human beings. This developed into a clearer more third person view of God within monotheistic Christianity. In this later belief system dualisms developed, such as soul and body – often with connotations of good and evil. However, music was seen as a key part in spirituality/religion in the writings of figures like the twelfth-century Abbess Hildegard von Bingen:

1 In my model explained later these are subsumed in Construction, Expression and Values.

> Music is the echo of the glory and beauty of heaven. And in echoing that glory and beauty, it carries human praise back to heaven. (Van der Weyer 1997 p. 79)

This was still true in the seventeenth century with writers like Sir Thomas Browne:

> There is a musick wherever there is a harmony, order or proportion, ... even that vulgar and tavern Musick, which makes one man merry another mad, strikes in me a deep fit of devotion and a profound contemplation of the First Composer. There is something in it of Divinity more than the ear discovers; it is an Hieroglyphical and shadowed lesson of the whole world and creatures of God ... In brief, it is a sensible fit of that Harmony, which intellectually sounds in the ears of God. (Harvey 1996 p. 7)

As religion in Europe lost its power, there was a loss of interest in the animating power of life; the arts became secularised and demoted to mere entertainment.[2] The Cartesian split reinforced the body/mind dichotomies implicit within Christian thought. However, the Romantics like Schiller often looked back to the ancient Greeks for their model of the unity between humanity and nature most clearly expressed in Schiller's poem *The Gods of Greece* (quoted in Charles Taylor, 2007 page not available).

At the end of the nineteenth century Nietzsche declared God dead and the anima mundi became identified as aspects of a culture which carries on today in the idea of memes (Blackmore 1999). Chief among these for Nietzsche were the concepts of Apollonian and Dionysian. Dionysus, Greek god of theatre, wine and ecstasy, Nietzsche viewed as suppressed in Western culture and revealed by journeys to the underworld where dark, primordial, irrational, or unconscious functions of experience resided. Apollo (associated with higher civilisation, music, healing, prophecy and law) he related to reason, harmony and beauty (Huskinson 2004 pp. 16–18). Nietzsche saw theatre as integrating these elements (Luchte 2004) and, in particular, tragedy. It is perhaps limited by Nietzsche's time when the merger and juxtaposition of comedy and tragedy in Greek drama had been forgotten (Hyers 2007). There is a transcendent quality given to this integration for the resulting union is seen as 'beyond'. The

2 Although the original meaning of the word entertainment was to nourish.

integration of these apparently opposing elements became inspirational for both dramatists and visual artists. Nietzsche associated music with the Apollonian. However, I will argue that by rethinking the musical experience in its totality, it too has the capacity to integrate the Apollonian and Dionysian aspects – the personal and archetypal, mind and body – the mysterious and the rational.

In Europe the psyche found a new place in the developing field of psychoanalysis (D. Muir 2000 pp. 237–8) which even acquired Psyche's name in its title. Jung defined the psyche as the totality of the unconscious in the face of a culture that was focussing concentration on the consciousness of the ego:

> The unconscious is not simply the unknown, it is rather the *unknown psychic*; ... so defined the unconscious depicts an extremely fluid state of affairs: everything of which I know, but of which I am not at the moment thinking; everything of which I was once conscious but have now forgotten: everything perceived by my senses, but not noted by my conscious mind; everything which involuntarily and without paying attention to it, I feel, think, remember, want and do; all the future things that are taking shape in me and will sometime come to consciousness; all this is the content of the unconscious. (Jung 1991 p. 95)

The unconscious was everything 'I feel, think, remember, want and do' (Jung 2004 p. 61). The myth of Psyche still fascinated thinkers. C.S Lewis's *Till we have faces* (1956/80) used it to address the complexity of loving. Derrida in his reading (1987 in Derrida and Kamuf 1991 p. 204) explored psyche (a French word for a mirror) as self-reflection. These texts reflect the century's location of the soul within the human unconscious. In art it was occasionally personified, but gradually the Greek anima mundi became related to human motivation (Vitz 1979) and more abstract. Composers' accounts of their inspiration become located in the unconscious (Harvey 1999 p. 71) rather than in some in a divine realm:

> Such musical journeys into the land of the unconscious and subconscious are so numerous in the contemporary music scene ... with sounds which leave no doubt that those seas and deserts and landscapes are all symbols of that inner landscape which reveals itself to the meditator. (Berendt, Joachim Ernst quoted Hamel 1978 pp. 134–5)

Deep in Greek philosophy and the Pantheon were the unities of The Good, The True and The Beautiful (personified in Psyche) but gradually over the course of European history these have been fractured:

- The Good – morality
- The True – authenticity
- The Beautiful – objectivity

Aesthetics after the Enlightenment became subjective expression for its own sake, with nothing auratic about it. Subjectivity, objectivity and morality become separated, and music lost its ancient Greek telos for fusing together The Good, The True and The Beautiful. Western classical traditions could develop notions of being value free[3] (no longer concerned with The Good) and objectivity (views of The Beautiful, often culturally limited) held sway in musical judgement. Subjectivity[4] (The True) became marginalised in traditional musicology as the discipline attempted to accommodate rational/scientific views of truth; the auratic was dismissed as superstitious. Now part of self-actualisation the musical experience could be seen as the last remaining place for the soul in Western society (Hay 1982, Hills and Argyle 2000). In Maslow's hierarchy of human needs (Maslow 1967) he included the aesthetic – the need for beauty, order, symmetry. It was placed immediately below self-actualisation with its peak experiences which included characteristics previously associated with the soul – such as an intense experience of the present, concentration, self-forgetfulness, a lessening of defences and inhibitions, empowerment, trust, spontaneity, and a fusion of a person with the world. It fitted well with notions of self-actualisation that came from American psychologists like Carl Rogers (1976) that came from inner exploration.

3 Here value-free is associated with no longer concerned with moral or ethical judgement around its context or intention as we shall see later.

4 Here subjectivity is defined as being concerned with the emotional, feelingful and intuitive life, where personal authenticity lies.

The Soul in Western Music

So what of Psyche have we lost in this view of music? What is still wandering around Western cultures seeking a home? The psychologist, Antonio Damasio describes Descartes' error as separating thinking from the body; he re-asserts 'being' as the essence of what it is to be human; thinking becomes simply a consequence of being (Damasio 1994 p. 248) not the very essence of our humanity. The so-called Cartesian 'error' has governed the development of Western education (Claxton, Lucas and Webster 2010) and this has coloured the way in which music has been conceptualised which is very different from its conceptualisation in the Europe of the Middle Ages (Boyce-Tillman 2000b). Guy Claxton (2002) identifies four characteristics that define the restoration of the psyche to our educational experience. If these are restored in our education systems they may start to be re-conceptualised within living itself. The first is an unusually strong sense of *aliveness* characterised by a heightened sense of vitality, clarity and strength of perception. The second quality he calls *belonging* – a sense of being at home in the world – which is a restoration of anima mundi. 'Attitudes of suspicion or competition are replaced with what appears to be an unforced inclination towards kindliness and care ... compassion, love' (Claxton 2002 unnumbered pages).

This challenges the place of competition in the world of music-making and hints at the restoration of The True – Values – to music making. Nel Noddings calls for an 'ethic of care'. She calls for an education of 'moral sensibilities', which is clearly an attempt to restore notions of The Good into education and calls on education to develop *human responses* (Noddings 2003 p. 163) to counter a culture of competition and war. The third quality Claxton calls an affinity with *mystery* – 'a curious, almost paradoxical sense that all is well with the world'. This is part of Turner's liminal state in which security in opinions and beliefs is replaced by an interest in the paradoxical nature of truth (Boyce-Tillman 2005a) and subsequently open-mindedness and inquisitiveness replace fundamentalism and dogma. Jonathan Harvey links this with music:

> The more we concentrate on the music *itself*, the more we *become* the music in *participation mystique*, with full consciousness, the more we sense its true nature to be the play of ambiguity and unity: 'one knowing'. (Harvey 1996, p. 9. Author's italics)

This calls for some restoration of a sense of the auratic – call it god, gods, the Great Spirit, or whatever is deemed appropriate in a particular context. Creativity becomes as important as success with its sense of delight and heightened sense of trust and spontaneity. Fourthly, Claxton identifies an enhanced *peace of mind* – the shedding of mundane anxiety and confusion. This Prelude maintains that musicking can transport us to a different state:

> What then does aesthetic experience mean for Dewey? Together with aspects of artistic doings and contextualism of this doing, the aesthetic aspect of experience means a qualitatively different, fulfilling and inherently meaningful mode of engagement in contrast to the mechanical, the fragmentary, the nonintegrated and all other nonmeaningful forms of engagement. (Westerlund 2002 p. 191)

Psychagogia

We can interrogate this search further through the lens of the Greek figure of Hermes – inventor of the lyre and the original psychagogue – the leader of souls from the Underworld. Hermes was characterised as managing change, love and reflexivity. Psychagogia was part of ancient Greek dramatic practice developed by Aristotle in relation to Greek tragedy (Aristotle 1992 p. 197 [Aristotle, *Poetics* 1450a33]) and was related to rhetoric. This was seen to move the human soul to understanding and empathy. Plato in *Phaedrus* described good rhetoric as the art of leading the soul by means of words performed with love – love of the forms and love of those to whom the rhetorician speaks (McCoy 2007).

In theatre psychagogia was associated with change (the butterfly image) in the psyche of the spectator (Arnott 1991 p. 79) – a move towards reflection. Within Greek society the actor is seen 'as a kind of mouthpiece for powers beyond control whose role is to enchant the listener' (Easterling and Hall 2002 p. 354). Theatre was part of the treatment at the sanctuary of Asclepius, the god of healing where it was seen as expanding the mind through dreaming (Hartigan 2009) – a valuing of the intuitive. It was deeply grounded in the notion of self-reflexivity – 'the awareness of our existence which involves the ability to stand back and look at life' (Grainger 2004 p. 6). Aristotle drew on Socrates to use it in relation to education – the educational art of leading the soul to a dialectical examination of The Good (D. Muir 2000) – one of Socrates' three components of Truth – The Good, The True and The Beautiful. The end of education was to enable the sense that The Good is to come from within the person not from an external authority. His conception of love included three levels – one for the person or object itself, another of a generic type and the third the transcendent 'being which truly is' (D. Muir 2000) which goes beyond the individual:

> [T]he movement of two souls toward each other, and then together toward knowledge of the good, constitutes not only a binding friendship but also the process of mutual education of the two friends. This mutual education culminates, ultimately, in these friends' participation in the philosophical (and according to Socrates, the best) life. (D. Muir 2000 p. 240)

Education's role was to develop *ethos* which was created by the actor (*ethiopos*) who had the skill to explore *mythos* – the metaphysical, irrational, and spiritual.

This concept of spirituality as uniting The Good, The True and The Beautiful continued in Europe in morality, education, religion, the arts and mysticism until the rationalism of Descartes and Darwin pushed it aside. In my concept of the spiritual, the psyche is restored to its meaning of integrating conscious and unconscious, rational and intuitive – The Good, The True and The Beautiful. Music draws people because of its psychagogic qualities (Cook 1998):

> The starting-point [of music education] must be how we (and that includes you and me) actually—use, internalise, or otherwise care about music, whether by going to concerts or discos, relaxing to it in the sitting-room, or whistling it at work ... This insight has been a driving force in the dramatic changes that have taken place during recent years in academic thinking about music. (Cook 1998)

Yet musicology today stays with the rational elements of music such as theory and history. Reimer (1970) defines the 'practical, religious, therapeutic, moral, political and commercial' aspects as nonmusical. Widening approaches to the philosophy of music, drawing on Dewey (1934), have called for more holistic approaches to music education which see the meaning of a musical experience composed of many interacting parts:

> The aesthetic in the arts needs to be examined in the *continuum* where every consummatory phase of experience, a normally complete experience, is aesthetic in its primary form, and in which aesthetic experience in art is an *intentionally cultivated development* of this primary aesthetic phase. (Westerlund 2002 p. 191. Author's italics)

The birth of somaesthetics represents another attempt to bring at least the body into the concept of the experience (Shusterman 2008) which embraces a diversity of forms of knowledge, social practices, cultural traditions, value systems and bodily disciplines to understand how this might be done.

I am going to use the phenomenographic/crystalline map (Marton and Booth 1997), that I have developed from numerous accounts of the musicking experience (Tillman 1987, Boyce-Tillman 1996, 2000a, 2007a, 2009a) to retrieve some of the wandering parts of Psyche and investigate how teachers may become psychagogues. This postulates that the spiritual experience is one based on the musicker establishing a relationship with the four domains in musicking – the Materials, the Expression, the Construction and the Values (see Figure Four).

The Four Domains of the Musical Experience

This will be dealt with in much greater detail as the book progresses. Music consists of organisations of concrete Materials drawn both from the human body and the environment which will be explored in more detail in Chapter Four. These include musical instruments of various kinds, the infinite variety of tone colours associated with the human voice and the sounds of the natural world as available in different locations. Choices here will also dictate musical pitches and rhythms available with their associated motifs and melodic and rhythmic patterns. The relation to the whole body is often ignored. Carl Orff saw this as a significant element in the musical experience (Hamel 1978 p. 18):

> Elemental Music is never just music. It is bound up with movement, dance and speech, and so it is a form of music in which one must participate, in which one is involved not as a listener but as a co-performer. It is pre-rational, has no over-all form, no architectonics, involves no set sequences, ostinati or minor rondo-forms. (Orff quoted in Hamel 1978 p. 18)

The ethnomusicologist, John Blacking, linked it with dance:

> If there are forms intrinsic to music and dance that are not modelled on language, we may look beyond the 'language' of dancing, for instance, to the dances of language and thought. As conscious movement is in our thinking, so thinking may come from movement, and especially shared, or conceptual, thought from communal movement. And just as the ultimate aim of dancing is to be able to move without thinking, to be danced, so the ultimate achievement in thinking is to be moved to think, to be thought ... essentially it is a form of unconscious cerebration, a movement of the body. We are moved into thinking. Body and mind are one. (Blacking 1977 pp. 22–3)

The close relation to the natural world is similarly ignored along with the acoustic space (Abrams 1996, Boyce-Tillman 2010). And so the linkage of this area to the material of the wider cosmos – the anima mundi – has been lost.

We could transform ecological understanding at a stroke if we taught all our violin students to open their violin cases and honour the tree that gave its life for the instrument. In traditional societies, the process of making an instrument involved a reverence towards, for example, the tree that gave its wood for the making of the drum, and the player would regard him or herself as continually in relationship to that tree every time the instrument was played. Our industrialised society with its production lines for musical instruments dislocates the connection between the natural world and the materials of sound. The role of instrument maker is dislocated from the roles of composer and performer.

The acoustic space[5] is an important part of the Materials of music. Composers for ancient cathedrals knew that each building accentuated certain tones and wrote their pieces with this in mind. There is now a return to including the venues in the natural world for musical performances including the natural sounds found in them as part of the piece. Composers like Pauline Oliveros have demonstrated their concern for acoustic space by recording in spaces like the old cistern used for her CD entitled *Deep Listening* (Oliveros 1989).

The domain of Expression – explored in Chapter Five – is where the subjectivity of composer/performer and listener intersect to provide facets of The True. The truth of the experiences of the composer/performer and listener interact here to give a variety of truths derived from the interplay between the intrinsic and extrinsic. Whatever the intention of one party (the intrinsic meaning) may have been, others in the process of listening/composing/performing will bring extrinsic meaning to the music – meaning that has been locked onto that particular piece or style or musical tradition because of its association with certain events in their own lives or their own enculturation (Green 1988, 1997). This has often been downplayed by classical theorists (Rahn 1994 p. 55) but this is where the hidden aspects of personality or psyche reside. It includes qualities of being where identity resides (Westheimer 2003). Here is a domain where insights from music therapy can be used differently in the context of education:

> The facilitation of the process aims towards a deeper inner self-exploration rather than therapeutic attendance of the participants' psychopathological needs. This relationship is interpersonal and inter-psychic, happening verbally or non-verbally with the whole group and each individual separately. (Batzoglou 2011)

It is in the domain of Construction – explored in Chapter Six – that the Academy often concentrates in its pursuit of The Beautiful. Effectiveness

5 Michael Deason Barrow describes how he started as a cathedral chorister in the 60's. He describes himself as a Wiltshire bumpkin who was shot very quickly into cathedral singing in which he developed a sense of the spiritual that was to last for a lifetime. The beautiful acoustic space of the cathedral played a significant part in this.

in this domain usually depends on the right management of repetition and contrast within a particular idiom. The way in which contrast is handled within a tradition – how much or how little can be tolerated – is often carefully regulated by the elders of the various traditions. However, the emphasis in musicology has been on the composers and theoreticians of the Western classical tradition rather than the master drummers of Yoruba traditions with the result that orate musical cultures have been subjected to the principles of the Western classical canon (Goehr 1992) usually to their detriment – and the concept of The Beautiful, became limited and confined. It has meant the marginalisation of improvisatory elements with their delight in spontaneity, play and the carnivalesque (Bakhtin 1993, Boyce-Tillman 2012a) and their ability to unite Apollo with Dionysus.

The domain of Values – explored in Chapter Seven – reflects a search for The Good. Classical Greek literature is filled with stories embodying the potential ethical power of music (Godwin 1987 p. 45) but theorists, such as Reimer (1970), have often preferred to see individual works of art as if they were dislocated from their social context. So he did not see musical understanding as being enriched by knowing the life of the composer or the context for which the piece was composed. However, for me, the sounds of music both serve, express, challenge and create cultures:

> The sounds of music serve as well to *create* those structures, and to create them in a dialectic of perception and action *consistent* with the quintessentially symbolic character of human worlds. (Shepherd and Wicke 1997 pp. 138–9. Author's italics)

Philosophers such as Subotnik (1996) and Westerlund have attempted to restore these cultural dimensions, seeing the potential of music to create and construct social situations by attending to the ethical dimension (Westerlund 2002 p. 144). The structure of the classical orchestra and choir reflect the European cultures that produced them – ruled by benevolent dictators now embodied in a conductor but where in our music curricula is this domain discussed? Where do we discuss community building through music? A ten-year old boy started his reflections on a performance (Boyce-Tillman 2001c) that was not controlled by a single conductor and included a multiplicity of pieces by the children themselves (and therefore was not the product of a single composer) with:

> It was like peace on earth. Everyone did their own thing but it all fitted together.

Of the same performance the teachers often commented on music's ability to develop community building skills:

> It improved the children's co-operative skills. I saw them supporting one another and encouraging other schools in their work. This is unusual for our children whose poverty often makes them quite self-centred.

The domain of Values also has intrinsic and extrinsic elements. In the intrinsic area, some traditions will edge towards more democratic practices in the creation process with everyone involved in the decisions while others will be more hierarchical. Notions of intrinsic Values are a subject of debate in musicological circles (McClary 1991, 2001) but as soon as a text or story are present, intrinsic Value systems will be more explicit, such as the including of the religious narratives in sacred music. Pieces composed for a religious context will necessarily embody the Values of that tradition. Extrinsic Values are present in the context of the performance such as finance and ticket pricing. Many community musicians today are very explicit about their Values, indeed the growth of the community choir can be seen as a challenge to the dominant Values system. Musicians working in the area of cultural fusion look towards music as a route to justice and peace (Boyce-Tillman 1996, 2001a, 2007c), such as Paul Simon in his recording *Graceland* in the context of apartheid in South Africa (Simon 1994). In my own piece *The Call of the Ancestors* (Boyce-Tillman 1998) I used Western classical traditions but left spaces for improvisation by groups from other cultures – at the first performance, Kenyan drums, Thai piphat and rock group. The use of a mixture of notated sections and 'holes' in the score where improvisation could take place, enabled the traditions to be true to their underlying principles of Construction. There are many narratives on musicking with declared ethical intention but are these stories in our music curricula? This domain shifts attention from individual acts of cognition to the wider context in which musicking is situated:

> The thesis of this book is that Reimer's theory and also to some extent Elliott's theory does not pay enough attention to the actual social-cultural context of education, to the situatedness of music as experience ... My attempt has been to widen the view of music education from the solipsistic inward subjectivity or performing individual cognition to shared musical events as particular kinds of social realities in educational contexts ... The last chapters have emphasized musical events that are meant to be socially enjoyed, collectively created and communally significant. (Westerlund 2002 p. 227)

This thinking critiques research in music which concentrates exclusively on individual acts of cognition. The link with notions of community is still there in government documents in the UK with the delivery of the citizenship agenda in particular (Department for Education and Skills 2002), including religious, moral, cultural, personal, social and health issues. Reflection in this area could prepare pupils for understanding about the use of music in shopping malls, military parades and political rallies – comparing its manipulative and transformative Values, for example. Anthony Storr in his book *Music and the Mind* saw the creation of community as the main reason for the presence of music in world cultures. He sees parallels between religious and warfare rituals and Western coronations and state funerals (Storr 1993 p. 23). And within religious rituals community creation has been a prime function for music:

> Religious music adapts its sacrality and redemptive power to new cultural expressions encountered through colonialism, immigration and market forces (such as advertising or distribution systems). In this way, each contributor discloses important correspondences between religious music and other fundamental realities in the cultural world of the performers, including: patterns of history or social organization or emotion; conditions of the soul; powers of the state; histories of material production; structures of law; motivations that vitalize new generations; manifestations of ethnicity and class; models of cultural memory; and even local conflicts and forms of disenfranchisement provoked by the politics of globalism itself (as evident in global economies of music recording and distribution as well as in universalising forms of analysis). These elements and more are found in religious musics and transported within their performed expressions. (Sullivan 1997 pp. 9–10)

Spirituality

I am calling the moment when all the other domains fuse – Spirituality:[6]

> For the first twenty-five minutes I was totally unaware of any subtlety ... What did happen was magic! (Dunmore 1983 pp. 20–1)

It represents the reintegration of the body (Materials), the emotions (Expression), the intellect (Construction), the culture (Values). These moments resemble Maslow's peak experience (Maslow 1962) or Csikszentmihalyi's 'flow' (M. Csíkszentmihályi and I.S. Csíkszentmihályi 1988, M. Csíkszentmihályi 1993).

Philosophers such as Catherine Ellis (1985) have brought ethnomusicological insights into relationship with Western classical traditions to offer us insight into the Spiritual domain. She distinguishes between three levels of learning – informal, formal and spiritual/visionary which are acknowledged in aboriginal traditions (Ellis 1985 p. 200). The musickers – be they composers, performers or listeners – enter a different time/space dimension – leaving everyday reality for 'another world – the liminal space of Victor Turner (1969, 1974). I have subsumed the following states within my description of spirituality:

- flow, coming in from psychologists of creativity (Csikszentmihalyi M. and Csikszentmihalyi I.S. 1988, Csikszentmihalyi, 1993, Custodero 2002, 2005)
- ecstasy, often associated with idea of 'the holy' coming from the religious/spiritual literature (R. Otto 1923, Laski 1961)
- trance coming from anthropological (Rouget 1987), New Age (Collin 1997, Goldman 1992, Stewart 1987) and psychotherapeutic literature (Inglis 1990)

6 Later (in Chapter Eight) I shall discuss in more detail the relation of this term to Turner's term liminality which is perhaps a more secularised descriptor of this experience.

- mysticism, coming from religious traditions, especially Christianity (Underhill in Rankin 2008)
- peak experiences (Maslow 1967)
- the religious experience (Rankin 2008)
- the spiritual experience of children (Hay and Nye 1998, Erricker, Erricker, Ota, Sullivan and Fletcher, 1997, Hay, 1982, E. Robinson 1977)
- liminality (V. Turner 1969, 1974)

Drawn from an analysis of ritual (V. Turner 1982 p. 44), a 'limen' – a threshold – is crossed into a different time/space dimension:

> A limen is, of course, literally a 'threshold.' A pilgrimage centre, from the standpoint of the believing actor, also represents a threshold, a place and moment 'in and out of time,' and such an actor – as the evidence of many pilgrims of many religions attests – hopes to have there direct experience of the sacred, invisible or supernatural order, either in the material aspect of miraculous healing or in the immaterial aspect of inward transformation of spirit or personality.[7]

This liminal/spiritual space is potentially transformative (Boyce-Tillman 2009a) – recalling the Greek image for the psyche of the butterfly. Turner (2004) focused his attention on the second stage of rites of passage, the crossing of a threshold or limen to a sacred moment 'in and out of time.' He also discussed its quality of communitas – the bond that develops between pilgrims. He concentrates on a sense of intimacy and I-Thou awareness – a feeling of being united with the universe, other beings and the natural world. It is a way of knowing that is different from everyday (propositional) knowing. It is a both/and logic which may appear as a way of not knowing because its central feature is paradox (I. Clarke 2005). Tom Driver brings together a number of our themes explored above:

> One of the ways in which ritual, religion, and liberative action are alike is that they all construct alternative worlds, nourishing themselves with imaginative visions. Different from ordinary life, they move in a kind of liminal space, at the edge of, or

7 <http://www.creativeresistance.ca/communitas/defining-liminality-and-communitas-with-excerpts-by-victor-turner.htm> Accessed June 25th 2004

> in the cracks between, the mapped regions of what we like to call 'the real world'. (Driver 1998 p. 82)

Here the 'beyond' is present as the whole person or community experiences the reintegrating of themselves; anima mundi is restored.

The discipline of musicology has carefully defended its somewhat limited view of the musical experience by creating new disciplines. So the emotional elements of the domain of Expression have, in general, been shunted into the discipline of music therapy. The domain of Values, with its concern for context, became situated in ethnomusicology in order to preserve the idea that the Western classical curriculum is value-free. So to examine the totality of the musical experience we need to put together insights from Ethnomusicology, Musicology and Music Therapy. That is what the rest of this book will be about – the restoration of a holistic approach to the liminal musical experience.[8]

Conclusion

We come to the last of the Greek myths – Orpheus – often called the father of song – who used song along with Hermes' invention of the lyre to charm the birds, fish and wild beasts, coax the trees and rocks into dance, and divert the course of rivers. Can we restore this thinking to our views on music and musicking? My argument here is that we can restore psyche to our music by adopting a philosophy that includes the totality of the music experience within it, both practically and theoretically. Towards the end of his life the French social theorist, Michel Foucault, saw the need

8 Calls for this are coming from various quarters. Salazar (Salazar and Randles 2015) explains how attendance at a conference on the sociology of music education revealed how the pedagogy into which he had been initiated as a music education student based on Western classical traditions ignored totally 'the social context of music and separates learning from students' vernacular experiences' (p. 287).

for the development of a desire to reinvigorate our ethical imaginations by challenging the status quo:

> The values that sustained his work were the refusal of the self-evident, the curiosity of knowing what is possible, and the courage to seek out what had yet to be done … To live autonomously is just to refuse the given, to uncover what is possible and to have the courage to master one's life. (Thompson 2003 p. 133)

The inclusion of the domains of Values and Expression gives us the potential for reintegration of human beings within the wider cosmos in the very deepest aspects of our being – both personal and communal – like the psychagogues in drama. By including these domains in our understanding of the musical experience we unlock greater possibilities for music in the development of people's autonomy and the development of identities of integrity. It gives the possibility of music as a source of hope for humanity. It means rethinking music as process not product (Suanda 2012). Estelle Jorgensen (2008 pages unavailable) calls for a musical pedagogy related to lived life, and calls for matters of character, disposition, value, personality, and musicality to feature in pedagogical training to encourage teachers 'to think and act artfully, imaginatively, hopefully, and courageously toward creating a better world.'

If our philosophies can help Psyche re-unite with Eros, Western musickers may be closer to fulfilling their role as psychagogues. Late capitalism and neo-liberalism has invented many underworlds to keep people trapped in cultures of consumerism, inequality, addiction and control. If we can grasp the totality of music's potential these subjugated groups may have further strategies of resistance that will give them autonomy, identities of integrity and hope. Music has often played an important part in these subjugated cultures and this book may enable us to understand more fully how and why and how we may use music for our own integrity.

CHAPTER ONE

The Development of Religionless Spirituality

A Poem

Did we see that day the unseeable
One glory of the everlasting world
Perpetually at work, though never seen?
(Edwin Muir 1963) *The Transfiguration*

Introduction

I recently visited Bali. Everywhere there were signs of religious observance – offerings to the gods, the environment, people disappearing to perform the devotions, cars held up to honour a funeral procession. It was strange to see religion in a dominant position in a culture. We have already seen how the soul got lost in Western culture. The butterfly image of transformation and the notion of the soul as anima mundi have surfaced again in the developments in the area of 'spiritual but not religious'. The rising interest in spirituality is a quest for ways of knowing that have been neglected or subjugated in Western culture – a call for dissent. Evidence suggests that, although subjugated by what many describe as a secularising age, the religious/spiritual experience is still as alive and well as in previous ages (Badham 2012).

The tension around where spirituality authority resides in the Christian religious tradition appears to have been there in the very beginning of Christianity. Certain ways of thinking appear to have become subjugated at the very beginning of the story. *The Gospel of Mary Magdalene* (Marjanen 1996) reveals that she claimed her authority from the visionary experience; however, Peter was concerned at setting up the hierarchy that we associate with the Church basing it on Jesus' words 'Upon this rock I will found my church'. The tension between dogma and experience is reflected in the tussles between sapiential theology and the church authorities as in the lives of such exponents as Dionysius the Areopagite, Hildegard of Bingen, Meister Eckhart and Teilhard de Chardin.

The distinction between *spiritual* and *religious* is becoming more commonplace in advanced modern societies. Within the United States, for example, the number of people claiming to be 'spiritual but not religious' is estimated variously (but with differing empirical measures) as 14 per cent (Roof 1999) and 31 per cent (Wuthnow 2005) of the adult population, because 'studying spirituality appears akin to shovelling fog' (Bender 2010 p. 182). Anthony Palmer quotes from the Noetic Sciences review:

> A common theme is that wisdom emerges from 'inner authority' – often called 'soul' or 'spirit' – and in its purest forms is completely free of reliance on any dogma or system of belief. (Palmer 2000 p. 102)

Rowan Williams (2012) distinguishes in the contemporary mind between religion with attributes of limits, with doctrine and regulated corporate life and the spiritual associated with self-development, wisdom and loose communal structures (R. Williams 2012 p. 320). Does this rediscovery of the subjugated Wisdom tradition within Christian thought enable us to uncouple religion and spirituality? Although the rest of this chapter will deal with developing notions of spirituality generally, readers may need to apply the findings to their own personal situation, bearing in mind that this is a rapidly changing area. This is part of the seeking that is an important strand in the literature on spirituality:

> While there has been a growing normalisation of the idea that a person can be 'spiritual but not religious', this designation may actually compound the problem of intellectual embarrassment … If spirituality is to be recognised as something with ontological weight and social standing it also needs an injunction that is culturally recognised, as it was for centuries in the Christian west and still is in many societies worldwide. (Rowson 2013 pp. 42–3)

My experience is primarily in the UK, although in the last five years I have conducted a number of interviews with people working in a variety of contexts in the US about their view of the spiritual. These interviews have informed this writing as well. This chapter moves from an analysis of the rise in the usage of the term spirituality in contemporary society to an examination of the relationship between religion and spirituality. It identifies a number of different strands in the literature including seeking, different ways of knowing, plurality, the relationship between the animate and inanimate, images of the Divine, various spiritual practices, the valuing of process and the rejection of creed and dogma. Although the literature is various and disparate, a list of strands are suggested towards the end that will be used to form the links between music and spirituality.

The Confusion in Secularisation

Although in the Prelude we saw this originating in Nietzsche's statement about the death of God, Charles Taylor in his significant text entitled *The Secular Age* (2007) charts the move towards secularisation as starting with the separation of the immanent from the transcendent:

> It became possible to relate certain realities as purely 'natural', and disintricate them from the transcendent whereby it eventually becomes possible to see the immediate surroundings of our lives as existing on this 'natural' plane, however much we might believe they indicate something beyond. (C. Taylor 2007 p. 43)

He sees this process starting in the seventeenth and eighteenth centuries and as accompanied by an intensification of religious faith as a new Christianity of personal commitment increased in a secularising society that was embracing disenchantment. In his opinion, this was part of the individualisation of faith.

Theorists are gradually bringing into their models an element of the spiritual in an effort to identify the limitations in the dominant machine models of what it means to be human. Rowson calls this unease spiritual embarrassment:

> Spiritual embarrassment is grounded in confusion about human nature and human needs ... Surely religions are the particular cultural doctrinal and institutional expressions of human spiritual needs which are universal? ... Compare the designations 'educated, but not due to schooling' or 'healthy but not because of medicine.' (Rowson, 2013 p. 42)

He goes on to identify some of the problems which our current systems are not tackling effectively as spiritual:

> When you consider how we might. for instance, become less vulnerable to terrorism, care for an aging population, address the rise in obesity or face up to climate change, you see that we are – individually and collectively – deeply conflicted by competing commitments and struggling to align our actions with our values ... The best way to characterise problems at that level is spiritual. (Rowson, 2013 p. 40)

Rowan Williams (2012) describes clearly how secularism was challenged both by the violent events of 9/11 and also the rise of Islam in Western cultures. He sees this situation as problematic for both religion and the arts because of the fear of imaginative awareness (R. Williams 2012 p. 13) that might challenge dominant assumptions. He sees traditional religious institutions and vocabularies as 'carriers of those practices of facing and absorbing disruption without panic that allow imagination to flourish' (R. Williams 2012, p. 21).

This challenge has led to the rise of the term post-secular. This was invented byCharles Taylor (2007) and was taken up by Pope Benedict XVI. What Charles Taylor meant by the term is not entirely clear – whether he was pointing out that Western society never did fully secularize or that a new phenomenon is appearing. The term reflects a society which is having to come to terms with the peaceful co-existence of sacred and secular world views and a shift from seeing the religious simply as a remnant of an older world order. This is reinforced in the West by the upsurge in migratory communities with differing world views which include a notion of the sacred. It is reflected in the growth of de-institutionalised religious groups, both fundamentalist and more liberal. Habermas (2008) critiques the failure of the secularism that characterised modernity and calls for a dialogue between differing world views.[1]

So the steady rise of secularisation in the twentieth century is being challenged in the twenty-first century and has contributed to the growth of interest in spirituality.

Missing God

As we saw in the Prelude, there was an increasing marginalisation of the sacred from the Enlightenment onwards, culminating with Nietzsche's assertion that God is dead. This led to a deep sense of loss. Spirituality (Heelas and Woodhead 2005) may be seen as an attempt by Western culture to sort itself out after Nietzsche's assertion that God is dead; but Nietzsche himself realised the cost of the loss of God:

> Do we not feel the breath of empty space? Has it not become colder? Is not night continually closing in on us? Do we not need to light lanterns in the morning? (Nietzsche, 1976 p. 181)

So there is deep in our society a sense that without God we are bereft of something. This is expressed in these verses from Dennis O'Driscoll's powerful poem entitled *Missing God*:

His grace is no longer called for
before meals: farmed fish multiply
without his intercession.
bread production rises through
disease-resistant grains devised
scientifically to mitigate His faults.

1 Habermas, Jürgen (2008), Secularism's Crisis of Faith: Notes on Post-Secular Society, *New Perspectives Quarterly*. vol. 25 p. 17–29

> Yet, though we rebelled against Him
> like adolescents, uplifted to see
> an oppressive father banished –
> a bearded hermit-to the desert,
> we confess to missing Him at times … …
>
> Miss Him when the radio catches a snatch
> of plainchant from some echoey priory;
> when the gospel choir raises its collective voice […]
>
> Miss Him when a choked voice
> at the crematorium recites the poem
> about fearing no more the heat of the sun …
>
> Miss Him when we stumble on the breast lump
> for the first time and an involuntary prayer
> escapes our lips […].
> (O'Driscoll 2002 p. 29)

In the Alister Hardy project this searching for comfort is present as in these responses from Turkey:

> The most common form of religious experience reported was described as 'receiving God's help in answer to prayer or response to desperate need', closely followed by 'awareness of God's presence' or 'awareness of God's guidance in life.' (Yaran 2007)

This human need has caused a rethinking of the meaning of art, which Csikszentmihalyi sees as losing its supernatural moorings along with play and life in general:

> The cosmic order that in the past helped interpret and give meaning to human history has broken down into disconnected fragments. Many ideologies are now competing to provide the best explanation for the way we behave. (Csikszentmihalyi 1990 p. 77)

So the question underpinning this book becomes whether the musical experience, and possibly the arts in general, also provide us with this nurture? There is a possibility here that the popularity of sacred music in a secular society helps to fill this gap by restoring cultural memories of God, as we shall discuss below in relation to religious narratives.

The Story of Spirituality

The concept of 'spirituality' can be traced through Church history in connection with the Holy Spirit (Sheldrake 1998). Robert Fuller, in his book *Spiritual but not Religious* (2001), traces its roots into the nineteenth century, linking it with such movements in the US as Transcendentalism, Swedenborgianism, Theosophy, Spiritualism and Eastern Religions. Swedenborgianism was a system of philosophical and religious doctrines created by Emanuel Swedenborg, who was a Swedish scientist and theologian (1688–1772). He asserted the divinity of Christ, the spiritual nature of the universe, and the possibility of contact with the world of spirits. On the basis of this his followers built the New Jerusalem Church. Chief amongst the Transcendentalists was Ralph Waldo Emerson who in his 1842 lecture describes the Transcendentalist as believing in miracle, inspiration, ecstasy and the essentially spiritual nature of humanity (Emerson 1842).[2] He drew on Kant's use of the word transcendental which was invented to counteract the basis of the philosopher Locke's thought that there was nothing beyond sensual reality. Emerson declared that there was a class of ideas that coloured the way we viewed experience. He called these transcendental ideas 'intuitions of the mind', so saw them as belonging in the area of intuition.

Another set of roots is found in the development of Theosophy. The title of this movement brings together the Greek words for God and Wisdom and makes claim to ancient roots. It claims its origins in ancient spiritual entities who delivered to Earth an esoteric belief system. This strand, Gnosticism, stresses the independent spiritual search. The Theosophical Society was founded in 1875 in New York City by Helena P. Blavatsky (1831–91) and its central tenet was the oneness of all life, sometimes known as pantheism. It spread worldwide. From this base, Rudolf Steiner developed Anthroposophy which stresses the centrality of the human being to the quest.

2 The essay 'The Transcendentalist' is on pages 305–35. In <http://www.amazon.co.uk/Nature-Addresses-Lectures-Ralph-Emerson/dp/1150688203/ref=sr_1_1?s=books&ie=UTF8&qid=1441989754&sr=1-1&keywords=emerson+nature+addresses+and+lectures>

Alongside all of this there was an increasing interest in the occult which formed the basis of Spiritualism. This was also concerned with the relationship between spirit and matter. Central to the movement is the interest in paranormal and psychic beliefs about the existence of various spiritual entities which exist in a parallel universe and can be contacted by mediums or psychics. Their practices resemble those of traditional shamanic practice.

In 1902 William James produced *The Varieties of Religious Experience*, which became a seminal text in such areas as expanded states of consciousness, mysticism and psychic phenomena such as telepathy. His work on theories of consciousness was carried forward by organisations such as the Alister Hardy Trust with its considerable archive of writings in this area now located in Trinity St David's University at Lampeter.

The word 'spirituality' is now commonly used and much debated. Shops are filled with books on the hidden self and inner child and these nestle alongside the vitamins and herbal remedies of the health food stores. According to Fuller (2001), more people look towards New Age traditions, yoga, ecospirituality, witchcraft, near death experiences, the Tarot, astrology and neo-paganism than towards a more Christian-based religiosity for their spiritual wellbeing.

So the loss of a clear concept of the divine has resulted in a rise of diverse spiritualities from a variety of sources.

The Perennial Philosophy

Throughout the twentieth century – within the philosophy of religion – the notion of the perennial philosophy moved forward. It saw the various religious traditions as underpinned by a universal truth which is the basis of religious search, particularly in the areas of reality, humanity and consciousness. In this world view, each religion is simply a different cultural interpretation of this truth. Organised religions such as Christianity, Taoism, Buddhism, Sikhism, Hinduism and Islam are derived from this universal truth and there are traces of it in less developed belief systems. This seeking for a perennial philosophy looks for universals which were described and justified by Aldous Huxley (1945) in his book *The Perennial Philosophy*. In it he sets out a psychology that sees the soul as linked with this universal reality which is an 'immanent and transcendent Ground of All Being' (Huxley 1945 p. vii).

Huxley struggles with the absence of an ultimate Divine Reality but saw the strength of Buddhism in the concentration on the nature of the spiritual experience in which the knower, the known and the knowledge are all one. In the Upanishads of Hinduism he sees the principle most clearly expressed in the Sanskrit formula usually translated as 'That thou art':

> The Atman, or immanent eternal Self, is one with Brahman, the Absolute Principle of all existence; and the last end of every human being, is to discover the fact for himself, to find out who he really is. (Huxley 1945 p. 2)

The psychiatrist and philosopher Karl Jaspers (1883–1969) summarises the philosophy:

> Despite the wide variety of philosophical thought, despite all the contradictions and mutually exclusive claims to truth, there is in all philosophy a One, which no man [sic] possesses but about which all serious efforts have at all times gravitated: the one eternal philosophy, the *philosophia perennis*. (*Perennial Philosophy* 2012)

In 1984, Ninian Smart charted some of this landscape, attempting to define the nature of the experience in *The Religious Experience of Mankind*. The notion of a philosophy that underpins the world's faiths underpins much of the work of the Alister Hardy Religious Experience Research Centre. This was founded in 1969 by Sir Alister Hardy who had been a Professor of Zoology at Oxford. He had devoted his academic career to careful examination of the habits of marine animals and decided that he would apply the same kind of scientific and empirical investigation into the phenomenon of human religious experiencing. This he did through the following question:

> Have you ever had a spiritual or religious experience or felt a presence or power, whether you call it God or not, which is different from, or more than, your everyday self? (Rankin 2008 p. 234)

The responses form the basis of the collection of over six thousand cases of contemporary religious experiences. Robert Runcie, as Archbishop of Canterbury, saw the importance of the search and launched an appeal for the Centre in 1990. Paul Badham was for a considerable time Director of the Centre and identifies the importance of the notion of a common core:

> If it can be shown that there is a 'common core' or 'ultimate sameness' to all religious experience, irrespective of creed, race or society, this could have profound implications for the evolution of common understanding across many of the current barriers which divide people in our world. (Badham 2012 p. 19)

Badham used this concept in a number of research projects using a lengthy questionnaire for people from a range of traditions – Christians, Buddhists, Confucians, Folk Religionists, and Daoists – and in a variety of cultures including Muslims in Turkey and Hindus in Tamil Nadu. He describes the hypothesis that underpins his work:

> The pluralist hypothesis set forward by John Hick and Sir Alister Hardy predicts that religious experiencing as a human response to a transcendent Reality tend to be more comparable ... across different traditions and cultures than doctrinal systems and religious institutions ... It seems clear that there is indeed much common ground between religions at the experiential level. (Badham 2012 p. 25)

The common core project sets out to see the commonalities in the experience; this has meant concentrating on the character of this experience sometimes linked with altered states of consciousness. The belief in a perennial philosophy underpins a great deal of the work in the area of spirituality.

The Common Core

The common core is an extension of the perennial philosophy. William James (1902) was concerned with its character. He identified four characteristics of the religious/mystical experience:

- *Transient* — This refers to the temporary nature of the experience. In time the everyday state of mind will return and replace the experience which is outside normal space/time perceptions.

- *Ineffable* — The spiritual experience defies verbal expression.
- *Noetic* — There is a sense that the person has learned something of value from the experience. What is learned is something normally hidden from human knowledge.
- *Passive* — There is a sense of givenness about the experience which cannot be controlled, although certain activities such as meditation make it more likely.

Habel seeks to link religion back to spirituality (Habel, O'Donoghue and Maddox 1993) as a way of distinguishing helpful and unhelpful mystical experiences. He sees religious experiences as being beyond the natural order of the everyday; he attempts to distinguish within them psychopathological states and those induced by drugs because these are not in a religious context. Moore and Habel (1982 p. 193) do distinguish between immediate and mediated religious experiences. The mediated are obtained via mediators such as sacred objects, rituals, special people or the natural world. The immediate involves an experiencing of the divine directly without an intervening mediator.

The philosopher, Richard Swinburne in *Faith and Reason* (1981) categorises religious experiences into five kinds – two of them private and three public:

- *Public* — This centres on a meaning given by the viewer to an event that can be explained otherwise, like seeing God's hand at work in a beautiful sunrise.
- *Public* — Some event breaches natural laws like walking on water.
- *Private* — An event can be described in words like Jacob's vision of a ladder.
- *Private* — An event defies description in normal language such as a mystical experience.
- *Private* — There is a generalised feeling of the divine at work in one's life.

Classical definitions of the spiritual experience include Rudolf Otto's (1869–1937) idea of the numinous. In his book *The Idea of the Holy* (1923), he identifies two characteristics in the spiritual experience. One he calls *mysterium tremendum*, associated with being afraid and the other *mysterium fascinans*, associated with attraction and fascination. There is also a sense of contact with a 'holy other'. He sees religion as necessarily including the numinous.

The Alister Hardy Religious Experience Research Centre has pursued this exploration of the spiritual/religious experience by sponsoring research to find out how common the experience is in modern society (as we saw in Paul Badham's work earlier) and the kinds of experiences people today have. The surveys over the past thirty years showed that between 31 per cent and 49 per cent of British people claimed to have had direct personal awareness of 'a power or presence different from everyday life' (Argyle 1997 p. 2). Similar responses were found in Australia and the US (Hay 1990 p. 79). The accounts in the archive suggest that religious experiences today can be as significant to those who have them as those reported in previous centuries (Badham 2012 p. 19). The evidence is that 'for the majority of people in western society, religious interpretations of reality are not mere abstractions, but are rooted in personal experience' (Hay quoted in Badham 2012 p. 19). This confirms, as we saw earlier, that the process of secularisation has not progressed as fast as some writers would suppose.

The common core project has resulted in a number of descriptors of the characteristics of the spiritual/religious experience.

Naming the Experience

Alister Hardy chose the descriptor 'religious experience' but various names have appeared for it in the literature. Ecstasy is one; it is used in two ways but always with a sense that the soul leaves the body for a transcendental realm. It is associated both with Christianity and shamanism and explored in a secular context by Marghanita Laski (1961). Enthusiasm too is found as a concept in various religious traditions. It is conceived as a sacred power entering a person from a space outside of the recipient. A distinction is often made in the context of differentiating between shamanic and spirit-possession traditions. The shamanic concept sees a shaman as visiting another world and the other – spirit possession-sees traffic from the other world into this world, often without control on the part of the person possessed. Lewis (1971) argues that these distinctions are false and that issues of who controls the experience are not as clear as the traditional positions would indicate.

The definition of the word mysticism or mystical is similarly complex. Some would make a distinction between these experiences and the numinous. This distinction lies in a similar area to that found in enthusiasm – whether the experiencer sees it as an encounter or a fusion with the 'other'. Two types of mystical experiences are identified by Zaehner (1957). One is associated with a religious tradition where the oneness is with a Divine being of one kind and the other is associated with a deep feeling of complete oneness with the natural world (Charlesworth 1988). Here we see a distinction between natural mysticism which is spiritual and religious mysticism which is both spiritual and religious.

Some events in this area are termed by their recipients' spiritual awakenings. These are more about a moment of relation to a sacred dimension in living and having a life changing impact. Near death, born again, conversion and enlightenment experiences fall into this category such as that of St Paul on the road to Damascus. These may or may not be religious in character (Charlesworth 1988). These may include corporate revelations in which entire groups may experience the sacred simultaneously as in the Toronto Blessing of 1994.

Naming the experience has produced a variety of words many of them having a religious origin.

Ways of Knowing and Wellbeing

Particularly interesting for the development of my thinking on spirituality has been the work of Isabel Clarke and her concept of the transliminal. In *Madness, Mystery and the Survival of God* (2008) she sees the necessity for human wellbeing of what she calls the transliminal or relational knowing. Clarke's notion of the transliminal is drawn from cognitive psychology (Thalbourne et al 1997). In her thinking, this way of knowing is to do with our 'porous' relation to other beings. It is in contrast to 'propositional knowing' which characterises the analytically sophisticated individual that our culture prizes so highly. To access the transliminal way of knowing we cross an internal 'limen' or threshold. She contrasts the two ways of knowing; the propositional is characterised by either/or logic and the relational or transliminal is characterised by paradox and both/and logic; the main characteristic of the transliminal is the ability to handle paradox (or plurality):

> I have floated the hypothesis that we are only partly individual; through our relational minds we are part of the whole. This brings responsibility and pain. It also brings wonder and joy ... And the deepest and widest of those circles of relationship which we both are, and are beyond us, is god or whatever label you choose. (I. Clarke 2008 p. 172)

In this hypothesis she validates the two ways of knowing as of equal worth and value, including the relational/transliminal. She sees the latter as most regularly accessed through the artistic and the religious:

> From about age of 36 onwards when listening to certain passages – Beethoven's late quartets I have had the feeling that he had touched a realm of experience beyond our normal consciousness, full of serenity and joy, the uplands of the Spirit, and through his music, I could reach not so much a sense of God, as of another world.[3]

The paradoxical nature of this way of knowing enables it to encompass conflicting emotions. Langer (1942) also suggested a 'non-discursive' form of communication that characterised music and religion which is different from propositional ways of knowing. Writers such as Shankar, Casals, and Jung often have extreme difficulty in expressing what they want to say about the spiritual/visionary aspects of their performance because words cannot contain paradoxical thinking easily (Ellis 1985). It is pure sound existing in

3 Religious Experience Research Centre from a 59 year old woman.

time; unlike written texts it passes on relentlessly with no stop or division as seen in a clock face or a calendar (Ong 1982 p. 75).

The complexity of describing the transliminal, which I have equated with the spiritual state, indicates that maybe there is a great variety of spiritual states of one kind or another – ranged along a continuum and depending on context. Some of them are more in the control of the experiencer than others. They include a brief moment of day-dreaming or reverie in a busy day, intuitive initiations of a poem or a song, subliminal perception, an ability to dissociate from a boring situation to create a poem or plan a musical piece, a period of incubation in the creative process as we shall see in Chapter Two (Wallas 1926), the induced trance states of hypnotherapy, the trance states of the shamanic drumming journey and the elaborate visions of the medieval mystic. There are indications that highly creative people are perhaps more at ease with these states. This is suggested by the EEG patterns of more creative people which reveal a dramatic de-focusing of their awareness. This may enable them to enter these states more readily. Guy Claxton (2002) summarises this in relation to religion, suggesting that 'spiritual development involves cultivating a wider range of states of mind or attentional modes' (Claxton 2002 pages unavilable). Dewey linked the aesthetic experience with everyday consciousness:

> What then does aesthetic experience mean for Dewey? Together with aspects of artistic doings and contextualism of this doing, the aesthetic aspect of experience means a qualitatively different, fulfilling and inherently meaningful mode of engagement in contrast to the mechanical, the fragmentary, the nonintegrated and all other non-meaningful forms of engagement. Aesthetic is a transformational concept meaning increased unity of experience. (Westerlund 2002 p. 191)

Dewey describes the aesthetic as an experience 'in excelsis', and as simply an intensification of ordinary experience. He is concerned to link the aesthetic experience into a continuum which is cultivated intentionally in art works.[4]

4 Morton Klass suggests that the sacred/profane distinction is an invention of western religious systems and may not be true of other religious systems (Klass 1995).

Sometimes the cultivation of altered states of consciousness has been deliberately linked with music such as in therapeutic hypnosis; this is based on the knowledge that music can lead to altered states of awareness, such as colour-synaesthesia. In this work (Hamel 1978 p. 168) it was established that patients tended to have negative experiences before the music appeared but after the introduction of the music happier images appeared. It was also found that several years later the same pieces of music could be used to induce the feelings of happiness; the music seemed to have been retained in the memory as associated with this happier state following the hypnotherapy.

All of these descriptors imply that human beings are capable of a variety of ways of knowing. Indications of this come from anthropologists and psychologists working in the area of consciousness. The current development of consciousness studies has entered the area of the interconnectedness of creation with works like Ken Wilber's *The Eye of Spirit* (1997) and *Integral Psychology* (2000). Here the search for the perennial philosophy drawing on a variety of traditions looks at a spectrum of consciousness often called *The Great Chain of Being* (Wilber 1997) to develop a hierarchy of consciousness. In the area of embodied cognition there has been a concern to link this with neuro-biology:

> Scientists now largely agree that consciousness, though mysterious, is a product of the activity of bodies with complex nervous systems going about their business in the world. When certain bodily events occur – sleep, a blow to the head, a stroke – consciousness is lost or changed. But the intact Brain-Body-Context System generates conscious experiences of knowing (or believing or seeing or feeling) of many different kinds. (Claxton, Lucas, and Webster 2010 p. 24)

They go on to distinguish between the content of the experiences; some relate to words and reason and others seem more concerned with feeling and emotion; some are linked with the body in some way and others use images or memories (which may be termed hallucinations). They develop descriptors for these states like intuitions and hunches and adjectives like being moved or impulsive, so therefore setting up something resembling the continuum already suggested.

The increasing acknowledgement of a variety of ways of knowing in human beings has opened up the possibility of a continuum of states of awareness linking the everyday with spiritual awareness.

Altered States of Consciousness and their Association with Religion

There have been suggestions that the twelfth-century mystic Hildegard's visions were a product of migraine (O. Sacks 1985); but Sacks adds that this does not invalidate the insights she was given in them. Indeed, the notion of an encounter with God and activity in the frontal lobes of the brain may simply be different ways of describing the same thing. Guy Claxton (2002) identifies a sense of dissatisfaction with ordinary states of consciousness, critiquing the Church for moving away from validating forms of consciousness like the mystical experience.

Very helpful to the understanding of the interface between states of consciousness and religion is the work of Brian Lancaster (2004). He looks at the variety of experiences of the mystics, and asks if the variety of methods and details of the experience invalidates the study of this area through the lens of consciousness. He decides that there is a sufficient common core to uphold their value for the study of consciousness and that this common core lies in the area of the overcoming of self-centredness:

> Spiritual and mystical teachings can reveal to us ways in which the self intrudes as a limiting factor on consciousness, together with insights into the form consciousness takes when such a limitation is transcended. (Lancaster 2004 pp. 81–2)

Lancaster manages to maintain a position where understanding the psychological origins of spiritual states does not necessarily invalidate the belief claims associated with them. He associates them with the state of what he calls deep memory processes. These processes necessarily engender multiple activations through their associative and hermeneutic logic (Lancaster 2004 p. 267). This diversity of associations, irrational and symbolic relations he identifies with Jewish Midrashic logic (Lancaster 2004 p. 266). This enables access to the preconscious – as described by William James and Rudolph Otto – which is normally inaccessible. Lancaster links this with the Aristotelian Active Intellect, the precursor to Divine Intellect and imbued with some of its essence. The Active Intellect he equates with the primordial Torah, source of all potential meanings and root of hermeneutic diversity. He sees this as both oiling the marketplaces of spiritual practice but also aligning itself with traditional mystics' view of God. Bauer and Blanchard link the realisation of the Rabbinic dream with our genetic inheritance – our genetic wiring:

> Brain research undercuts the claim that our present economic, political, and educational systems are the only realistic option. There are naturally satisfying alternatives to legal, economic, political, and educational institutions built on aggressive competition and/or the humiliation of others. (Bauer and Blanchard 2010 p. 72)

In the end Lancaster comes to an understanding that the experience is contentless and represents the apophatic way of not knowing. To place names on it he considers to be idolatry – akin to making an image of the divine (Lancaster 2004 p. 273). In music we can envisage a realm of contentless experience that is transformational in character which individual cultures or persons may want to name in some way (in the domain I call Values later). Lancaster's thinking takes him to a place potentially of a religionless spirituality which religion may want to enculturate in some way.

Later we shall compare this with the musical experience. So developments in the area of consciousness studies have supported the notion of a variety of ways of knowing from a different perspective.

Ways of Knowing in Education

In valuing these diverse ways of knowing, we challenge current educational practice with its focus on single-mindedness and its invention of pathologies like ADHD.[5] The philosopher, Michael Polanyi, said that 'we know much

5 On April 5th on Radio 4 an adult diagnosed with Asperger's syndrome described how, as a child, he liked to spin as it took him into a state of reverie and peace. This was frowned on by his school. It is interesting to reflect that this is the way the whirling dervishes of Sufism attain their states of awareness. James Davies (2013) explores in great detail how the pathologies of the DSM – the Diagnostic and Statistical Manual of Mental Disorders were invented by men with links to the pharmaceutical industry.

more than we know we know' and we access this by being less focused, less questing, less impatient and less controlled, which increases the ability to access other ways of knowing in which mystery and intuition are valued. A survey by Ference Marton (cited in Claxton 2002) has shown that taking your intuition seriously is almost a pre-requisite for a Nobel Prize in science. There is a place for inhibition and excitation in the brain and, if we link this with the findings of neuro-science, this can be seen as the turning on and off of neurons. When we are thinking in a focused way, the frontal lobes build short-term inhibitory stockades round the centres of activity (Claxton 2002). If we link this with social constructionism, these inhibitions could be seen as the process of inputting the internal policing which is necessary for ordinary life; but at certain times this restraint needs withdrawing to realise our full humanity. This is similar to Freud's idea of repression and is revisited in Chapter Two. So an education with a concept of spirit in it – 'spirited education' (Claxton 2002) – may enable students to access different ways of knowing. People need to develop at least two and probably many more ways of knowing to be fully alive (as discussed in Dweck 1999 and C. Clarke 2005).

The valuing of one way of knowing in education has powered a search beyond the classroom for a wider view of human potential.

Music, Spirituality and the Human Potential Movement

The growth of the human potential movement saw the spiritual emerge in a new form. Rogers, Maslow, and Howard Gardner attempted to explain where the religious sits in the hierarchy of human needs. In their writing, the spiritual becomes part of the process of self-actualisation. This was often associated with a notion of transcendence of or within the self and led people to look for places where or strategies by which transcendent experiences may be achieved. Not only did this include the rise of the various spiritual practices that we shall examine in the next section, but also to some looking towards the musical experience as the last remaining place for the spiritual in Western society (Hills and Argyle 2000 pp. 61–75, Hay 1982).[6] It is this that we shall explore in this section, examining how music can be a trigger for the spiritual, because of qualities within the experience that may be regarded as self-transcending or mystical, and also that an experience of the spiritual is important for realising our full humanity.

These may be regarded as peak experiences within the context of the human potential movement. It is in the context of self-actualisation and realisation, that Cindy Wigglesworth (2012) produced her book *Spiritual Intelligence*. She develops this from Howard Gardner's (1999) idea of various intelligences. She sees these as lying in everyone, and able to be developed. She brings together ethical concerns with the transcendental. In line with the thinking described above, she concludes with a section on developing your own spiritual intelligence, especially the Nine Steps to Higher Self and the Three Core Exercises. Kenneth Leech also saw religion as associated with the growth of human potential:

> True religion helps us to grow, but pseudo-religion hinders growth, for it creates and maintains obstacles and barriers. Thus it is that much religion merely censors experience and does not liberate it, stifles human potential and does not allow it to blossom. Much religion is superficial and does not help the journey inwards which is so necessary to spiritual health. There has to be a movement towards the still centre, the depths of our being, where, according to the mystics, we find the presence of God. (Leech 1995 p. 39)

Rowan Williams (2012) sees a profound difference between a spirituality based in the self-actualisation movement and one based in religion, as lying in what is considered important. Spirituality without religion is concerned with deploying religious/spiritual skills 'to settle and assure the self' (R. Williams 2012 p. 321), whereas in religion the self is concerned to locate itself in a territory defined by the love of God. So the grasp of the beyondness of the deepest meaning is part of the realisation of the fullest human potential and may or may not be helped by religion.

6 Some of the ideas, however, survived through such figures as the harmonic astrologer John Addey (1920–82), Gurdjieff (1866–1949) and Rudolph Steiner (1861–1925).

Conrad Hyers (2007), in his book on *The Spirituality of Comedy*, also links spirituality tightly with the realisation of our full humanity. Hyers sees comedy as linked with mystery and as a guard against human arrogance. This humility is linked with a deeper but concealed meaning that will always be beyond human comprehension. Here spirituality means exploring the full range of human experience:

> Tragic action runs through only one arc of the full cycle of the drama ... Consequently the range of comedy is wider than the tragic range ... The comic cycle is the only fulfilled and redemptive action ... The drama of the struggle, death and rising – Gethsemane, Calvary, Easter – actually belongs in the comic rather than the tragic domain. (Sypher 1956 p. 220)

This thinking would link the spirituality of comedy with that of music, in that both explore this wide range of feeling, sometimes involving paradoxical and conflicting emotions. It is this characteristic that probably led William James in 1902, to consider music as the most spiritual of the arts:

> Not conceptual speech but music rather, is the element through which we are best spoken to by mystical truth. (James 1902 p. 322)

This is probably the thinking that led Alf Gabrielsson to include a category entitled transcendental and existential in his descriptions of strong experiences in music (Gabrielsson and Lindstrom 1993); here he starts to develop a typology of musical experiences that might be seen as of a spiritual or religious character, or at least as having similar characteristics to the spiritual/religious experience. The experiences that he includes demonstrate the synergy between the aesthetic and the spiritual; words such as magical, mysterious, supernatural and extra-terrestrial appear regularly in the accounts:

> The narrator feels as if he/she is put in a trance or ecstasy; there may be a feeling of totally merging with something bigger and of glimpsing other worlds or existences. (Gabrielsson 2011 p. 159)

Some of them have a visionary quality as in this experience of the Adagietto movement of Mahler's fifth symphony:

> You lose grasp of time and to a certain extent of space too, in the sense that the whole room I am lying in starts to revolve. In the fortissimo on the dominant in the last bars, it is like a light passes over my closed eyes, fading out more and more in the following diminuendo. (Gabrielsson 2011 p. 175)

Sometimes there is a direct message from God, such as 'It was as if his voice was there in the prayer of God' during a performance of Kodaly's *Psalmus Hungaricus* (Gabrielsson 2011 p. 180). Gabrielsson (Gabrielsson 2011 p. 402) also identifies a category he entitled Music and Existence, which is a state of 'just being' often described as 'holy' (Gabrielsson 2011 p. 149). These are sometimes seen as transformative:

> [A pop ballad] meant an end to years of battling with myself and all the others and everyone around me ... Ah! I found my way home. (Gabrielsson 2011 p. 157)

Hills and Argyle (1998) concluded that religious and musical were very similar, including such characteristics as 'glimpsing another world' and 'loss of sense of self'. This account from a 65 year old woman draws similar parallels:

> Countless are the times great music has brought me spellbound to the 'gates of Heaven' – the hush during a Beethoven symphony, a sermon in itself. I've often said that to me, a good concert was far more full of awe – God, if you like, than many a church service.[7]

Gabrielsson (2011) also identifies similarities with religious experiences:

> In experiences of God I often feel completely broken-hearted and at the same time eternally grateful to God who wants to come so close to me. So it was shocking to experience the same feelings but from a totally different cause, namely music. The music was not sacral, but it gave me the same feeling as in the meeting with God. (Gabrielsson 2011 p. 454)

So, we have in these accounts of people's intense experiences, many examples of parallels between transcendental, aesthetic, spiritual and musical experiences; these we shall examine in more detail in Chapter Eight.

7 Religious Experience Research Centre archive.

So the human potential movement has seen the centring of the spiritual within the self rather than within the Divine in some way; this would place music as a significant generator of these transformative peak experiences.

The Re-emergence of Spiritual Intention

The human potential movement with its notion of wellbeing, particularly in New Age contexts, saw the re-emergence of musicking with spiritual intention outside of religious liturgy (Boyce-Tillman, 2000a, pp. 155–66). Some areas of rock and jazz traditions (Hamel, 1978, pp. 134–5) drew on Eastern religious ideas with a more holistic view of the mind/body/spirit relationship. Elsewhere, transcendence was approached through physical practices such as chanting (Gass and Brehony 1999) or dancing. Many New Age traditions pursue their spiritual intentions through linking dance and movement with music, such as Gabrielle Roth: in a way which echoes the sense of being played by something beyond oneself that we saw in Hildegard:

> I wasn't controlling the dance – I was being danced ... The dancer disappeared inside the dance and I'd find that divine part, divine spirit, the spark of infinite beat ... This was my prayer. I was sweating my prayer. (Roth 1992)

There are increasing numbers of music making groups with spiritual intention. Groups of overtone chanters meet regularly with spiritual and healing intentions. Jill Purce runs regular workshops helping people to develop the technique for their own healing. Her workshops include group overtone chanting as well as a range of vocal techniques to connect with oneself, with others and with the cosmos which she sees as re-enchanting Western society by creating an enchanted singing community (Purce 1998).

So music became one of the spiritual practices that support a person's spiritual journeying.

Spirituality as Practice rather than Dogma

As part of this inclusion of spirituality as part of personal development, the last part of the twentieth century saw a number of religious practices separating themselves from their religious roots and entering the secularised marketplace. The first of these was Transcendental Meditation often known as TM. It appeared in India in 1955 under the tutelage of the Maharishi Mahesh Yogi (1914–2008) which he then disseminated worldwide in a series of world tours starting in 1957. His association with the Beatles in the UK gave him a considerable following. The worldwide following identified as practising the technique is variously quoted as between six and ten thousand and include the practitioner Deepak Chopra. It consists of sitting for 15–20 minutes twice a day with eyes closed and using a sound or mantra to centre. Although it is regarded by some as religious, the marketing of TM stresses its scientific research basis. It makes many claims to improve health and is linked with the Maharishi Vedic Centre for Health. It claims to produce higher levels of consciousness; it is, however, primarily seen as a technique to increase stress relief and relaxation without chemical help. It is taught for a variety of fees as a seven step course by qualified practitioners worldwide (*Transcendental Meditation* 2012). Deepak Chopra has developed from this technique his own primordial sound meditation.

Mindfulness has a similar history at the beginning of the twenty-first century. Its origin is in the heart of Buddhist psychology and practice. Now separated from its religious roots and marketed in a seven week course as a purely secular discipline, it still uses many quotations from the Dalai Lama. It is widely used in mainstream healthcare and is often defined as 'paying attention on purpose moment by moment without judging' (Kabat-Zinn 1990 pp. 31–4).

> Mindfulness can help us to work directly with the struggle we sometimes have in relating to life's experience and in doing so we can really improve our quality of life. (*Mindfulness* 2011)

The meditation skills taught are based on awareness of the breath and body in both stillness and movement. Websites cite the benefits of it in various contexts including education.

> Mindfulness helps children, students and teachers to improve their concentration, attention, conflict resolution and empathy. (*Mindfulness* 2011)

These private practices are seen 'to electrify the spiritual impulse that animates all of life' (Wuthnow 1998 p. 198). Spirituality becomes process, with notions of God replaced by notions of being-ness.

Rowan Williams (2012) critiques the misrepresentation of the place and role of dogma in religion. He draws on David Martin's Eucharistic theology to set out a vision of a ritual that makes people whole 'by absorbing and imbibing its brokenness and its violence' (Martin 1997 pp. 153–4). He sees the Eucharist as misrepresented as an audio-visual representation of a set of propositions (R. Williams 2012 p. 92) rather than entry into this place of wellbeing. Despite this, the perception on the part of those who self-define as spiritual but not religious is that the Church doctrine was exclusionist, clearly set out by Danah Zohar and Ian Marshall in *Spiritual Capital: Wealth We Can Live By*:

> The broader kind of spiritual capital needed for organisations, communities, and cultures participating in today's pluralist and global society must draw on deeper, non-sectarian meanings, values, purposes, and motivations that might be sacred to any human being. (Zohar and Marshall 2004 p. 3)

A variety of spiritual practices have been developed and separated from their religious roots. These have often replaced church attendance and belief in certain creedal statements as central to a person's spirituality.

The Seekers

We have already seen how seeking was part of the gnostic strand in Theosophy. It is a recurrent theme in this literature. To be religious implies faith in God or the divine, participation in institutionally based practices, and respect for the teachings of a tradition; but we have already seen how many of the seekers have abandoned the creeds and narratives of Christianity. According to Fuller (2001), the seeking is primarily done in the New Age traditions, yoga, ecospirituality, witchcraft, near death experiences, the Tarot, astrology and neo-paganism rather than a Christian heaven for their spiritual wellbeing. To be spiritual puts emphasis upon the experience of connectedness, relationship, or oneness with God/Christ/a higher power/the sacred/nature together with an appreciation for personal growth and inner awareness in one's life journey. Richard Dawkins (2012) in a BBC interview claimed that although many people are in favour of religion, what they usually mean is that they are in favour of only one religion, the one that they believe in. It is then possible to see the development of 'spiritual but not religious' as an attempt to see the validity of a sacred dimension to life without subscribing to a particular belief system.

Some of these seekers are feminists, disappointed by the lack of spiritual authority in the traditional patriarchal faiths; their search sometimes leads them to goddess and Wiccan traditions. Many of the interviews I conducted in the area of Spirituality at Work in the US saw Oprah Winfrey as a crucial populariser of a religionless spirituality and the extraction of virtues from a religious context. She took from the black churches qualities such as community, self-examination, gratitude, generosity, forgiveness, simplicity and listening (Nelson 2005). Kwok Pui Lan sees a new sort of person emerging from traditional religious contexts – seekers who 'dream of new possibilities and follow their hearts' desire' (Kwok 2002 p. 4). Wade Clark Roof (1993) entitles his book *A Generation of Seekers: The Spiritual Journeys of the Baby Boomer Generation*. This study based on a large survey saw this generation as involved in the 50s with institutional religion, dropping out in the 70s. The 80s saw a rise in born-again Christianity, the New Age and complete defection from organised religion; then, in the 1990s, some religious observance returned as part of child rearing. In the end, Wade Clark Roof describes four characteristics of the baby boomers' religious/spiritual identity:

- The re-emergence of spirituality – with various names such as creation spirituality, Goddess spirituality, feminist spirituality
- Religious and cultural pluralism – a religion was what one chose at a time when normative faiths were challenged by the Vietnam war and the Watergate scandal
- Multi-layered belief and practice – mixing and matching citing the growth in the possibility of reincarnation within Christian frames

- Transformed selves which he sees as increased sense of commitment and sense of finding oneself in a wider network of relationships. (Roof 1993 p. 245)

The study reveals a deeply spiritually divided generation with some still attached to traditional religious communities.

Leigh Eric Schmidt – in *Restless Souls: The Making of American Spirituality* (2005) – traces a line we have already plotted to the Transcendentalists and William James. In attempting to define the characteristics of the present day, he cites the rudiments of spiritually inclined progressives, according to Horatio Dresser (1919 pp. 4–12):

- Individual aspiration after mystical experience or religious feeling
- The valuing of silence, solitude and serene meditation
- The immanence of the transcendent – in each person and in nature
- The cosmopolitan appreciation of religious variety as well as unity in diversity
- Ethical earnestness in pursuit of justice-producing reforms or 'social salvation'
- An emphasis on self-expression and adventuresome seeking

Schmidt sees these as an interlocking group of precepts and practices which passed under various names – from the Transcendentalist Newness to the Universal Religion to the New Spirituality. He claims that the term *Religious liberalism* 'remains particularly serviceable as shorthand for this conglomeration' (Schmidt 2005 p. 13).

Yet despite the apparently individualised nature of the spiritual search, there was also within the movement a search for community which is committed to the understanding of difference and varying identities. Links are seen as needing to be established across global divisions. In this approach the health of the person and the healing of the wider community are seen as linked:

> The point of spiritual practice is not to elevate an isolated set of activities over the rest of life but to electrify the spiritual impulse that animates all of life. (Wuthnow 1998 p. 198)

It is a spirituality that contains paradoxes, thus offering the possibility:

> not of the finished work of salvation, but of the incomplete labor of democratic freedom and cosmopolitan progressivism. (Schmidt 2005 p. 290)

So seeking is a characteristic identified widely in the literature – both individual and global. Robert Wuthnow (1998) identifies a move 'from dwelling to seeking'. He describes the difficulties of writing about spirituality in the US because faith is considered a private matter in tune with widely held libertarian views.

> Spirituality consists not only of implicit assumptions about life, but also of the things people talk about and the things they do; the stories they construct about their spiritual journeys, the prayers they offer, the inspirational books they read, the time they spend meditating, their participation in retreats and at worship services, the conversations they have about it with their friends, and the energy they spend thinking about it ... But spirituality is not just the creation of individuals; it is shaped by larger social circumstances and by the beliefs and values present in the wider culture. (Wuthnow 1998 pp. vii–viii)

His study draws on a wide variety of people and he sees a new spirituality emerging which he calls practice-based. He sees how the dwelling spirituality rooted in religious traditions is giving way to one orientated towards seeking. The new one he sees as taking seeking further, adding 'a vital element of sustained commitment' (Wuthnow 1998 p. 198). It provides 'a more orderly, disciplined, and focused approach to the sacred' (Wuthnow 1998 p. 196). These people see practice rather than dwelling as a way of generating a balanced perspective on the sacredness of all the world, as Joan Chittister describes:

> Contemplative prayer ... is a prayer that sees the whole world through incense – a holy place, a place where the sacred dwells, a place to be made different by those who pray, a place where God sweetens living with the beauty of all life. Contemplative prayer ... unstops our ears to hear the poverty of widows, the loneliness of widowers, the cry of women, the vulnerability, the struggle of outcasts. (Chittister 1991 p. 35)

The seeking is often coupled by a loosening of the hold of particular dogma – or what I shall call below Narrative. Brian McLaren (2010) finds four characteristics of the spiritual seeker that are similar to Wuthnow. In a book interestingly called *Naked Spirituality*, he describes a move from trusting sciences for all the answers, distrust of organised religion, a sense of universal sacredness, and spiritual practices such as meditating.

Kwok Pui Lan sees a new sort of ecumenism emerging from traditional religious contexts:

> The Catholics and Protestants would not easily mingle with one another or visit each other's churches in the same neighbourhood. On the contrary nomadic seekers do not have an identifiable place which they can call a spiritual home – they are explorers and sojourners but not dwellers. (Kwok 2002 p. 4)

However, Grace Davie (2005 p. 46) sees a lingering love of religion which she calls 'vicarious religion'. This sees a relationship with the Church that is at a distance; they cherish the Church because of links with their own past, a resonance with some future need, such as a funeral, and as a source of comfort in the context of a collective disaster. We shall explore this later in the second interlude on Christian theology and music.

Miner and Dowson (2012) draw a number of these themes together in their definition of spirituality:

> In the context of spiritual experience, spirituality is the search, beyond psychology and physicality, for meaning transformation, and connectedness (trait), success in which leads to new patterns of understanding, becoming and relating (start). (Miner and Dowson 2012 p. 18)

They distinguish between three modalities – meaning, transformation and connectedness – and the traits which characterise the search and finally the behaviours which indicate the traits such as prayer, reflection, self-denial and surrender (Miner and Dowson 2012 pp. 18–19).

Many writers see searching as a central feature of contemporary spirituality. This contrasts with the dwelling that characterises religious affiliation.

The Secularisation and Commodification of religion

Developments in religionless spirituality can be related to secularism. Rowan Williams sees fundamentalism as religion's answer to secularism and sees the two feeding off one another and colluding in a contest between secularist certainties and religiously controlled ones (R. Williams 2012 pp. 18–19). Religionless spirituality is rooted in answers to questions that once religious narratives were seen as answering. In a religious context Williams distinguishes between patrons (visiting but not committed) and subscribers (those who are committed to the religious community) to religion (R. Williams 2012 p. 87). This is summarised below in the way in which narratives function in the definition of spirituality in various ways.

Miner and Dowson distinguish between philosophy-based and religious-based behaviours in the area of the focus of the action – either the material-social world or on the metaphysical 'next world' (Miner and Dowson 2012 p. 18). These distinctions are part of a wider movement to secularise religion/spirituality. Rowan Williams also sees the pressure on traditionally conceived religious communities to look 'credible and attractive, marketable' (Williams 2012 p. 87); and in the religionless spirituality group the teachers of the meditation techniques described above are regularly critiqued for the fees charged for their courses.

Courtney Bender's study in Cambridge Massachusetts concentrates on the relationship between the shaping of spirituality and a complex secular context:

> Spirituality is produced in multiple social institutions, including many that we do not consider religious … This calls us to investigate the multiple spaces (including secular ones) where religious sensitivities and selves are robustly explored and cultivated … It makes clear that the binaries of religious and secular institutions are inadequate to our analysis of religious life in America. (Bender 2010 pp. 182–3)

For him religion is so integrated into society in the US that the sacred/secular divide is challenged:

> Nation, race and religion are tied together in rituals, histories and narratives and practices, as well as through legal claims to land, self-governance, and the like (Bender 2010 p. 223).

This coincides with some of Bakhtin's thinking about the forgotten origins of contemporary rituals which are reinvigorated in a renewed form in contemporary performances (Bakhtin, 1996 quoted in Bender 2010 p. 229).

A warning note is struck by Carrette and King (2005) as they describe spirituality as the privatisation of religion which took place in two stages – individualisation (through psycho-political normalisation) and corporatisation (through neo-liberalism). They see religion as commodified and commercialised through being repackaged as spirituality and is critical of its use in workplace situations as simply supporting its capitalist aims. They conclude in a way that contrasts with some of the other literature. They see:

> the silencing of a concern for community, social justice and the extension of an ethical ideal of selfless love and compassion towards others ... The use of an idea such as 'spirituality' is *always* bound up with political questions even when the term is defined in apolitical terms (in which case it supports the status quo). (Carrette and King 2005 pp. 171–2)

This placing of the term within a capitalist frame draws on the religious dimensions of capitalism.[8] In the behaviour of capitalism, the 'market' can often be seen as functioning as God once did in writings such as the Hebrew Scriptures. Phrases such as 'The market will not like it' resemble phrases such as 'The Lord will be angry'. In a Foucauldian analysis Carrette and King look always for the manifestations of power and seek out strategies of resistance. They draw on Ken Wilber's analysis of the translative and transformative aspects of religion. They see religion as serving translative (Intrapersonal-within the self) rather than transformative (Extrapersonal – cultural) ends (Carrette and King 2005 p. 182), thus linking it with the human potential movement. The translative aspects, enabling people to live their lives better, were condemned by Marx as an opiate. The transformative aspects led to social reforms such as the abolition of slavery. They condemn the accommodationist aspects of religion and call for a breakdown of the

8 There is a considerable literature in the area of business studies and management on the secularisation of the sacred and the sacralisation of the secular within capitalism. The boundaries between sacred and secular (unknown in many societies) are becoming increasingly blurred. Spirituality has certainly entered the marketplace.

divide between sacred and secular to challenge the injustices of capitalism and its attempts to commodify everything:

> The emergence of new forms of engaged spirituality grounded in an awareness of our mutual interdependence, the need for social justice and economically sustainable lifestyles, may yet prove our best hope. (Carrette and King 2005 p. 182)

Rowan Williams also sees the fragmentation of religious communities into privatised spirituality as the destruction of a community of people who are not 'simply at the mercy of this culture, to be absorbed into its stories about the autonomous self and its choices and which can challenge global systems by proposing an "imagined society"' (R. Williams 2012 p. 96).

However, in the twenty-first century an atheist spirituality has developed that acknowledges the useful functions of religion, both Extrapersonal and Intrapersonal:

> [First] the need to live together in communities in harmony, despite our deeply rooted selfish and violent impulses, and second, the need to cope with terrifying degrees of pain which arise from our vulnerability to professional failure, to troubled relationships, to the death of loved ones and tour decay and demise ... The error of modern atheism is how many aspects of the faiths remain relevant even after their central tenets have been dismissed ... There might be a way to engage with religion without having to subscribe to its supernatural content. (De Botton 2012 pp. 5–6)

This coincides in some respects with Geertz's definition of religion as a system of symbols that encourage human motivation, provide meaning and a factual narrative to support faith (Geertz 1971 p. 4). De Botton's hope is that that the arts might be as effective as religion in their ability to guide, humanise and console. He searches for meaning without superstition via art:

> The maxims of Marcus Aurelius, the poetry of Boccaccio, the operas of Wagner and the paintings of Turner should be secular society's sacraments ... We are unwilling to consider secular culture *religiously* enough, in other words, as a source of guidance. (De Botton 2012 pp. 32–7)

He argues that we no longer need a set of religious or doctrinal beliefs in a God of any kind. However, he suggests that people in this modern age should not feel embarrassed about re-appropriating for the secular realm those 'consoling, subtle or just charming' religious rituals that inspire, such as gratitude, beautiful spaces, pilgrimages and singing; all of which he says can nourish the spirit and soul. Here we see again the possibility of a similarity between the place of religious thinking and artistic knowing within the context of a capitalist and secularising society. It is similar to Jonathan Arnold's 'genius' view of sacred music in a secular society which sees great music as pointing towards 'themes, ideas and ideals of mystery, transcendence, sin and forgiveness, love and hope that are eternal' (Arnold 2014 p. 10).

Secularisation has resulted in a change in the relationship between religion and spirituality. On the one hand, religion may be seen as fragmented and commodified. On the other hand, the absence of a clear concept of the divine has established a form of spirituality uncoupled from the divine and rooted in desires for meaning and companionship.

The Separation of Animate and Inanimate: An Interconnected World

So the development of the many spiritualities of the twenty-first century can be seen as an attempt to enrich an increasingly impoverished Western culture. This impoverishment is nowhere clearer than in our attitude to the natural world particularly in the division between animate and inanimate. Modernism traditionally denied the connection with the environment (Charles Taylor 2007) for a world of abstraction. Within western theology, human beings became alienated from the natural world – or, indeed, superior to it based on one interpretation of the Genesis creation myth. This has resulted at best in a patronising stewardship and at worst domination and outright rape. Traditional societies would not subscribe to the animate/inanimate division of contemporary science; however, Western European colonialism has attempted to subjugate this more conservative view of the cosmos wherever it found it. In this subjugated cosmic view, the entire world has its own energy or quality and human beings and the natural world are in constant interplay. If any of these ways of viewing nature were alive in our culture today would we not have a greater reverence for the musical instruments that we make and play and for the bodies that we use to make musical sounds? This will be further explored in Chapter Four.

Some Westerners are relearning their connection with the land from traditional cultures in a way that involves musicking. Writers like Chris Clarke (2002 p. 266) endeavour to merge scientific and indigenous paradigms by weakening the notion of hierarchies of being. He draws on quantum physics to explore the notion of the difference between humans and worms as not being the degree of awareness but its content. Chris Clarke's thinking provides a very helpful paradigm on which to build a theory of the vibrations of the different elements of the cosmos to produce a cosmic symphony based on music as a uniting force for creation as a whole. The medieval mystic Hildegard of Bingen (1098–1179) saw music as recreating the original harmony of God and the world in the Garden of Eden (which has echoes of the opening Edwin Muir poem):

> Music expresses the unity of the world as God first made it, and the unity which is restored through repentance and reconciliation. (Van de Weyer 1990 p. 80)

Sam Keen attempts to secularise Christian spirituality by means of environmental awareness:

> The Logos, the Word ... that informs the cosmos – all things great and small – is still spoken in sparrow song, wind sigh, and leaf fall. An electron is a single letter, an atom a complex word, a molecule a sentence, and a mockingbird an entire epistle in the great ongoing saga. The ocean still whispers the song that originated with the big bang. Listen in the longing inner heart for love and justice, and you may hear the sacred word. (Keen 2010 p. 74)

Ken Wilson emphasises the feeling of connection through the practice of prayer:

> Prayer is what the brain does or wants to do to transcend the boundaries of the self, to sense a connection with what lies beyond the praying self. (Wilson 2009 p. 6)

Dominic White in dealing with *The Lost Knowledge of Christ* (2015) links the purpose of Jewish law 'to bring harmony between people and between humanity and creation' (p. 107) with Sabbath rest, the seven year sabbatical, to enable the earth to rest and singing in church as a harmony creating exercise.

So in much contemporary spirituality there is a longing in an increasingly fragmented culture for a wider connection with both the human and the other-than-human world. Christian theologians like Mary Grey (2007) and Andrew Linzey (1994) are seeing redemption as cosmic and including the environment. So the indigenous pagan traditions, current philosophers and theologians challenge the division between animate and inanimate matter and have found a variety of frames for seeing the essential interconnectedness on the cosmos, but whereas indigenous frames have included music, the Western ones reflect the fragmentation of knowledge that characterises Western culture.

Spirituality and Religion

So, in the contemporary world, spirituality takes increasingly diverse forms in response to changing social and cultural realities. Descriptors of spiritual but not religious can be summarised as:

- A rejection of creed and dogma as a source of truth
- A valuing of experience over received tradition
- A rejection of the Augustinian notion of original sin, replacing it with original blessing (drawing on C. Taylor 2007 pp. 698–771)[9]
- An embracing of plurality in belief frames and postulating a link with the idea of a perennial philosophy

9 John Stuart Mill exalts 'Pagan self-assertion' over 'Christian self-denial'. It links with Nietzsche's idea of opposing Dionysianism that we saw in the Prelude to 'the Crucified One'. Referred to in Taylor, Charles (2007).

- An awareness of various forms of consciousness which can be cultivated by spiritual practices such as meditation
- A celebration of the mysterious and paradoxical linked with experiences of awe and wonder (Yob 2001) – the 'sacred ignorance' of the theology of liberation theologians (Keller and Danielle 2002, Christ 2003)
- A notion of spirituality as potentially transformative both personally and culturally
- An awareness of a wider connectivity in the universe
- A sense of journeying or seeking which draws on process philosophy and theology (Whitehead 1929), underpinning the aesthetics of Dewey (1934) and Shusterman (2008)

In contrast to this, to be religious has within it a concept of God and a trust in a religious institution with its associated practices and traditions. It is then possible to see the development of 'spiritual but not religious' as an attempt to see the validity of a sacred dimension to life without subscribing to a particular belief system. Dawkins may have inadvertently encouraged this development in the area of spirituality. It is certainly true of the English composer, John Tavener, whose perspective has overtones of the common core explored earlier:

> I think I had a vision. I can't explain it, but I had a kind of vision of a Sufi who seemed to be telling me that no religion can be exclusive any more. Of course, I remain an Orthodox Christian. We have a small Chapel in the stable at our house, and we have regular services there, and I remain an Orthodox Christian. You can't be synchronistic in one's prayer life. You can't pray to Allah through the great Spirits of Krishna and Christ. For Christians, Christ is God. One prays to Christ, but in my work it's possible to celebrate other religions, and I'm trying to think about an opera for children at the moment – well, not an opera – a masque on the life of Krishna, but no way can it be seen as a betrayal of Christianity. After all, Krishna was another manifestation of God. I just see them as manifestations of God – all, all the same. (Tavener 2005)

Out of these cultural developments, several patterns emerge. One that we have seen above could be described as *post-traditional*, characterised by searching and experimenting. Here, individuals are acting with a great degree of autonomy to explore spiritual truths from many sources, mixing and matching elements by their own choice. Globalisation has resulted in high levels of exposure in many places to religious diversity. This has contributed to the mixing of the religious codes. Cross-national research in Western countries suggests that this pattern holds broadly for the post-World War II (1945-present) generation (Roof and Carroll 1995), especially in the US. Seeker-oriented spirituality is compatible with life in modern, rapidly paced societies and also, in these settings, ties to established faith traditions are often weak. Social and religious conditions thus make for a thriving 'spiritual marketplace' where innovative entrepreneurs compete with one another in defining spiritual needs and in supplying meaning and practices—all intended to assist the individual in his or her spiritual journey. Drawing upon the spiritual resources available to them, both within and outside of organised religion, people assume a considerable amount of self-direction in cultivating their spiritual lives.

Various empirical measures of self-rated religionless spirituality are increasingly used by social scientists as a means of analysing these differing responses. Self-rated religiousness is related to attendance at religious services and orthodox belief, whereas self-rated spirituality is associated with mystical experiences and New Age beliefs and practices, particularly among those with higher levels of education and income. An expanding body of research links these two to a broad range of social, psychological, and behavioural correlates, particularly in the areas of psychotherapy, child-rearing philosophy, and lifestyle research (Zinnbauer et al. 1997). Research also suggests that the vast majority of those claiming to be religious see themselves also as spiritual; indeed, they see the spiritual as lying at the core of their religious life.

However, if the post-traditional spiritual quests described above represent shifting styles of individual religious expression, a second pattern might be called *re-traditionalising*, or the deliberate cultivation of spiritual meaning through committed religious life and practice. Described as *engaged spirituality*, this effort is deeply grounded within congregational religious life and thus is less individualistic in style, and seeks to combine spiritual depth with social concern and responsibility (Wuthnow 1998, Stanczak 2006). It is often a way of rooting the free-floating aspects of religionless spirituality within a secure tradition.

A third, quite different pattern is the *neotraditional* response, or the attempt at reconstructing and enforcing older religious beliefs and values throughout a sociopolitical order. Protesting the erosions of modernity, efforts such as these typically arise in close alignment with political ideologies and mass movements, as with the mobilisation of the Religious Right in the United States or the rise of radical Islamic militants in various parts of the world. Spirituality of this kind arises out of 'a re-mythologising of narratives of God, people and nationality, in search of religious certainty and a more secure moral universe.'[10] Anthony Giddens (1999) sees this rise of fundamentalisms as a product of a de-traditionalising society where people avoid the choices necessary for identity construction by taking on the pre-set package of creeds and dogmas offered by fundamentalist traditions of many kinds (Shapiro 2011).

So various alliances between religion and spiritual have been and are still being formed.

The Place of Narratives in Spirituality

There is considerable debate about the relationship between spirituality and religiosity. We have seen above what some term a humanist spirituality (Gross 2012 pp. 199–200). McLaughlin distinguishes between what he called 'tethered' and 'un-tethered' spiritualities. Religiously 'tethered' spirituality is shaped by the religion which has shaped and formed it (McLaughlin 2003, p. 191). Here the narratives are included but as we shall see below are treated in a variety of ways. Some children in any class may already be committed to a religious tradition (what Williams called above 'subscribers') while others will simply be 'patrons' drawing on them to illuminate their lives.

McLaughlin contrasts this approach with religiously 'un-tethered' spirituality, which, as we saw above, often deliberately dissociates itself from

10 Dr Anna King in an email to the author: 29th November 2010.

religion including its narratives (McLaughlin 2003 p. 192). Best (2004) sees these as attractive in educational contexts, drawing on the work of Jane and Clive Erricker (2001). So meditation practices and experiences such as 'stilling' and 'silent sitting', are sometimes used in practices like Circle Time, and in some curricular schemes such as that of the Human Values Foundation. These neatly avoid any objection (especially in countries like the US where religion is banned in public schools) or offence that might be given; accusations of indoctrination are avoided. They are facilitated by a raft of meditative techniques like Transcendental Meditation and Mindfulness which have, as we have seen, an origin in a particular religion but then desire to market themselves without religious overtones. So these systems still have links with religiosity and maybe fall into a category that I would call 'semi-tethered'. The notion of semi-tethered spiritualities will be particularly useful when we come to discuss the current popularity of music with sacred texts in Interlude Two.

In an age of measurement, however, in educational contexts, McLaughlin sees the problems of defining criteria for spiritual development in the context of untethered spirituality (McLaughlin 2003 p. 192). Adrian Thatcher asserts: 'Once wrenched from its religious meaning, it has to be *assigned* a meaning by its advocates, and there is lack of agreement about what it signifies' (Thatcher 1999 p. 3). Best (2004) argues that the word spiritual overlaps with words such as aesthetic, affective, psychological and philosophical (in its relationship with meaning and purpose), drawing on Roger Marples (2006). At the end of this chapter, I attempt to set out a phenomenology of spirituality consisting of a set of interlocking strands which each person shapes for themselves.

The God Delusion and the Christian tradition

Into this debate around religiosity come, from time to time, further assertions of Nietzsche's ideas, now defended by scientific methodologies. These assertions depend on a pre-existing religious view which can be negated.

These views are often presented in an evolutionary view of the development of humanity; this position sees it as necessary to transcend views of God for human beings to reach new heights of rationality:

> Unbelief and exclusive humanism defined itself in relation to earlier modes of belief, both orthodox theism and enchanted understandings of the world. (C. Taylor 2007 p. 269)

This humanistic system was part of a search for order and discipline in the context of human freedom. These were contrasted with the intuitive and irrational forms of what are seen as magical and intuitive schemes of cosmic understanding.

The word God delusion comes from a text by Richard Dawkins (2006) in which he claims that a personal belief in a supernatural creator is a delusion. This leads him to a description of religion as a shared insanity. The sales of this book – which reached 2 million copies by January 2010 – indicate the popularity of the ideas that he sets out. He is following in the footsteps of authors like Philip Pullman (2000) who similarly describes God in *The Amber Spyglass*, as a puny male divine figure. This aged male image draws on Western iconography of some 1500 years, including the popular one representing the creation of the world painted on the ceiling of the Sistine Chapel by Michelangelo. But such iconic human figures appeared long after the death of the historical Jesus. The narrative of Christianity developed this anthropomorphic view of God only after 300 years of Christianity during which symbols such as the fish were used. Having invented anthropomorphic images, the Christian authorities supported these idolatrous representations with creeds and dogmas; these are still reflected in the patriarchal hierarchical structures of many of the Christian traditions. The move in our culture towards a personal descriptor of spiritual but not religious has, in general, rebelled against the systematisation of the supposed teachings of the founding figures of religious traditions which are often initially passed on orally. It is this systemisation – particularly of the teaching of Jesus – that underpins the atheism of people such as Pullman and Dawkins.

The problematic nature of the images of God that I was initiated into as a child I expressed in a hymn which reworks one that I regularly sang as a child:

Finding God

1. A child once loved the story,
Which angel voices tell,
How once the King of Glory
Came down on earth to dwell.

2. Now, Father God, I miss you –
Your beard, your robes, your crown –
But you have served us badly
And let us humans down.

3. So easy to disprove you
And doubt your truthfulness;
For you were just an idol
That kept Your power suppressed.

4. For You are deep within us –
Revealed within our deeds,
Incarnate in our living
And not within our creeds.

5. No image cannot hold you;
And, if to one we hold,
We keep some from your loving
And leave them in the cold.

6. Excluded groups are legion –
Disabled, female, gay –
Old Father of the heavens,
Your picture moves away.

7. Life's processes reveal You –
In prison, death and war,
In people who are different,
In gatherings of the poor.

8. For Godding means encounter,
Gives dignity to all,
Has every shape and no shape –
In temple, tree and wall.

9. So we will go a-godding
And birth You in our world;
In sacrificial loving
We find Your strength unfurled.[11]

So my position set out in this hymn is that we in Christianity have lived with a God delusion for a long time and that the nature of the delusion has been revealed to us by the prominent atheist writers of our day; their position would be impossible without this particular representation and narrative of the Divine. My conclusion is that if we change our view of the spiritual to process rather than product, the atheistic position would be much more difficult to defend; this change would open much wider possibilities for accessing ways of knowing beyond the rational and every day – a condition longed for by the human products of a post-Nietzschean, God-is-dead, pseudo-secularised society.

Going a-Godding

The notion of beingness as the essence of Christianity rather than a commitment to a certain set of facts set in a particular narrative has been a strand in Christian thought for some time. Christological scholars have been rethinking Jesus's development of the idea of the Kingdom in a more process-based light – not as a thing to be achieved, but as an on-going co-operation between human beings and God which John Crossan likens to art (Crossan 1992 p. 29). He roots this in the concept of time, with a

11 June Boyce-Tillman November 2012 based on hymn by Mrs Emily Huntington Miller, unpublished.

concentration on the present rather than the past and future (Crossan 1992 p. 32). The Kingdom is a collaborative artistic project involving human and divine co-operation.[12] So, within the developments in theology, there is a move towards a process model of Divine/human interaction.

Dewey (1934) in a text that has been seminal in the writing of this book – *Art as Experience* – was drawing on process philosophers and found the concept of musical rhythm as helpful to the development of his own philosophy (Lafferty 2013). Although he was drawing on the Western classical music traditions (which as we shall see later may behave differently from orate traditions in this area), he nonetheless highlights the temporality of the musical experience and the appropriateness of using process thought as a philosophical way of understanding it.

Feminist theologians have drawn on the development of process thought (Daly 1973, Grey 1989). Ruth Mantin writes that she wishes to see spirituality as process and sacrality as performative (Mantin 2002); for her the process is never completed. Carol Christ (2003) has drawn on the process philosophers such as Charles Hartshorne to see God as verb, which I have attempted to capture in this song:

CHORUS And we'll all go a-godding
To bring the world to birth.

1. New life is calling;
Help set it free.
And we'll all go a-godding
With a song of liberty.
CHORUS

2. Hunger is calling,
Find food to share;
And we'll all go a-godding
To give out abundant care.
CHORUS

12 This relates to the feminist theologians' renaming it as a kindom. It is about the process of establishing the kinship (Fiorenza 2000) between human beings and the Divine.

3. Hopelessness calling,
Lonely and drear;
And we'll all go a-godding,
In warm friendship drawing near.
CHORUS

4. Warfare is calling.
When will it cease?
And we'll all go a-godding,
In our arms, the flowers of peace.
CHORUS

5. Justice is calling,
Scales in her hand;
And we'll all go a-godding;
In her strength we'll take a stand.
CHORUS

6. Wisdom is calling;
Search out her ways;
And we'll all go a-godding,
To the ending of our days.
CHORUS
(Boyce-Tillman 2006c p. 97)

Carol Christ's theology – epitomised in the title of her book *She who changes* (2003) – concerns itself with change in the world, creation as in constant transformation, rather than fixed eternal laws. She concentrates on life in the body and associates this with the finitude of life on earth. In contrast to philosophies rooted in the Platonic tradition, which see change as negative because the Divine does not change, she sees the need to affirm change – hence God as verb, movement and fluidity.

Philip Sheldrake (1995) sees the attraction of Celtic spirituality for our times in the notion of wandering. This sits well with the flexibility of a spirituality based in journeying (Sheldrake 1995 p. 69). Celtic Christianity was the seat of the Pelagian heresy which is rooted in virtue theology; as such, it has many of the characteristics that we now associate with spirituality:

> I suspect that the Celts may also have been led towards an affirmative view of human nature and its destiny through their own experience as a people living on the margins and constantly under threat ... There has always been a great concern in this country about good behaviour and individual morality. (I. Bradley 1993 pp. 61–4)

I was reminded of this when my seven year old grand-daughter came round with her opening question: 'Grandma, I don't need to go to church to be a Christian, do I? I just need to be good.'

> In Britain, the primary test of faith is not religious observance but daily behaviour towards our neighbours and pets! (Van de Weyer 1990 p. 113)

John Wolffe, in *God and Greater Britain* (1994), describes the development of a diffusive Christianity in the late nineteenth and early twentieth century as an unofficial popular religion, which is characterised by a non-doctrinal belief in God; it sees Christ as a good man setting us an example of how to behave. Its attitude to the church is not hostile but apathetic. It sees the function of the church as primarily social because of its role in cementing communities and providing rites of passage; in these hymn singing played a significant part. 'The emphasis was on the practical and communal rather than on the theological and the individual' (Wolffe 1994 pp. 92–3).

Many of the ideas appearing in the literature on spirituality today are examples of ideas that have been termed heretical at various points in Christian history. Sister Fidelma – the fictional creation of Peter Tremayne a leading Celtic authority – summarises the process by which heresies are created:

> What does heresy really mean? It is simply the Greek word for choice. It is in our nature to make a free choice, therefore we are all heretics ... We are a people who question all things and only through our questions can we hope to arrive at the Great Truth and we must stand by the Truth even if we stand against the world. (Tremayne 1997 pp. 127–8)

Strands in current spiritualities have downgraded thinking in favour of action. They include that it is in the doing/being not the thinking that spirituality lies. Here, process theology/spirituality finds its expression in breaking down the sacred/secular divide as we encounter the Divine in unusual places, including our work – it is not separate.

A process-based spirituality is much more able to encapsulate failure within its remit – as we saw in the Pelagian heresy and its challenge of the doctrine of original sin. This links with the creative process, that we shall examine in Chapter Two, with its need for risk taking and the embracing of times of unclarity. There is an ancient saying that you cannot find light unless you are prepared to enter the darkness and that these times or uncertainty and potential error are part of the process of life. To adopt this view we need to revisit views of success and its relation to the idea of human progress. This is well expressed by Leonard Cohen in his song *Anthem*:

> Ring the bells that still can ring
> Forget your perfect offering
> There is a crack, a crack in everything
> That's how the light gets in.
> (Leonard Cohen 1985)

Isabel Clarke takes this as title for her chapter on Psychosis and Spirituality in *Ways of Knowing* (2005) in which she explores a way of knowing that embraces paradox and contradiction.

In 1974, John Navone brought out a book entitled *A Theology of Failure*, in which he critiques the legacy of the Renaissance in the formulating of the cult of progress. His view of the biblical text is that the concept of failure is a central theme of life which enables the God of liberation to appear. Professor Beverley Clack (2012) suggests that we should construct philosophy as a discipline that offers medicine for the sick soul as it struggles to engage with the loss of meaning. That we are on a journey and can therefore learn from our mistakes is much more in keeping with a process model of the Divine.

So the development of process philosophy and contemporary atheism have affected a growing field of process theology and establishing the notion of God as verb. The emphasis on being fits well with the temporal nature of music.

Plurality

Earlier in this chapter, we examined the notion that there is a perennial philosophy underpinning the variety of religious belief systems; but in the early twenty-first century diversity reasserts itself, as Ursula King suggests:

> It is ... much more appropriate to speak of 'spiritualities' rather than spirituality in the singular. Christian spirituality differs from Jewish, Muslim, Hindu or Buddhist spirituality ... Many contemporary spiritualities have come into existence which are not defined by traditional religions but are secular or newly created. (King 2009 p. 4)

This process is a move towards an individualised piety constructed by each person on their own rather than the communities that characterised established religions. So these processes are producing multiple spiritualities; indeed it might be said that, in many cases, each person creates a distinctive personalised spirituality.

The fragmenting of the narratives of Christianity is seen by Charles Taylor (2007) in the development of humanism as an alternative to Christianity in the late eighteenth century:

> It's as though the original duality ... set in train a dynamic, something like a nova effect, spawning an ever-widening variety of moral/spiritual options ... The fractured culture of the nova ... reaches its culmination in the latter half of the twentieth century ... Integral to it, there arises in Western societies a generalised culture of 'authenticity', or expressive individualism, in which people are encouraged to find their own way ... The connection between pursuing a moral or spiritual path and belonging to larger ensembles – state, church, even denomination – has been further loosened; and as a result the nova effect has been intensified. We are now living in a spiritual super-nova, a kind of galloping pluralism on the spiritual plane. (C. Taylor 2007 pp. 299–300)

We have already seen in the work of Carrette and King (2005) that this process can be linked with the commodification of spirituality that enables it to find a place in the marketplace of capitalism.

Process theology/philosophy accommodates diversity much more easily than more dogmatic systems. Significant for this embracing of plurality is Catherine Keller's idea of multiplicity which she defines as polydoxy 'considered as the teaching of the manifold, stretched orthodoxy through the pluralism it fears' (Keller 2011 p. 1). Catherine Keller's lecture title – *And truth so manifold* – illustrates this well. In this she examines the nature of transfeminism through the lens of polydoxy which she describes as comprising a trinity of 'relationality, mystery and multiplicity' (Keller 2011 p. 1). Relationality she calls entanglement – a term which covers the vast range of relationships from intimacy to infinitude. Mystery, she links with apophatic mysticism and describes as including a spectrum ranging from ignorance to wisdom. In the book she edited with Laurel Schneider (2010) – *Polydoxy: Theology of Multiplicity and Relation* – she sees Gregory of Nyssa's establishment of the Trinitarian conception of divinity as an attempt to combine the diversity of paganism with the monotheism of Judaism and so to establish a distinct identity for Christianity. She sees the idea of the Trinity as a dialogical principle at work. So her development of the idea of polydoxy is the rediscovery of the diversity possible within a Christian frame. This links current developments in spiritualities to a Christian frame:

> Can we imagine the trinity as a site for interreligious exchange rather than as a prefabricated solution to the problem of religious diversity? My sense is that the trinity can indeed be an open site for interreligious dialogue and exchange but not so long as Christians bring to dialogue a finished conception of the trinity that can in no way be enriched by way of dialogue and comparative theology.[13]

Despite this, plurality often serves to resist the definition religion – a characteristic that sets Hinduism apart from the apparently monotheistic Abrahamic faiths. Following this line, notions of spirituality now include a variety of faith traditions as in *World Spirituality: An Encyclopaedic History of Religious Quest* (Dupre 1990) which includes twenty-five diverse examples of spirituality that cross a variety of historical eras and different faiths.

13 Keller and Schneider <http://depts.drew.edu/tsfac/colloquium/2010/TTCChapter%2013%20-%20Thatamanil.pdf>. Accessed November 24th 2014.

So the development of a journeying spirituality and process models has meant a proliferation of a plurality of spiritualities. These are often built on the fragmentation of traditional religions. This is particularly useful in the area of meaning and music as we will explore in Chapter Five.

Pulling the Strands together

So spirituality or spiritualities can be seen as containing a number of very various strands. From the Titus Brandsma Institute based in Nijmegen University comes the SPIRIN project – Spirituality International – 'an academic forum, multi-disciplinary in structure and multicultural in approach' (Huls 2011 p. 141). Within the SPIRIN Encyclopaedia they distinguish ten dimensions of spirituality: words, things, arts, texts, forms, connections, processes, professions, disciplines and theories. The words are taken from different periods, contexts and spiritual backgrounds. The dimension things includes both the natural world and artefacts which leads directly into spiritual aesthetics and a whole range of artistic practices including symbolic representations of the divine/human relationship, entities imbued with divine values and presence. The dimension called texts is comprised of a vast array of literatures including holy books, sermons, prayers and so on. The dimension entitled forms concentrates on historical forms, models and traditions. It is the dimension of connections that I have concentrated on in my work and they have come up with a similar range including interpersonal, intrapersonal, cosmic, divine/human, society and so on. Processes include ways of developing spiritual authenticity and maturity. The dimension called professions includes the way spiritual accompaniment is structured including ministry, education, health care, hospitality, religious life and so on. The dimension discipline is particularly interesting in this context because it challenges researchers to 'reflect on spirituality as a discipline from intradisciplinary, monodisciplinary and interdisciplinary perspectives' (Huls 2011 p. 152). The theories dimension replaces a medieval and renaissance moral and spiritual hierarchy with modern attempts at a theory 'in the twilight of conscious articulated concepts and unconscious presuppositions and interests' (Huls 2011 p. 152).

The SPIRIN theory of dimensions is one of various attempts that have been made by theorists to chart the area of spirituality. These often concentrate on particular combinations of the SPIRIN domains. Douglas Pratt (2012) concentrates on the domains of words, texts, connections and forms as he distinguishes between three interlocking elements in religion – narrative, metaphysical and ethical. Sternberg's (2003) balance theory of wisdom concentrates on connections as he lists three interests – within the person, between persons and outside the person (culturally).

Of the SPIRIN categories the following dimensions are useful for me: the arts, connections and process. The forms dimension is helpful when analysing the place of music in sacred contexts and the domain of disciplines shows how we need to cross disciplinary fields to examine the phenomenon of music. Some of these are ones that have developed within the study of music such as musicology, ethnomusicology, community music and music therapy. But we also need to examine cultural studies, theology and liturgy.

From these, I have developed the headings below for the strands drawing on the dimensions of texts, connections, forms and processes – Metaphysical, Narrative (codifying the Metaphysical and situating it in a particular faith tradition), Intrapersonal/Expressive (within the person), Interpersonal (relational), InterGaian (relationship with the natural world) and Extrapersonal/Ethical. These are overlapping concepts. Many of these themes are concerned with processes (particularly those of interrelationship), rather than the product-based dogmas or creeds of the established faiths.

METAPHYSICAL

1. The questions firing the search are: 'Who or what can I serve? How can I know God? What is the source of my strength?' (Kaldor and Miner 2012 p. 183).
2. There is a sense of encounter which can be with mystery. This links with the experience of what Heidegger called 'contemplative thinking' (Lancaster 2004).

3. There is a sense of the beyond – the 'All shall be well' of the mystic, Julian of Norwich – a releasing of control – a sense of connection to a life-force, God, higher power or purpose (Tisdell 2007).

NARRATIVE

4. This 'refers to the fund of 'story' in which an individual 'dwells' and that constitutes the primary reference for religious identity' (Pratt 2012 p. 4). This is usually seen as relating the person to a particular tradition and enables them to define their religious identity in terms of Islam, Buddhism, Christianity and so on. However, it also seems that people are constructing hybrid narratives for themselves, such as the establishment of a separation between Jesus and Christ in such developments as 'Christ-consciousness'.

INTRAPERSONAL

5. This is powered by the questions: 'Who am I? Where do I belong? How do I deal with suffering?' (Kaldor and Miner 2012 p. 187).
6. There is a sense of empowerment, bliss and realisation. Guy Claxton (2002) links it with being energised and a sense of great clarity like 'a high-spirited child, or a spirited horse'. Gregory Bateson calls the union of being and doing (as in a musical performance) as aliveness (Bateson 1972 p. 522). This is sometimes called expanded discourse leading to such virtues as hope (C. Cohen 2008a):

> A sense of coming home to be at peace and at one with ourselves ... the joy and reconciliation of better knowing ourselves ... and the unity of being at peace with ourselves. (Jorgensen 2008 p. 280)

7. An evanescent and fleeting quality that cannot be controlled, may result in a sense of givenness with a mixture of grace, insight and effort, to shed some of the mundane anxiety and confusion that Buddhists call *dhukkha*. This may include an element of surprise (Tisdell 2007 p. 533). This means that we can only set up situations in which it is likely to happen and never be sure of its happening. Within music education, Bernard states that 'it is not possible to make either flow experiences

or transcendent religious experiences happen at a particular moment' (Bernard 2009 p. 11).

8. The sense of freedom feels like an opening-up in the experiencer as boundaries start to dissolve and an expansion in the sense of identity.
9. The intuitive faculties are opened up.
10. There is an opportunity for experiment. Open-mindedness and curiosity replaces fundamentalisms of all kinds, leading to creativity born from unusual associations (Koestler 1964). This is made from largely unconscious and symbolic processes (Tisdell 2007) so that diversity can exist within it easily. These may be manifested in image, symbol, music, and other enculturated expressions. Paradox is tolerated or even celebrated (I. Clarke 2008).
11. Transformation and change occurs (Boyce-Tillman 2007e, 2009a, Mezirow et al 2000).

INTERPERSONAL

12. The underlying question of the search here concerns how I relate to others (Kaldor and Miner 2012 p. 187).
13. Empathy arises. A sense of belonging and being at ease in the world replaces competition with caring and attempts to bless.

INTERGAIAN[14]

14. The main question empowering the search is my relationship with the natural world (Kaldor and Miner 2012 p. 187).
15. There is an experience of a sense of oneness and deep relationship with the other-than-human world (Boyce-Tillman 2010).

EXTRAPERSONAL/ETHICAL

16. Communitas arises – a feeling of unity with other beings, people and the wider cosmos.
17. Peace is built within the mind and beyond. Tisdell (2007) describes this as a sense of wholeness, healing, and the interconnectedness of

14 This is drawing on the usage of Anne Primavesi (2008) and other ecologists.

all things resulting in the finding of ultimate meaning. This results in ethical choices.

The Place of the Narrative

It is the presence or absence of the religious narrative strand in a person's spirituality that determines whether a person will define themselves as spiritual and religious or spiritual and not religious. If they need a faith narrative in their view of spirituality then they would self-define as religious; if these are not necessary then they will not use the descriptor religious.

But this area is complex. In this analysis it includes a variety of approaches that people may take to the narratives of the various faith traditions. These can be broadly defined as

- Devotional
- Storying
- Cultural

The most traditional religious approaches to the narratives are the devotional ones and this approach usually involves taking the interpretations given to them by the particular faith traditions as well – becoming a 'subscriber'. So the narrative is accompanied by a collection of dogma and creedal statements.

But there are two other possible positions. One is simply to see them as good stories and rate them alongside other good stories like Tristan and Isolde and Grace Darling. In this case, the narrative simply gives the emotional colour to the music, as we shall see later.

The cultural reading of the narrative is somewhere between these two readings. It sees the narratives as significant for a particular culture which can be personal and national/international. Paul Tillich saw an inextricable link between religion and culture (Tillich 1964) as we saw with the American theorists above. The narratives therefore become part of a variety of identities. Here the narrative may have been believed in the past by a person, particularly in childhood; or at least they will acknowledge that it has shaped the culture which shaped them. As such, it may well still have significance for a person but no longer be part of their current belief system; or they may have synthesised part of the narrative into a new one. In this group would be the 'patrons' who take from the religious traditions what they think will enrich them rather than subscribing completely to the religion's demands. This is a common position in Western classical music traditions, where the music has a Christian text. We have already seen how it may be linked with the idea of missing God. It will be further developed in the Second Interlude.

Summary

This chapter has attempted to identify strands in developments in the area of spirituality while acknowledging that this is very difficult. It has adopted a social constructionist perspective and seen how spirituality behaves as a subjugated way of knowing in Western culture defining itself as both separate from and as part of the dominant Christian and humanist traditions. Later in the book, we will see how this colours the Values that dominate musical understanding. From a social constructionist perspective we are seeing a change in the dominant culture's embracing of Christian theology. I have charted how the narrative of religion has fragmented under pressure from a variety of sources, resulting in a multiplicity of spiritualities.

In line with the crystallisation methodology (Richardson 2000) set out in the introduction, it has embraced a knowledge that is situated, partial, constructed, multiple and embodied. It has seen the complex landscape as made up of pieces similar to those of a jigsaw without a completed image. It does not make claims to a definitive truth (Haraway 1988), but a survey of the landscape. It has examined the competing truth claims of various traditions and individuals. It has examined competing power relations and where spirituality/spiritualities fit within them. It suggests the existence of a variety of ways of knowing encompassed within the concept of spirituality.

This chapter has looked at the rise of environmental issues based on the division of the animate and inanimate and how ecotheology and paganism have informed this strand in spirituality/spiritualities. It has examined the history of the descriptor spiritual but not religious and the relation between experience, dogma and the common core experience. The role of interfaith dialogue has included the concepts of the perennial philosophy; alongside this, the secularisation and commodification of various meditation techniques have been critiqued in relation to the development of a market economy. The development of a generation of seekers and the development of the human potential movement have played a part in spirituality/spiritualities concerned with transformation. These diverse elements have produced a concept of spirituality/spiritualities as containing various strands which behave rather like a smorgasbord from which various individuals and groups select various combinations. So the Extrapersonal is popular in the area of business and management and the Metaphysical and Interpersonal with arts practitioners. If the Narrative strand is present in a person's conceptualisation, then they may well identify themselves as spiritual and religious. If that is not an essential part of a person's conceptualisation they may well self-define as spiritual but not religious. The dilemma of the place of narratives will be further debated in the domain of Values within the musical experience and the historical relationships between musicking and various religious traditions. A more process based view of spirituality separates it from the more formulated belief codifications of many established religions and will prove very useful in establishing the role of music as similar to that of religion in former ages.

CHAPTER TWO

The Cult of Creativity

> In the beginning God created the heaven and the earth. And the earth was without form and void; and darkness was upon the face of the deep. And the Spirit of God moved upon the face of the waters. And God said 'Let there be light!' and there was light. And God saw the light, that it was good; and God divided the light from the darkness. And God called the light Day, and the darkness he called Night. And the evening and the morning were the first day. And God said, Let there be a firmament in the midst of the waters, and let it divide the waters from the waters. And God made the firmament, and divided the waters which were under the firmament from the waters which were above the firmament: and it was so. And God called the firmament Heaven. And the evening and the morning were the second day. And God said, Let the waters under the heaven be gathered together unto one place, and let the dry land appear: and it was so. And God called the dry land Earth; and the gathering together of the waters called the Seas: and God saw that it was good. And God said, Let the earth bring forth grass, the herb yielding seed, and the fruit tree yielding fruit after his kind, whose seed is in itself, upon the earth: and it was so. And the earth brought forth grass, and herb yielding seed after his kind, and the tree yielding fruit, whose seed was in itself, after his kind: and God saw that it was good. And the evening and the morning were the third day. (Genesis 1 vv 1–13 King James Bible)

Introduction

This story which opens the Christian Bible has influenced much Western thinking on creativity; and this is an area where concepts of the spiritual have survived in Western culture. This chapter will examine why this should be, relating recent literature on creativity to older spiritual strands in Western culture. Creativity and creative have been buzzwords in this culture since the 1960s. At this time there appeared catalogues of creative percussion and handbooks of 'creative activities'. Courses for releasing creative potential still have titles like 'Release the child within and find your creativity'.[1] It has become a bandwagon, a rallying cry for the converted and a bastion against the upholders of traditions. However, if we look at its meaning we find that, like spirituality, it is as multi-faceted as a diamond/crystal; so each writer on the subject appears to be looking at the collection of facets that happen to be facing him/her at the time. Golann summarises this in his *Psychological Study of Creativity*:

> A striking feature of the literature on creativity is the diversity of interests, motives and approaches characteristic of many investigators. Creativity has been viewed as a normally distributed trait, an aptitude trait, an intrapsychic process, and as a style of life. It has been described as that which is seen in all children, but few adults. It has been described as that which leads to innovation in science, performance in fine arts, or new thoughts. Creativity has been described as related to, or equitable with, intelligence, productivity, positive mental health, and originality. It has been described as being caused by self-actualisation and by sublimation and restitution of destructive impulses. (Golann 1963 p. 548)

This chapter will look at the concepts that make-up the construct of creativity. Some of these still seem to be drawn from the Genesis myth at the opening of the chapter:

- Mystery
- Darkness
- Chaos
- Enlightenment
- Ordering
- Playing
- Freedom
- Self-expression and transformation
- The need for courage and risk taking

1 These usually involved activities such as painting, dancing or moving freely, improvising music or sounds.

Strands in the Literature

We shall trace these strands through the literature which can broadly be divided into four areas – the creative person, the creative process, the creative product and the environment that encourages creativity. This chapter will concentrate on the creative process and then look at these motifs in the rest of the literature. This will draw on accounts of artists and scientists, but they will be related to the writings of musicians mostly from the European classical tradition but with some from jazz.

It is possible to identify five strands of creativity within this literature.[2] In one – the traditional – the links with the myth of Divine creation are much clearer. It is the bringing of something new into being or from some very primitive material like God in the creation of the world (R. K. Elliott 1971 p. 140). Charles Taylor calls this position 'Deism'. He sees the development of this into humanism through two further stages. The first he sees in developing in the seventeenth and eighteenth centuries into an anthropocentric tradition which he calls 'Providential Deism'. This is characterised by a 'shift towards an impersonal order', linked with an order that we can 'easily grasp, if not misled by false or superstitious notions'. The third phase is linked with the perennial philosophy that we saw in the previous chapter, and involves the uncovering of natural religion without 'accretions and corruptions' (C. Taylor 2007 p. 221). Here we can see the fragmenting of the Christian narrative already encountered in Chapter One.

The second strand in the literature is alive in Hanns Sachs *The Creative Unconscious* who saw this modification as starting with Rousseau, in an attempt to control nature, which is no longer conceived of as a gift from God (H. Sachs 1947 pp. 211–15). Humans could now control nature which could be compelled by creative human beings to deliver its gifts. This links with the animate/inanimate division explored in Chapter One. Creativity is associated with the ability to manipulate the natural world. So the creative

2 I am indebted to R.K. Elliott's article entitled *Versions of Creativity* (1971) for much of this analysis.

self now took the place held in the traditional view by God; the re-creation of humankind now was seen to rest not with God but with the re-creation of the individual self – artistic exploration became an exploration of oneself. In a powerful book entitled *Psychology as Religion: The Cult of Self-worship*, Vitz (1979) deals with the four major theorists of the view linked as we saw in Chapter One with the human potential movement – Eric Fromm, Carl Rogers, Abraham Maslow and Rollo May. Their concept of artistic creation being somehow a process of self-realisation arose from this particular modification of the divine concept.

Out of this, a third concept of creativity emerged in the first two decades after World War II. It had its origin in the 1930s in the US with the Progressive Education Movement; in this movement, teachers and parents observed children's natural curiosity, experimenting and exploration. It included such spokespeople as William James, John Dewey, William Heard Kilpatrick (the leader of the movement), Francis Parker, Boyd Bode and George Counts. It was a counter-cultural movement centred on the interests of the child; it emphasised democratic ways of behaving and used problem-solving enquiry as a pedagogic strategy. It favoured self-motivated learning, emphasising purposeful activity, intrinsic motivation, planning, open-mindedness, honesty, group action and child-centredness. The stress here is on the process of learning rather than its products. Psychologists, such as G. Stanley Hall (1907), stressed creativity, placing emotions above intellect and intuition above reason. He also thought that too much analysis of the process destroyed spontaneity. He believed in the rich potential of human beings and deplored time spent in school orderliness, standing, sitting, etc. He criticised teachers for helping children over difficulties rather than spurring them to self-activity. The movement favoured characteristics marginalised by the dominant culture of the day. John Dewey was one of its most prolific writers in this area and showed how the scientific method could be applied to all fields of enquiry. To this movement the word 'creative' was applied. It has featured highly, though often unacknowledged, in many educational debates from the mid-twentieth century onwards.

A fourth and harder concept of creativity was very different in fundamental motivation from the versions already examined. It originated with the concerns of the military, government and industry. In the US it became linked with the arms race against the USSR:

> In World War II creativity was forgotten. After it, the atomic bomb demonstrated the power of science and technology and other innovations in industry and projects like Sputnik demonstrated what development was possible by having many creative people at work in a constant effort to transcend what had already been done with accomplishments still more novel and powerful. Figures like J.P. Guilford, Frank Barron and Paul Torrance (Myers and Torrance 1965 p. 20) made the link between the 'creative' education movement and potentiality for producing men and women of genius and produced books to encourage 'creative' thinking. (Guilford 1962 pp. 156–7)

Here the link between problem solving and creativity developed and this split into two strands. One was linked with the identification of problems – situations where no current knowledge was available – and their solution, which would be achieved through new methods and technologies. The second was much more linked with the notion of genius and acknowledged the role of the free play of fantasy in the process, during which a novel idea might arise that would solve the problem, thus linking artistic creation with problem solving. From this view came the development of such techniques as brainstorming[3] in which people wrote down every idea they had, however bizarre and apparently unrelated. A relationship between creativity and healing developed – problem solving became linked with solving life's problems.

The place in the artistic process where these problems were situated varied. Some saw the artist as solving inner emotional problems by means of creativity while others saw the problems being more 'art' centred and limited to the problems presented by the artistic materials in use. If we relate it to the concept of music as operating in four related domains – Materials, Expression, Construction and Values which are explored in the second half of the book – we shall see that the two are interrelated; it may also be that the creative process can start in different domains which are then brought together as the process moves forward.

3 The use of this term was critiqued by mental health practitioners.

A fifth concept of creativity, synthesising some of the ideas above, emerged as the ideas of the New Age took hold in the late 1970s and 1980s and linked with Charles Taylor's third development within Deism. This restored an element of the sacred. To resolve problems is seen as an important part of the soul's journey; this may be done partly with the help of spiritual beings. However, the notion of a single primordial principle (God) and of creation from nothing are replaced by a post-modern delight in diversity and individuality and notions of working with the stuff of personality (into which are often wound ideas of karma and past lives). It links powerfully with the notions of spirituality developed in the last chapter. It draws on notions already found in the concept of the perennial philosophy and the core experience. It sees a relationship to a Higher Self which is construed as being part of a Higher Consciousness. This is summarised in an epilogue from *The Well of Creativity*:

> [Julia] Cameron believes that one of the ways to connect with the greater spirit of the world is through our creativity. No traditional concept of God is necessary to succeed, only a sense that our personal creativity reflects that of the universe, and as we express our artistic impulses we come in touch with a spiritual world of infinite size and power. (Toms 1997 p. 19)

To summarise, the ancient concept of creativity saw its origins in the Divine very explicitly. At the Enlightenment human creativity assumed an independent life and also included a notion of *controlling* nature. In the early twentieth century, in the hands of educationalists it became linked with the young child's natural curiosity and involved challenging traditional educational methods. Through being creative people would realise their human potential and so an area of psychology of this name came to be developed encouraging lateral thinking and right brain activity. After the Second World War these concepts came to be linked with industrial and military progress, especially in the Cold War between the US and the USSR. Techniques for producing 'original' solutions to problems were developed. With the advent of New Age philosophies the notion of an element of the Divine or Spiritual came to be reintroduced into the notion.

The Creative Process

However, the patterns of the creative process – whichever of the above concepts is embraced – in the literature follow quite tightly the track of the Genesis 1 myth including phases of disorder which lead to the creation of a new order (Sinnott 1970 p. 111). There is a notion of reintegration of the personality in some way – a transformation within the person. In artistic terms this makes the starting point of the creative person a desire for a re-ordering of the personality. Creativity grows out of 'a state of disequilibrium' (Stein 1967 p. 110). The creative person (who is seen as more sensitive than others) is seen as working from a sense of dissatisfaction with the established order to the attainment of a new one:

> The creative process is the process of change, of development, of evolution, in the organisation of subjective life. (Ghiselin 1952 p. 110)

In order to do this, the artist draws on ideas from previous experience (Patrick 1949 p. 266). Drawing on the model that will be explored below, in the preparation stage ideas occur that draw on past experience to address the problem; but these do not yet fulfil the need within the personality. After a time of chaotic exploration of ideas, the unfulfilled need is met; illumination then occurs and the solution is reached; this is then revised to be aligned with culturally accepted standards involving processes of perception and judgement.

As we have already seen, views of where the motivation originates vary. Sometimes its origin is seen as being within the emotional domain of the person (later called Expression); in other views the motivation lies in the desire to explore particular musical Materials out of the desire to explore a certain way of constructing an art work. These follow the problem-solving model of creativity and are common to both scientific and artistic creation:

> This sequence of labour, quiescence, illumination, and further labour has turned out to be common to the experience of creative workers of all sorts. (Ghiselin 1956 p. 200)

There are various models of the creative process (both artistic and scientific) that exist in various forms in the literature. The basis of them all is a model created by Wallas (1926), in which he drew on the writings of the physicist, Helmholtz and the mathematician, Poincaré. It contains four stages:

1. Preparation, in which the problem is investigated fully in all directions
2. Incubation, in which the problem is not thought about consciously
3. Illumination, which is the appearance of a happy idea
4. Verification, in which the idea is elaborated and tested. (Wallas 1926 p. 9)

These are common to the analyses of the work of creative artists (Patrick 1935 and 1937, Sparshott 1981), inventors (Rossman 1931) and thinkers (Dewey 1910). Most writers, especially those associated with the arts, see an overlapping between the stages. The elements identified by Wallas are evident in musicians' accounts of their working, even if not in a clear order. These accounts produced less linear models, illustrated by Sparshott's (1981) account of Collingwood's (1938) artistic expression:

> Here there is no determinate first stage, no known structured message to be encoded. There is only an encoding that is at the same time an act of deciphering. The creative process is a passage from unclarity to clarity, the imparting of structures to inchoate feeling ... So there is and there is not a process. (Collingwood quoted in Sparshott 1981 p. 50)

Such accounts show how order and disorder, unity and disunity play significant parts in the process. Birthing is another metaphor used for the experience of the process (Sparshott 1981 p. 50); this model sometimes contains Metaphysical strands in some of its stages, especially that of illumination; this strand originates in the oldest version of creativity already discussed.

Other descriptions are more interconnective with the stages less clearly defined. Mooney (1962) encompasses a number of ideas that link process, person, product and environment. His is a very 'connected' view of creativity which bears marked similarity to the domains of the musical experience to be explored in later chapters. He sees the living being as having four essential conditions:

1. 'Out' – 'his [sic] belonging to the universe as a whole' (the environment),
2. 'In' – 'his being integrative of the whole' (the person),
3. 'Out and in and out and in again and again' – 'his continual coming to be through give and take, incoming and outgoing' (the process),
4. 'Fit' – 'his continued fitting of specific incomings and outgoings, his rendering potentialities actual in concrete sequential instances' (the product). (Mooney 1962 p. 76)

These relate to the preceding chapter with the first linking with the InterGaian and the second with the Intrapersonal. The last two relate to the Interpersonal and the Extrapersonal. In the end he uses a musical metaphor to create a fourfold unity within the processes of creativity in the works of artists:

- harmony, which signifies belonging to the universe
- melody, reordering the self
- rhythm, the fitting of which makes
- a song (Mooney 1962 p. 78)

In musicians' accounts of their process there is often specific preparation for a particular work. Here composers stress the need for openness to the flow of ideas which form the Materials of their piece:

> The process of execution is first of all that of listening inwardly to the music as it shapes itself: of allowing the music to grow, of following both inspiration and conception wherever they may lead. A phrase, a motif, a rhythm, even a chord may contain within itself, in the composer's imagination, the energy which produces movement. It will lead the composer on, through the force of its own momentum or tension. to other phrases, other motifs, other chords. (Sessions 1955 p. 46)

There is also, an openness, a sense of discovery which is difficult to describe and includes hints at divinity or transcendence in the use of words like vision or inspiration:

> I have been using the word 'vision'. It is strange that our language doesn't have a word for aural imaginings. All the words 'revelation', 'insight', even 'imagination' itself, stem from the visual sense. Only 'inspiration' is different, and comes from breathing ... We

> need a word. Wanted – a word to convey both the vivid, direct experience of music in the mind, and the sense of excitement and discovery. As in 'insight', what about 'insound'? (Fowler 1985 p. 4)

Every creative act involves therefore an initial starting point and a retrieval of ideas from the memory, but in such a way as to make new connections. Opinion is divided about the role of memory in the preparation phase. In one model, the memories are considered as being stacked or accumulated in the unconscious from which evocation can remove them at will. In another model the link is made between the operation of memory and the reorganisation of the personality. This links with the domain of Expression discussed in Chapter Five.

I was helped in understanding this by my four year old grand-daughter – Scarlett Tillman. She had been singing her considerable repertoire of English and Slovak nursery rhymes; she then launched into a long narrative style song that is common in children of that age (Tillman 1987) describing herself sleeping and having frightening dreams and waking up. I said to her, when she had finished her singings: 'Did you make that one up?' She thought for a little; and then she said: 'Oh no, Grandma. I found it somewhere in my life.'

The incubation phase is less well documented, possibly because this is where the chaos of the process is situated. However, what becomes clear is that a descent into chaos in necessary to discover anything new and creative people need to find ways of managing this (Ward and Wild 1995). Different people have different ways of managing it. Voluntary abstention from conscious work is often recommended and Wallas (1926) recommends physical exercise. Here it is seen as important to allow the barriers between ideas to drop and the boundaries of the self to become more permeable:

> What is clear is that the censorship of the mind has to be withdrawn. (Schiller quoted in Ball 1938 p. 193)

Aid for this process can be provided by various strategies, such as:

> by selecting specific working environments, by taking oranges, drinking liquors or it may occur when the person is distracted or devoting himself to activities other than those that are specifically relevant to his creative work. (Stein 1962 p. 89)

Stein illustrates this with examples such as Schiller keeping rotten apples in his desk, Milton, Descartes, Leibniz and Rossini lying stretched out and Mozart finding it easier to work after exercise. Current models of mental health have seen the presence of psychoneurotic symptoms (Hutchinson 1949), sometimes quite mild, as the creator strives to realise the goals which will restore balance in the self.

There are many terms in use to describe where the activity takes place in the incubation phase. Some (Wallas 1926, Ghiselin 1952) prefer the term unconscious, involuntary or fringe-consciousness, which does not have the same meaning for them as it does for psychoanalysts. Psychoanalysts like Kris (1953) and Kubie (1958) prefer preconscious. Psychologists like Woodworth (1934) question the use of these terms at all and relate it to the process of recall. This can be linked with the re-ordering of the ideas or the re-membering – in other words, putting them into new combinations, not just pure recall. This may link with the work of Brian Lancaster and Midrashic logic that we explored in Chapter One. For this is the time where, in the adult, there is reference to the use of childhood memories and processes. The boundaries that block the inner personal region from consciousness are permeated and the artist goes into a deep subjective experience. There are accounts of powerful feelings, sometimes accompanied by the notion that an outside agent has whispered productive ideas to them, such as Socrates' 'daemon' (with hints of the Divine in this concept). Koestler (1964) talks of underground games:

> The period of incubation represents a *reculer pour mieux sauter*. Just as in the dream the codes of logical reasoning are suspended, so 'thinking aside' is a temporary liberation from the tyranny of over-precise verbal concepts of the axioms and prejudices ingrained in the very texture of specialised ways of thought. It allows the mind to discard the straitjacket of habit, to shrug off apparent contradictions, to unlearn and forget and to acquire, in exchange, a greater fluidity, versatility and gullibility. (Koestler 1964 p. 210)

This dreamlike state was heavily emphasised in the writing in the 1950s and 1960s and links as we have seen with strands in spirituality. Maslow (1962) called it a return to primary processes (as opposed to the secondary processes of reason and logic), encouraging people to let loose, to be crazy privately. He saw this as a voluntary act made possible by not being afraid of the unconscious. In the childbirth model of the creative act it was likened to the agony of labour. It is out of this apparent disorder that the moment of illumination comes which is often accompanied by alternating states of pain and joy. As we saw in Isabel Clarke's work in Chapter One, it contains plurality and paradox. It also sees an intuitive re-ordering within the self, as in this writing from Ken Robinson:

> Discovery in science often results from unexpected leaps of imagination: the sudden jumping of a logical gap, in which the solution of a problem is illuminated by a new insight, a new association of ideas or a vision of unforeseen possibilities. There is a point in scientific inquiry where logic is not the best instrument. Many of the discoveries were made intuitively ... [quoting a professor of mathematics] 'The other key factor [in mathematical discovery] is aesthetic. It is the elegance of the proof, the beauty of the argument' ... The aesthetic dimension of science is a powerful motivating factor for scientists, just as it is for mathematicians, painters and poets. (K. Robinson 2001 p. 152)

In the successful completion of an act of creation an artist can have a sense of satisfaction from having been freed from a heavy burden. There is often sudden change of mood with the 'eureka' experience. This is the moment of inspiration generating its own energy which enables the creator to make the original idea take shape in the material of the chosen art form. This is associated with a new combination – a reintegration (Koestler 1964 p. 211). Central to Koestler's theory is the combining of two different sets of rules, living on two different planes. The creative act for him is the bringing together simultaneously of activities occurring at several levels of the mind previously distant from one another. The mind is conceived as a pyramid in which habits or skills at various levels and distances from one another can suddenly come into contact. The term 'bisociative' refers to the sudden integration of two dissimilar hierarchically ordered habits or skills in the pyramid. He calls the moment of illumination, the bisociative click (Koestler 1981 p. 14). Loane illustrates this well in a musical composition by 12/13 year olds:

> All this said, however, the new techniques did not come out of the blue, nor were they entirely unprepared. Each is in some way an extension of a technique already familiar,

> or perhaps the result of putting together of two previously learned but previously separate ideas. Thus the flute player already had the performance skill of adjusting intonation by adjusting barrel position. In describing the composition of *Midnight Delirium* ... she recalled having been reminded to adjust her intonation in this way, during a wind band rehearsal. And she had the composition skill of employing an unexpected note to increase tension. We might say that she has put the two together by a leap of understanding that she could use her barrel-twisting technique to make a note unexpected in a new way – sliding flat. She thus creates something new (at least to her) by putting together two things which had previously been apart, a process perhaps close to Koestler's notion of 'bisociation'. (Loane 1984 p. 210)

In the notion that the eureka experience is a reordering of the personality in some way, the literature on creativity draws heavily on the problem-solving model, which is interpreted in various ways – as a form of therapy, as a working out of neuroses (Freud 1949), as a solution to an inner sensate problem (Storr 1972, Witkin 1974), as part of the drive to self-duplication (Gutman 1967), as a bringing about of an internal order (Laub-Novak 1976), as a means of relating to the outer world (Dudek 1974), as an expression of one's own personality (Maslow 1962, Cottle 1973). Most of these draw heavily on psychoanalytic theory. Indeed Julia Cameron writes:

> When *The Artist's Way* [her book] came out, therapists all over America started using it. Their clients started getting better in droves and it's because a lot of what we think of as neurosis in this country is simply people who are unhappy because they're not using their creative endowment. I think most of us are far healthier than our 70-year-old paradigm of therapy would tell us. (Cameron 1997 p. 16)

All stress the newness of the creative product to the person and it is often in this aspect of the process that the notion of Intrapersonal transformation originates. It could be that the embracing of a new way of knowing (as we saw in Chapter One) enables healing to take place. This links the creative process to one of wellbeing through artistic creativity.

So, in these accounts, we see that different sorts of thinking or consciousness are required in the process. The times characterised by freedom are often situated in the incubation phase; the phase of elaboration often includes a greater measure of restriction of freedom as the ideas are contained in a particular Construction pattern. Often, as in the Genesis myth, a new world is created – for the self, a particular group, or the cosmos.

To summarise, all accounts of the creative process include a measure of chaos or disorder within them. This can be located in a particular phase in some models; less linear models show a more subtle relationship between ordering and disorder in the whole process. The goal nonetheless does seem to be order of a new kind – whether this is a scientific theory, an artistic creation or a re-formation of the personality achieved by means of the creative process. This effectively links creativity with ideas of healing and transformation. This in turn can be seen as a development from Deism of a notion of an impersonal ordering as underpinning the cosmos and revealed in this process.

The Place of Playing

For the rest of the chapter we shall examine other characteristics in this literature and see how even the more secularised version of creativity contain elements found in the Genesis creation myth. The first concerns the role of playing in the process which is clearly linked with the incubation phase just described. Indeed, in children playfulness and creativity are often seen as almost synonymous for educationalists. Winnicott (1971) sees the origin of play in the space between mother and child, in a reality intermediate between subjective and objective experience. He calls this the 'potential space' between mother and child; at first it is the mother who creates it. Then with the help of transitional objects the child develops independent, social and symbolic play:

> The concept of transitional spaces originates in the idea of transitional object, as developed by Donald Winnicott and Melanie Klein in the context of child developmental psychology: here the transitional object allows the child to move away safely from the confining security of the mother, into the wider reality, a transitional space. A transitional space, then, in the context of conflict studies, refers to the building of a safe space where even antagonists in a violent conflict can meet as protagonists in generating and allowing the emergence of sustainable peace relationships and processes. In transitional spaces visions and renewed relations can be enacted and tested for their life-giving capacity and sustainability. Here also smothered and neglected

> voices will be heard. Multiparty dialogues and praxes aim at the inclusion of the excluded, victim and perpetrator. (Bouwen et al. 2008 p. 2)

This space is the site of all creative and cultural experiences; it sets up a potentially creative situation:

> The searching (for the self) can only come from desultory, formless functioning or perhaps from rudimentary playing as if in a neutral zone. It is only here, in his unintegrated state of personality, that which can be designed and creative can appear. This, if reflected back, *but only if reflected* back becomes part of the organised individual personality. (Winnicott 1971 p. 15. Author's italics)

Roger Grainger (2010) links the work of children and adults by means of the verb pretending. He draws on the work of Saralea Chazan (2002) to show how therapeutic play is for children because it is a 'safe arena in which to explore overwhelming feelings' (Chazan 2002 p. 119). He unpacks this:

> The secret lies in the realisation that we are actually pretending; and this depends on the ability to stand back from ourselves and see what we are doing ... What adults dismiss as 'pretending', children use as the way to learn to cope with real life ... This, of course, leads on to drama, and the shared game of theatre. (Grainger 2010 pp. 68–9)

The notion of 'make believe' being a part of the creative space is reflected in the comment of a young person from Ukraine who declared that it was easier for her to realise when she had painted them.

Sometimes this pretending is set in contradistinction to such attributes in the process as analysis and logical interpretation (Huizinga 1955 p. 2). It is certainly linked with the suspension of the critical and evaluative faculties. Sometimes the aspect of repetition is stressed (Erikson 1963 p. 153), as in the phase called Mastery by Piaget (1951). Lieberman (1977) defines playfulness as social and cognitive spontaneity, joy and a sense of humour; he says that it might aid early identification of the divergent thinker. He has a developmental approach to play and sees it as combinatorial in essence (Lieberman 1977 p. 120). In the writings on creativity in education great stress is laid on playfulness in the classroom atmosphere (Tillman 1983).[4]

4 However, there is an increasing tendency to use the diagnosis Attention Deficit Hyperactivity Disorder (ADHD) as a descriptor of young people with these attributes

For adults, the arts can be a place in which they can play freely. The adult chooses deliberately to enter their unconscious/subconscious and explore its contents. This is where the courage referred to in the literature comes in. The arts are places where adults are free to make mistakes which we saw in the process based models explored in Chapter One. The characteristics of play are a safe place where experimentation can be made without fear. This involves the freedom to make mistakes (de Saint Exupery 1950 pp. 33–45). It also contains the notion of cultural rebellion.

> The person has control of the elements and is free to create and change rules by common or individual consent. In this notion is a rebellious element, a way of challenging the rules of society (Metzger 1997 p. 57)

Safe playgrounds for adults are rare in our society. So creativity in adults can be seen as a return to the freedom of the idealised childhood (Laub-Novak 1976 p. 15). It is in this phenomenon that the title 'Releasing the inner child' for courses on creativity originates. So, the idea of a creative safe playground contains the concept of risk taking and the embracing of paradox and failure that is implicit in play. It offers a place of freedom in a constrained society.

Freedom

Close to the idea of playing are the characteristics that Maslow calls peak experiences. These will be further explored in relation to music in Chapter Eight:

(Davies 2013). Prescription drugs are used to 'normalise' young people displaying these so-called symptoms. In so doing we may be disempowering some of our most creative young people.

- Giving up the past
- Giving up the future
- Innocence (without shoulds and oughts)
- Narrowing of consciousness (concentration)
- Loss of ego (self forgetfulness)
- Disappearance of fears
- Lessening of defences and inhibitions
- Strength and courage
- Acceptance
- Trust versus trying
- Taoistic receptivity
- Permission to dip into primary processes
- Fullest spontaneity
- Fullest expressiveness
- Fusion of person with the world (summarised from Maslow 1967 pp. 45–7)

The notion of giving up and yielding oneself up to some other power may have its origins in Heidegger's concept of 'being'; here we encounter aspects of spirituality again, for he is drawing on the medieval mystic Meister Eckhart. It has aspects of the virtue of surrender to a Higher Power as described in the influential book on the New Age – *A Course in Miracles* (Schucman and Thetford 1992). Duarte (2013) describes it as a release into the open expanse of freedom, a surrendering that mixes willing and non-willing. It is the yielding up of a representational form of thinking that releases being within the person. This is picked up later by the wisdom theologian Cynthia Bourgeault in her work on the need to welcome sensations like fear and pain. Paradoxically, she sees part of this process as letting go desires for such notions as security and survival, esteem and affection, power and control and a desire to change a particular situation (Bourgeault 2008 pp. 178–80). Although this would seem to be in contrast with Maslow, the idea of surrendering to a different way of knowing in which paradox exists is there in both concepts; this links it back to ideas of a Higher Power in the first ideas around creativity explored at the beginning of this chapter. This is further explored in Isabel Clarke's book, revealingly entitled *Madness, Mystery and the Survival of God.* (2008).[5]

Chaos and Darkness

This features in many accounts of the creative process, especially in the incubation phase. John Cage is a composer who was influenced by John Dewey, moving from a piece of music being a thing to an experience. His writing about his own processes includes a description of the 'formless experience' not unlike the character of the Winnicott passage (1971 p. 15):

> What we need is to fumble around in the darkness because that's where our lives (not necessarily all the time, but at least some of the time, and particularly when life gets problematical for us) take place; in the darkness, or, as they say in Christianity 'the dark night of the soul'. It is in these situations that Art must act and then it won't be judged Art but will be useful to our lives. (Cage 1978 quoted in Ross 1978 p. 10)

It is in this phase that we have the notions of an element of confusion, madness and dreaming:

> Generally speaking the germ of a future composition comes suddenly and unexpectedly. If the soil is ready – that is to say, if the disposition for work is there – it takes root, with extraordinary force and rapidity, shoots up through the earth, puts forth branches, leaves, and, finally, blossoms ... It would be vain to try and put into words the immeasurable sense of bliss which comes over me directly a new idea awakens in me and begins to assume a definite form. I forget everything and behave like a madman. Everything within me starts pulsing and quivering; hardly have I begun the sketch when one thought follows another. In the midst of this magic process it frequently happens that some external interruption wakens me from my somnambulistic state; a ring at the bell, the entrance of a servant, the

5 This is clearly picked up in the first stage of the twelve-step programmes where the participant admits their own powerlessness and surrenders themselves to a Higher Power.

> striking of the clock, reminding me that it is time to leave off. Dreadful, indeed are such interruptions. Sometimes they break the thread of inspiration for a considerable time so that I have to seek it again – often in vain. (Tchaikovsky 1878 in Vernon 1970 p. 58)

When such a great stress is laid in musicology on the domain of Construction, these elements in the creative process are often ignored or discouraged. This is particularly true when creativity has to take place in traditional examination contexts. Jorge Ferrer sees chaos as needed to be included in education:

> Because of the widely undeveloped, undifferentiated, or dissociated state of many of those worlds in the modern self, this process [participatory education] may involve temporary periods of chaos and confusion, but we suggest that they be regarded as fertile steps toward the achievement of genuinely integrated cognition and higher orders of complexity in our creative apprehension of life and the world. (Ferrer, Romero, Albareda 2005 p. 20)

So, there is a need for a descent into chaos and unknowing as part of the creative process.

Ordering

If we look at the accounts from musicians of their creative processes we see different emphases in terms of constraints and freedoms. Indeed, the phases of the creative process can be identified as differing degrees of constraint and freedom. The regression to primary processes described above could be identified with the first and second phases when the initial ideas are collected and then allowed to form themselves often during a time when the creator is not consciously thinking about them.

It is often in the final stages of the process after the moment of illumination that the notion of the ordering or containment of these ideas into a musical construction becomes apparent. Western classical musicians often wrestle with the process of encompassing their free-flowing original ideas within formal structures. Sinnott explains this in terms that resemble the Genesis myth when he writes that creativity is:

> A searching ... for something still inchoate, unformed, which is seeking, so to speak, to reach expression. (Sinnott 1970 p. 110)

Composers stress the challenges in this process. Tchaikovsky writes of the verification phase when he has to allow his ideas to take an appropriate musical form:

> Yesterday when I wrote to you about my methods of composing. I did not sufficiently enter into that phase of work which relates to the working out of the sketch. This phase is of primary importance ... Only after strenuous labour have I at last succeeded in making the form of my compositions correspond, more or less, with their contents. Formerly I was careless and did not give sufficient attention to the critical overhauling of my sketches. Consequently my *seams* showed and there was no organic union between my individual episodes. This was a very serious defect, and I only improved gradually as time went on; but the form of my works will never be *exemplary*, because, although I can modify, I cannot radically alter the essential qualities of my musical temperament. (Tchaikovsky 1878 in Vernon 1970 p. 58. Author's italics)

Other composers, working at the containment of their feelings within a formal structure, stress the constant interaction with his/her medium and the dilemma of incarnating the original idea or vision in a material form:

> Not only will he (the composer) [sic] have the gift of seeing ... the complete musical form ... He will have the energy, persistence and skill to bring this envisioned form into existence, so that even after months of work not one of its details will be lost or fail to fit into his photo-mental picture. (Hindemith 1952 p. 71)

Hindemith goes on to describe the importance of the initial vision and how skill, although important in its working out, is no replacement for it – showing the interface between the intuitive and the rational in the creative process. The account of the composer Jennifer Fowler also illustrates the complex relationship between the process and the original inspiration

> So, in the beginning there is an idea, a plan: partly map, partly seed. It has to be flexible enough to allow things to happen. As one makes progress into the piece, so

> one constantly returns to the beginning to allow that first page to carry the right implications. Through writing the piece, one modifies the original plan, so for a long time there is constant interaction between the plan in advance and the piece as it actually emerges. (Fowler 1985 p. 4)

Busoni writes about the crucial role that notation plays in the encapsulating of ideas in the European Western classical tradition in a formal score:

> The moment that the pen takes possession of it the thought loses its original form. The intention of writing down an idea necessitates already a choice of time and key. The composer is obliged to decide on the form and the key and they determine more and more clearly the course to be taken and the limitations. (Busoni 1957 pp. 87–8)

There is, in many Western European classical composers' accounts of their processes, this tension between the ordering of ideas into a form and the need for the originality of the product. Because of the stress of innovation in the European classical tradition, here the concept is more of a freedom from the restraints of current musical culture than of a personal freedom. So the balancing of order and chaos and reason and intuition is seen clearly within the creative process (Boyce-Tillman 2007b).

Enlightenment

This is often associated in the work of professional composers with originality or the illumination moment. The need for a constant search for originality has been central to much of the writing about the Western European classical tradition. Jennifer Fowler outlines what originality means for a composer:

> Someone has asked for a piece for violin and piano. I think of the sound of a violin, the sound of a piano. Stale. These are instruments which have been constantly 'worked over'. It is a bit like the 'big bang' development of the universe. First the middle, strongest and most resonant sounds are explored, then the edge are expanded; composers pushing out constantly to the edges of register, to the peripheral sounds of

> whispers and grittiness ... Why always seek the new? We have to do battle against the inertia of the human mind which is biased towards travelling along known paths in known directions. Ask anyone to think up a bit of music and it so easily comes out as yet another version of the familiar. Even in the great composers' notebooks, this is sometimes true of the first attempts. One's own expectations, like everybody else's, are formed by the known. Somehow one has to trick the imagination into making a step – see a vision outside itself – communicate the excitement – have something to say. (Fowler 1985 pp. 3–4)

In the non-notated orate improvised traditions the concept of innovation is slightly different. The freedom in jazz, for example, is linked with ideas of courage. The jazz musician Keith Jarrett (1997) describes it as jumping in:

> At that moment when the piece is being played, I jump anyway. I am trusting in the discipline that I have already been going through ... I must say, though, that you cannot constantly be jumping. You know, you do land occasionally. (Jarrett 1997 pp. 80–2)

Both of these accounts, however, stress the tension between the tradition in the process of ordering or containment within a form and the need for innovation and freedom. It is on the basis of an acquired discipline that the courageous leap of faith is made. The existential philosophers connected the possibility of human freedom to the possibility of human creativity – human beings are free precisely because they both can and must create themselves, as their existence precedes their 'essence'. Sartre (1947) rejected notions of determinism to declare that the human being is free; the essence of humanity is freedom which is fostered by creativity.

To summarise, there is a clear emphasis on freedom as a necessary part of the creative process. This is often linked with a return to the processes of childhood especially play. The operation of these processes in adulthood is different from those of the child, in that it is a conscious choice on the part of the adult. The arts are a place where adults can play, where they are free to explore their own innermost expressive world and also to make mistakes without serious consequences. This requires a degree of courage and the capacity to take risks. The notion of a creative imagination is related to these characteristics. The creative process also contains the characteristics of Maslow's peak experience where there is a sense of transcendence that contains a sense of freedom. Containment is seen in childhood play in the development of rule based play. In the accounts of Western European classical composers, it appears to be an important part of various phases of the creative process, often in the area of formal construction and notation. In jazz traditions, it is illustrated by the situating of their playing within the discipline of the tradition. Innovation is often associated with a notion of a counter cultural rebellion, a challenging of the conventions of society in the exploration of new ideas.

Self-expression and Transformation

In the Genesis narrative there is a notion that God expressed Godself through the creation of the world. This section will examine the importance placed on Expression in the literature and debates about what is being expressed. Notions of self-expression are very clear in the contemporary literature; but in the first version of creativity what is being expressed is of Metaphysical character – of God. The German abbess composer, Hildegard (1098–1179), for example, saw all her songs coming straight from God and resisted any attempt to change them in any way (Boyce-Tillman, 2000b). Many of the creators of the sacred music of the Western classical musical tradition would see the prime source of their creativity as God, whom they would also seek to glorify in the works that they create.

Creativity is seen as accessing the deepest areas of the personality where – as we saw in the Prelude – the soul may be seen as residing. Psychoanalysts see it in terms of an artist trying to solve a personal problem (Kris 1953), so forming the link with the problem-solving strand in the literature, or as a product of relationships in childhood (Gowan 1967). The term self-actualisation was coined by the writers of the 1950s and 1960s, such as Maslow (1958) and Rogers (1970). This was refined by theorists like Witkin (1974) who defined the driving force as a desire to solve a sensate problem.

So the process of creation becomes potentially transformative. Alice Miller (1987) was very clear on the links between violence and creativity.

She saw the psychic energy that could be used for aggressive behaviour as potentially transformed into creativity (Miller 1987 p. 270). The personal emotional conflict involved in creativity is seen by some writers as potentially resolved through an act of regression, in which we recover our pre- or aesthetic modes of structuring experience and or the adaptive operation which is the title of Witkin's book – *The Intelligence of Feeling* (1974). This relates well to the work of Lancaster (2004) and Midrashic logic that we explored in Chapter One. The experience contains a feeling of discomfort as a new structure is created – which links with the drive towards balance and stability within the personality. Kris (1952) develops a concept that the process of regression serves the development of the ego and stresses the use of primitive modes of thinking in the first phase of the creative process. But the regression of the adult is different from the playing child, in that it is voluntary and consciously and deliberately chosen. Ross sees the second developmental crisis for individual creativity as occurring at adolescence; the first he sees occurring when the child discovers the potential space between him/herself and his/her mother; this is the time when adults have to take the risk of returning to primary processes (Ross 1978 pp. 11–12).

Mihaly Csikszentmihalyi (1997) resolves this by stressing the paradoxes within the creative personality and the fluidity necessary for the creative process (Lieberman 1977 p. 125). The creative adult can effectively access the child's way of knowing while remaining a responsible adult. The notion of challenging the values of the dominant culture, especially in the area of gender, is very clear in his work when he describes playful people as 'both playful and responsible at the same time', as rebellious yet based in tradition and as reworking stereotypes (Csikszentmihalyi 1997 pp. 128–9). So here creativity may be seen as accessing the soul through accessing the deepest recesses of the personality.

The notion of music as *self*-expression (rather than expression of the Divine) became possible after the Enlightenment. With the growth of the new concept of creativity, human beings gradually acquired the central position formerly occupied by God. The hierarchy that had come to be associated with God (mediated largely through the hierarchical structures of the Church) also broke down and the way was open for the establishment of creativity as a universal attribute in line with thinking about the common core experience and the perennial philosophy that we explored in Chapter One. There is a tension here between a more elitist view which set up the concept of genius – a category for special people with attributes often described as godlike – and the concept of creativity as a universal attribute.

It was in the writers on creativity from the beginning of the twentieth century, that the possibility that all were creative became a possibility. As educationalists increasingly used the descriptor creative of all children, so it seemed possible that all adults were potentially creative. It became apparent to groups such as industrialists that it might be possible for education to provide the vast numbers of people needed for creative developments in the future. In a few years, public opinion about creativity had changed so that it became the potential property of all people. Vinacke, for example, in 1952 asserts that:

> with respect to personality there is no reason to suppose that artists as artists, are different to non-artists. (Vinacke 1952 p. 241)

This came to be applied to music. The upsurge in 'creativity' that characterised British music education in 1960s and 70s was full of statements like:

> It [creative] is not a word used about music at all: it is human beings who are, in varying degrees, creative. All music is, or has been, created by wonderfully made humans. It is only when a teacher realises this that he can tap the sources of power that lie within every pupil we teach. (Addison 1975 p. 60)

The link between creativity and the process of everyday living (as we saw in the discussion of altered states of consciousness in Chapter One) is emphasised by many writers (drawing on ideas found in Dewey on the relationship between the aesthetic and the everyday). It enables people to be flexible, free from fixations, and live their lives to the full. This links with a statement from a Christian theologian, Irenaeus: 'The joy of God is men [sic] fully alive.' Sometimes this was linked with music. Evans under the heading *Creative expression by adults* points to how people use music in their ordinary lives:

> Most people at some time in the safety of their bathroom indulge in a form of singing. Relations and neighbours might vary in the name they give this vocal exploration, but the fact remains that, relieved of the inhibitions caused by the external environment and stimulated by the physical process of towelling, a great many people indulge in some form of bathroom vocalising. If the atmosphere of the bathroom extravaganza could be taken on to the primary classroom of this land, a musical revolution would thrust itself upon us overnight. (Evans 1971 p. 10)

This theme is taken up by the Department for Education and Employment (National Advisory Committee for Creative and Cultural Education) in *All our futures: Creativity, Culture and Education*:

> In our view, all people are capable of creative achievement in some area of activity, provided the conditions are right and they have acquired the relevant knowledge and skills. Moreover, a democratic society should provide opportunities for everyone to succeed according to their own strengths and abilities ... In our view:
>
> a. creative possibilities are pervasive in the concerns of everyday life, its purposes and problems;
> b. creative activity is also pervasive; many people who are creative do not recognise that this is what they are doing;
> c. creativity can be expressed in collaborative as well as individual activities, in teamwork, in organisations, in communities and in governments. (K. Robinson 1999 p. 28)

The writers of this report contrast this with what they call the elite definition – rooted in the eighteenth-century literature on genius – which stressed innate personality characteristics. Creativity is now seen as being an educational issue. Genius could and should be 'nurtured' by the right educational environment. Others tried to steer more of a middle course in the nature/nurture debate, trying to bring the two together in terms of qualitative measures:

> At one end of the scale it covers that rare quality, original genius. But a high degree of originality is only one aspect of creativity. Also included is the ordinary, everyday inventiveness which grows from a combination of necessity, awareness and imagination. In this sense, creativity is something we all possess and employ to some extent, every day of our lives. (Paynter 1977 p. 4)

The conclusion to be drawn from such writing is that the aim of the process of fostering creativity is not to create geniuses but more integrated people who will be able to live their more fully and with greater insight and use this process as a strategy for living their lives more effectively. The creativity of the 'ordinary' people is in terms of entry into a process not the production of a product; this is in keeping with the idea of spirituality as process that we discussed in Chapter One. By concentrating on the process rather than the product the way was open for all to be creative.

Other writers suggest that what most people lack is not the ability to generate original ideas, but the ability to elaborate or verify imaginative ideas. The German composer, Hindemith calls the motifs from which compositions are generated Einfaelle

> When we talk about Einfaelle, we usually mean little motifs, consisting of a few tones not often even felt as tones but felt merely as a vague curve of sound. They are common to all people, professionals and laymen alike: but while in the layman's mind they die away unused in their earliest infancy, as before, the creative musician knows how to catch them and subject them to further treatment. (Hindemith 1952 p. 68)

This implies that untrained musicians can enter the first phase of the creative process but lack the skills to go further – into the elaboration phase described above, where a grasp of musical construction is necessary. The development of music technology has enabled more people to enter this process than when the main form of working in the European classical tradition was a grasp of Western classical notation.

This was confirmed by my own research into children's improvisations/compositions where at a certain point they wanted to learn the conventions of their musical culture (Tillman 1987c). The varied approaches to the place of skill-giving in creativity in music is nowhere more clearly seen than in the literature on music therapy. In the project *Music Lessons on prescription* that we ran in the 1990s from the University of Winchester (then King Alfred's College) with children with chronic anxiety, music lessons not therapy were being given (Walker and Boyce-Tillman 2002). Alongside other intentions it was intended that these would give the children the skills to refine their expression into a contained and satisfying shape. These young people were enabled to go beyond the generation of musical ideas by means of the lessons that included improvisation.

Self-expression is seen as a powerful motive in the literature on motivation. Some writers see expression as a basic human need. Ribot (1906 p. 315) sees the origin of the creative process in human needs, appetites, tendencies and desires, including those for individual preservation (resulting in food getting, housing etc.), individual and social expression (resulting in military, commercial, industrial inventions); in a disinterested form, the creative process results in aesthetic creation, sexual fulfilment in art and everyday life, and the need of knowing and explaining, leading to myths, religion, philosophical systems and hypotheses. He concludes that this need finds its expression in some form of physical activity:

> Every want, tendency or desire may, then, become creative, by itself or associated with others, and into these final elements it is that analysis must resolve 'creative spontaneity'. This vague expression corresponds to a *sum*, not to a special property. Every invention, then, has a motor origin; *the ultimate base of the constructive imagination is motor*. (Ribot 1906 p. 315 Author's emphases)

He then goes on to see the necessary role of the imagination to generate the images that will govern the action:

> But needs and desires by themselves cannot create; they are only a stimulus and a spring. Whence arises the need of the second condition – the spontaneous arrival of images. (Ribot 1906 p. 315)

To summarise, the notion that creativity involves the making of some object (including music) from the less readily available parts of the self is deep in the literature. This is considered de facto as desirable and a universal human trait. It may indeed be related to everyday processes and be a useful way of overcoming blocks within our personal lives. The need finds its expression in the action of making an object; it is the process of making that is significant as the poem *I Love all beauteous things* by Robert Bridges exemplifies.

I too will something make
And joy in the making!

Altho' tomorrow it seem
Like the empty words of a dream
Remembered, on waking. (Bridges 1932)

Creativity is regarded as potential for most, if not all, people. It is, however, possible that in the area of music, most people are able to generate ideas but need some skill to work them out in larger musical forms.

The Place of the Community

The place of the wider community in creativity is a complex one in the literature. The concept of the creator is closely linked with a single God in a monotheistic faith. When linked with the notion of self-expression it becomes part of the favourite European archetypal narrative of the heroic journey (Boyce-Tillman 2000a, 2007b). It is this alliance of ideas that generate the notion of self-realisation and self-actualisation. The origins of the current notions of creativity were very much situated in the heroic journey of the individual fulfilling his or her potential, which is still alive in the seeking model of spirituality. In the literature, the prime role for the community is particularly related to the validation of the value of the product. In the Western classical music traditions, the community is a sounding board for ideas, particularly how they need to be refined. It is also a recipient of them in the form of an audience, which includes the place of critics. Maurice Stein summarises it well, in a way that links the innovation of the composer/artist/inventor well with the audience/recipients:

> By accepting the product and regarding it as creative, the group indicates that it accepts and implicitly approves of the needs which initially motivated the creative person to deviate from the accepted patterns and to probe the unknown. In the process of accepting the creative product the group manifests similarity and identification between its own wishes and those of the creative individual ... and that it has, in a sense, joined the individual in the creative process and become co-creator

> (Kris 1952). For the group the creative product has fulfilled or given expression to certain needs. The creative product 'says' things that the group has wanted to say but has been unable to. (Stein 1962 p. 87)

He starts by affirming the part played by scientific and professional organisations, art and drama critics, curators of museums, literary agents and so on in defining what is creative. This can be further enriched by a Foucauldian analysis, examining how the dominant culture validates who and what it will regard as innovative (Foucault/Gordon 1980, Boyce-Tillman 2007b), particularly in the area of gender and ethnicity (Boyce-Tillman 1996). The degree of innovation required by a work or invention to be described as creative is an important element stressed by Jerome Bruner, which he defines as 'effective surprise.' This is clearly related to Koestler's (1964) idea of bisociation, discussed earlier. In the context of community, the new creation provides a new perspective for the community as a whole (Bruner 1966 p. 23).

If we apply this writing specifically to music we find an interesting thesis arising that supports the notion of the composer as potentially a therapist for a particular group; it opens up the potential for creative listening that is transformative (Boyce-Tillman 2007e). The composer – in going into his own resources, coming up with new solutions and combinations and resolving his/her own issues – is able to act in a similar way on behalf of a group of people. The group, when listening to the piece, is taken into new areas. Insofar as these are congruent with their own needs and desires (their own personal journey) they are guided into new processes and new solutions of their own. The task of the successful composer/improviser is to keep in touch with the surrounding needs; but they need to stay a little way ahead presenting them with some challenge but not so great as to lose track of the audience. We shall examine this further when we look at the domain of Construction.

This was clear in the thinking of Leonard Meyer. He makes a very closely argued case for the evaluating of compositions along the line of information theory, that requires the presence of the unexpected in a piece for meaning to be attributed to it. Musical meaning is created out of a contrast between the expected and the actual (Meyer 1967 p. 11). So the relation of the composer to the audience is reinforced by the management of surprise (innovation) and repetition in the work. This holds their attention.

In some orate traditions, such as Irish folk traditions, the relationship may be more subtle and the audience can be seen as having a hand in the shaping of the performance in terms of repetition and contrast. Carson describes the relationship between the performer and audience:

> The inexperienced punter may be somewhat disconcerted by the custom whereby little whoops and screams are uttered while the music is in progress. These expressions of appreciation may not be as random as they seem. An attentive punter may, for example, make a little yelp at that point where the tune has been played once and is now to be played again (tunes are played at least twice round), indicating a) that he knows where a tune ends and b) that he would like to hear it again, which he will anyway. On the other hand, the yelp may come at a point in the tune which is determined by the punter's perception of a particularly fine melodic variation; to the musician who just played it, it may have been a mistake. Or it may not. (Carson 1986 p. 56)

So the relationship between player/composer/improviser/audience in other traditions is much more co-operative and connected. This relationship is carried by a wide range of subtle signals often incoherent to the listener outside of the tradition (Carson 1986 p. 55). Carson goes on to describe this interactive process as an art in its own right, claiming that:

> the song, after all, is one expression of whatever is going on at that particular social gathering. (Carson 1986 p. 50)

When we turn to education and children, this area shows immense complexity, in that the creation may be new to the child but not to society; these ideas play against one another in the literature. Randall Allsup (2013) distinguishes between open and closed forms in music teaching, linking the notion of the closed more with traditional forms of teaching and musical construction and the open forms with more innovative and experimental pedagogies. In my own experience, as part of my doctoral thesis, I saw and heard children move from pieces that appeared more innovative to my adult mind, to pieces showing them wanting to learn the conventions of our society. They would explore freely at first, and then acquire the skill to execute a musical convention like a steady pulse. Having grasped that securely, they would go on to explore it more freely and then they would edge towards other conventions, such as melodies familiar within their own culture. This was clearly illustrated in the story of a seven-year old who previously had produced many attractive and idiosyncratic improvised songs. This time, when I asked her to sing a song, she offered *London's burning*. 'No. One of your own' I said. However, she replied: 'But I want to sing this one'. And so she did, I realised that she now wanted to embrace the vernacular which was innovative to her but not to me. If she had obeyed me, she would have been trapped in a 'Peter Pan' position of perpetual musical childhood, not learning cultural conventions which form the tunnel she had to go through, in order to enter musical adulthood. Later, she would produce variations on *London's burning*; but you cannot produce variations on a tune that you have not grasped in its conventional form. These debates echoed around the early literature on children composing and improvising; they are only solved by embracing both tradition and innovation within a classroom context and acknowledging that there is a difference between new to the child and new to the surrounding culture.

To summarise, a powerful notion in the concept of creativity, linked to the individual heroic journey, is that of self-realisation; this developed in the early twentieth century in the context of psychoanalysis and the human potential movement. Innovation was an important aspect of this notion. This necessarily links creativity with a particular group of people in a particular place at a particular time. In music, this link is between the composer/improviser/performer and the audience in which is the community of critics and gatekeepers to performance venues. In other often orate traditions, such as the folk traditions, the audience seem to have more of a hand in shaping the piece each time it is performed, through an intricate system of audible signals linking performer and audience together in a symbiotic relationship; this links the degree of innovation with the needs of a particular audience directly.

The Creative Environment

When we look at the area of the creative environment, the essence of it is to encourage empowerment and a safe, nurturing place to undertake the challenge of creating. Where creativity is used in association with music (especially music education) in the literature it almost always refers to the act of composing or improvising. There is little reference to creative listening or performing (although hints at it have already been part of the discussions above). The underlying assumption is that it is in the act of composing/improvising that we engage most deeply with the materials of sound and so achieve the maximum degree of creative fulfilment and therefore self-transformation. This links it very tightly to the act of making that is the central feature of the Genesis myth.

Earlier educators had also supported the notion of empowerment through methods involving risk taking and discovery. Froebel (Froebel 1879) suggested that educators took their cues from the early learning activities of children. He encouraged people to focus on the earliest activity of the child, to support children's spontaneous and personal activity, to encourage the impulse to self-culture and self-instruction through self-shaping, self-observation and self-testing. He considered knowing, feeling and willing as the three activities of the mind. He advocated the involvement of the child with as many sensory experiences as possible – sound (song and rhythmic bodily movement), modelling, drawing, painting and printing. He believed that nothing is more contrary to nature than to forbid a young child the use of its hand.

Yorke Trotter wrote from a similar position at the beginning of the century working out its implications in music education:

> The aim of the teacher should always be to develop the innate feeling for music in the child. This can best be brought about by causing the pupil to do things himself. One of the best means of developing the feeling is to cause the pupil to finish a theme, as soon as sufficient material has been given. The teacher sings or plays a phrase, the pupil at once sings an answer to it. From the answer the teacher learns if the first principles of musical construction are in the child's mind. If the answer is a suitable response to what is given, the tonalitive principle of key centre is present. It will be found that the principle of reiteration appears when a certain stage is reached. The child will reproduce the material that appears in the question, not generally as mere repetition, but as development. The length of the phrase that is offered depends on how much the child can hold in his mind. Obviously, a very young child can only assimilate a very short phrase; an older child can understand long phrases; and will be able to sing complete melodies without modulation to different keys. In every case the answer must be given without premeditation. It must be the intuitive expression of the pupil's feelings. Answers made by consideration of the various factors

> of the given theme are of no service in developing musical feeling. Unless there is spontaneity, there can be no good results. (Trotter, published at the beginning of the twentieth century, p. xc)

It is interesting to note here how he stresses the role of intuition and the suspension of evaluative faculties, two strands to be found in the American literature from much later and examined above. Such methods encouraging pupils to find their own route through active immersion in the Materials of sound, saw the real importance of nurture to enable this to happen.

Similarly, the literature encouraging adult creativity lays great stress on a supportive environment where people are supported through their own choices and there is a climate where mistakes can be made 'safely'. There is sometimes a notion that people (and children) need to be given new and 'challenging' experiences in order to trigger the creative process or even to give them a subject for creative work. In more recent literature, particularly that associated with the New Age, this can be the natural world (Boyce-Tillman 2010). So the environment to encourage creativity needs to be safe and protected to give people the impetus to engage in the creative process with its risks and potential failures.

The Place of the Metaphysical

This final section of the chapter will examine how far the notion of the divine or metaphysical is still part of the concept of creativity and how much the process is conceived of as being psychological and whether there are physical components. The myth of Divine creation is the oldest strand in the literature on creativity and is still present in the twentieth century in the writing of people such as Tolstoy (1930) – even in some of the very 'secular' literature. It has resurfaced in the fusions of concepts that have arisen in the so-called New Age. Pope Paul Xll linked God with scientific discovery, when he spoke to astronautical scientists in his justification for research:

> All creation has been committed and offered to the human spirit, that man [sic] may penetrate it and thus be able to understand more and more fully the infinite grandeur of his Creator. (Barron 1963 p. 290)

The traditional link is most clearly worked out in the work of Dorothy Sayers. The speech of Archangel Michael at the end of *The Zeal of Thy House* sums up her thinking which she worked out in more detail in *The Mind of the Maker* (1941/47). In this, she establishes a model of Divine creative power based on her observation of her own creative process:

> Praise Him that He hath made man in His own image, a maker and craftsman like Himself, a little mirror of His triune majesty.
>
> For every work of creation is threefold, an earthly trinity to match the heavenly.
>
> First: there is the Creative Idea; passionless, timeless, beholding the whole work complete at one, the end in the beginning, and this is the image of the Father.
>
> Second: there is the Creative Energy, begotten of that Idea, working in time from the beginning to the end, with sweat and passion, being, incarnate in the bonds of matter; and this is the image of the Word.
>
> Third: there is the Creative Power, the meaning of the work and its response in the lovely soul; and this is the image of the indwelling Spirit.
>
> And these three are one, each equally in itself the whole work, whereof none can exist without other and this is the image of the Trinity. (Sayers quoted in Brabazon 1981 p. 206)

It is, however, from such writing that the concept of the godlike genius occurs. This is in contradistinction to the more democratic views of creativity discussed earlier in the chapter. These geniuses have divine qualities in that they are said to create a world (e.g. Shakespeare, Dostoyevsky). The creation of the world is seen as the model of artistic creation. 'Creating a job' (out of nothing), 'creating havoc' (out of nowhere) and so on, are examples of the use of the term in this sense. Very good scientists that reconstruct our understanding of the world fall into this category (e.g. Newton, Einstein and Freud), but not lesser ones. All successful artists fall into it. There is one view that sees artists as set apart – as having God-given qualities.

> The creator 'par excellence' is God, and whenever we create some new thing we feel we are God-like and achieving immortality. (Lytton, 1971 quoted in Plummeridge 1980 p. 35)

Lorenz (1972 p. 68) coined and redefined the term 'fulguration' for creative acts. It is a term used by mediaeval mystics for God's creative acts and contains the idea that it is God's lightning that causes new things to come into existence.

This divine aspect of creativity has fascinated human beings down the ages. One early explanation of the flash of inspiration that leads to the reinterpreting of human experience was that it was a divine madness, a seizure of the individual by the gods. The Greeks called it 'enthusiasmos' (from which came their word for inspiring creators, 'enthusiasts') – or God within; we have already seen this in the literature on spirituality in Chapter One. It is found in contemporary literature too and is clearest around the idea of inspiration. Deanne Bogdan, in her 2013 panel presentation, describes her idea of the 'shiver-shimmer factor' in relation to a professional Russian pianist; in her thinking all these elements are clearly present as she draws on Plato's idea of divine madness (related to enthusiasmos – the God within) and possession by a daemon. In the discussion that followed, this was linked with ideas on shamanic practice and their influence on the construction of genius in the Romantic period when the first text on the nature of genius was published in Europe. Fanny Waterman in an interview on BBC Radio 4 (2010) described the great classical composers as being able to 'commune with the gods'. Levi Strauss (1970) sees this strand in creativity lying in the mysterious nature of music:

> Music is a language by whose means messages are elaborated ... Since music is the only language with the contradictory attributes of being at once intelligible and untranslatable, the musical creator is a being comparable to the gods, and music itself is the supreme mystery of the science of man [sic]. All other branches of knowledge stumble into it; it holds the key to their progress. (Levi Strauss 1970 p. 18)

Creative states are likened to states of ecstasy, or, as Maslow calls it, a 'peak experience'. In the psychological writing, religious ideas, such as ecstasy, are brought together with the language of psychoanalysis:

> What had been projected as a vision, God, is now in ecstasy taken back into the ego, but not as an antithesis between ego and superego, or between ego and God: ego and God are one. (Kris 1965 p. 40)

This view explains how some people are reluctant to inquire into the sources of creativeness; it is a feeling almost of sacrilege and a fear that such inquiry will cause the departure of God within. There is a vast literature on the subject starting with Homer and Socrates. It is this line of thinking that leads to the position taken by some researchers into creativity that creative acts cannot and should not be analysed because doing so will destroy the very essence of the act of creation. It can be observed and appreciated but not caught. This is often linked with the notion of transcendence within the self:

> The creative artist or scientist does not simply produce a transcendent product; in a certain sense he actually transcends himself on producing something he could not have willed, which he could not know he has the ability to produce. As a bearer of a tradition he has not only gone beyond it, he has gone beyond himself, he has transcended himself. One is reminded of the beautiful story about Haydn who listening for the first time to his Creation, broke into tears and said: 'I have not written this.' (Briskman 1981 p. 131)

It is in this mystery that antagonism towards research projects into creativity lies. Barron (1963) says that a fifth of the writers approached to take part in his survey saw researching into the process as intrinsically evil. Here, however, the grounds are the relation of academic research to the normativity of the dominant society:

> The objections to such research are mainly on these counts: it is an expression of the effort of organised society to encroach upon the individual and rob him of his fruits; it is presumptuous because it seeks to describe and to understand what is intrinsically a mystery. Psychological diagnosis is, moreover, a form of name-calling; it is the way of having the last word; it does not respect the individual. Finally, it is the present

> seeking to impose itself upon the future and to perpetrate the status quo through techniques which will identify the potentially constructive deviant and permit society to control him. (Barron 1963 p. 290)

Here we see the suspicion that creative people have about the way pathology is constructed by the dominant culture (Foucault ([1963] 1973); many creative people, such as Alan Turing, have fallen into the hands of mental health services. On the same grounds, a number of artists have resisted therapy which they would see as designed to inhibit their processes. Their evidence that psychiatry does not deal well with highly creative people (Boyce-Tillman 2013d). To analyse their creativity would be to destroy it. This is borne out by a *Desert Island Discs* interview with Stephen Fry who, asked if he would like to be free of his diagnosed bipolar illness, replied: 'If you get rid of my demons, the angels may also leave.'[6]

When the theological views of creativity were replaced by philosophical views, a notion of the Metaphysical that involves a world beyond this world, mediated by our mind, was retained:

> For Popper this world of 'objective mind' (his '3rd World') interacts both with the world of mental states (his '2nd World') and with the world of physical states (his '1st World') – the latter interaction being mediated through the '2nd World'. It follows that both the mental world, and more importantly, the physical world are also open; and this rules out physical determinism and, in time, kicks open the door to the possibility of human freedom. In other words, for Popper, the creative potentiality of human thought, the possibility of genuinely creative, unpredictable additions to his '3rd World', opens up the door to human freedom. (Popper 1950 quoted in Briskman 1981 p. 131)

The mediation of the 3rd world through the mind into the 1st world of physical states illustrates well the inextricable link between the transcendent and the material. The 3rd world has to find its expression in material form. Popper's views have real parallels with Platonic thought and medieval theologies of creation.

6 Stephen Fry in an Interview on *Desert Island Discs*, BBC Radio 4 June 26th 9am, 2015.

If the pre-Enlightenment culture stressed the transcendent aspects of creation, later philosophical systems stressed the notion of immanence. Powers once attributed to a transcendent Person outside the order of nature, are now regarded as being *immanent* in nature, especially human nature. There is a notion of a power at the heart, the hidden centre of nature (as something natural and not needing a Divine explanation). This links well with the thinking around the perennial philosophy in Chapter One. This shift in perception enables the power to be available to everyone. Music is somehow a reflection of a reality at the heart of the universe. This has been clear in analytical systems attempting to link musical systems to the laws of acoustics (Boyce-Tillman 2007e) and so uncoupling these from notions of the Divine (to which they would have been linked in the Middle Ages).

The philosopher Whitehead saw creativity as at the very heart of reality because of its relationship to time. Murray outlines Whitehead's position on this:

> Whitehead adumbrated a theoretical system of systems in which creativity is a metaphysical ultimate. His conception is that of a procession of over-lapping and inter-dependent events, or actual concrete occasions, in space-time ... A fine micro-analysis would yield a sequence of occasions, or actual entities, each of which with a duration, say of a fraction of a second, would perish at the instant of its composition and then be immediately succeeded by another actual occasion ... Translated to the mind, this could be illustrated by the composition of an image which is immediately decomposed, only to be followed by the composition of another image, or with the formation of a word which dies as another word succeeds it, and so forth. Our senses being less acute than certain delicate instruments, we are scarcely aware of these individual 'drops' of mental life and are more prone to choose metaphors of fluid continuity, such as the 'stream' of consciousness or the 'flow' of thought. One might say that a 'wave theory' is closer to our immediate experience than a 'corpuscular theory'. The latter, however, may prove more serviceable in the end. (Murray 1958 p. 99. Author's emphasis)

So, for Whitehead, every moment is one of innovation; we are continually moving into novelty. This enables him to see everything – from a sentence to a ten-year conversation – as unique, in that they consist of an integration of novel elements. By applying this study to the very nature of time and, in particular, the relationship between past, present and future, these philosophers enter into the very heart of the musical experience, which is, in essence, a structuring of time. They also make music an icon of the way in which the universe functions; this notion links Whitehead's philosophy with Hildegard's theology of music and its relationship to the wider cosmos in the Middle Ages, thus linking it back directly to the Genesis myth.

Such views connect human beings with the very nature of the universe and conflict with some thinking about the relationship between human beings and the natural world. Some claim that it is creativity that sets human beings apart from animals, thus reinforcing the traditional theological view of human beings as the pinnacle of God's creation. Claims were made that human beings were the only creatures to create musical sounds purposefully and use music to control their environment. This is by no means now a universal view. Chisholm (1966) makes the case for the creative element in bird, fish and insect sounds and claims that, apart from social reasons such as mating, identifying a territory etc., some sounds are made simply out of a pure pleasure in creating; some writers see music being a uniting factor with the universe – a way of uniting us with the natural world in which animals and plants would also have their songs (Abrams 1996). Lorenz (1972 pp. 57–9) does see the link between animals and art in the area of perfecting rituals. (The beautiful colours of fish and birds may have evolved in order to enhance particular ritualised movements.) In an account in the Alister Hardy archive a listener hears a birdsong as a concert. A 54-year-old woman suffered a nervous breakdown followed victimisation in her job as a teacher and describes a beautiful experience:

> As I sat by the back door on a garden seat and looked down the sloping lawn to the trees in the valley and the hills beyond. A blackbird sang loud and clear from the top of a nearby tree. 'This is my concert' I thought.[7]

The New Age has rediscovered some of these ideas. Lorenz (1972) says that we cannot know whether emotions are involved in animals, but has a feeling that they may be. The performance theories of Richard Schechner (2003)

7 Religious Experience Research Centre Archive. Written about 1970

carry this thinking further and are taken up by Baz Kershaw in looking at the parallels between human and animal performance (Kershaw 2010).

To summarise, the oldest view of creativity contained a strong sense of its origin in the notion of the Christian and Jewish Divine, and such Metaphysical notions are still to be found in the literature. It is sometimes associated with notions of genius; this has led to a suspicion about research into the area, which some think should remain a mystery. When creativity is limited to human beings, there can be a suspicion that it will be destroyed by linking it with a normalising society. Philosophers, in explaining the temporal laws at the heart of the universe, contain transcendent notions in their thinking; these link music with the central core of the universe.

Summary

This chapter has looked at the concept of creativity as found in a variety of literatures. The development of the concept has been traced from one rooted in Christian and Greek ideas of the Divine to one that is essentially rooted in the human condition. The two views have been brought together by some of the literature arising from New Age ideas. The creative process is seen to be similar in all forms of creativity and to include phases of preparation, incubation, illumination and elaboration. It is possible for all to enter into the process, but, how far they proceed, is limited by their level of skill; there is a more elite view linked with the notion of genius which is seen as both individual and godlike. The more universal view of the attribute of creativity sees the process as part of the flow of living and part of the process of growth and change. This involves a degree of courage on the person who needs to be free to enter playful processes in order to achieve a re-ordering of personality. The result is a sense of empowerment, which can be nurtured by encouragement and an environment that encourages acceptance, risk taking and spontaneity. Philosophers and psychologists have linked creativity to states of ecstasy and transcendence, traditionally linked with spirituality. We have seen how many of these ideas can be linked back into the Genesis creation myth and can be found even in those that are more secularised. It is these links with a seminal myth for Western culture, that would explain the link often made in popular consciousness between creativity and spirituality.

CHAPTER THREE

The Development of a Phenomenography of the Musical Experience

As I developed a critique of Western music, drawing on my experience at Oxford University and the underpinning constructs of musicking in the wider community, my concern was to develop a model of musicking that might restore some of the elements lost in the academic study of music. It started in the area of music education; but it soon expanded beyond that, following my appointment as a music lecturer at what was then King Alfred's College but later became the University of Winchester. It also developed from my increasing personal development and involvement in the area of the spirituality of music and as a church musician; finally I became ordained as an Anglican priest.

A spiral model of children's musical development had been developed as part of my PhD research in association with my supervisor Keith Swanwick (Swanwick and Tillman 1986, Boyce-Tillman 1991a and b). It was a helix showing the main concerns of children at various points in their development as composers/improvisers. It described children exploring sounds freely individually and in groups in what came to be known as creative music making. My own work charted how pupils developed musically in this environment based on ten years of observation and experiment:

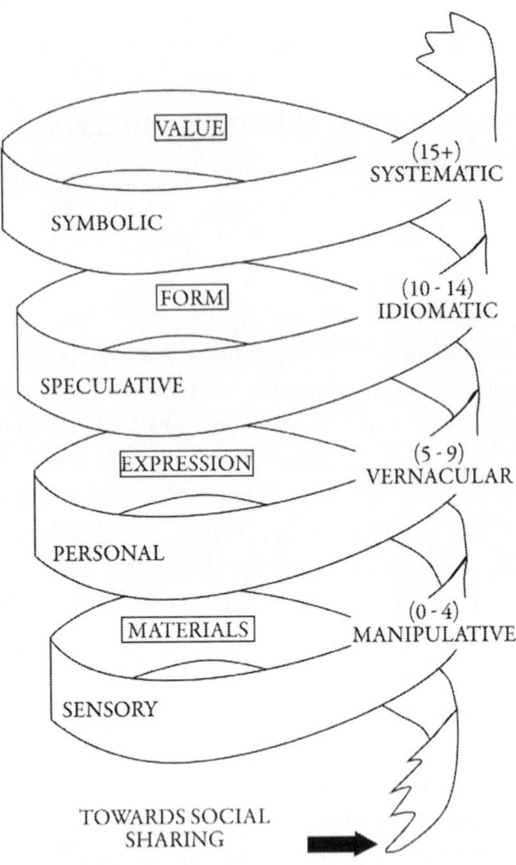

Figure One: The Sequence of Musical Development (Swanwick and Tillman 1986).

It showed how the youngest children explore sound freely as part of a wider sensory exploration of the world and how the development of the ability to control bodily movements is linked with the ability to control sound (Materials). The developing capacity for self-expression through music is clearly seen and needs supporting by a sensitive and authoritative teacher (Expression). It shows how children need at certain times to experiment freely and at other times to be part of traditions. A time of embracing a tradition may well be followed by one of breaking the boundaries that were once freely accepted.[1] In this need for both tradition and experimentation a balance is maintained between freedom and containment. Children become increasingly able to handle musical ideas and motifs (musical gestures) in the construction of musical form (Form). The turn of the helix entitled Values was less well-researched because of the age of the students within the research.

Because of the critiques of this model, which soon became interpreted as a stage-by-stage model, particularly because it was originally linked with Piagetian stages (which was probably unwise), I decided to rethink the model to make it of a more general application and a way of examining the musical experience more holistically. In my original thesis there was an upper level of the spiral which included Transcendence and was my first foray into the area of music and spirituality. It was – very interestingly in the light of the argument of this book and its relation to the values of the Academy – deleted, as too speculative for an academic thesis. I feel as if I have spent the rest of my academic life exploring the meaning of those two deleted pages!

What became known as the Swanwick and Tillman model of children's music development (1986) never included spirituality; but I kept my original work on this carefully and continued to explore it. I did this partly by leaving the world of music education and working in depth on the medieval abbess, Hildegard of Bingen (Boyce-Tillman 2000b); she saw her songs as coming directly from the Divine as part of the visionary experience. So prolonged research into her work gave me insight to a time in European music history, when the spiritual nature of music would not have been questioned.

I was also deeply involved in multi-cultural and interfaith work as you will see in the Chapter Ten; I developed new models to help with the understanding of this work. These did not use the spiral/helical format at all. They included tree and funnel shapes and bore little relation to the original model. These were used and published in the book that emerged from the World Musics Course at the University of Winchester – *World Musics in Education* (Floyd 1996, Boyce-Tillman 1996):

1 This has parallels in the area of spiritual development where a time of embracing a particular tradition may be followed by its fragmentation.

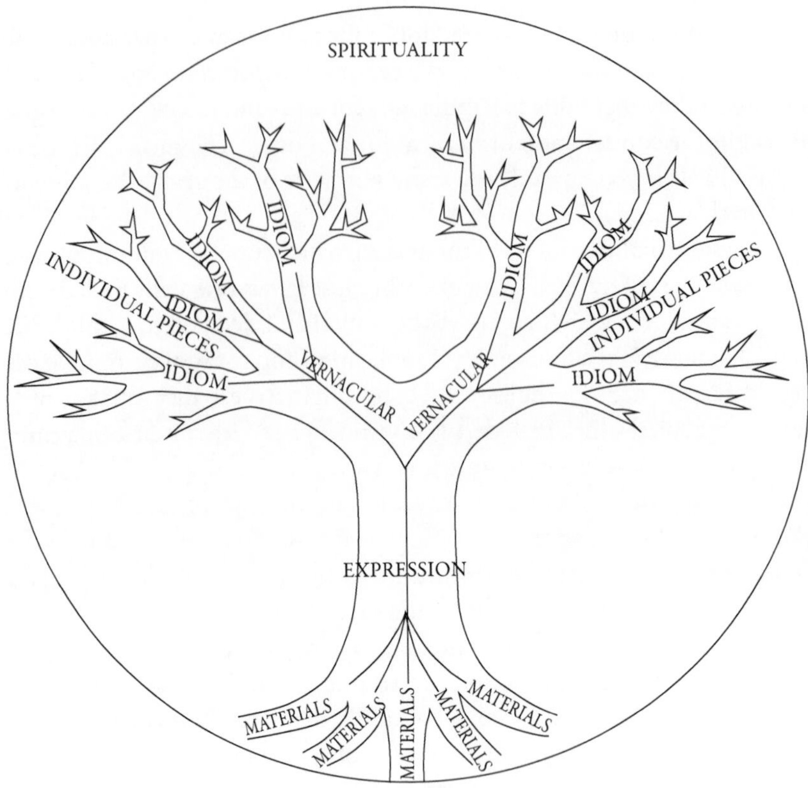

Figure Two: A Model of Enculturation (Boyce-Tillman 1996).

I was also working with feminist theory at the time (Boyce-Tillman 1993, 1994). This turned my attention to musical Value systems; I brought together the social constructionism of Michel Foucault with the way in which music and healing had been united in various cultures to produce a model for relating individual well-being to the values of the wider society. This was fully explored in my book *Constructing Musical Healing: The Wounds that Sing* (Boyce-Tillman 2000a). Here I concentrated on the Values implicit in music and how these impinged on the individual self. This led to a more detailed exploration resulting in a model of subjugated ways of knowing (Boyce-Tillman 2002a, 2005a).

This thinking enabled me to understand the domain of Values more fully and its interface with the other domains of the experience. My new thinking eventually bore fruit in a model of five interlocking circles using two of the terms I had used in the helical model but essentially showing the musical experience from a different angle – much more holistically and with less risk of being interpreted in a linear manner. I imagined looking down through the spiral model and how it would appear as interlocking circles. The notion of Transcendence was now included as a Spirituality circle within a model of five interlocking circles of Materials, Expression, Construction, Values and Spirituality (Boyce-Tillman 2004):

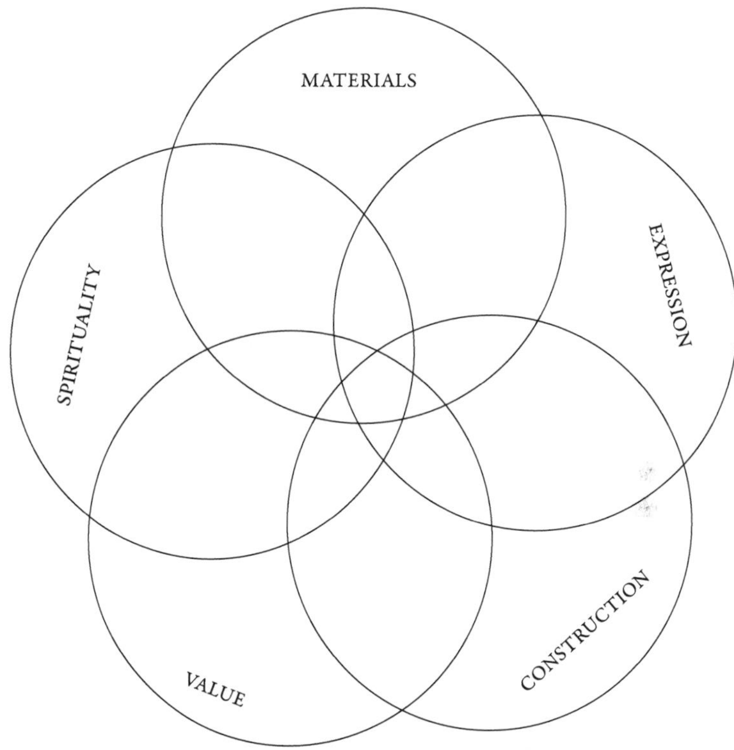

Figure Three: The Five Domains of the Musical Experience (Boyce-Tillman 2004).

This model was then more deeply explored in relation to the domain of Values[2] to look at the role of music in promoting well-being and how adjustments in the Values domain changed the nature of the other domains (Boyce-Tillman 2002b, 2002c). I saw this as a phenomenography of the musical experience for adults and children (Marton and Booth 1997 p. 129). By this time, I had encountered numerous accounts of the musical experience from a variety of sources and spheres. For my PhD I observed forty children composing and improvising for seven years. I had examined numerous mystical accounts of the musical experience from the Middle Ages to the present day. I had received and assessed many undergraduate accounts of their experience of composing, performing and listening-in-audience. So the sources for the model are:

- The way the phenomenon is reviewed in research traditions
- How it appears in the literature, treatises and textbooks
- How it has been handled in different cultures
- Discourses and accounts of musical experiences
- Interviews and accounts where an interviewee is in a state of 'meta-awareness'

As I worked on Turner's concept of liminality and anti-structure (V. Turner 1964 a and c), I started to see that the spiritual experience was a sum of the other domains of the musical experience and not a separate circle. This led to the model underpinning this book (Boyce-Tillman 2006a, 2006c):

2 In later models I used the term Values in the plural as I wished to include a variety of Values in the concept.

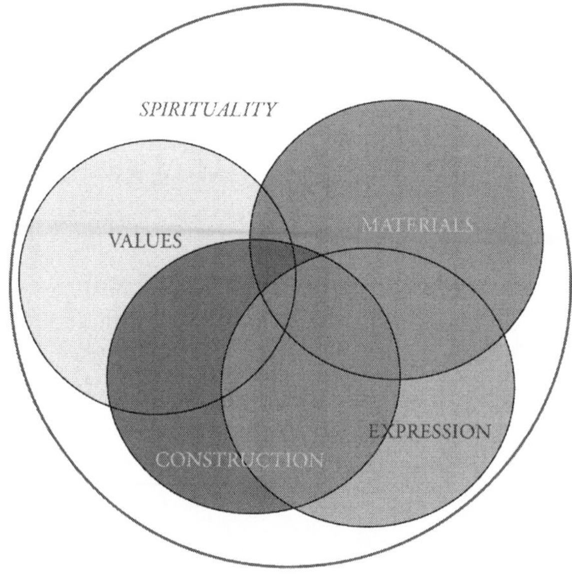

Figure Four: The Spiritual Experience in Music (Boyce-Tillman 2006a and c).

These texts were not concerned with music education but the totality of the musical experience in a variety of contexts. I turned my attention to its use in educational contexts (Boyce-Tillman 2007a, 2007g). It has also been used to interrogate work in the area of music and reconciliation (Boyce-Tillman 2007c, 2007d, 2013b).

So the route into this book started in enculturation into the Western classical musical tradition at Oxford University, which was challenged by my work in education. World Musics and intercultural work and a deeper understanding of orate traditions gave it a new shape. Feminist studies then led me to a social constructionist approach to music and a revisiting of the model in relation to various contexts and Values systems. Immersion in medieval musical and mystical traditions led to a deeper understanding of the spiritual and its place in music alongside Victor Turner's concept of the liminal.

Broadening the Concept of the Musical Experience

The domains that I have developed in this model reflect the varied focus of the experiencer during the experience (which here includes a variety of ways of musicking – listening-in-audience, composing/improvising and performing/improvising). The stress on product ('doing' rather than 'being' in the typology described above) is dominant in western culture and has led to a devaluing of process. The joy of the models I encountered that were offered by Victor Turner (1969, 1974), is that what he describes as liminoid/liminal acts are seen as processual. Process is more significant than product. The performance, the concert are to be evaluated in what they do for those participating and draws on a variety of disciplines previously separated in the study of music, as we saw at the end of the Prelude. His ideas are an example of crystallisaton:

> The scholar draws freely on his or her productions from literary, artistic, and scientific genres, often breaking the boundaries of each of those as well. In these productions, the scholar might have different 'takes' on the same topic ... I propose that the central image for 'validity' for postmodern texts is not the triangle—a rigid, fixed, two-dimensional object. Rather, the central imaginary is the crystal, which combines symmetry and substance with an infinite variety of shapes, substances, transmutations, multidimensionalities, and angles of approach ... Crystallization provides us with a deepened, complex, thoroughly partial, understanding of the topic. Paradoxically, we know more and doubt what we know. Ingeniously, we know there is always more to know. (Richardson 2000 p. 934)

The model enables us to examine the complexity of the musical experience with its diverse facets which we may experience with different intensities at different times and in different contexts. It helpfully maps onto the strands of spirituality explored in Chapter One, with the InterGaian strand sitting in the domain of Materials, the Intrapersonal in the domain of Expression, the Interpersonal in the domain of Construction, the Extrapersonal in the domain of Values and the Metaphysical in the domain of Spirituality, which is now encountered through these different domains acting together like different facets of a crystal.

The research that led to this model was multi-faceted and each facet has its own methodological strategies attached to it. The strategies and methodologies for examining the various circles differ: traditional musicological techniques for notated music are clearly appropriate in the Construction domain; techniques drawing on the literature on music therapy help considerably to illuminate the Expression domain; ethnomusicological methodologies illuminate the domain of Values; organology is a clear part of the Materials domain as is the physiology of the body found in such disciplines as somaesthetics. I have tried to present this book in a crystalline way, using song, story, poem, commentary and academic theological and philosophical texts, interwoven with one another.

The model offers a thick description of the musical experience (Geertz 1973) and accepts the essential subjectivity of the experience – with different aspects becoming apparent, depending on the domain of the crystal through which the experience is being viewed. So, for example, quantitative psychological methodologies, such as testing, to explore how certain music always makes people sad, may be appropriate through one lens; but looked at through another lens it will look very different. It generates a deepened, complex interpretation (Richardson 2000):

> Crystallization provides another way of achieving depth, through the compilation not only of many details but also of different forms of representing, organizing, and analysing those details. (Ellingson 2008 p. 11)

The fluidity of the model[3] enables it to interrogate the process of musicking through different lenses accepting that some present us with paradoxes. In the process of developing this, I used Buber's (1970) idea of encounter with the Other. The notion of encounter with something or someone other also flickers through Rowan Williams' thinking about the

3 Other scholars were working in a similar area. Richerme (2013) found four areas very similar to the domains of Materials, Expression, Construction and Values. Smite and Kasha (2013) developed descriptors for teaching the musical experience to composers that encompassed these domains – motion/stasis, unity/variety, sound/silence, tension/release, and stability/instability.

arts, when he talks of the encounter with other perspectives, noting 'the interiority and inaccessibility that this entails and the necessary time and understanding in such a light' (R. Williams 2012 p. 17). This presupposes 'a commitment to looking, thus a self-investment, even self-dispossession, in respect of what is seen or read' (R. Williams 2012 p. 17) – or in this case heard. This, he says, means encountering new perspectives. The notion here is that a musicker encounters a variety of domains within any musical experience. They are:

- Expression – an Other self
- Values – an Other culture
- Construction – the world of abstract ideas
- Materials – the environment

Insofar as these domains form part of all musical experiences, music serves to reunite the division resulting from Descartes' Error, because of its complex, multi-dimensional nature.[4]

Naomi Cumming (1997), in exploring the subjectivity of the musical experience, similarly saw the experience as encounter with a subject who is absent but present behind the music. She draws on Hans-George Gadamer (1986, 1988) who sees works of art as changing their experiencers and Suzanne Langer (1942) with her sense of music illuminating our interior lives; Cumming sees 'a "subjectivity" in the work itself, with which the listener may become actively engaged, not following his or her own impulses but guided by those of the work' (Cumming 1997 p. 7). The interior self of the musicker encounters a subjective other in the music which is constructed partly by the active engagement of the listener (Hull 2015 p. 5).

4 There are limits to any model which can in itself only encapsulate certain aspects of truth. I hope, however, that the one set out in this book will enable people to understand the relationship between spirituality and the musical experience more clearly.

Summary: The Implications for Musicking

How then can this model enable us to see how the relationship between music and spirituality might be working? The model suggests that all the areas within ourselves and the music need to resonate to produce the spiritual experience. So all need to be honoured. Music is not just the excitation of the frontal lobes of the brain, as some accounts of the experience might imply.[5] It is not just the awakening of emotions and feelings. It is not just a debate of musical ideas. It is not just a way of reinforcing or challenging a culture; but potentially it resonates in all of these simultaneously; so all these ways of experiencing need honouring and respecting.

The model I have developed for looking at music enables us to see where the narrowing of the understanding of music to the domain of Construction for musicology and Materials for instrumental technique have marginalised the spiritual experience. The universals in music cannot be limited to one domain, however objective; the study of Construction in our curricula is broken into durations, scales, tonalities, chords and forms such as ternary and sonata. I claim that it is in the contentless spiritual experience – a state of being – that the universal may well reside; but it is approached by culturally specific works in which the resonance of all aspects of the sounds resonate simultaneously within the musicker.

I initiate an exercise called a humming bath regularly, in workshops on music and spirituality, to demonstrate the power of spiritual intention.

5 Ray [a medical student] read about the elderly under the bold-face heading 'The conditions of death'. It described a study done in nursing homes in which a large percentage of patients saw someone standing at the end of their bed at night. Often this person tried to talk to them or call their name. Sometimes the patients were in such a state of agitation during these delusions that they had to be given a sedative or strapped to their beds. The text went on to explain that these visions were a result of small strokes that often preceded death. 'What is commonly thought by the layman as the Angel of Death, when discussed at all with the patient's family should be presented to them as a series of small strokes compounding an already precipitous state of decline.' (Sebold 2002 p. 223)

People gather around two people and hum any note they choose with the intention of communicating love. The experience is usually blissful but, on reporting what has happened, participants often choose one resonance level:

I felt I was vibrating (Materials)
I felt a sense of warmth and enfolding (Expression)
I loved the harmony forming around me (Construction)
I felt part of the community in a powerful way (Values)

All the levels resonate – our bodies/instruments/the environment, our emotions/feelings, our sense of order and structure and our sense of belonging. The experience may be contentless – but we may use terms from any of the domains to describe the experience.

The model, as we shall see in the ensuing chapters, concerns:

- Honouring the subjective experience of the music
- Talking of musicians' writing about their own religious experiences
- Giving a place for identity where Expression, Values, Materials and Construction interact powerfully
- Acknowledging the relationship between ethics and action in the wider community when Construction and Values interact
- Restoring communality as an important musical value
- Carefully setting up the experience of listening-in-audience
- Reconnecting body/mind and spirit

INTERLUDE ONE

A Place of Transformation: *A Midsummer Night's Dream*

Synopsis

This play is about an encounter between four groups – the aristocracy, the tradesmen, the fairies and the natural world of the midsummer wood. Celebrations are planned to mark the marriage of Theseus, Duke of Athens and Hippolyta, Queen of the Amazons. Egeus brings his rebellious daughter Hermia in front of the Duke. She is refusing to marry Demetrius, her father's choice, because she is in love with Lysander. The Duke orders Hermia to obey her father or, according to Athenian law, she must face either death or a convent. Hermia and Lysander decide to elope that night. They confide in their friend Helena and she, in love with Demetrius and hoping to win his affection, tells him of the plan. That night, all four lovers steal away into the wood. Rehearsing that midsummer night in the same wood is a group of Athenian tradesmen, led by Peter Quince, who are planning to perform a play, *The Tragedy of Pyramus and Thisbe*, in celebration of the Duke's wedding.

Also in the wood are Oberon and Titania, King and Queen of the Fairies, who have quarrelled over Titania's refusal to give up her changeling boy to Oberon. He sends Puck to find a magic plant, the juice of which, squeezed on the eyes of someone sleeping, will cause them to fall in love with the first creature they see on waking. Oberon uses the juice on Titania who falls rapturously in love with Bottom, one of the tradesmen who has been bewitched by Puck. Oberon also tells Puck to use the juice on Demetrius so that he will fall in love with Helena, but Puck mistaking the two Athenian youths, uses it on Lysander instead, who falls in love with Helena.

Eventually all the enchantments are lifted, the human lovers are happily paired and Titania and Oberon are reconciled. The three couples are married and Bottom's troupe perform their play at the wedding.

Analysing the Drama

The central core of the play takes place primarily in the liminal space of the wood on the highly magical night of the midsummer solstice. This natural environment both contrasts and interfaces with the world of the city, as does the night with the day and imagination with reason. Jonathan Bate (2000), Professor of Shakespeare and Renaissance Literature at the University of Warwick, sees Shakespeare as on the cusp of the religious and feudal ways of the Middle Ages and the growth of the bourgeoisie and rationalism. So the two areas in which the play takes place represent the co-existence of the rational, civilised city with the marginal, intuitive, dark forest. So the wood is constructed as a magical space which is still related to the everyday world. The characters leave this everyday world, only to re-enter it transformed by the time in the magical wood:

> But on reflection in the cold light of morning, the strangeness of the night has effected a material transformation leading lovers to a truer place than the one where they were at court the day before ... The action in the forest fills the space between the betrothal and the wedding celebration of Theseus and Hyppolyta. For the young lovers it is also a time-between, the time, that is, to say, of maturation, of discerning who they are and whom they really love. (Bate 2008)

What do they encounter in the wood? They encounter not only various people some of whom they knew before, but also the magical realm of the fairies and the natural world of the wood with its possibilities of magic potions from the plant world. The wood space is boundaried but within it the players lose their boundaries, Bottom even becoming half animal.

They interact with the fairies and the natural world; the normally clear dividing lines are blurred and fractured, so Bottom makes love to a fairy and potions are used to influence behaviour. It is like the magical world of the carnival (Bakhtin 1993). The wood is dark – an entry into the intuitive way of knowing, counter balancing the rational world of everyday.

Here, Shakespeare drew on the philosophy of Ovid who, in his use of magic and vision in works like *Metamorphoses*, ran counter to the rationality of Roman thinking in his exploration of the inevitability of change:

> From here Shakespeare got many of those images of transience that roll through his Sonnets, but in the Dream he celebrates the transfiguring and enduring power of night vision, of second sight. (Bate 2008 no pages)

In the wood the humans lose their power to a band of fairies; so their responsibility is temporarily removed and they are in the power of something beyond the patriarchy of the prevailing culture. They enter the realm of their own vulnerability and they enter it together:

> Magical thinking answers a deep human need. It is a way of making sense of things that would otherwise seem painfully arbitrary – things like love and beauty. (Bate 2008 no pages)

As a result of this, people can try out new personas, like Bottom the weaver. He, the bad actor in the real play of *Pyramus and Thisbe*, becomes an inspired actor, because he accesses his childlike ability to play. Linked with the animal world as an ass, he is outstanding. Here is perhaps the essence of transformation – that in this magical place everyone can play with new identities, have fun and discover joy.

So, from this analysis, we can see various themes emerging that can help us to understand the potentially transformative effect of the liminal/spiritual space, which I shall apply to music:

- It is *related to everyday world* which is left and then re-entered in a transformed state.
- There is a variety of *encounters* in the wood – with the natural world, other people, the magical and new ways of thinking.

- Within the boundaried space of the wood, there is a *loss of traditional boundaries*.
- The heightening of *intuitive faculties* brings an awareness of hidden areas (alterities) within the self.
- As in play, there is a handing over to or acknowledgement of the *responsibility of higher powers* – here the fairies – but this gives a strange freedom to the humans.
- They enter a space of *empathy*, where they are collectively vulnerable.
- This enables them to try out new personas, which may be useful in the other world such as the transformation of Bottom.
- Each group encounters *new discourses*, the humans meeting fairies and the aristocrats meeting the tradesmen.
- They are *energised* by the encounter and return to the ordinary world empowered by their new insights.

It is these potentially transformative elements of the liminal/spiritual space that I shall relate to the possibility of music as psychagogia – personal and societal transformation.

CHAPTER FOUR

The Environment

A Poem

After a Poetry Reading in Winchester Cathedral by Doreen Pearce

These huge Quarr stones
have stood for centuries
soaking up sounds, divine and secular,
thinning the human voice to a mere thread,
de-thundering the organ, damping down the choir.

But when the last trump comes
and graves give up their dead,
when kings and bishops, saints and noblemen
rise from their chests,
sort out their bones, and are re-fleshed,
will then the transept walls give up their sounds,
poems re-echo round the arches
pillars resound with Benedictine psalms?
Will youth guitars, visiting choirs,
sermons of deans and Handel's hallelujahs
all combine with organ notes
in one triumphant shout of praise
before the world dissolves?

For me the process began last night.
Thank you. (2009 unpublished email)

Introduction

There is a renewed interest in embodied cognition with the development of Performance as Research (Boyce-Tillman et al 2012c) and Work-based learning (Boyce-Tillman 2013c). This aspect of music making has often been ignored. All music consists of organisations of concrete Materials drawn both from the human body and the environment including the crystals that vibrate in digital technology. Lori Custodero sees the musical motifs as musical Materials and calls the experience 'aesthetic:

> I propose that 'being with' *music* [author's italics] generates a sense of the aesthetic as we both transform musical materials – timbres, pitches, rhythms. Phrases, harmonies – and are transformed by our experiences with them. (Custodero 2005b p. 36)

We have already seen how both Dewey (1934) and Shusterman (1995) have sought to reinstate the body in the construct of the musical experience, because it includes the infinite variety of tone colours associated with the human voice. It also includes musical instruments of various kinds and the sounds of the natural world which we find increasingly used in New Age type recordings, especially those designed for meditation and relaxation. It also includes the acoustic space in all its infinite varieties, as we saw in the opening poem. This domain of the musical experience is one that can re-establish the role of the Material world in the spiritual experience. Here spirituality is embodied and incarnated in Material form. The domain of the Materials of sound has been devalued in musicology in favour of Construction – a much more disembodied concept and allied with the debating of ideas. This domain links clearly with the InterGaian strand in the analysis of spirituality set out in Chapter One.

The Place of the Body

There has developed in Western society a distinct mind/body split; the result of this is that much Western education has become disembodied, reflecting Descartes' error. Many more ancient Wisdom systems, now subjugated within Western culture, see the spiritual as rooted in the body. In the development of the collection of spiritualities, often referred to as the New Age, there is a very real upsurge of interest in more esoteric systems involving the body. However, we have often concentrated on disembodied aspects of music making. Cognition is embodied. Through neuro-scientific research, Damasio directly links the conscious (cognitive) awareness and bodily experience, suggesting that 'consciousness begins as the feeling of what happens when we see or hear or touch' (Damasio 1999, p. 26). The body comes into play in the teaching of instrumental and, sometimes, of singing technique; but often here it is often simply a limited part of the body and the whole flow of energy through the body by means of breath and posture is ignored. Singers concentrate on whether the next note is a crotchet or a quaver, a G or a G sharp, rather than on the breath flowing through the body. The meditative repetition of a mantra on a single note or a single sound like the 'ohm' have reappeared in the meditative chanting practices of the New Age.

It is in branches of Western popular music that the relationship is often to be found. The trance and rave music traditions have seen music and dance re-united with notions of transcendence (Collin 1997); these were often criminalised in their early days by the dominant value system – often because of their association with hallucinogenic drugs. It is true that in these traditions transcendence has been commodified by a capitalist value system that enables the recording industry and the drug cartels to exploit what is a fundamental human need (Maslow 1967). There is also no shared spiritual frame in which the young participants can place their experiences of the Spiritual; indeed they may have no frame at all. At least there needs to be an examination of these as a cultural phenomenon to explain their popularity and investigate their relationship to the domain of Spirituality within the musical experience. Accounts of transcendence are still found in the Western classical tradition but now often dissociated from the body; the concept is still one often associated with the mind and approached cognitively. Concert halls have fixed seats with all of the body except the head (the perceived location of the brain!) trapped in a seat.

The place of the body has been rediscovered in the area of somaesthetics. Shusterman drew on many different traditions and disciplines such a Bourdieu, Foucault, Nietzsche, American body therapy (such as Feldenkrais and Alexander technique), as well as East-Asian Confucian philosophy to create a meta-philosophy, that sees philosophy as the art of living. As in the development of mindfulness, both Shusterman (2008) and Dewey (1934) saw the possibility of Eastern meditation practices in the restoration of psyche to contemporary society. Underpinning somaesthetics are Shusterman's beliefs that:

1) The senses can be improved through heightened awareness and focused attention, thus also improving our knowledge of the world;
2) Self-knowledge is facilitated through improved awareness of our feelings and lived experience in the world;
3) The power of our will, toward right action, depends on somatic efficacy;
4) Philosophy's concern with the pursuit of happiness suggests that the body as a site and medium of pleasure deserves philosophical attention; and
5) As a site of power's inscription, the body can play a role in political philosophy and in exploring questions of justice.

> The highest forms of pragmatic somaesthetics combine such delights of self-transformational self-surrender with strict disciplines of somatic self-control (of posture, breathing, ritualised movement, etc.) and, importantly, that disciplined training prepares and structures peak experience. (Powell 2010 no pages)

Shusterman's philosophy seeks the aesthetic legitimation of popular art. He follows critical theorists such as Herbert Marcuse (1978) in identifying the source of the loss of the sense of the aesthetic in the everyday in the emergence of privileged high art alongside the emergence of a popular culture governed by exploitative economic practices. 'Low' forms of distraction and entertainment in modern life are inferior substitutes for the aesthetic existence that was characteristic of earlier eras (Tabaczynski 2009). Shusterman sees these developments as necessary to prevent insight into the negative effects of the market (Shusterman 1995 p. 204). Putting his principles into practice, Shusterman sees a philosophy of art as experience as validating traditions like rap, so providing counterarguments to theorists like Adorno (1970/1997); he also seeks to re-establish the important role of entertainment as a nourishing force. His tradition of somaesthetics is designed to restore the notion of the body into philosophy. Shusterman uses the term soma rather than body to declare that the bodily and mental (as well as cultural and biological) dimensions of human being are essentially inseparable.

It aims as a discipline to improve how we understand the aesthetics of the interactions of our bodies and the environments in which we function and form which gather both energy and meaning (Shusterman 2012).

In summary, the development of somaesthetics, brings the totality of the musical experience under scrutiny and sees the body as a central part of it. It sees the possibilities of the transformative power of the musical experience which is now viewed holistically; it brings the experiencer into intimate relationship with the experienced.

Organology

The rise of ethnomusicology engendered a renewed awareness of the place of instruments in the domain of Materials, as instruments from different cultures became available to Western eyes and ears with new woods, seeds and reeds appearing in our culture. The invention of the typologies of organology such as membranophones and lithophones reflected this. This coincided in the 1960s with an increasing interest in the Materials of sound. Avant-garde composers reached for new and sometimes startling sonic worlds. Following them, music education developed ways of enabling pupils to engage with the Materials of sound through improvising and composing activities. Titles of pieces like Stockhausen's *Mixtur* and books with titles like *Exploring Sound* (Tillman 1976) reflected this trend.

Instrumental Technique

What is used in a particular piece or tradition depends on the availability of materials in certain geographical locations and the technical abilities of those involved. The choice of instruments and vocal colours and ranges will also dictate musical pitches and rhythms – the keys and scales that can be used and associated motifs and melodic and rhythmic patterns. Different traditions also value quite distinct vocal and instrumental colours such as the distinctions between European bel canto and the vocal techniques of Chinese opera. The development of certain technical skills on the part of players and singers of various traditions is associated with this domain and intimately linked with the development of certain instrument shapes and vocal tone colours.

What is often identified in performance assessment as 'technical skills' are located within the domain of Materials. Instrumental and vocal studies show a concentration in this domain of the musical experience. My observation of the products of the individualised music examination system is that this is the only domain that they master – those of Expression and Construction are often not addressed. The results of this are epitomised by a comment from a product of the system: 'I have never performed on the piano. I have only done the grades.' In one episode of *Sesame Street*, a sad 'virtuoso' violinist sits sadly in a corner before a concert. When asked by a puzzled friend why he is so sad, he replies that he can play all the scales and arpeggios very fast, but that in the pieces they are all muddled up! Here is someone able to handle the Materials domain of performance very well but unable to use these technical skills to enter any of the other domains of musical experience. This is evident to some degree in some contemporary performances that display a pyrotechnic level of technical skill with little expressive understanding or grasp of the construction of the music. There are some aspiring performers who wait in this position for a lifetime with their books of studies, unable to move from this domain into the others.

And yet, it is possible with the most basic technical skills to enter the totality of the musical experience, if these domains are regarded as interlocking and not hierarchical. A good example of this is the instrument called the singing bowl. The instrument itself comes from Middle East and requires the mastery of the technique of running the stick around the outside of the metal bowl to produce a 'singing' sound full of complex overtones. This sound produced with reverence, an understanding of and connection with the 'feel' of a particular group and with the intention of calming and healing the people present, can have an amazing effect. I similarly remember a young boy about nine years old, who attended a workshop of mine preceding a performance of my one-woman show based on the life of St Hild of Whitby. He brought with him a Scottish pipe that he wished to learn to play. As part of the workshop he learned three notes. These he used in a piece depicting air in the performance which took place in an ancient chapel, full of intense atmosphere and lit only with candles. In this piece he used his very limited and newly acquired technical skill to make unbelievably expressive sounds within the structure we had worked at in the workshop. His father attended the performance and looked across at his son with an attitude of rapt attention that drew father and son together in a moment that I expect neither will ever forget. It was a deeply spiritual and personal experience, that involved all the domains, but which was entered with limited expertise in the domain of Materials.

The Natural World

A musical instrument provides an intimate relationship with the other-than-human world – perhaps the most intimate after the process of eating it as food. The Materials from which instruments are made, with link human beings and the natural world. As we saw in the Prelude, traditional societies, honoured the tree that would be used in the making of the drum; the player would have various ways of keeping a relationship with the wood of the drum. Our industrialised society with its production lines for musical instruments dislocates the connection between the natural world and the Materials of sound: the role of instrument maker is dislocated from the roles of composer and performer. Sadly in the west this loss of the connection with the natural world has been reflected in the way we treat and regard instruments. We need to re-establish this reverence in relation to instruments in our Western fragmented culture.

The use of natural material, unrefined by manufacture, is growing, as interest in the environment grows. In a piece, entitled *Between*, I used quantities of stones knocked together. There is a rediscovery of lithophones – instruments constructed from struck stones. One example of the construction of a contemporary instrument is by Ela Lamblin and Leah Mann. The instrument is created from one hundred river rocks suspended by music wire from a wing-shaped sound box and hanging in a steep arch. The strings (vibrating longitudinally) release their music as the performers dance and, with rosin-covered gloves, stroke, caress, and tug the strings:

> Stearns and Sunsinger recorded the rocks on a portable digital audio system – equipment that was designed to record vibrations within the Earth near volcanoes and recorded the sounds of rocks 'singing.' They discovered that a wide variety of sounds could be produced by striking or stroking rocks with different items, including their hands and other rocks. It is also possible to purchase magnetic Hematite singing power stones, which will make 'most mysterious singing sounds' when thrown in the air. (Boyce-Tillman 2010 pp. 165–6)

The rise of a new interest in paganism and pre-Christian history has led to a renewed interest in sacred sites involving sound. For example, the *Clach a' Choire* on Tiree's coast is an Ice Age boulder which produces a metallic clang when struck. It is called a Ringing Stone. There is evidence of current veneration in the form of coins left in a little hollow on the top which recalls perhaps that this was a megalithic portal to another world (Sharkey 1975). Ringing stones are now known to be in Central, Eastern, Southern-Eastern and Western Asia, Africa, South America and Europe. These could be like indigenous mythic points where myths and stories begin and end. There are historical accounts of singing statues, such as the two statues of the Egyptian Pharaoh Amenhotep III, split by an earthquake, which emitted a hum at dawn. Music sits as a profound power in societies where there is a profound connection with place:

> To the Western mind music is essentially something created by man [sic], although it may be an unconscious process. For the shaman, music is something separate, a form of spiritual power that has an autonomous being apart from human minds. (Frowen-Williams, 1997 pages unavailable)

Contemporary science is rediscovering the notion of a sound coming from the earth itself:

> a relentless hum of countless notes completely imperceptible to the human ear, like a giant, exceptionally quiet symphony, but the origin of this sound remains a mystery

> ... unexpected powerful tunes have been discovered in this hum ... This sound, first discovered a decade ago, is one that only scientific instruments – seismometers – can detect. Researchers call it Earth's Hum. (Boyce-Tillman 2010 p. 158)

This represents a rediscovery of vibration as the essential stuff of the universe, with molecule and atoms circulating in apparently static matter, and vibrations of liquid crystal giving the colour to digital displays. However, the fracturing of the link between arts and sciences has meant that this is not extended to see music again as a powerful agent of destruction or creation. It can bring down fragile church spires but less work has been done on its capacity to build and heal.[1]

Science is showing us that stones – the mineral – do have an energy, which has been channelled into our technology. Early radios were called crystal sets, because at the heart of them was a crystal, which took the incoming signal and helped to convert it into intelligible sounds. Quartz crystals are still part of transmitters and receivers. Some of us will have made a glass sing with a moistened fingertip; glass is a form of stone and, in both the Baroque period and the twentieth century, this has been used as the basis of musical instruments. Rock contains iron ore, which, when crushed with limestone and coal, produces steel. So steel, like that used on a steel string guitar, is made of ground up stones with some carbon (coal) thrown in and heated up. So it could be said that in both the gong rocks described above and the steel guitar strings, rocks have a 'voice'. In some cases, this does not require human agency.

In summary, there is a rediscovery of the sounds emanating from the earth and these can be used to establish a reconnection between human beings and the natural world.

1 The development of cymatics has produced claims for vibrations to heal and mend organs of the body. <http://www.cymatics.co.uk/>. Greater work has been done on music and the mind in the area of music therapy.

The Separation of Animate and Inanimate

We saw, in Chapter One, the cost of the separation between the human and the other-than-human world and the longing in contemporary society to re-establish this link. It is powerfully related with the 'I/Thou' experience described by Martin Buber (1970) and included by Nel Noddings (2003) in her category 'spiritual':

> But it can also happen, if will and grace are joined, that as I contemplate the tree I am drawn into a relation, and the tree ceases to be an it. (Buber 1970 p. 57)

Nowhere is this truer than when musicians play an instrument made of wood, if they are encouraged to meditate on the Materials of which their instrument is made. We have seen how traditional societies did not see the animate and inanimate worlds as separate. In this view, the entire world has its own energy or quality; human beings and the natural world are in constant interplay to continue the theme started in Chapter One:

> Did you know that trees talk? Well they do. They talk to each other, and they'll talk to you if you listen ... Trouble is, white people don't listen. They never learned to listen to the Indians, so I don't suppose they'll listen to other voices in nature. But I have learned a lot from trees; sometimes about the weather, sometimes about animals, sometimes about the Great Spirit ... I think that Western people who come into an Indian environment and attempt to preach, take along their own set of categories and use it to deal with Indian people they meet. Anthropologists, summarizing what they find in the Indian tradition, always call us animists, and that view is accepted by a great many people in the field of religion. We are put in a cultural evolutionary framework, and then we are supposed to move from animism to some great abstract conception of one god. (Tinker 2004 pp. 105–25)

If this alternative way of viewing nature were alive in our culture today would we not have a greater reverence for the instruments that we make and play, and for the bodies that we use to make musical sounds? A drum can do no more than a human player can require of it (technique) and the human player can do no more than the drum – a mixture of tree and skin – will allow it to do. Were this not so, we would not wish to acquire a better instrument when we have technical skills of a certain level, such as a Stradivarius violin replacing a cheaper instrument.

Some Westerners are relearning their connection with the land from traditional cultures and sometimes this involves musicking. David K. Turner describes how in playing the didgeridoo he realised his own connection not with Australia but with his own land:

> I was where my own spiritual stuff was – in Canada where I had grown up, where I always returned and where parts of me were buried. (D. Turner 2001 p. 49)

This represents a rediscovery of these subjugated values for music. It is now much more acceptable, for example, to sing to plants to encourage growth than it would have been twenty years ago. There is a greater acceptance of vibration being the substance of the planet and that when we make music we deal with the very stuff of the natural world, as set out by Daniel Barenboim in his Reith lectures (2006). Below, we shall see how the theory of the Music of the Spheres attempted to articulate this – to build a theory of the vibrations of the different elements of the cosmos producing a cosmic symphony based on music as a uniting force for creation as a whole.

The Music of the Spheres

Sophie Drinker in her remarkable book *Music and Women* situates the loss of a relational view of music to the entire world in the loss of matriarchal religions (Drinker 1948/95 pp. 68–9). But this view became subjugated as the patriarchal religions dominated Europe (Boyce-Tillman 2006c, 2014). A musical pattern underpinning the cosmos dominated a great deal of thinking in the Classical World; but it became subjugated at the Enlightenment. It is difficult to examine the complexities of the ideas as part of a chapter; it is dealt with in greater detail in *The Music of the Spheres: Music, Science and the Natural Order of the Universe* by Jamie James (1995). The circling planets were seen to generate a music which was not audible and formed the harmony of the universe. It was related to Greek mathematical theory, and also related to the idea of the ascension by ladder from earth to heaven. Each planet was understood to generate a particular note which was related to the rotation of the earth.

Pythagoras saw the entire universe as a system of complete relationships; the theory of music was an essential part of the scheme. The ancient Greek philosophers developed the idea of music and the spiritual philosophically, as we saw in the Prelude. Pythagoras, in his notion of three sorts of music, saw a resolution of the perceived division between body, mind and spirit (J. James 1995 p. 31). He was followed by Plato, Cicero, Pliny and Ptolemy; the theories filtered into medieval Europe via such writers as Boethius (c480–524/5). His *Principles of Music* became the primary textbook for music in the Middle Ages (Godwin 1987 p. 43). Because the fundamental nature of the universe is music, then music in their system became an important tool to heal the body and lift the soul (Godwin 1987 p. 130). A numerological system was developed from this and moved through mystical movements such as the Rosicrucians and figures such as Robert Fludd (1574–1637) and Johannes Kepler, who wrote, in 1619, his *Harmonice Mundi* (Godwin 1979).

The theologians of the Middle Ages drew heavily on these theories. The medieval mystic Hildegard of Bingen (1098–1179) saw music as recreating the original harmony of God and the world in the Garden of Eden:

> Music expresses the unity of the world as God first made it, and the unity which is restored through repentance and reconciliation. (Van der Weyer 1997 p. 80)

These ideas were clearly linked with the basic medicinal frame that was in use in medieval Europe – the Doctrine of Humours; this saw the human being as inextricably linked with the natural world because humanity is made of the same basic elements. Music plays an important part in what Hildegard calls the greening power:

> Just as the power of God extends everywhere, surrounding all things and encountering no resistance, so too the sound of human voices singing God's praise can spread everywhere, surrounding all things and encountering no resistance. It can rouse the soul lost in apathy, and soften the soul hardened by pride. (Van der Weyer 1997 p. 80)

Hildegard connected singing with embodiment as an act of incarnation (Baird and Ehrman 1994 p. 79). Music developed a profound spiritual significance in Judaism:

> One post-Diaspora Jewish tradition where music played an important and positive role was in the mysticism and messianism of the Kabbalah. The strains were woven into the *Zohor* the thirteenth-century text so central to the study of Kabbalah, where music is emphasised as a means to a kind of religious transcendence and ecstasy. (Westheimer 2003 pp. 26–7)

At the Enlightenment, these ideas gradually moved from being part of the dominant way of knowing to being subjugated (Boyce-Tillman 2007a) by the development of the scientific rationalist paradigm and the dominance of humanity in the cosmic schema. This meant that music lost its central place as the stuff of the universe and the notion of the aesthetic developed which was about individual achievement rather than relatedness, as we saw in Chapter Two. A barrier was set in place between human beings and the natural world which now becomes 'inanimate' – lacking a soul. What was lost essentially was the connection between the earth – the material world – with human beings.

The development of and centrality of notation systems to European music also led to a process of separating music from context. In the case of indigenous traditions each place and its associated music will have its own soundscape of the natural world with animals, birds and sounds of wind and sea. Songs were reworked for each occasion and were related to particular holy sites and the mineral and animal world:

> In North Russia, where the song leaders (stihovoditzi) are particularly musical, the chantress conducts the old rites ... She knows by heart the ancient portions of the incantations and invocations ... She improvises new texts and new melodic lines to suit the emergency. (Drinker 1948/95 p. 13)

Once notation was developed, music could be conceived of as a separate entity, lacking a body or a specific place. The score of the classical piece became 'the music' and music became separated from:

- The body of its creator
- The place of its creation
- The context (time, place, event) of its first intended performance

Western classical music became about the abstraction of dots on a page; often its connection with anything other than its own internal construction systems became fractured. The twentieth-century composer Janacek (2008) complained, in a musical analysis class, that music was not about a page of a score but about life, passion and nature. The other domains of the musical experience became subjugated in importance and Construction became the dominant domain of interest for musicologists (see Chapter Six). The development of recording techniques has enabled this to happen for more improvisatory and non-notated traditions as well. They too now face a situation where their music can be taken anywhere, by anyone, for any purpose (Boyce-Tillman 2001a).

To develop a philosophy of music related to the environment, we need to rediscover music theories from:

- medieval Europe with its notion of the Music of the Spheres, described briefly above
- indigenous musical traditions often entering the West through the phenomenon of the New Age
- the area of music therapy, particularly in the area of entrainment, when our bodies adjust our heart rate to the speed of the music (Boyce-Tillman 2000a)
- post-modern feminist theorists in the area of embodiment and music (Isherwood 2000)

We have already charted, in Chapter One, how the current development of consciousness studies has also entered the area of the interconnectedness of creation in writing such as Ken Wilber's *The Eye of Spirit* (1997) and *Integral Psychology* (2000); but seldom does music hold a significant place in notions of consciousness. E.F. Schumacher set out four great Levels of Being, in which matter (m), life (x), consciousness (y) and self-awareness (z) (Schumacher 1977 pp. 27–8) are interrelated as follows:

> 'Man' [sic] can be written $m+x+y+z$
> 'Animal' can be written $m+x+y$
> 'Plant' can be written $m+x$
> 'Mineral' can be written m (Schumacher 1977 pp. 32–3)

If, in this model, we establish the mineral level as vibrating, we have a sense that it is vibration that links all these levels of being together.

So, in pre-patriarchal as well as pre-Enlightenment Europe, music was considered central to the cosmic schema, but the development of scientific rationalism replaced these ideas with theories based on evidence from the material world. Although ideas of the interconnectedness of the cosmos remained in subjugated form, the centrality of music became lost; the subjects, formerly held together by the notion of the Music of the Spheres, were fragmented in contemporary knowledge systems. The development of musical notation and recording weakened the link of music to place and context.

Place Memory

Some of the reconnections of music with place are connected with ideas developed around place memory. In human experience certain memories are regularly attached to certain places. Visitors to the Holy Land are often overwhelmed by the fact that they may be walking on the same stones as Jesus walked on. The Wailing Wall in Jerusalem holds the tears of many Jews. Gravestones in a million cemeteries bear testimony to many unanswered prayers. We can harness and transform these energies. Community drama groups, for example, have performed dramatic rituals to purify places in Serbia where terrible massacres occurred. I remember visiting Romsey Abbey and wondering at an Anglo-Saxon crucifix, in which it appeared to me that all the devotion from past ages were contained and gave me the inspiration for future action:

SOLO:	A Cross on a wall in an old market town looks down with love.
YOUNG PEOPLE:	Holy Cross, Holy Rood, what do you see, what do you see?
	Holy Cross, Holy Rood, what do you see, what do you see?

SOLO:

1. I see a world broken and torn,
Where the hungry stay hungry
And the paupers are scorned,
Where the mothers are crying
And the children stillborn.
Is this your world?

2. I see a world broken and torn,
Where justice reigns
And the poor are supported
And the slaves lose their chains,
Where the children are nurtured
And the sick lose their pain.
Is this your world?

3. I see a world struggling for truth,
Where along the road's winding
The trees start to root,
Where the people are caring
And the children bear fruit.
Is this your world?

Michael Perry (1987), in his book on *Deliverance*, tells how the memories held in a place can join with later human experience to produce paranormal phenomena. He tells the story of a young father of two children. Three weeks after the cot death of a child, he was woken by what he thought was burglars. He opened the bedroom door to find groups of people walking along the landing of the house and disappearing through the far wall. They were dressed in seventeenth-century costume and looked very sad. They were carrying bundles. A young police officer saw the phenomenon as well and the police dog would not enter the house. Perry describes how the man's grief and the memory in the place combined to produce the phenomenon; he sees the necessity to bless the place as well as counsel the person to deal with the phenomenon (Perry 1987 p. 34).

So places do appear to hold the memory of events that have happened there in the past. It is, therefore, possible to explore ways of working with these. It is suggested that music can be a way of accessing and redeeming the memories. Certainly, in the area of music and reconciliation, musicians are playing and singing at venues where acts of violence have occurred to redeem the memories associated with the place.

Acoustic Spaces

The acoustic space is an important part of the Materials of music as we saw in the opening poem. Composers for ancient cathedrals knew that each building accentuated certain tones and wrote their pieces with this in mind. There is now a return to including the venues in the natural world for musical performances including the natural sounds found in them as part of the piece. Composers like Pauline Oliveros have demonstrated their concern for acoustic space by recording in spaces like the old cistern used for her CD entitled *Deep Listening* (Oliveros 1989).

In an age of recording techniques we are aware of the need to create acoustic space artificially. In recording an opera of mine we had the singer stand at different distances from the microphone to simulate the movement on the stage; in a recording I made of my own songs we used three different levels of reverberation to suggest a small room, a concert and a larger, sacred space.

The ideas associated with the Music of The Spheres also filtered into the Church and underpinned the design of many of the great cathedrals of medieval Europe producing spaces of unparalleled resonances which are still there to be rediscovered. One theory sees each building having a particular note. I experienced this in 1999 in a piece written for York Minster. The piece centred around a single note. In rehearsal the piece appeared somewhat drab and uninteresting. In the cathedral the repeated sounding of the note were taken up by the building. What such theories restore is the building itself as an intrinsic part of the musical experience.

In my compositions, I have been concerned to include the building as an important 'instrument' or player in a musical experience. Traditionally musicians have been placed in the middle of spaces and the walls have been used as places against which the sounds bounce to produce resonance and echo. I have become fascinated by placing musicians around spaces and close to the walls so that the walls support the sounds from behind and are coaxed in resonating. In this I have learned a great deal from the music of John Tavener. In Winchester cathedral, I started with a piece called *The Call of the Ancestors* (Boyce-Tillman 1998), in which a rock group, Thai gongs and African drums were placed around the cathedral. For Liverpool Metropolitan cathedral, I wrote *Ecological Celebration* (Boyce-Tillman 2007f) in which small groups of singers were placed around the circular building. This proved immensely successful, as they were singing into the widest part of the building, rather than performing from the middle and therefore singing into the narrowest part. *PeaceSong* (Boyce-Tillman 2005b), in Winchester cathedral, used twelve different choirs scattered all over the cathedral for the first movement; they were singing fragments of song that might have been sung in the cathedral in the past, separated by periods of silence. I called it *If these walls could only speak;* I felt I was making unheard sounds stored in the stones audible. Before the performances of these pieces, I go down to the cathedral and sit on the stones and pray that they will play their part in the pieces. It has never failed me, and before one *Space for Peace* I saw a gold cloud rise from the floor of the cathedral, as if it had responded.

Space for Peace (Boyce-Tillman 2009b) was my most radical piece so far and is described in more detail in Chapter Ten. It was not really a piece but a frame for an event (Boyce-Tillman 2011a, 2012a). For this we assembled together local choral groups from a variety of sources – community choirs, schools, the university, the cathedral choristers and quiristers and Rabbi Mark Solomon, who chanted the Hebrew Scriptures. The effect was beyond my imaginings. Everyone present (and the stones of the building) had a part in the creation of an experience of beauty and togetherness and experienced intuitive ways of relating to and co-operating with others. Children singing *I think to myself what a wonderful world*, merged with plainchant, Jewish cantillation, Taizé chants and motets, in a way that saw diversity held in a unity that was not a uniformity. Many saw the interaction between space and sound:

> I think the fact that the cathedral had been emptied of chairs was an important factor in the experience. First, it created a root to its past back to a time when cathedrals were masses of movement and diverse activities going on at the same time. Second, it literally created the space for sound and movement ... I thought this must be what heaven is like, a space where diversity finds its unity and unity blossoms into diversity ... As the whole event drew to a close I noticed a child near me sitting on the floor in the classic Eastern meditation position. (2009 unpublished email)

It would not be unlike the soundscape of the medieval cathedral, when masses were celebrated simultaneously in the chantry chapels. It represented a unique co-operation between stone and human agency.

Neurobiology

The developing area of neuroscience and music provides an overlap with the next chapter. Oliver Sacks links the brain with musical training. He examines the claim that a brief exposure to Western classical music stimulates mathematical, verbal and visuospatial abilities in children, critiquing the literature on the Mozart effect:

> The Mozart effect ... not only aroused scientific controversy but excited intense journalistic attention and, perhaps unavoidably exaggerated claims beyond anything intimated in the researchers' original modest reports. The validity of such a Mozart effect has been disputed by Schellenberg and others, but what is beyond dispute is the effect of intensive early music training on the young, plastic brain. Takako Fujioka and her colleagues used magnetoencephalography to examine striking changes in the left hemisphere of children who have had only a single year of violin training, compared to children with no training. (O. Sacks 2011 pp. 101–2)

Adamek, in the area of singing, makes claims for the relationship between music and psychic balance:

> People seem to be capable of employing singing as an aid for maintaining for regaining their psychic balance in specific situations, and thereby experiencing the bodily stimulation or, in contrast, relaxation that comes with it. People appear to be capable

> of initiating changed states of self-consciousness through singing and also utilizing it as a door to places of spiritual experience. (Adamek 1996 p. 25)

So, it is possible that there are physical effects within the structure of the brain, including, as we shall see in the next chapter, pain control, from engaging in the processes of musicking.

Summary

This chapter has set out a philosophy of environmental connectedness including embodiment. It can be seen in people's accounts of musical experiences:

> [*Space for Peace*] made me realise that when I go to a concert, I focus on the performers and what is coming from them; but last night it was as if the very stone was sounding out itself into that wonderful space ... as if it was joining in. (2009 unpublished email)

The greater concern with environmental issues in the wider society can mean an increase in interest in this domain. Projects on creating instruments out of recycled materials including weapons,[2] which are increasingly popular in a variety of contexts, reflect an increasing awareness of this domain. Also, there is the exploration of a wider range of vocal sounds than have traditionally been sanctioned in classical music traditions (Bonenfant 2014). Concentration on this domain in musical studies could lead to greater connection of music making to the body and the other-than-human world.

2 While working on this book, I attended an exhibition entitled *Disarm*. In the next two years we had the commemoration of two wars in the UK: the First World War (1914–18) and the Battle of Waterloo (1815). My piece *From Conflict to Chorus* (2015) used recycled rifles as a percussion instrument and a flute.

CHAPTER FIVE

Music and Expression

A Story

In the popular UK radio drama, *Old Harry's Game* Satan is training a young devil called Scumspawn in hell. Scumspawn calls him up saying that there is a problem in the Reception Pit. 'Master, we need your wisdom and experience!' When Satan responds Scumspawn explains that following a gas explosion at the Grand Ole Opry, they have taken unexpected delivery of a country and western band. 'Obviously we set about giving them their introductory scourging but now we are in trouble, because every time we subject them to more suffering and pain ... they just write a song about it.' In the background, the country and western band are singing:

> 'We're standing in a lake of fire
> And the flames are a-getting higher.'

'You see how horrendous it is', says Scumspawn. 'At the moment they're stuck for a rhyme for "inferno", but it's only a brief respite.' Satan responds with offering the help of his new assistant, Nero. Scumspawn protests: 'But he is a mere mortal.' Nero retorts that actually he is a god. At this Satan is cross: 'No, you're not actually a god, Nero.' Nero protests: 'I am a god. The Senate declared me a god.' Satan invalidates this claim by retorting that his status was only given by a certificate from bunch of fat Italians wearing sheets. Nonetheless he dispatches Nero to deal with Scumspawn's problem. 'Any idea how you're going to deal with it?' 'Simple.' Says Nero 'I shall just remove their vocal chords.' Satan praises Nero's natural aptitude for his devilish role. 'You can't teach that. Logic combined with sadism.' Scumspawn protests that the other demons will not be very keen on obeying a mortal. The female singer of the country and western band embarks on a singalong song about her 'D-I-V-O-R-C-E becoming final today. Other souls in hell join in with:

> 'Me and little J-O-E.'

She continues:

> 'We'll be going away
> I love you both and this will be ...
> Sheer H-E-double L for me.
> I wish that we could stop this D-I-Eurgh!'

Nero has succeeded in his task and the singing stops. (Based on Hamilton 1998)

Introduction

We have already seen how the soul became located over the course of European history in the inner world of the musician:

> Music – at once so seemingly tangible and yet so mysterious in its potency – seems to stand on the cusp of the noumenal and the material world, and in so far as we can identify the emotional geometry that constitute its laws, offers us a glimpse into the true nature of our selves. (Robertson 1996 p. 35)

The domain of Expression is where the subjectivity of composer/performer and listener intersect to provide facets of The True, which I have defined in the Prelude as the authentic. It is the domain in which self-awareness and self-reflexivity can be developed. Rowan Williams draws on Raimond Gaita (1999) – *A Common Humanity* – to see art as a loving encounter with a subjectivity not one's own (R. Williams (2012 p. 17). The presence of the soul in the Jungian notion of the psyche opened up the notion of exploring inner landscapes in the seeking process, as we identified in many of the spiritualities in Chapter One. If this was once done externally by means of such ritual events as pilgrimages, it is now to be carried out internally; this might be in response to internal threats and opportunities, as we saw in Chapter Two. The journey is now to the subconscious and unconscious with a view to finding a real self, freed from the neuroses created by early traumas. However, there was also in the Jungian system the notion of the universal unconscious and the utilisation of images and symbols which were viewed as being of a transcultural nature (Jung 1964). Within the Jungian philosophy there was a great sense of becoming a unique person within the context of culture.

It was the link between this domain and self-actualisation – which we identified in Chapter One – that led to notions of spirituality being present in the world of jazz and popular musics through the 1970s in the work of people such as the guitarist John McLaughlin and Carlos Santana, leader of the American group, *Santana*. Quotations from Eastern gurus permeate the sleeve notes to the records produced. The truth and the intentions of the composer/performer and listener interact here to give a variety of truths and diversity within the concept of The True. But the problem of interpreting musical events is well documented and explored further in intrinsic and extrinsic meaning below. Here is one of many examples:

> Loud playing could indicate a release of physical tension or a desire to communicate aggressive and frustrated feelings. It could also indicate confidence, focused attention and internal strength. (Langer 1942 p. 27)

This domain is concerned with the evocation of mood, emotion (individual or corporate), images, memories and atmosphere on the part of all those involved in the musical performance. It is where deep joy resides, such as in this musical encounter with an autistic girl:

> Stepping rhythmically from foot to foot, she throws her body as far as she can from one side to the other. Her face shows utter joy and release matched in spirit by the joyfulness in Carol's [the music therapist] stimulating and playing. (Robbins 1993 p. 15)

We have already seen, in Chapter One, the potential link between humour and spirituality; this contains within it, the experience of deep joy when it is infused with love:

> It is important not to undervalue *joy*. Joy is more than fun, more than just having a good time. There is something transcendent about the purity of joy, something that relates to an original realisation of one's full humanness. For a child as developmentally disabled as Nicole, joy in discovering self-expression or in achieving musical creation with a therapist can be momentous ... Joy is nourishment. (Robbins 1993 pp. 15–16. Author's italics)

So Expression is the domain where emotions are validated within the experience, which was crucial in William James' writing about the spiritual experience (W. James 1902/1997).

The domain of Expression was explored, in great detail, by Suzanne Langer summarised in her sentence: 'Music is a tonal analogue of emotive life' (Langer 1953 p. 27). It has played a greater part in women's writing about music than the male leaders of traditional musicology (Rahn1994 p. 55). This has been further developed by Silvan Tomkins as he deals with emotion and affect:

> Music is the art form par excellence of the affects, just because it can duplicate these subtle, complex, ever-changing combinations of affective components by analogy, through variations which both mimic and evoke affects. (Tomkins 1962 p. 191)

It has perhaps been this fluidity, as well as the difficulty of capturing it in words, that has led to the exclusion of this domain from musical study, even though it may be the main entry route into experiencing music.

The Meaning of Music: Intrinsic or Extrinsic

The debate between absolute and referentialist views of music has raged long and hard among the theorists and composers in Western culture. This is evidenced by the Schumann/Brahms debate over programme music in the nineteenth century. Whereas traditions like those of the Far East have instrumental pieces with titles such as *The Crane's Story* and *Water on a Lotus leaf*, Western classical music, particularly post Enlightenment, has used titles concentrating on the Construction domain such as *Sonata* and *Symphony*. Indeed, children have often seen pieces with such titles as being of more value than those with titles in the domain of Expression. For example, in an unpublished story entitled *Mexican Beans*, the author describes her favourite piano piece, when aged twelve, which bore the title *Mexican Beans*. She writes of her shame at announcing the title and how she wished it had been called something like *Sonata No 2*.

However, musicology has concentrated on intrinsic meaning – the meaning located within the sounds themselves – linking it closely with the domain of Construction. It is very difficult to ascertain where the intrinsic emotion comes from, as Kingsley Price discusses in his article *How can music be merry* (Price 2000 pp. 59–66). But it is here that the subjectivity of all those involved in the musical event intersect. The intrinsic meaning of the music, reflecting the subjectivity of composer and performer, is often completely changed by its intersection with the subjective experience of the listener. The listener may well bring extrinsic meaning to the music – meaning that has been locked onto that particular piece or style or musical tradition because of its association with certain events in their own lives or their culture. This immensely important component has often been ridiculed or ignored by musical theorists. It is beautifully expressed in Ivor Gurney's poem from the First World War, entitled *Bach and the Sentry*:

Watching the dark, my spirit rose in flood
On that most dearest Prelude of my delight.
The low-lying mist lifted its hood,
The October stars showed nobly in clear night,

When I return, and to real music-making,
And play that Prelude, how will it happen then?
Shall I fear as I felt, a sentry hardly waking,
With a dull sense of No Man's Land again?[1]

Silvan Tomkins writes of the complexity of the intersection between emotion, meaning and memory in this domain:

1 <http://www.poemhunter.com/best-poems/ivor-gurney/bach-and-the-sentry/> Accessed January 2009.

> This does not imply that music triggers the *same emotions* [author's italics] in different individuals. Emotions are always culturally conditioned, subjective experience ... Thus, music will often trigger the same effect in different individuals, but they will often experience different emotions – based on their idiosyncratic biographies. It is also possible that different individuals can experience the same or very similar emotions, when special conditions are present. In other words, this implies that affect and even emotional material may be shared directly through music. (Quoted in Jordanger 2008 p. 15)

It is on powerful life experiences – such as falling in love or abuse of some kind – that the listener often draws to produce extrinsic meaning to the music. Popular music, in particular, often conjures up a range of associations, as does hymnody, which is often associated with significant rites of passage like baptism, marriage and death. The phrase 'They are playing our tune' reflects the association of certain emotional events with certain pieces.

Some theorists prefer to link these meanings with personal characteristics in the listener. Michael Sadgrove describes how Jean Langlais's *Messe Solennelle* was to one person 'a bold piece, bold, exhilarating, and driven ... by a furious energy;' another perceived it as 'violent, conflicted, disintegrating, pulling in the opposite direction of a liturgy that is meant to put us back together again as human beings' (Sadgrove 2000 pp. xviii–xix). Wheeler (1985) found five personal characteristics that would affect personal musical preference (and therefore the effect of music). These were gender, age, musical training, personality and mood. Other researchers have linked personal preferences with personality characteristics. Extroverts, for example, were found by Stephen Dollinger (1993) to prefer arousing music like jazz. Downplayed by classical theorists (Rahn 1994 p. 55), Lucy Green's books *Music on Deaf Ears: Musical Meaning, Ideology and Education* (1988) and *Gender, Music, Education* (1997) make a very useful contribution to this debate in defining two different meanings within the music itself, which she calls inherent and delineated. What is clear, however, is that extrinsic meaning – that is, expressive meaning drawn from the listener's own previous experiences – is an immensely important component in this domain.

The Intrapersonal: Music and Emotion

It is the strand of the Intrapersonal with the notion of transformation where the domain of Expression can be seen as transformative. The relationship of music to emotions has a complex literature associated with it. John Tavener, for example, distances himself from raw emotion:

> I don't think it's the job of the artist – I don't think it ever was – to show his existential angst or his existential pain. I think it can contain melancholy and a haunting melancholy – a sadness, because the world is sad on one level. Extremely sad. One can express the sadness, this yearning, but one should not, I think, express in one's music the existential angst that one may well have as a person. One has to transcend it, but by the time the music has left my study, I want none of this angst left in it. (Tavener 2005)

However, we have already seen, in Chapter Two, the role of music might play in the expression of powerful potentially destructive emotions. In the literature on psycho-analysis, there is a sense in which really powerful emotions can only be expressed musically. Problems played out unsatisfactorily in words, can be worked out effectively through musicking:

> The structured, non-verbal nature of many musical activities and improvisations can be very re-assuring for families who have become entangled in verbal conflicts, and the delicate issues of control can then be readdressed. (Oldfield 1993, p. 54)

Western society desperately needs tools for expressing powerful emotions safely; in this domain, we see the potential fusion of the Dionysian and Apollonian, which Nietzsche saw as the role of tragedy; this fusion might generate a moment of healing transcendence, as we saw in the Prelude. We have seen how Freud's notion of the sublimation of potentially destructive emotions is present in some of the therapeutic writing about the processes of musical creativity. The concept of integration was central to Jung's theory of the personality; but others, such as Thomas Fordham (1986), have emphasised a rhythm of integration and de-integration, in a way that we saw in Chapter Two. Music can play an important part in this. De Backer describes how, through music, his client, David, joins elements together in his personality by means of musical motifs and phrases in a way that echoes Koestler's idea of bisociation (1964):

> David expresses his synthesis: death and life ... death is a chaotic and alarming game, life is a peaceful and melancholic one. Thus, the presence and absence is not expressed in words, but symbolised in a musical game ... In this way one is no longer a victim of these circumstances and no longer subject to the contingency of the parents' absence. (De Backer 1993, p. 37)

As we saw in Chapter Two, music is sometimes seen as a container for difficult emotions – a way of managing chaos:

> He [the music therapist] will, as it were, stretch a skin over the patient's experience – an acoustic skin – which binds and shapes the expression of chaos. (De Backer 1993 p. 36)

As a non-verbal medium, music in its 'free-flowing awareness' (Kortegaard 1993 p. 61) has a wider potential than words. I remember a student I was tutoring over a two year composition programme. At the beginning of it, her mother was gradually dying from a brain tumour. She gradually composed a bleak piano trio. When we were putting her portfolio together at the end of the course, some one and a half years later after the death of her mother, her perceptive comment was: 'I do not like it; but it says what I wanted it to say.' This is a clear example of the role music can play in the area of self-awareness and reflexivity and the re-evaluation of the arts in education that is called for by theorists like De Botton (2012). Judith Bell's paper (2012) *Nurturing Students in School Music programme after a Natural Disaster* describes how the continuance of these programmes helped students come to terms with the earthquake in Christchurch, New Zealand. John Tavener describes how a composer can encapsulate a profound experience in a piece of music – how a fragment of life was captured:

> It was a piece that came to me while I was sitting on the harbour in France – in Chartres in Normandy. It was the day of the Assumption, and the church bells were ringing and there was a general air of festivity in the town, and instead of praying in words, I wrote down, as it were, the words of the prayer. It was rather an impassioned prayer, I think, and I wrote it down and then went back to the little place where I was staying and wrote out the whole piece. (Tavener 2005)

Ruth Westheimer, a German Jew separated permanently from her parents in World War II, describes the power of singing songs from her Jewish heritage to deal with her deepest emotions:

> What I do know is that the hopelessness I felt was so deep, I could admit it only in song. (Westheimer 2003 p. 64)

So music enables us to reach and express parts of the personality otherwise unreachable and inexpressible but how this is encapsulated in the sounds is varied.

The Intrapersonal: Music and Freedom

We have identified, in Chapter Two, the freeing power of creativity. Paul Robertson in his video *Music and the Mind* (1996) describes Tony Blois who is a musical savant. This means that he has very limited intellectual resources in most areas, but an immense musical gift. For Tony, who is blind and autistic due to brain damage at birth, music is his chosen means of expression and for some time his only one. His immense talent became apparent when he was given a keyboard at the age of two. His mother describes how at first he embarked on an intense programme of musical exploration. After six weeks, with help from his mother, he mastered *Twinkle, twinkle, little star*. He now has seven thousand songs in his repertoire; his musical talent has enabled him to expand his other abilities so that now he has more conversation:

> His language may be rather literal, but through his music he can directly express very powerful feelings ... When I asked Tony how he felt about his mother, he played *Twinkle, twinkle little star* as a Bach two-part invention (a short piece working out a single idea). It was both impressive and beautiful and showed how profound musical communication can and should be. How could many of us express our emotions so eloquently? (Robertson 1996 pp. 13–14)

Work with patients with Alzheimer's disease show its capacity to free people from the limitations of their diminishing world and to bring some order by recalling former experiences in their lives:

> As their lives seem to ebb away, and their faculties fade, music appears to be a ray of light in their dimming world. It beckons them slowly out of their anguish, out of their 'absences'. It touches them, and gently nudges them into song, speech, movement, moments of alertness, peace and pleasure. When caught in their frantic, rapid shuffling along the corridors, it slows them down to a comfortable pace. When their joints and limbs seem to freeze and block, music brings about a thaw. It gives them glimpses of the past, as memories emerge, prompted by songs, sound and rhythms. (Gaertner 1998)

This freeing process can initiate hope, which is one of the 'curative factors' of the therapeutic session highlighted by Irvin Yalom (1985 pp. 3–4).

The Intrapersonal: Music and Reminiscence

It is these associations that make music a powerful medium for reminiscing. Ruth Bright has several examples of how personal associations can interrupt 'normal' reactions:

> For example, the song 'Danny Boy', because of its words and its harmony pitch, speed of performance and general structure, is generally perceived as a sad song. In one seminar, a participant began to laugh when the song was played. He explained that in his office it was used as a request for someone else to answer the phone whilst you went to the bathroom, based on the line in the song, 'The pipes, the pipes are calling'. (Bright 1993 p. 199)

I was working with a woman who was looking for calming music. The woman had found slow Baroque pieces particularly helpful and it would have seemed a logical step to Bach's *Air on a G string*. However, on hearing this, she became extremely agitated. It transpired that the piece had been associated with a traumatic memory. The music had clearly developed personal meanings in these stories, which overrode the intrinsic meaning of the sounds.

This enables it to play an important role in reminiscence therapy with older people. Both pleasant and painful memories can be recalled by carefully chosen pieces of music. Creative arts activities in Wellington, New Zealand, are personalised to meet clients' needs. One 83-year-old resident used playing the piano as part of reminiscence therapy to evoke visual memories (Eames 1999 p. 35). This is particularly useful for older patients, where confusion can be caused by unresolved grieving. Music can help to recall these events and the associated emotions. Anthi Agrotou (1993) sees the possibility of group mourning using music. Here she examines the link between 'religious rituals, certain ritualisms, certain kinds of ritualisation and ritualised play' and examines the transformative space in her sessions (Agrotou 1993 pp. 175–91).[2] Her analysis has clear links with Turner's concept of the creation of a liminal space. Agrotou ends her chapter with a passage exploring the religious dimension of the music therapy session, linking it with the resurrection story of people such as Christ (Agrotou 1993 p. 191). Dr Elizabeth Kubler Ross (1983) gives a moving account of how a live performer, dancing to a piece of Tchaikovsky in an old people's home, enabled people, who had not moved for years, to remember dance moves from their past.

What is clear for anyone working in the area of musicking is that there are multiple meanings that a single piece of music may have, that need to be respected and explored.

The Intrapersonal: Music and Empowerment

The notion of empowerment is deep in the Jungian version of the heroic quest and links with the Vygotskyian (Holzman 2008) idea of scaffolding. An experienced musicker – be they an improvising music therapist or a supportive music teacher – might be seen as holding and supporting people on their own particular journey. Various forms of imaging to music have been developed for musical journeying, especially the method developed

2 We shall examine how the recordings of the Requiem may do this.

by Helen Bonney where music is deliberately used to induce images which are therapeutic to the client and which can be used by the client in the week following the musicking session.

Therapists have developed musical ways of supporting clients. In his work with David, Jos De Backer (Smeijsters and van den Hurk, 1993 pp. 257–8) identifies a return to humming and singing like a mother comforting a child when a client needed love and security. Claire Flower describes how a client used the theme from *EastEnders* as 'a musical hand to hold' and a safe starting point for exploring more difficult areas (Flower 1993 p. 42). When with a class of five-year-olds, we discussed what various instruments made us feel, one five-year-old wanted to take the rainmaker with her to help her sleep. So certain instruments are seen as endowed with particular qualities, or as evoking particular emotional reactions like a bass drum and the cymbal being frightening (De Backer 1993 p. 35). Johannes Kneutgen in his centre *Neue Wege der Musiktherapie* in Dusseldorf in 1974 used tape-recorded lullabies in place of sleeping tablets to soothe debilitated children at night and reduced bed-wetting by two-thirds. George Hengesch, in Bonn, allowed schizophrenic psychotics to play classroom percussion instruments. This calmed them enough to enable him to resume his speech therapy programme with them (Hamel 1978 p. 167). Liz Wilcock, a music therapist, studied the reactions of a hundred and twenty clients at the Bristol Cancer Help Centre to the Tibetan Bowls. The bowls resonated in the mind, body and spirit of the patients (Wilcock 1997 p. 25) to give a sensation of healing. Leslie Bunt (1994 p. 31) cites a number of studies in this area showing, for example, that fast music affects children's play activity and that calming and exciting music can be linked with changes in the electrical resistance of the skin.

The word spirituality is beginning to appear in the literature associated with this area, with titles such as *Music and Soul-making* (Crowe 2004). The term Crowe uses – soul making – is described as the ability of music to heal what makes us vital, whole, alive, and balanced. Her theory is based on twenty-five years of experience as a music therapist. She shows how music touches the four facets of human functioning: mind, body, emotion, and spirit, linking it with the development of Threshold Choirs, who work in hospices with the dying.

In the world of community choirs, from the late twentieth century into the first two decades of the twenty-first century, we see a move towards a nurturing empowering environment, although Sarah Morgan disagrees with this terminology:

> I prefer not to use the term 'empowering', as to me that implies that people lack a power which I can mysteriously bestow on them. I do strongly believe that everyone has the ability to experience and enjoy singing in some way, and I see my role as helping to remind people of that, and trying to remove barriers, where they exist, whether they relate to musical technicality, terminology, accessibility or skills. (Morgan 2013 pp. 27–8)

The need for a sense of nurturing runs through all the literature on leading community choirs, which means revisiting the idea of failure, as we saw in Chapter One:

> At a practical level, one of the most useful skills I acquired was an ability to look around a group and quickly notice people who looked uneasy or uncomfortable, and make it acceptable for people to voice their unease, as well as finding ways of making mistakes an accepted and even a positive part of the process of learning. (Morgan 2013 p. 18)

All of this shows the valuing of process:

> Because much of my material is folk based, I also explain that the music is usually just a guideline or a reminder, not a set of precise instructions – a river rather than a road. (Morgan 2013 p. 28)

This mean that the qualities required of leaders of community choirs are many and various, and include personal as well as musical skills:

- Musically skilled
- Socially skilled/receptive
- Sensitive to specific needs, circumstances and capacities of individuals
- Knowledgeable about specific health condition
- Organised
- Creative
- Flexible
- Humble (Vella-Burrows and Hancox 2012 p. 16)

The result of this philosophy is that many people in the UK of the twenty-first century find their most profound spiritual experience in the world of community choirs as we shall explore further in the final chapter.

The Intrapersonal/Interpersonal: Music as Companionship

We have seen how Alain de Botton (2012) and Tina Beattie (2007) have made an impassioned plea to artists to rethink their teaching to enable the music to fill the void left by God in comforting and supporting people in life's difficulties. This is echoed by Jill Dolan in her writing about music theatre:

> *Utopia in Performance* argues that live performance provides a place where people come together, embodied and passionate, to share experiences of meaning making and imagination that can describe or capture fleeting intimations of a better world. (Dolan 2005 p. 2)

Millie Taylor develops this idea in her inaugural lecture:

> The utopia that Dolan outlines, is not a stabilized model nor a self-determined system, not a narrative or realistic representation of a better world, but something always in process, always slightly out of reach, as an approach toward, a momentary experience, and yet as powerfully real as hopes, desires and 'concrete fantasy' (Dolan 2005 p. 7). These utopian performatives are momentary experiences. (M. Taylor 2013. No page numbers)

Millie Taylor illustrates this with Stephen Sondheim's song *Into the Woods* (1987) based on journeying into difficult places. Here she suggests that the audience finds meaning in their own journeying and accompaniment on their journeys through their experience in the theatre. Here musical theatre becomes a form of companionship along the journeys of life and a guide in negotiating them in the same way as God once was.

There is a similar literature in the area of hymnody. Stephan Reinke (2015) draws on Jung's notion of archetypes to see childhood hymns as a form of self-help, because they open up a 'symbolic mediating space that is filled with inner images and perceptions' (Klessmann 2005 p. 232). This is the tune rather than the text:

> Instead of doing all manner of excessive rationalizing about the text one might well give the power and effect to the entirety of text and melody. It is there that, in veritable echo, the entire fullness of the richness of both is revealed. Viewed accurately, for most of the chorales the edification lies more in the speaking soul of the melody than in the body of the text. (Heymel 2012 p. 13)

There are some examples of the deliberate use of techniques drawn from religious traditions in therapy to support people's journey. The German clarinettists and psychotherapist Ernst Flackus used Zen meditation music in his treatment programmes for drug addicts in the 1970s. Here he combined music listening with methods of autogenous training:

> During the exercise, I played the Zen meditation music softly over a loudspeaker system, but nevertheless made it clear beforehand that the patient should not listen to the music but simply concentrate on the weight and warmth of his body. (Flackus, Trug der Drogen 1974, quoted in Hamel 1978 p. 169)

In an age where addiction is a considerable problem, situations where the power of music to influence the mood of pupils becomes evident could be of great value to students. Current research is into the role of music in the developing practice of mindfulness.

The Interpersonal: Encounter and Empathy

As we move to the strand of the Interpersonal we meet the experience of encounter; this may be with the music itself or with another person within the musical experience. This, for Levinas (1969), represented an encounter with infinity, and a way of being in which the spirituality resides in the flow between the two others who retain their differences in the meeting, which I call difference-in-relationship. This links with Derrida's notion of 'differance' (Derrida 1972 p. 19) and Dewey's of experience as an interaction that is potentially transformative (Dewey 1934 p. 22). This interpersonal encounter is well described by Rudolf Steiner in a lecture from 1919:

> If you meet another person the following occurs: For a short period you perceive a person, a being comparable to yourself, and he or she makes an impression on you. The impression disturbs you inwardly, you resist this attack and become inwardly aggressive toward the person. In this aggression you become crippled and aggression ceases. Then the other person can again make an impression upon you, and after you thus have time to regain your aggressive strength, you carry out another act of aggression. Again, you become numb, and the other person again makes an impression upon you, and so forth. This is the relationship that exists when one person meets another and perceives the other I – that is, devotion to the other – inner resistance; sympathy-antipathy. I am not speaking now of feeling, but just the perception of meeting. The soul vibrates; it vibrates sympathy-antipathy, sympathy-antipathy, sympathy-antipathy. (Steiner 1919/1996)

He goes on to describe the process to be like waking and sleeping and, by using this analogy, he highlights its similarity with the altered time/space dimension of the liminal space. The ability of musical experience to contain a flow between the more rational and the intuitive more dreamlike states makes it a particularly useful medium for facilitating relationships. By using the term vibration, there is a hint in Steiner's writing at the potential role for music in this process.

This is an area of empathy (Laurence 2008), imagination and identity creation. The description of this process varies. Words like sympathy and compassion are defined differently by different authors. Hauerwas (2004 p. 62) draws on Adam Smith's *Theory of Moral Sentiments*, to see sympathy as dependent on the imagination; this he sees as projecting what we might feel, if we were to undergo the same experience. Laurence (2008) sets out a careful definition of empathy, encompassing individualism and community:

> In empathizing, we, while retaining fully our sense of our own distinct consciousness, enter actively and imaginatively into others' inner states to understand how they experience their world and how they are feeling, reaching out to what we perceive as similar, while accepting difference. (Laurence 2008 p. 25)

It enables us to access a sense of mutual vulnerability (Richard 2000 p. 52); this is a significant part of reconciliation work using music. So sympathy is part of making oneself available, essential to engaging with another's vulnerability (Niebuhr 1941 pp. 115–16). Feelings, memories and cultural prejudices are activated to promote empathy and imagination. The use of music and reminiscence with elders is one example, as is a 10-year old girl who sings a setting of an African prayer every night:

> I felt close to the people in Africa whose prayer we sang. Now I continue to sing it and think of them.

In my two collections of songs from various cultures, I give the background to the songs – contextualising the material (Tillman 1987a and 1987b) to enable this process to happen.

Rik Palieri describes the power of his song, entitled *Fathers and Sons*, which he wrote to heal violent abuse by his father:

> As the years passed I continued singing this song and I had some remarkable results. I found it was a great way to address this difficult topic and even in a few cases reunite families. (Palieri 2008 p. 201)

I have had a similar experience with a song written to heal the relationship with my mother (Boyce-Tillman 2006c pp. 110–11). So the musical experience, seen as encounter, invites sympathy and empathy among the participants.

The Interpersonal: Meaning and Context

The meaning of a piece of music to the participants can also be changed by the context; this is where this domain can interact powerfully with the domain of Values. Christopher Small writes of the transformation achieved by the singing of Pete Seeger's and Lee Hays' song *If I had a hammer* in the context of a right-wing republican gathering (Small 2010 pp. 1–8); this established a new meaning for the word Hammer which had been used to represent the right-wing value system that they embraced. We have already seen, in Interlude One, how music is a place where new identities are discovered or old ones rediscovered. Music can give people an experience of identity. Ruth Westheimer used a lullaby to establish her Jewish identity which was lost when her parents gave her away to escape the Nazi regime:

> I sang that lullaby – which has a melody written by Heinrich Isaak back in 1490 – to my children. And maybe I mangled the melody, but I felt – and still feel –the sweetness of it in my bones. (Westheimer 2003 p. 13)

From the First World War, we find a moving letter which shows how singing hymns from his homeland was used to strengthen the cultural roots of a young soldier, who at age 25 wrote the following account just before he died on September 7, 1918:

> Here we try to keep our spirits up through all the firing. We have short services here in the trenches and in all the mud. I turn to sing the verses that I learnt at dear Mynydd Gwyn. I hope that I will be back there soon.[3]

The Interpersonal: Music and vulnerability

It is also a place where group integration can be explored – a place of interpersonal encounter. Finn Tschudi develops the idea of collective vulnerability:

> I have here tried to draw in experiences of vulnerability and shame both in concrete conflicts and as aspects of larger culture. When such experiences are recognized in art, myth and religion, this may facilitate recognition of joint humanity in concrete conflicts– what we have called collective vulnerability. This may again inspire joint, creative ways out of deadlocks. (Tschudi 2005 No pages available)

Sensitivity, at a personal level, facilitates group integration through musicking:

3 I am indebted to John Roberts for this translation from the Welsh of a letter from Griffith Roberts written September 3, 1918.

> Music is very much a social act: people can listen, imitate, learn from each other, even trying out and discarding different styles of interacting. Alternative ways of behaving can be explored in the safety of the musical setting ... Many observers, even of one session, comment on the fact that music can quite quickly bring people together and provide a sense of group cohesion, a sense of immediate belonging ... Whether we listen to music or make music together, the very structure of organised sounds themselves provides a unique opportunity for such integration. (Bunt 1994 pp. 27–8)

As we saw in Chapter Two and Interlude One, this involves risk-taking. Here it is important that the Expression is accepted, encouraged and even praised by someone. This resembles the Vygotskyan idea (Holzman 2008) of scaffolding which enables in this example, the musickers to take the risks that we saw were necessary to the creative process in Chapter Two:

> The group members were beginning to show signs of accepting and encouraging one another. Over a period of time, in more extended work, some of the patterns and habits from earlier in life that may have contributed towards particular problems can be explored in the trusting setting of the group. In music, it is possible to try out different ways of playing. Taking risks may be easier for some people in a musical rather than a verbal medium. (Bunt 1994 p. 27)

In the context of drama therapy, Roger Grainger describes a similar process. He calls it group holism where 'the group is felt to be more than the sum of the interactions of its members' and how one person can become the focus of group awareness within the 'relational area' which he claims represents the 'spiritual identity of the group' (Grainger 1995 p. 31). These skills, developed through musicking, such as sensitivity and mutual support, are seen as transferable (Bunt 1994 p. 7). This increases people's own self-awareness, causing them to look in the mirror form of the psyche, as we saw in the Prelude:

> Music is more than a temporary diversion: it presents people with a challenging opportunity to look at aspects of themselves in a different light. As in any therapy, such a process can be painful. (Bunt 1994 p. 35)

I remember an improvising group of nine-year-olds, in which one member of the group had to hold a steady pulse on a drum, while the other members improvised in turn on their instruments. A nine-year-old boy had the drum to hold the pulse and played loudly throughout. At the end of the piece we discussed any problems with the improvisation. 'The girls were too soft' he said. 'What should we do?' I asked. 'Well, they must play louder' he replied. The girls had small glockenspiels; so I asked him if he could think of another solution. He could think of nothing. 'Perhaps you could play softer?' I suggested. We did the exercise again, and he proved to be an incredibly sensitive accompanist to other people's offerings. It had simply never occurred to him to be more sensitive. I think that that music lesson taught him far more about awareness to other people – especially in the area of gender[4] – than any discussion might have done. So musicking is a place of encounter, in which we can learn a great deal about group cohesion, risk taking, empathy and vulnerability. This opens up the opportunity of new ways of interacting and the healing of old conflicts.

Summary

Music has immense power to access and manage deep emotions and feelings. It is an important way of exploring an inner landscape through a medium that has expressive possibilities beyond those of words. It is, therefore, the domain of Expression that is important for the development of self-awareness and the development of authenticity – a person's sense of what constitutes The True for them. Psychoanalytic traditions, especially Jung, behaviourist traditions and the humanistic psychology of Carl Rogers, in association with music, have revealed a number of ways in which reflexivity can be developed through musicking. The notion of music initiating internal change is deep in the underpinning philosophies of psychoanalysis, especially that of Jung. This links with interpersonal relationships through

4 This may be regarded as stereotyping gender differences; but there is a literature linking particular musical instruments to boys and girls – and, in general, boys are associated with drums.

participation in group musicking activities. In this process, acceptance and encouragement is important. Cultural and personal issues come into play in musicking because of the extrinsic associations that become associated with various actual pieces and styles of music.

As we move to the domain of Construction, Heidegger (1886–1976) helpfully reminds us of the two approaches to a work of art, so linking this chapter with the next. Ideas of The True started to appear in the Enlightenment, as the inner landscape met the world of cultural norms and structures – thus linking The True and The Beautiful:

> Heidegger approaches a work of art from two angles. On the one hand he asks what can make a human being see the world in a new light: on the other, he asks what the role of art actually is. The two questions turn out to be related. Heidegger's aim is to show how the work of art still – as in the aesthetics of the Romantics – is concerned with truth. Indeed, it emerges that the work of art is one of the few things that can seriously open our eyes to the world in which we live ... The true is what we human beings sense, purely and simply. (Nielsen in Beyer 1996 p. 174)

This chapter has attempted to bring together the traditional arguments between the camps of formalists and referentialists. The formalist approach favours what I have called intrinsic meaning and has been dominant in musicology. It sets up instrumental music as the purest form because the presence of a text always provides meanings which are beyond the musical sounds::

> Of what *instrumental music* cannot do, it ought never be said that *music* can do it, because only instrumental music is music purely and absolutely ... one will have to grant that the concept 'music' does not apply strictly to a piece of music composed to a verbal text. (Hanslick 1986 p. 14. Author's italics)

It is this concentration on intrinsic meaning that has made Construction so central to musicology. In the next chapter, we shall see that there is flow between expressive and structural elements, in the same way as we have seen the relationship between extrinsic and intrinsic meaning in this chapter.

CHAPTER SIX

Musical Construction

A Story

An African leader was taken by his British host to a concert of Mozart at the Royal Festival Hall. After listening politely he said to his host: 'Thank you for this but I thought your music was more complex than that.' His host was surprised.

Introduction

This is an interesting story when viewed from the assumed exalted position of the Western classical tradition. It shows the dilemma concerning how musical ideas are debated in various cultures. Many of the African traditions have chosen to debate them primarily in the area of rhythm (as we shall see below). The African was skilled in understanding them in that area; however, the Western classical European cultures have chosen melody and harmony as the prime areas for musical debate. The Mozart concert asked for skill in understanding ideas debated in those areas and the African leader was not experienced in understanding debate using melody and harmony. As the rhythm of Mozart was relatively simple, he perceived the argument as simple. The complexity was not in an area he could grasp. In the same way, Western classical theorists have regarded the African traditions as simple because they could not read complexity in the area of rhythm.

This domain is about the ordering of time in a particular culture, as we shall see when we compare orate and literate traditions. Charles Taylor sees a new form of time emerging from the processes of secularisation. He links this with Benedict Anderson's new sense of belonging to a nation under the category of simultaneity (Anderson 1991). This, according to Charles Taylor, is an exclusively secular view of time, which he contrasts with earlier more religious views of time; these religious views saw a certain verticality in its view of time which 'depended on a grounding in higher time' (C. Taylor 2007 p. 209). The way in which time functions is an essential part of how Construction functions in various musical cultures.

There is much writing about how musical ideas are debated in the Western classical tradition, such as how a string quartet, for example, is an intimate conversation between the players. In a recent keynote address on Music and Spirituality, at a conference on the spirituality of music education, Roger Scruton asked for the development of judgement within musical education; the standards that he set up for this, were entirely based in the Construction systems of Western classical traditions, which he also used to evaluate popular music traditions. When I asked if his system for judging good and bad music would be the same if he had been brought up in one of the drumming traditions of the African continent, he was forced to admit that they would probably would not. Brought up in a tradition that has valued Construction more highly than any other aspect of the musical experience, he was a prisoner of his own cultural upbringing.

The elegance of the debate and, indeed, what is regarded as an elegant structured argument, has long concerned theoreticians of the Western classical tradition. It is in the domain of Construction that our curricula in musicology concentrate, in their pursuit of The Beautiful. The unequivocal acceptance of some music as great and other as more inferior depends on the deep establishment of these norms of The Beautiful; these have governed how Western culture has created its criteria for the assessment of musical Beauty.

It could be argued that this view of The Beautiful had a spiritual or quasi-spiritual origin. A quotation from a novella by Wackenroder illustrates this well:

> When Joseph was at a grand concert he seated himself in a corner, without so much as glancing at the brilliant assent assembly of listeners, and listened with precisely the same reverence as if he were in church – just as still and motionless, his eyes cast down to the floor. Not the slightest sound escaped his notice, and his keen attention left him in the end quite limp and exhausted. (Wackenroder, cited in Dahlhaus 1989 p. 94)

This form of the concert was a new idea, originating in the early nineteenth century with the development of the public concert tradition. Chua (1999) describes the invention of the idea of absolute music with its claims for internal structural coherence and an abstract and intangible meaning:

> And if musical meaning is abstract, absolute, and ineffable then it is only a very short step to claims of universality and mystery, and this to the quasi-religious character of nineteenth and twentieth century concert listening practices, documented by Johnson (1995) in the history of listening in Paris. (E. Clarke 2005 p. 131)

The development of a canon of 'great works' in Western classical music depended on these supposedly 'universal' criteria for The Beautiful and these have long been the basis for Western music education. For it is through the processes of education that these norms are embedded deeply and sustained within a particular society. The dominating elders of Western classical music have controlled music education, with the result that Construction issues may be seen as over documented in the pieces that make up the classical canon (Goehr 1992) and form the basis of Western musicology. In fact, we might say that musicology has primarily been concerned with the way in which ideas are debated in Western classical traditions – what makes them understandable and what makes them incomprehensible. The curriculum through which my musical ability was nurtured consisted largely of understanding this domain in relation to Western classical music. When, later, I encountered the world of popular music, I began to realise the cultural limitations of what I had been taught. It downplayed, for example, my paternal grandfather's skill as the village dance pianist who, every Saturday night, played – largely by ear – the popular dance tunes of his day.

Sadly, the principles and terminologies developed in the Western classical tradition have often been applied to other cultures, without sufficient regard for how thinkers within those traditions have regarded their own processes of musical Construction. For example, the more circular structures of improvised traditions often sit uneasily with the use of the terminology associated with the more linear notated traditions.

Revisiting Values in Construction

One of the problems for this domain in music is the failure to locate the Value systems that underpin its concepts of Beauty in the context of the religious frame that generated them. This is because the meanings of music are more complex and less clear than the performing arts that use words. The philosopher, Rosi Braidotti acknowledges the contemporary power of the legacy of metaphysical symbols from the past in her provocative statement:

> God may be dead but the stench of his rotting corpse pervades all of Western culture. (Braidotti 1995 quoted in Mantin 2002 pages unavailable)

My explorations as a feminist theologian led me to interrogate more deeply the close relationship between music and theology. This was forged in the Middle Ages, when an overarching theological frame governed all knowledge.

My thinking in this domain led me to see how the traditional male metaphysical symbols for God originated in the description of a male Trinity in the Middle Ages; but these symbols moved to the mind of man (and I mean man) in the work of writers, such as Francis Bacon in the seventeenth century (Bacon 1973 p. 3). The values of triumphalism, dualism, unity, clarity and order are now construed as the highest human virtues and eternal in character. But, in reality, they simply reflect their origin in the maleness of God. Without God, who is now reduced to the side-lines, they can stand freely as an objective goodness – a powerful myth which maintains the status quo by claiming that they belong to a sphere outside temporality. They are now the standards of the Academy, peddled as free-standing and objective. How often are debates about equal opportunities of all kinds punctuated by the statement: it does not matter who wrote it but whether it is 'good' music? Other academics have seen similar linkages between ancient theological frames and the constructions of contemporary academic disciplines, such as Fiona Bowie, in the area of anthropology:

> Although cultural domains are culturally specific, they usually come with claims to universality that are seemingly nature-given and/or God-given and are made real through institutional arrangements and the discourses of everyday life. (Bowie 1998 pp. 52–3)

What these analyses show, is that values derived from the maleness of God have been crucial to the maintenance of a variety of patriarchal patterns for the judgement of The Beautiful to create a monoculture based on a limited monotheistic theology. These values have oppressed many groups, such as the 'foreign', the 'unusual', women and the natural world; so the re-empowering of subjugated groups is associated with a concern for social justice and the establishment of new and various criteria for The Beautiful.

But these were not always the values of Christianity. My research into early Christianity has shown that the hierarchies associated with these values, developed over the first six hundred years (Boyce-Tillman 2014). During this time, the emerging Christian church established its position as distinct from its Judaic roots and the surrounding pagan traditions. Early Christian gatherings were in the private space of the home – the woman's domestic sphere (Macdonald 1996 p. 217). As such, they were communal in their organisation and the worship was congregational and inclusive of all present. Margaret Lindley, in her fascinating article *Competing Trinities: The Great Mother and the Formation of the Christian Trinity*, charts how gradually the concept of a male Trinity was constructed in order to present a credible challenge to the worship of the great Mother (Lindley 1995 pp. 32–6). Sophie Drinker, in her remarkable book on *Women in Music*, links the establishment of hierarchical practices in music with the move to a male divinity (Drinker 1948/95 pp. 127–42). Indeed, the construction of and increasing dominance of the male Trinity, went hand in hand with a hierarchical organisation of the ministry (including the musical ministry) of the Church. It also reflected the increased embracing by the Church hierarchies of the values of Roman imperialism; these were, in the end, transferred to the spiritual domain. From then on, both the music and the liturgy of the developing Church remained tightly in the hands of male-dominated hierarchies. The dominant theology of medieval Christianity became that of a male God who made the world and then operates it, somewhat remotely, through the offices of an ordained priesthood, by means of the use of their understanding of a special, 'holy' language. This priesthood mediates God's wishes to a lay congregation whose task is simply to receive and obey God's commands. This model has coloured the way that musical composition is constructed in the Western classical tradition, with composers playing a role similar to that of God, remote and in control; the performer's role is similar to that of the priests, because they understand the 'special' language of the Western classical notation system; the audience play a role similar to that of the laity, whose task is simply to receive the mediated word of the composer.

The Church had to wait until the Protestant Reformation to attempt to share power more widely by means of a congregational-singing tradition. This challenged the hierarchies of the existing Church; it was based on the use of popular tunes to enable the engagement of a wider group of people with theology and started a move towards a community based on musicking. Forms such as the cantata saw the professional choir integrated with the hymn singing of a re-empowered congregation.

My work on the Wisdom (Boyce-Tillman 2007b, 2014) traditions (traditionally feminine) led me to challenge traditional theological hierarchies and its associated values of order, clarity and aesthetic perfection. Along with other feminist theologians such as Mary Grey (1993) and Carol Christ (1997), I embraced notions of God as process, working continually within creation, through the processes of renewal and restoration; from that came a challenge to musical hierarchies and the blurring of the boundaries between composer, performer and audience; this was based on a model of God as weaver rather than controlling autocrat (Boyce-Tillman 2006a p. 67).

Ordering and Chaos

We explored in Chapter Two how order and chaos are valued or devalued through the myth of creation in Genesis 1; as notions of God declined, there was the development of the idea of an impersonal order underpinning the universe and named the Aesthetic, which to some extent retained Values that were previously rooted in the male Divine. Most courses in music in the West have concentrated their tuition in this highly ordered approach to this domain, teaching Western classical notation as if it were a branch of mathematics. The compositional side of my music education at Oxford University, for example, consisted largely of the reproduction of empty shells of the musical forms of High Art European Music between 1550 and 1900.

In this domain, effectiveness usually depends on the right management of repetition and contrast within a particular idiom (Boyce-Tillman 2011a). The way in which contrast is handled within a tradition – how much or how little can be tolerated – is often carefully regulated by the elders of the various traditions – be they the composers or theoreticians of the Western classical tradition or the master drummers of Yoruba traditions:

> Music is a kind of organization of audible material in time. It is simultaneously unique and plural and it varies according to era, place, language, and culture. From this come the differences and even the oppositions between musical styles and the study and use of symbols that follow from it, peculiar to each people and each civilization. (Feki 2011 p. 52)

A particular culture sets up the ways in which ideas are to be debated musically; in this domain, we encounter a musical debate and need to be able to grasp the contours of the norms of the particular culture that we are being put into. At a micro level, each music piece will have an internal structure. Some of these will be quite simple like ternary from – ABA – where the first section recurs at the end. This can be extended to rondo to produce an ABACA shape, where one phrase acts as a recurring refrain. Other forms are more complex and associated with particular idioms and styles like the middle eight of the popular song and the repeated chord sequence of the twelve-bar blues. We shall see later how orate traditions function in this domain.

In Chapter Two, we discussed how ideas around originality coloured debates in the area of creativity, related to particular communities. However, different communities value a greater or lesser degree of innovation. Western classical culture has valued a high degree of innovation, whereas other cultures have valued a much closer adherence to tradition. The degree of repetition (in the domain of Construction) included will affect the domain of Expression that the piece will inhabit. Minimalist pieces, for example, create a meditative atmosphere by a great deal of repetition and limited changes of volume. A high degree of contrast which is always changing gives a restless feel, as in some contemporary classical pieces. Popular traditions use a greater degree of repetition which is why classical devotees tend to find them boring. The converse is also true when popular music addicts find Western classical music incomprehensible. Christian Friedrich Michaelis summarised his position well in the *Berlinische Musikalische Zeitung* (1805):

> The shaping of a coherent whole, is hampered in music in two principal ways. Firstly, by uniformity so great that it almost excludes variety: by the constant repetition of the same note or chord: by long, majestic, weighty, solemn notes and hence by very slow movement; by long pauses which hold up the progress of the melodic line, or impede the shape of a melody, thus underlining the lack of variety. Secondly the shaping of a coherent whole is hampered by too much diversity, as when innumerable impressions succeed one another too rapidly and the mind is too abruptly hurled into the thundering torrent of sounds or when ... The themes are developed together in so complex a manner that the imagination cannot easily and calmly integrate the diverse ideas into a coherent whole. Thus, in music, the sublime can only be that which seems too vast and significant, too strange and wonderful, to be easily assimilated by the imagination. (Le Huray and Day 1981 p. 290)

It is in this domain where many claims for a spirituality associated with order have been made, by traditional writers on aesthetics and spirituality, linked with William James's view of the religious experience as associated with harmony:

> Were one asked to characterize the life of religion in the broadest and most general terms possible, one might say that it consists of the belief that there is an unseen order, and that our supreme good lies in harmoniously adjusting ourselves thereto. (W. James 1902/1997 p. 59)

This has led to many people, at ease with the Western classical tradition, seeing these pieces as essentially spiritual:

> After 12 years I remarried a university deputy librarian with whom I often attended the Halle concerts. Countless are the times great music has brought me spellbound to the 'gates of Heaven' – the hush during a Beethoven symphony, a sermon in itself. I've often said that to me, a good concert was far more full of awe – God, if you like, than many a church service. But then it may be because I am artistic to a certain extent … I am convinced that there is a spiritual power beyond the material world, strengthening us and urging us on in the fight against evil and I find as I gain this strength I am able to give help to others – but not in a soppy sentimental way – rather by 'rooted optimism'.[1]

The Western Musical Canon: Monumentality

In the Alister Hardy archive, there are regular references of this kind to music by such composers as Mozart, Beethoven and Bach, all of whom feature prominently in the musical works that make up the canon of Western classical music. Many of the works are conceived on a large scale using orchestras and choirs. Because of the linking spirituality with notions of awe, mystery and transcendence it is easy to see how this has played out in seeing these works as the height of a spiritual tradition (Kanellopoulos 2013). Such elements were significant in the development of 'monolithic conceptions of canonic music in the nineteenth and twentieth centuries' (Kanellopoulos 2013). Rehding's study (2009) entitled *Commemoration and Wonderment in Nineteenth Century Germany*, sees musical monumentality as a central feature of nineteenth-century German repertoire. Here he sees an intersection between aesthetics and memory using examples from Liszt, Wagner and Bruckner. He shows how music history has portrayed this part of music history as communicating the sublime to a listening public. Monumentality will always excite awe and wonder:

> Monumental, gargantuan things captivate us. Whether it be the world's biggest ball of twine, the county's fattest pig, or the Grand Canyon, objects that are supersized

1 Alister Hardy Archive Woman aged 65.

> and beyond all reasonable scale thrill people ... The same is true with human creations of vast scale: they have the ability to exceed the parameters of normal, quotidian life. Like the mighty Redwood or the vertiginous canyons of the southwest, towering achievements of human ingenuity, endurance, creativity, and intellect can have an overwhelming, oceanic awe attached to them. And every discipline of human experience has its own equivalent to Mt. Everest. Literature lovers have Proust's 7-volume *In Search of Lost Time*; thespians have the 8-hour *Faust* by Goethe (and Japanese thespians have even longer *Noh* plays); opera fans love to get lost in 'The Ring' cycle; and for humble musicologists, we have Richard Taruskin's *The Oxford History of Western Music*. (Samples and Wallmark 2015)

Panos Kanellopoulos (2013) describes a powerful experience associated with monumentality:

> Athens, Spring 1990: Grigoris Semitekolo performs Yanni Christou's (1926–1970) *Araparastasis III: The pianist*, an extravagant music-theatrical ritual for actor, percussion and tape, a work that belongs to what the composer calls an enactment of proto-performance. The performance culminates in a cataclysmic climax, which leads the performers to stretch the limits of density, volume, speed, with the actor's metapraxis leading to near-paroxysm. The performance vanishes to silence and I sit still, overwhelmed by this experience. I do not think that I have ever again listened to a live performance with such intensity. This is my most vivid impression from the performance: a sense auditory, visual and bodily 'act of *latching-on*' (Mandoki 2007, in Regelski and Gates 2010, p. 199) to the struggle of Christou's pianist. I try to get up; my legs are not responding. At that very moment I realise that my fingers are stretched. Even today, after 23 years, I remember very well that I was trapped so to speak in a position where I was observing my body as if it did not belong to me. I am scared. I tell my friend that I can't get off the chair, but she does not take me seriously – after repeated attempts to get up, she *has* to take me seriously. (Kanellopoulos 2013 Author's emphasis)

Kanellopoulos goes on to reflect on this as an experience of 'beyond-ness', in this case by 'an exploration of the ineffable anxieties of human beings.' Christou had immersed himself in ancient mystical traditions (Lucciano 1999); Kanellopoulos does not link his experience with these strands, but with the monumentality of the music, describing it as:

> an act of latching-on to the performance's exploration of psychologically extreme conditions. (Kanellopoulos 2013)

We shall explore this notion further in Chapter Eight; but here it is the sheer scale of the work that enables this experience to happen.

Monumentality has another resonance simply in the amount of writing about a subject. This is very clear in Richard Taruskin's monumental study *The Oxford History of Western Music* which weighs in at five volumes and 3,856 pages (Samples and Wallmark 2015). In it, Taruskin (2009) does link classical music to spirituality when he talks of 'the spiritualised classical music of the turn-of-millennium', arguing that it has catered for an "art that reflects their [people that Taruskin refers to as 'bourgeois bohemians'] ethical self-image' that is characterised by the imperative of 'personal authenticity, constructed not in terms of a wholly original worldview but in terms of eclecticism' (Taruskin 2009 p. 287). His comments link with the critiques of versions of religionless spirituality, explored in Chapter One. But the very size of his work and the weight of musicological thought behind it serves to support the Western classical view of music; those who even know about it (without having read it) will see it as an affirmation of the 'greatness' of certain works. Monumentality is also attributed to the volume of writing by Taruskin; in *Text and Act* (1995,) he cites the example of *Don Giovanni* to which meanings have been attributed by Mozart, Da Ponte (the librettist), E.T.A. Hoffmann, Kierkegaard, Charles Rosen and Peter Sellars. Taruskin claims that these shine through the work and add to its richness. So the work grows in stature by acquiring a mass of meanings and interpretations. Denk (2011) likens these works to:

> certain alien beings in science fiction which draw detritus into themselves, and thereby become ever greater monsters, ever more powerful beings. (Denk 2011. Pages not available)

The converse of this is that fewer meanings have ben ascribed to folk or popular material (certainly in written form) and therefore they are perceived as less rich. This position was supported in many music curricula in the US and the UK by lessons in music appreciation, supported by *The Oxford Companion to Music* (Scholes 1938, Jorgensen 1987). This shaped the taste and values of people educated in this particular culture. Systems of analysis have been developed to support these claims and many will be convinced, especially when these claims are repeated in programme notes for classical concerts. Here we encounter the significance of words in dictating how a musical piece is viewed; these works are usually mediated by some form of words – academic texts, programme notes, sleeve notes – which prepares the listener for regarding these works as 'great' (Blake 1997). Such words as Taruskin's have been used to support a theory of the greatness of certain works, in some sort of third realm where abstract notions of The Beautiful, supported by Western criteria, exist independently of human experience.

But this book has set out to interrogate and challenge this view of the spiritual in music. I suggest that it is summarised in this vignette – that if you play Bach's Mass in B minor in the jungle, even the animals will worship God. It was this view that Dewey (1934) also sought to counter.

Construction and Mathematics

The linkage between Spirituality and Construction is related to the essential ordering of the universe as in the Genesis 1 myth we looked at in Chapter Two, where God brings order as part of the creation process. This ordering has often been related to mathematical formulae; so Construction issues in composers like Bartok are linked with numerical sequences in the nature of the universe like The Golden Mean or Golden Sequence. These have been taken further in the spirituality of Arvo Part where his notion of rhythmic infinity is generated from the Golden Sequence alongside infinity systems of melody and harmony. The linkage with the mathematical found itself becoming more complex as the twentieth century progressed with serialism and pitch-set theory.

It is now well represented by Paul Robertson's approach to the spiritual meaning of music. On his website he describes how Bach encoded many hidden religious meanings into the construction of his pieces for solo violin. His claim (supported by the German academic, Helga Thoene) is that embedded in sonatas and partitas for solo violin are a pattern of chorales associated with Christmas, Easter and Pentecost:

> These magnificent and often perplexing works are yielding this multitude of hidden meanings, expressing faith and hope in redemption and resurrection, and personal love and dedication to his wife and children in a musical, mathematical tapestry of creed, song, dance and magic. (Robertson 2015)[2]

Robertson claims that in the eighteenth century these mathematical encodings were common in verse as well and known as paragrams. Bach was also influenced by Jewish mysticism and numbers associated with various names including the name of Jesus:

> [Bach used] numerical/alphabetical 'Gematria' (a system for converting letters and words into numbers, most commonly associated with the mystical Jewish tradition of Cabbala) upon which the music is composed.[3]

The encoding into the music was done, Robertson claims, by a mixture of techniques, such as the proportions of the movements, the length of notes, note names and bar numbers. Pozzi Escot has done similar work on the compositions of Hildegard of Bingen (1999). She has written widely on the relationship of music and mathematics in books such as *The Poetics of Simple Mathematics in Music* and her journal *Sonus*.

I have heard many lectures claiming that the greatness of particular pieces – often from the Western classical canon – resides in the spirituality of various mathematical formulae, whether these be the modes of the Greek Orthodox Church, the Golden Sequence, particular tunings of instruments and their relationship to Greek mathematical concepts, to name but a few. This resulted in an Avant garde set of composers who were obsessed with mathematical bases for musical construction. John Tavener critiqued this complexity:

> First of all, there was an enormous thirst for complexity, and my music is rather simple, I suppose, and rather direct. Also, I think that the majority of artists living today want to show the world that it is, or appears to be that is, ugly and dissonant, and together it's an expression one could say of Hell, and many artists do it extraordinarily well. I'm thinking of Francis Bacon; Harrison Birtwistle in the musical

2 <http://www.musicmindspirit.org/new_paul2.html> Accessed August 19th 2015.

3 <http://www.musicmindspirit.org/new_paul2.html> Accessed August 19th 2015.

> world – they're masters of showing Hell, because, in a sense, they're in Hell, and this is a very sad state of affairs because I'm only interested, really, in representing Paradise, and it's very easy to mock that. Paradise is far more difficult than Hell ... it's much more difficult to try to represent the childlike state of Paradise that one hears in Mozart or the music of the Sufis, or any of the great religious musics. One is aware of an enormous childlike simplicity. (Tavener 2005)

Tavener here challenges the prevailing orthodoxy of the Avant-garde by his own simplicity of the domain of Construction.

The valuing of highly ordered Construction systems, fixed by a literate notation system, has tended to exclude the inclusion of more chaotic elements. Improvisatory elements with their delight in spontaneity, play and the carnivalesque (Bakhtin 1993, Boyce-Tillman 2012a) have been marginalised. But the combination of order and chaos offer the possibility of uniting the Apollonian and Dionysian elements of our culture, which is why I include improvisatory passages in many of my pieces. There are other attempts to rebalance the Construction systems of the Western classical systems:

> How? By integrating universal elements into the study of its objective without limiting the comparisons to include only the standards of European systemic norms, and without fearing to go beyond cultural frontiers. (Feki 2011 p. 50)

For example, the more circular structures of improvised traditions often sit uneasily with the use of the terminology associated with the more linear notated traditions. How musical form is perceived in orate musical cultures differs markedly from its perception in literate musical cultures, because time functions differently in those adopting a more circular shape.

The Relationship between the Inner and the Outer: Expression and Construction

I often reflect on this domain in my work in the area of Performance as Research stressing how important it is that this process is clear and coherent:

> So, I have no problem because that's the way the artist works, but I found myself asking about Musical Composition, 'How far is a symphony and the creating of a symphony a methodology?', and I think there's an interesting parallel here. One of the methodologies used for practice-led research, is Grounded Theory; what you do in Grounded Theory, you collect a whole load of data from a variety of sources and gradually you pull the main threads out of it to create a theory which is the end of the process ... I've got little ideas forming in my head and in my own mind I've got a mass of data flying around my head including, what size the orchestra is, how many children there's going to be, all of that's data in the same way the Grounded Theory is, and in a sense the *Titanic* piece is the theory, out of that mass of data I have constructed a coherent piece, or if one wants to have a parallel, it's a very good parallel that you have loads of data and often far more data than you're ever going to use in the piece, and you're selecting and rejecting stuff to produce and you could say that a work of art of some kind is a theory. (Boyce-Tillman et al 2012c pages unavailable)

We have already seen how the ordering of potentially chaotic emotions is seen by Leslie Bunt as central to music therapy; the idea is that emotions are released in a form that is constructive. There is a power in this domain to bring order to the potential unruly chaos of the world of feeling and emotion. David Aldridge distinguishes between catharsis and expression using this domain as his touchstone. He describes how the move from one to the other can be used to facilitate change as catharsis moves into shaped musical form:

> The creative expression is not the same as cathartic expression. Whereas personal emotive expression may be the first step in the process of healing, the continuing therapeutic process is to give articulation to a broad range of human feelings. While passionately playing music can lead to an emotional catharsis it lacks the intensity of form which articulates the whole range of personal aspiration. (Aldridge 1996 p. 18)

Leslie Bunt sees the need for form and structure in the setting up of a group session in an acute admissions ward in a psychiatric unit in a general hospital:

> Some musical structures will be set up, in the hope of providing a sense of security. But within such structures there is freedom to improvise and explore ... Boundaries are established at the start of the group. (Bunt 1994 p. 23)

David Aldridge picks up the idea of debate in discussing the need for intelligibility between musickers by using phrasing that they share, as in speech (Aldridge 1996 p. 55).

Jonathan Harvey sees the inner world meeting the outer world in this domain and sees the importance of being rooted in a tradition, so that 'the composer's "innate" inspiration collides with his "learned" technique' (Harvey 1999 p. 71). Charles Friedrich Michaelis in 1805 in the *Berlinische Musikalische Zeitung* defines true Beauty as the moment when emotions are fused into the whole (Le Huray and Day, 1981 p. 290). So here we see how the domains interact powerfully. The containment of the inner landscape in an appropriate form is the essence of the successful musical experience. As we turn to the orate tradition we see that the construction systems are different. Indeed, Roger Graef, talking about his discovery of relationship with Western classical music after a life time of jazz, described it as 'jazz with architecture'.[4]

One of the problems of notated traditions is the effort required to decode the symbols. The absence of these in improvised and orate traditions often makes them feel much more directly linked to emotions and physicality. One of the reasons for the stress on memorisation in the notated traditions, lies in that capacity to go beyond the symbols to the essence of the music, which is the sound. I am reminded of the verse of George Herbert's hymn:

A man that looks on glass,
on it may stay his eye;
or if he pleaseth, through it pass,
and then the heaven espy.
(George Herbert)

In notated traditions, the notation needs to be passed through to reach the spiritual, and much Western musical education stops at the point of decoding and never passes through it to see the spiritual beyond.

4 Graef, Roger (2014), Interview on *Desert Island Discs*, BBC Radio 4 Nov 2nd 2014.

Improvisation

The place of improvisation in the domain of Construction is much debated. Indeed, it is in the Christian liturgical traditions – particularly improvised organ episodes – that it has retained a place in the highly structured classical traditions of Western Europe. Of Pierre Cochereau, organist at Notre Dame, Paris (1924–84), it was written:

> He drew us into his joyous celebration, which makes a prayer become, easily and imperiously, a kind of jubilation, an exaltation before God ... Those final improvisations were not a conclusion, not a closing act. They opened doors; those of the cathedral on to the illuminated square and those of the celestial of Jerusalem on to the light that will always shine. (Cochereau 1994)

Charles Tournemire (1936), organist of Ste Clotilde, Paris, sees flashes of vision illuminating his soul, when improvising; this description resembles the illuminative aspects of the creative process explored in Chapter Two. Tournemire thought that these improvisations were greater than the pieces that he had worked at in notated form.

Andrew Love links improvisation with the biblical phenomenon of singing in tongues (Love 2003). This he relates biblically with metaphysical inspiration. He sees improvisation as a rebalancing of the West's reliance on the rational left brain, bringing into play the more intuitive right brain. This too links with strands in the literature on creativity that we explored in Chapter Two, particularly in the return to intuitive childhood processes. We know that babies are capable of entering creative musical improvisations with their carers (Trevarthen 1979); and there may well be a connection between early speech-song and improvisation, linked with Brian Lancaster's work that we examined in Chapter One. This is related to 'an undifferentiated method of communication' which linked speech and song by means of the features of pitch, stress and duration was a feature of earlier cultures (Nettl 1972 p. 136). James Macmillan sees himself wanting to 'give vent to that dreamlike state which only a child knows' (Macmillan 2000 p. 3). Tournemire (1936) claims that, in his inspired improvisations, the unconscious substitutes itself for the conscious. In Tournemire's writing, there are descriptions that we might associate with Csikszentmihalyi's flow (1993), which has elements of childhood experiences of playing.

This playful improvisatory experience is a zone, potentially, of reconciliation. Vegar Jordanger saw this happening in his peace-making work in Rostov:

> There was no time to mentally prepare for improvisation ... Once the musicians started playing on their instruments, we saw mental concentration and playfulness in their faces. In other words, once the musicians started playing they instantly entered the zone of risk and uncertainty – this is the zone of dialogue par excellence. (Jordanger 2008 p. 13)

This is possibly because play is linked with the forgetting of subjectivity (Ricoeur 1994 p. 186); this is a characteristic of many spiritual behaviours proposed by the great religions:

> Purposive rationality focuses on the survival of the individual organism, but the knowledge required for the survival of the whole group, or wisdom, is held in the non-conscious realms of the mind, accessible to conscious awareness through art and ritual. (C. Cohen 2008a p. 4)

In Judaeo/Christian theology this links with the Wisdom tradition, which is seen as playing with God at the beginning of time. Hugo Rahner links playing with the ability to fuse a spiritual unity between apparent opposites, such as joy and sadness; we saw this in Chapter One in relation to the spirituality of tragedy and comedy. A child's play is both serious and joyful (Rahner 1965 p. 21). This infant musicking is the way that infants start their understanding of time with an understanding of reality that is 'preconceptual and participatory' (Love 2003). This may be when a child has an experience of pure 'being' – Heidegger's concept of Dasein (Love 2001 p. 179); music brings together a more existential, wilder way of knowing, which continually rolls underneath the more intellectual, abstract knowing of conscious reasoning:

> Musical improvisation will continue to embody the same significance throughout the lifetime of the person, evoking a primordial memory, because musical

> improvisation is the activity in which unconscious memories of babbling are carried into later life. Musical improvisation will continue to link the person with his or her world ... For Heidegger, 'Being speaks' in language. Infant music is embryonic language. (Love 2001 p. 155)

So improvisation is a way of locating 'being' within time (Love 2001 p. 164); this Being-in-Time embraces emotion. 'Understanding always has its mood' (Heidegger 2002 p. 182). It also points to the future because of its moving, momentary evanescent quality, linking it with Whitehead's process philosophy, that we saw in Chapter One. The interface between the domains of Construction and Expression enables the fusion of understanding and emotion.

Stephen Nachmanovitch in *Free Play: Improvisation in Life and Art* (1990) makes similar claims for free improvisation which requires attentive awareness of the environment with mind, body, emotion and intuition. For Nachmanovitch, the free flowing energy that characterises improvisation is contained within the limitations of time and place. In doing this, we transcend ourselves, so establishing a deep link between living with integrity and musical improvisation. John Cage's saw his music as rooted in the present and freeing up the future:

> The masterpieces of Western music exemplify monarchies and dictatorships. Composer and conductor: king and prime minister. By making musical situations which are analogous to desirable social circumstances which we do not have, we make music suggestive and relevant to the serious questions which face Mankind [sic]. (Cage 1980 p. 178)

Music then becomes a vehicle of hope and possible transformation, important strands that we have seen in descriptions of spirituality. For example, Gerrit Jordaan (2015) saw group improvisation of the Taizé tradition as the most profound Expression of Christian community. So some improvisatory practices had survived in Western classical traditions; theorists have linked these with childhood musicking and to a time of 'pure' being which can be revisited by improvisation in later life. This state, which may be Midrashic, can be seen as deeply spiritual.

The Meeting of the Notated and the Improvisatory: Gospel Music

In the last two centuries we have seen a merger of notated and improvised traditions in the rise in popularity of gospel music and its associate, jazz. The wife of John Coltrane is credited with saying that playing jazz is to worship in church. It is perhaps epitomised in John Coltrane's *A Love Supreme*. In black churches notated hymns were taken and transformed:

> Rather than retaining the Euro-American structure, hymns were reshaped or improvised or 'blackenized' as a means of contextualisation. (Costen 1993 p. 98)

The Western hymns entered a new river – the orate traditions of the African-American culture:

> The oral tradition introduces itself again; the 'standard' or well-known, Euro-American hymns require no special instruction for black rendition. The Black religious community instinctively knows how to sing them. The mode of singing is common to the black religious experience and is passed from one generation to another via an oral tradition in Black sacred music. (Walker 1979 p. 98)

Here the fusion of the literate Western hymnody with the orate traditions of Africa have produced a cultural fusion that for many people represent an important contemporary tradition of spiritual music. It has produced a merger of freedom and containment that is an excellent metaphor for human living.

Orate Traditions

The absence of a literate form of a tradition means that the way it functions and is perceived is different from literate traditions. Community choirs in the UK have developed a considerable repertoire of pieces that can be taught and performed totally orally. This means that the way repetition and contrast are handled is different, as time behaves differently. The literate traditions are always looking backward and forward because notation fixes the past and future; the orate traditions are more aware of the present.

Traditionally the Western literate traditions have seen these cultures as 'simpler', because it looks as if repetition is more dominant. These judgements were often made without experiencing these cultures performatively and understanding the subtlety of variation that was happening with them. Olu Taiwo (2012) is a drummer/dancer with a basis in Yoruba traditions. His doctoral thesis identified the way in which the beat functions in the orate Yoruba drumming traditions. He sees the return beat as '*becoming*' within an experience of a curved rhythmic flux in a way that resembles Heidegger's ideas explored above. I am indebted to him for the ideas set out in the rest of this section.

So how we experience the 'points' and 'spaces between' beats in a rhythmic event or wave packet is culturally determined. The performing arts provide us with some processes of Construction that encourage individuals or groups to reflect their experiences of cultural becoming. An example of this is the difference between West African dance and European ballet. Whereas in ballet we see an emphasis on line, length and lightness in its placement, in West African dance, we see curves that are contained within weighted movements emphasising a complex relationship with drum rhythms. The former reflects a desire for individuals to fly and leave the material condition, while the latter reflects experiences that discover altered states through the material, through embodiment. Performative rhythm is a phenomenon that enables individuals or groups to predict, produce and maintain their cultural experience of becoming. This is achieved by embodying, anticipating and projecting those predetermined tacit parameters noted above, that underpin the culture into which they were born (Taiwo 1998).

Taiwo identifies two aspects of the beat – its being and its becoming:

1. How do we subjectively experience the liminal points at which the beats occur? Its being
2. How do we subjectively experience the temporal spaces between the beats? Its becoming

When we experience the beat in the two different cultures we compare the metric beat (a European perceptual flux) with that of the return beat (a West African perceptual flux). There are, according to Taiwo (2012), distinctive differences. These perceptions influence the play of consciousness, using the line and the circle or curve as metaphors. Taiwo concludes that experiences of points and spaces differ. He stresses the cultural nature of this distinction.

Beat	*Perceived Temporal and Spatial Flux*	*Perceived Experience of Points*
Metric	Linear	Static
Return	Curved	Dynamic

Figure Five: Table of Metric and Return Beat (Taiwo 2012).

The Metric Beat

The characteristic of the metric beat is the predominance of a linear flux, with an experience of static pulses. The main focus of attention is a point in the future.

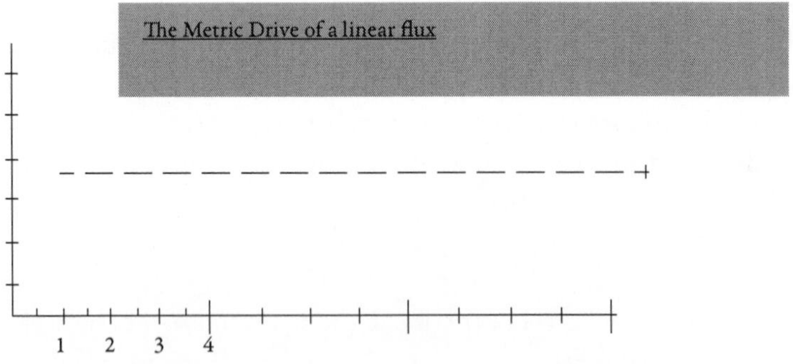

Figure Six: The Metric Beat (Taiwo 2012).

The metric drive of a linear flux is perceived as sequenced movement in one direction. Rigour and mathematical precision are highly regarded as a way to maintain the rhythmic measure (Taiwo 1998).

The Return Beat

The return beat is characterised by a predominance of a curved flux with an experience of dynamic pulses as references for the centrifugal and centripetal drives of the return beat.

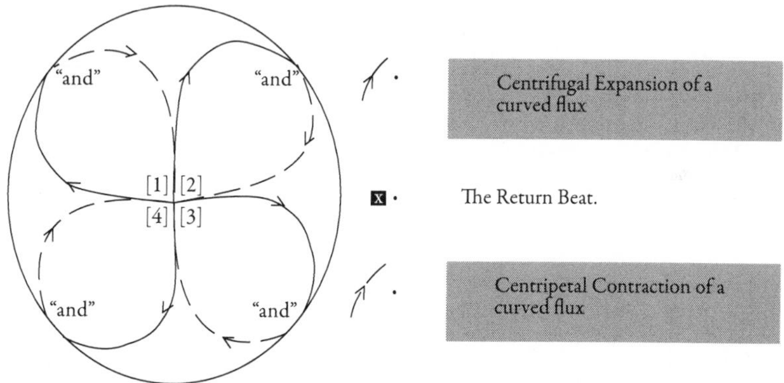

Figure Seven: The Return Beat (Taiwo 2012).

In traditional and contemporary West African societies, rhythm plays an important role in educating the community about notions surrounding balance. The curved flux in the drive of a return beat means that the spaces between the beats are experienced as a cycle. This creates an outgoing centrifugal and a returning centripetal aspect to the experience of space between the beats – the practice of returning to the 'self' in the 'here and now' (Taiwo 1998).

A Modified Model

Taiwo uses the metaphor of the flux of a magnetic field to describe the movement around the beat. The metaphor is intended to express the invisible and simultaneous bipolar movement of contraction and expansion. Taiwo links this with the interweave between his consciousness and his physical journal, which act metaphorically like a magnet influencing, and connected to events in temporal space. He turns to process thinking (as we saw in Chapter One) to explain what is happening. In this sense it is closer to Whitehead's concept of 'fundamental interrelatedness'. These events are processes that unfold, linking interior experience and exterior spatio-temporal structure; the result is the bringing together of 'matter' and 'mind'. This concept of fundamental interrelatedness means that actual events mutually co-create, interfacing and interpenetrating with one another (De Quincy 2002):

> My theory involves the entire abandonment of the notion that simple location is the primary way in which things are involved in space-time. In a certain sense, everything is everywhere at all times. For every location involves an aspect of itself in every other location. Thus every spatio-temporal standpoint mirrors the world. (Whitehead 1975 p. 91)

For Taiwo, the processes of communication and the maintenance of internal and external balance occur throughout the physical journal and facilitate his communication of complex performative codes which include balance, dignity and a feeling of bliss. His response to it is physical:

> The more balanced I am when I dance and respond to the oscillating sensation of flux within a return beat, the greater my subjective feeling of bliss. The feeling of bliss and balance is both simple and complex. It is simple because it creates a response to create more balance using the rudimentary processes of 'feedback' and adaptation. It is complex in that overwhelming arrays of simultaneous physical, psychological and performative phenomena are involved. (Taiwo 2012)

This is borne out in Paul Berliner's research into jazz, where he highlights the physical character of the listening, identifying different relationships with the beat, which at times has physical characteristics, as well as force:

> There's an edge I feel when I'm playing walking bass lines on top of the beat. It's like you're walking into the wind. (Berliner 1997 p. 14)

Eric Clarke (2005 p. 152) draws attention to how these insights from orate tradition highlight the relationship between autonomous and heteronomous perspectives on music.

Taiwo (2012) uses digital technology in his performances; here he claims that there is an important distinction to be made between a digital flux and an organic flux within a rhythmic event. The space between the beats in a digitally created rhythm is regulated electronically whilst the organic rhythm is produced and regulated by a physical journal's experience. This affects the aesthetic experience of 'metric' and 'return beat' rhythms. The homogenised cycles of a digitally created return beat underpin contemporary Hip Hop, House, Acid House, Techno, Trance, and Jungle popular rhythms. Each has a distinct rhythmic style, which relies heavily on evolving repetitious forms. Historically, in order to create a single rhythmic weave, a DJ would collect 'breakbeats' from obscure records and seamlessly weave them together, editing out the singing parts to focus on the dance section.

In this section, I have examined the profound differences in the way that time is handled in some orate traditions and the literate Western classical music tradition. There is great scope for similar comparisons to be made with other orate traditions.

Developing New Musical Structures

As a composer, I decided to explore new ways of structuring pieces, so that the Construction systems could embrace the literate and the orate. This was my intention in writing *The Call of the Ancestors* – to explore the meeting of various musical structures that could bring together various cultures with integrity. The musical structure was intended to mirror a just society by creating a structure that would reflect a respect for diversity. This, in turn, would influence the lives of the listeners. This was written for the Church Colleges Choirs Festival in March 1998 in Winchester Cathedral. Underpinning it at the spiritual level, was the notion of the call to Wisdom; I see this as a universal call which each culture has to rework within its own forms and structures; these will be diverse. In the domain of Materials different performing groups were used which included improvising groups of various kinds (non-notated traditions) and notated traditions (the brass quintet); in this performance the Materials were Kenyan drums, a rock group and Thai piphat, a Western brass quintet, the moot horn (an Anglo-Saxon instrument), a large four-part choir. In the Expression domain, the work brings together a number of different texts from differing cultures including King Alfred's (871–99) prose translation of Psalm 45 (the male ancestor) and the antiphon to Wisdom by Hildegard of Bingen (1098–1179) (the female ancestor). It was choreographed by Olu Taiwo who used movements taken from the Capoiera tradition. The four dancers represented shapes floating in space and also a combination of the awe and wonder generated by the large space alongside a childlike playfulness. These reflected in the domain of Expression the character of the carvings on the moot horn. The Construction I chose for the piece was that of a responsive psalm. Each verse is sung by the choir accompanied by brass quintet and responded to by an improvising group. These are held together by the notion of a fractal design, which is a pattern found in the natural world in plants like the cauliflower, in which each of the parts has the same shape as the whole. The groups were placed around the Cathedral with the choir and brass group at the East End, the rock group at the West End and the drums and piphat in the North and South aisles. The audience was thus enclosed by the music which appeared to 'move.' The domain of Values was reflected in letting the non-notated traditions make their own structures rather than forcing them into the structures of the notated Western classical traditions, which were used by the choir and brass group (Boyce-Tillman 1998).

My next piece explored how far this Construction that shares out function of composing among the performers to create community could be used with experienced choirs – to find out how they would respond to being asked to create some episodes. The piece was based on Hildegard's Hymn to the Virgin Mary *O viridissima virga* (Boyce-Tillman 2000b) and was written specially for the Church Colleges Choirs' Festival at St Mary's College, Twickenham. The piece fell into nine sections based on the nine verses of the hymn. Through it all ran an ostinato taken from the opening of the hymn. This is intended to suggest eternity against which a number of temporal episodes take place. Four themes were taken from the Hildegard hymn:

- The praise of Wisdom as revealed through the Virgin Mary
- The nativity (which I extended to include birth in general, as well as Jesus' birth)

- The earth (which was a real concern of Hildegard's and is reflected in the imagery of this hymn)
- The poor (drawn from the theme of generosity in the hymn)

Some sections were composed by me and some were composed by the participating choirs, using the texts set out in the score. The singers were situated around the audience who also had to sing. The piece was ultimately about making connections and minimising divisions. Semi-structured interviews following the performance revealed the following aspects of liminality/spirituality within the experience (which we will explore further in Chapter Eight):

- The effect of the circular layout:

> It was nice – it was nice to see everyone – to be in the circle ... and also because, sort of, the sounds coming from different areas in the Church, it made good use of the acoustics ... Plus it fits the concept of the piece really. It fits a sort of Eastern spirituality and, thinking along those lines, the circle does tie in with that.

- Shared responsibility. Several interviewees said that the role of leadership was as if a ball was thrown from one choir to the next or like passing a relay baton on as the authority passed from the main conductor to the conductors of the individual choirs:

> I thought, conceptually, it was a really good idea. I think the idea's excellent. I think one of the problems for me with such an idea, though, is when you give responsibility to other people to make inserts, then you lose control obviously, and you take that as read when you do it. So, as a piece, I think it was enormously successful, period, but then if I was going to go one stage further ... is that it becomes slightly disjointed. Not so much in terms of the sort of like the feeling that comes from each of the choir's inputs, but rather in terms of the scale of things. It becomes actually quite gargantuan as a piece.

- A sense of ownership

> I liked ... this circular idea ... It kind of goes through all kinds of different traditions of music at different times. However, I would like to say that there was lots of different types of music, and ... I think one of the successes was that there was a huge range ... Each choir played to its strengths...It was nice ... for the students to have a sense of

their own part ... Although you had written the framework into which everything fitted, which ... was easy to learn because it used the different musical idioms giving it fluidity ... then each small episode that the choirs individually produced ... gave them a sense of ownership of the piece.

- Engagement:

It's not, kind of like, entirely new to me because in Taizé ... I go back to this thing of attentiveness – it does refresh your attentiveness ... because that authority ... does pass from one to the other ... Your whole sort of attentiveness in music has been different.

- The role of the audience-inclusivity

We're back to this circular thing. I think it made it more interesting from the audience's point of view ... I thought that was a great idea. It had the feeling of more music-making for everybody.

- Simplicity:

It was great ... I thought that ... the choral composition itself, they were very attractive and very strong. I loved ... the idea of the very simple, you know, modal, mediaeval feel to it, and using forms that could, in themselves, be taken out independently ... O.K., our intellectual, musical friends would virtually, I'm sure, sort of tear your music and my music to shreds in terms of ... Well, what is this? This is very straightforward and very simple.

- The relationship to the Wisdom tradition of theology

As chaplain ... I really welcome the resurrection of this whole notion of Wisdom and the Sophia and the feminine qualities that it brings, but they're not necessarily gender-specific, 'cause I think ... feminine aesthetics can be found in the male gender just as much as in the female gender ... I think it brings back to the fore both in the thinking of women and men ... the whole nurturing, the nourishing, the birth and the re-birth.

- A sense of the Spiritual

I mean, the whole feeling of the choirs being together, I felt that was a kind of great religious thing anyway. Very spiritual, yes.

This was an experiment in democratic, collaborative ways of composing and challenging the individualistic models of the Western world.

PeaceSong was an extension of *The Greening branch* project, written for the same festival which took place in Winchester Cathedral in March 2006. It extended the use of the space more dramatically so that the cathedral building acted as an important creator in the piece. It also asked the various choirs to create episodes in the windows in the piece. It had five movements entitled:

- *If these walls could only speak*
- *Shalom*
- *Invocation*
- *Swords into ploughshares*
- *Natural Connection*

These represented

- Peace with the past – Extra- and Intrapersonal
- Peace with the Spiritual – Metaphysical
- Peace with other faith traditions – Extrapersonal
- Justice making – Extrapersonal
- Peace with the earth – InterGaian

The first movement represents the walls of the cathedral yielding up the sounds that have happened in that place. All the musicians were hidden in side chapels and sang pieces such as Bruckner's *Locus Iste* and *Praise God from all blessings flow*. The various conductors could not see one another and had to work intuitively. The pieces were fragmented as calls across the space. It started in darkness, with the no performers visible, creating an air of mystery out of which the piece emerged. The audience were encouraged to explore their own memories within this mysterious space.

In the second movement, the choirs moved around the building singing *shalom* on a single note and carrying candles. The building gradually filled with this pedal note, which sounded like an ohm with 'ssh' in it. Over it the instruments improvised of a Hildegard antiphon (Boyce-Tillman

2000b). The third movement included peace prayers from various faith traditions set by the various participating choirs. This was punctuated by the Hindu prayer for peace sung by choirs and congregation.[5] The fourth movement used a song on the theme of piece combined with a Nigerian drumming group moving from the back of the cathedral to the front. In the final movement the children arrived singing *Hevenu Shalom Aleichem*. It ended with *The Song of the Earth* sung by everyone, including the audience. The effect was stunning. The audience talked of being caught up in a 'golden vortex of sound.' The 'shalom' procession caused one student to be aware of the spiritual connection between song and her body:

> I have sung for many years but it always meant working out if the next note was a G sharp or G natural and a crotchet or a quaver. Because you only asked me to sing a single note I was aware of the breath entering and leaving my body and it became a meditative experience.

However, this piece was not uniformly well received. Before the performance after the scores had been sent out an email came from one choir leader sent, not to me but to all the heads of the church colleges. It asked why we were singing another rubbish piece, when there were so many worthy masterpieces for students to sing. Conversations following this bombshell included: 'You must be doing something important if you are exciting such ire' and 'We may not do it like you do, June. But what you do is to teach us to think outside the box'. It seemed to me that that was really universities were called to do.

Step into the Picture (Boyce-Tillman 2007h) was a collaborative project involving an orchestra, schools, a gospel choir and a visual artist. It was designed for a concert hall. An interdisciplinary project involving music, drama, improvisation and the visual arts, it included newly composed material combined with traditional material from a variety of cultures. It

5 Taken from *Peace seeds*, 12 prayers for peace prayed in Assisi, Italy on the Day of Prayer for World Peace during the United Nations International Year of Peace, 1986. They were taken to the US and entrusted to the care of the children at the Life Experience School. <http://www.peaceabbey.org> accessed August 5th 2005.

was based on a set of pictures of the Life of Jesus by the artist Paul Forsey and a commission from the Southern Sinfonia through my friend Kay Norrington. The idea was that the participants would be able to step into the story of Jesus in a variety of imaginative encounters involving song, instrumental pieces and episodes composed by the participants. The elements intertwined in the piece are:

- A Hildegard responsory for the Holy Innocents
- Episodes composed by the schools in the 'windows' in the piece
- Songs for the various choirs some using traditional material
- Audience participation, including singing and knocking two nails together for the crucifixion
- Performers moving in processions around the space including a long procession of palms with 150 children moving through the audience and a multicultural carnival for Pentecost with fifteen different songs from fifteen different faiths forming a giant multi-cultural quodlibet
- Instruments entering and leaving the space improvising and also being placed in galleries and around the audience

Again elements of liminality/spirituality coloured comments from those present:

> The journey of creative discovery that has taken shape over the time spent in preparation and in rehearsal, [was] reflected in the joy, faith, belief, contemplation and celebration in the eyes, faces, voices and movement of all the people taking part.
>
> Such a breath taking awe inspiring God praising Jesus breathing work ... I sat so on the edge of my chair with tears of complete joy, sadness and peace as the peoples woven in and out came together to create a splendid performance of truth!... I know many many people were blessed through listening and taking part in your vision.
>
> The whole evening was a magical experience.
>
> I've just been to see *Step Into the Picture* at the Anvil, and have to say it was one of the most amazing things I've ever seen onstage. A glimpse of what heaven might be like.

Summary

In the area of Western classical traditions the domain of Construction is a well-documented and well-represented domain in a musical tradition where literacy is central. It is a domain where we see how Interpersonal dialogue has been conducted within a particular culture – what is regarded as acceptable and not acceptable and culturally constructed notions of coherence. Eric Clarke highlights how an ecological approach to listening reshapes the autonomy of this construction-based Western classical musical tradition:

> The ecological approach to perception emphasises the perceiving organism's adaptation to its environment ... Accepting the idea of autonomy on its own terms. Music can be understood as constituting a 'virtual world' into which a listener is drawn ... An ecological approach can then help to understand the ways in which events of this virtual world (tonal events, metrical events, textural events, motivic events) are specified in sound. Second, ecological principles can contribute to the critique of autonomy while recognizing the pervasive influence of this cultural construct, and the listening practices with which it is associated. (E. Clarke 2005 pp. 154–5)

Eric Clarke goes on to see a possible link between the ecological and the 'unworldly'. However, the way of listening taught within the Western classical music tradition has yielded (and still yields) for many, what they would regard as the most authentic 'spiritual' experience.

This has been borne out by an exercise that I do regularly around the spiritual experience in music which will be reported in more detail in the next chapter. I play a recordings of a number of pieces and ask participants which would give them a spiritual experience. They include an Australian aboriginal ritual, a Salvation Army hymn and Leona Lewis's *A moment like this*. The one that British people aged upwards of fifty always choose is the slow movement of Mozart's Clarinet Concerto. They have been initiated, through the cultural approach to musical appreciation, into this 'other worldly' experience in pieces from the classical canon. They also know well how they function and can enter into the debate of musical ideas within the Construction of this tradition easily. I am not denying the validity of such an experience, but simply placing it in a cultural context which has been supported by school music curricula, a considerable volume of literature and by such phenomena as programme notes.

There is far less work done on the orate traditions and the way in which ideas are debated in these. When popular musics began to enter the curriculum in the UK the weaknesses of applying constructional principles developed in the literate classical traditions to a different tradition began to be apparent.[6] The introduction of other traditions – such as folk traditions – into the curriculum encourage this further and lead us into the next chapter, revising our value systems to include a valuing of a greater plurality of traditions. I have shown how I have tried to reflect both literate and orate in my own composing and how this led to people's musical/spiritual experience changing. It has shown how these experimental pieces – new in the domain of Construction to the local culture – were able to induce spiritual experiences. It is not intending to define these constructions as 'better', but rather as 'different'. It sets out how these traditional constructions embody different value systems from other cultures with more orate traditions and so leads to the next chapter. When we combine the thinking with the next chapter, it makes possible the redefining of 'greatness' in music as appropriateness for purpose.

6 I remember vividly trying to work out whether the final cadence of a pop song was plagal or perfect. As I tried to analyse the complex nature of the chords that made it up, I realised that, not only was the exercise difficult, but also fruitless.

CHAPTER SEVEN

Values in Musicking

A Story of Values

> When a woman in a certain African tribe knows she is pregnant, she goes out into the wilderness with a few friends and together they pray and meditate until they hear the song of the child. They recognize that every soul has its own vibration that expresses its unique flavour and purpose. When the women attune to the song, they sing it out loud. Then they return to the tribe and teach it to everyone else.
>
> When the child is born, the community gathers and sings the child's song to him or her. Later, when the child enters education, the village gathers and chants the child's song. When the child passes through the initiation to adulthood, the people again come together and sing. At the time of marriage, the person hears his or her song and, finally, when the soul is about to pass from this world, the family and friends gather at the person's bed, just as they did at their birth, and they sing the person to the next life. (A. Cohen 2003)

The author of this story also relates how, in this African tradition, there is one other occasion upon which the villagers sing to the person. If at any time during his or her life, the person commits a crime or an aberrant social act, the individual is called to the centre of the village and the people in the community form a circle around him or her. Then they sing the person's song to them. The tribe recognises that the correction for antisocial behaviour is not punishment; it is love and the remembrance of identity. In a similar vein more rooted in Western culture:

> When you really recognize your own song, you have no desire or need to do anything that would hurt another. A real friend is someone who knows your song and sings it to you when you have forgotten it. Those who love you are not fooled by mistakes you have made or dark images you hold about yourself. They remember your beauty when you feel ugly; your wholeness when you are

> broken; your innocence when you feel guilty; and your purpose when you are confused. And finally, after you've found your own song, help your loved ones find theirs. (Melanson 2003)

Introduction

The domain of Values is related to the context of the music-making experience – both its creation and its reception. It is the domain where Extra-personal relations are worked out, as we encounter other cultures. All musical experiences are culturally related. Indeed, the structure of the classical orchestra and choir reflect the European cultures that produced them – ruled by benevolent dictators, now embodied in a conductor.

Musical performances contain both intrinsic and extrinsic Value systems. Some are within the sounds of the music itself and some are to do with the context of the music making. However, these two interact powerfully. Notions of intrinsic Values are a subject of debate in musicological circles (McClary 1991, 2001); but as soon as a text or story are present, Value systems will be declared and so be intrinsic to the music, like the heterosexual Values of the traditional love song and the maternal love of the lullaby. All musical pieces stand in relation to the culture in which they are created, even if that relationship, like the protest songs of the sixties, is to challenge. Various forms in the history of music theatre have reflected the racism, sexism and elitism of their cultures, as illustrated in the elitism of opera or the sexism of some contemporary rap traditions. In a conversation with the conductor, Jane Ring Frank, I found that she included in some programmes only musical pieces that she would consider as empowering of women; in other programmes she would highlight the Value systems underpinning the Western canon.[1] This domain shifts

1 Frank, Jane Ring (January 2003) Unpublished conversation with the author in Cambridge, Massachusetts.

attention from individual acts of cognition to the wider context in which musicking is situated (Westerlund 2002 p. 227).

Is Music Value-free?

The opening story takes us to a society with a very different Value system from our own. Society is beginning to rediscover its loss here. Singing to babies in the womb represents a rediscovery of the Value systems underpinning the opening story. The rise of community choirs represents a challenge to the Value systems underpinning the Western classical choral tradition.

There are numerous articles asserting that music is value-free, often in relation to Western classical music. Charles Taylor links an epistemology that is value-free with the development of individualisation:

> Just as, in modern epistemological thinking, a neutral description of things is thought to impinge first on us, and then 'values' are 'added'; so here, we see ourselves first as individuals, then become aware of others, and forms of sociality. (C. Taylor 2007 p. 157)

A number of arguments have focused on Wagner's anti-Semitic views and whether these are reflected in his music. This was debated very hotly when, in 2013, as a celebration, a version of Tannhäuser was staged in a Nazi Holocaust setting. Such was the outrage that the production ran only for one night. Daniel Barenboim has engaged with this discussion:

> Barenboim himself has waged a lonely struggle to introduce the music of Wagner to the concert halls of Israel. The conductor makes the simple point that while Wagner himself was a vile anti-Semite, 'his music isn't anti-Semitic' and 'as a musician you can't simply ignore him'. Others have quibbled with this, arguing that certain of the characters in some of Wagner's operas conform to anti-Semitic stereotypes; but Barenboim is right – the music itself is no more anti-Semitic than it could be described as right-wing or left-wing. The arrangement of musical notes is an aesthetic phenomenon, entirely divorced from the world of politics, and indeed morality. (Lawson 2013 p. 12)

He goes on to link this with a 'celebrity' model of composers and performers who have to reveal a great deal of their motivations, concluding that:

> There is no valid connection, whatever, between the inner abstract world of music and the outer world of things and political parties, even if at times each exploits the other. (Lawson 2013 p. 12)

However, in my opinion, the domain of Values reflects not only an individual's Value system, but also that of a particular culture – a particular society's search for The Good, as we explored in Plato in the Prelude; the totality of the experience includes the domain of Values; this may be intrinsic or extrinsic to the music.

Intrinsic Values

Elsewhere in the same article, he locates all the greatness of the music, as we saw in the previous chapter, in the domain of Construction; however, he does describe this as subjective:

> Obviously, we can talk about good and bad music. At least, to the extent of saying, for example, that J.S. Bach was a better composer than any of his children who followed in the family business. But when we talk about a 'bad' piece of music, we never use the word in the moral sense; we only mean that it doesn't work well, as an arrangement of notes and harmonies – and even that is necessarily subjective. (Lawson 2013 pp. 12–13)

Many other theorists, such as Reimer (1970), have shared Lawson's view, preferring to see individual works of art dislocated from their social context. Even though John Rahn downplays what he calls functionalism in music and excludes it from his notion of aesthetic value, he nonetheless acknowledges its existence, calling it 'induced aesthetic value' (Rahn 1994 p. 55). He gives the examples of the song associated with falling in love and with memories of a homeland:

> The powerful and deep emotions evoked may well spill over into the aesthetic domain, investing the music with a beauty not pertinent to it in the old country. (Rahn 1994 p. 55)

However, an essentially contextualised view of music has been taken by ethnomusicologists. This chapter suggests that we now need to use ethnomusicological methodology on our own musics, rather than simply on the musics of Others. Music and culture are inextricably linked. In musicking we encounter another culture:

> As we have argued, music is capable of evoking, in a concrete and direct, yet mediated and symbolic fashion, the structures of the world and the states of being that flow from them and sustain them. (Shepherd and Wicke 1997 pp. 138–9)

The British composer, Michael Finnissy, sees the Western classical canon as an encounter with our history, as we saw in Chapter One in relation to cultural approaches to religious narratives:

> Musical metaphors also propagate the world-views of their particular era. From the beginning of a Handel piece, you can see how the people walked, you can see the clothes and you know what their attitude to the world was, at least the attitude that they wanted to have. (Fox, Brougham and Pace 1997 p. 20)

The call to see the domain of Values as a significant domain in the musical experience has come from many great performers, such as Ravi Shankar and Pablo Casals (Ellis 1985, p. 35). Pascale (2005 p. 162) describes how the Values ascribed to various singing traditions in the Western classical tradition have alienated many people from their birth right to sing. Culturally this means engaging with the Extrapersonal strand of spirituality explored in Chapter One. There are strengths and dangers in this encounter which involves feelings such as awe and wonder:

> The historiography of music and culture begins with the moment of encounter. Intensifying encounter is the awareness of difference, and that awareness engenders wonder and awe, which, however, lie precariously close to fear and danger. Music marks the moment of encounter, for it stands out as the form of communication that is at once most familiar and most incomprehensible. (Bohlman 2003 pp. 46–7)

The failure to acknowledge the presence of Values within musical events has enabled them to be used for colonial and appropriation purposes with impunity, as we shall see in Chapter Nine.

There is a powerful interaction between the domain of Values and the other domains of the musical experience. The creative process itself will also contain a particular Value system. The level of democracy involved in the process will be reflected in the Values intrinsic to the final product. A truly democratic process will involve many people in the decision-making process. Some musical idioms use more democratic processes than others and value those processes and their integrity, as discussed in Chapter One. The Western classical tradition has been quite hierarchical in its structures with a single composer constructing a piece alone, while jazz and many orate traditions are more democratic in their creating processes.

Extrinsic Values

At the end of Lawson's article, quoted earlier, he describes a recording by Furtwängler of Beethoven's Ninth Symphony. The film was made for broadcast by the Nazi's and swastikas are visible around the audience which includes Goebbels. It is now on YouTube and he suggests listening with eyes shut when it is beyond good and evil 'like Wagner's greatest music' (Lawson 2013 p. 12). But when actually do we listen to music in this way – unaware of our surroundings? Extrinsic values are present in the context of the performance. There is a difference between a carol performed in a school nativity play and in a High Mass in Westminster Cathedral. We shall see in Chapter Ten how this will affect the entry into the Spiritual domain.

The available finance is another Value issue which will be culturally determined and affect the context. Opera, for example, as a form, requires a large amount of money, and a particular venue – hence the problems with the maintenance of the tradition when the power and wealth of the aristocracy, who supported its development, is now reduced. Factors like the cost of tickets will have cultural implications in the domain of Values that will be reflected in the piece itself and in the way people receive it. The availability of large resources to certain groups of people, such as women and certain ethnic groups, has influenced the Construction of their pieces and meant that the characteristic of monumentality, set out in the previous chapter, has not been open to them.

The Idea of Intention

The creative processes employed will reflect the intention of the musickers and their underpinning Value systems. I have already described one exercise that I use regularly, called a humming bath in which a group of people surround two of their number with hummed sounds; here the intention of the participants to communicate love is central to the activity. This always produces feelings of great joy and uplift. Music has the potential of transmitting love; but in much of Western culture we have lost the notion of intention in musical performance. Kay Gardner explores this by using Hildegard's concept of viriditas – a greening energising power that runs through the entire cosmos, giving it life and vitality – to construct a piece composed for 'people with life-threatening dis-ease' (K. Gardner 1990 p. 229). As the aesthetic and analytical became dominant value systems in Western culture, Values such as connecting with the natural world, healing, peace and reconciliation became subjugated. They are now being rediscovered, as can be seen in the books edited by Olivier Urbain (Urbain 2007, Laurence and Urbain 2011):

> Peace education, I believe, is at once a task that demands a critical intellect, an ethic of justice and compassion, and a spiritual recognition of the precious and inviolable nature of human life, as well as the web of being that connects all life. (Shapiro 2011)

Musicians working in the area of cultural fusion are often very clear about their intention and look towards music as route to justice and peace (Boyce-Tillman 1996, 2001a, 2007b). Examples include Paul Simon in his recording *Graceland* in the context of apartheid in South Africa (Simon 1994) and we have already seen how I showed respect for different Construction systems in *The Call of the Ancestors* (Boyce-Tillman 1998).

Music and Morality

It is not my intention in this chapter to establish a relationship between music and what I would regard as good or correct morality. I have deliberately used the word Values for the domain; as in other domains the emphasis is on the relationship between the Value systems that underpin the music itself and those of the musicker. I personally could not manage to establish a relationship with much of Eminem's work because of its misogynist content, but his popularity would indicate that many people can. David Carr attacks the Rolling Stones' 'vanity, egotism, personal squalor, and disreputable social responsibility' (2010 p. 142). Again such Values might not be acceptable for him, but clearly others could establish a lasting bond with it. Music can be used to reinforce certain Values by its very power – the monumentality explored in the previous chapter. One example is Hitler's use of music to reinforce Nazi Values by means of large-scale multi-disciplinary events. Individuals and groups may want to define certain Values as better than others. My writing so far has probably already shown the ones that I embrace, and the ones I reject; however, this book is not about the moral rectitude of certain Values but about the ability of musickers to relate to the Value systems of a particular piece. The logic of this is that Spirituality in my model is not necessarily moral in the eyes of some people. Hitler was an extremely skilful manipulator of the spiritual experience; this means that all musickers – in whatever role they are – need to look clearly at the underlying Value systems of an event, before they are taken up into the liminal experience.

Music with Text

We have interrogated in previous chapters the formalist/referentialist debate concerning the meaning of music. The presence of a text or associations outside the sounds makes music less pure in the view of the formalists. Text, in this view, weakens a piece because Construction is dictated by the demands of the text and not by the abstract debate of ideas. Clearly religious ideas are most clearly present when there is a text present that has religious origins or implications.

Peter Kivy (2002 p. 14) sees a dichotomy between text and music. This problematises the notion that music is religious when the text it sets is religious. Indeed, Suzanne Langer sees an intimate relation between feeling and sound (Expression and Construction) that is more problematic in pieces with a text (Langer 1953 p. 85). This position can see liturgical music as a less pure genre than the symphony. It is supported by Stravinsky's view on the setting of sacred Latin texts, that:

> the text thus becomes purely phonetic material for the composer. He can dissect it at will and concentrate all his attention on its primary constituent element – the syllable. (Stravinsky 1938 p. 128)

This position denies the intention of many composers to convey religious ideas (Ridley 2004 pp. 88–9). Ridley is much more in tune with my thinking, in saying that composers heighten the textual meaning by their musical setting. As a composer of liturgical music, I not only strive to enhance to text, but to set up a set of extrinsic associations. So, for example, if I write a text to an existing well known hymn tune, I will make the new text interact with the old text; here I use the power of association – sometimes to enhance, sometimes to create a satirical relationship with the original. One hymn that I wrote replaces the original chorus of 'One church, one faith, one Lord' with 'May we being drawing nearer in love and with respect'; here an imperialist unity is replaced with a valuing of diversity. In *Conflict to Chorus* I use a powerful Elgar tune (*Pomp and Circumstance March No. 4*) with all its nationalist associations (epitomised in the use of Elgar's music in the Last Night of the Promenade concerts) for a song about the Flowers of Peace. This is similar to Coroniti's idea (Coroniti 1992 p. 11) that Steve Reich's setting of the Hebrew psalms in *Thallium* is a sceptical interpretation – close to my idea of satire:

> Song is the reincarnation of a poem which was destroyed in order to live again in music. The composer, no matter how respectful, must treat poetry as a skeleton on which to bestow flesh, breaking a few bones in the process. He does not render a

> poem more *musical* (poetry isn't music, it's poetry); he weds it to sound, creating a third entity of different and sometimes greater magnitude than either parent. (Rorem 1970 p. 26 Author's italics)

The formalist position, denying any association outside the domain of Construction, does not, therefore, see any music as religious. However, it is extremely difficult to separate word and music in such traditions as chant with a single melodic line tightly bound up with the text; this is the characteristic of much ritual music. Here the words are heightened by the music. Indeed in the debates in the Church over the years, an important strand has been that the words were often lost when the music became too complex. This was the reason for restrictions being placed on polyphony by papal decree in the thirteenth century. In early Christianity, St Augustine (Augustine 1961 p. 239)[2] was happy with the text on its own; but he was concerned that the music might awake religious fervour, of which he was suspicious, because he associated with sensuality (Boyce-Tillman 2014). Indeed, the Protestant congregational hymn is a simple form intended to inform the singers' understanding of the theology of the text. So, in my thinking, an overtly religious text gives a particular musical event a set of Values associated with a particular faith tradition.

Values and Religion

In this domain we encounter the strand that I called Narrative in Chapter One. We saw there how there were three possible relationships with it:

- Devotional
- Storying
- Cultural

2 'When I find the singing itself more moving than the truth it conveys, I confess that this is a grievous sin.' (Augustine 1961 p. 239)

In different musical traditions, we can see all three approaches adopted. Liturgical music, in general, sets itself in a devotional context and was often written for groups of people who subscribed to a particular belief system, with such musical forms as hymn tunes or Palestrina's motets. Sometimes, as in the Bach's Passions and cantatas, they involved the congregation joining in in devotional mode with parts of the music. Music designed for liturgical or ceremonial use will also be constrained in the domain of Construction by the demands of the ritual.

But the two other positions are quite significant. The narratives of religious traditions embedded in their texts will certainly colour the domain of Expression. The development of the oratorio enabled stories to be told as stories that can be observed by the audience who are not asked for a devotional response. The move from the liturgical Requiem Mass to Elgar's *Dream of Gerontius* shows this clearly; here the Requiem Mass is now part of the telling of the story of the death of a human being, rtaher than a liturgucal event requiring devotion. When I asked the audience to sing in an opera on Julian of Norwich, one person (alongside many who loved the experience) said that I asked for more commitment than he was prepared to give.

However, the cultural treatment of the faith stories is of great significance for music. Works like the Bach Passions are now often heard as cultural artefacts, which the audience receive as a glimpse into a distant culture. Hence, very few contemporary performances of the Bach Passions and cantatas ask the audience to participate. They are significant works for the musickers, but not in terms of a belief system. The debates intensify when the nature of the belief systems of composers and performers enter the debate. In the context of a college carol service which had previously been sung by the university choir with all its shades of beliefs and spirituality, about which the participants were never questioned. A new chaplain decided that only Christians could sing in the choir for a service. This aroused a huge level of debate amongst students about the belief systems of such phenomena as cathedral choirs. In school contexts, concerns are expressed about asking pupils to enter too fully into religious narratives, such as the passion narratives of Jesus. This could be seen as moving from a cultural view to a devotional view. I found this boundary difficult when I wrote the piece *Step into the Picture* (Boyce-Tillman 2007h) – telling the story of Jesus for schools. Most of the time, I stayed with the storytelling mode; but in the text around the John the Baptist narrative, the last verse had the line 'We will gather by the river' which some thought was asking for a devotional response from the children who were singing. It is likely that composers setting religious narrative have worked out their own relationship to them, which may be any of the three approaches outlined above. However, within an audience, there will be a variety of responses to the story being told. Some will find the narrative acceptable but the Construction of the music too difficult. Others will find the religious narratives, especially when treated devotionally, as simply a domain that prevents them entering into a total commitment to the experience.

The cultural view may also reflect the notion of Missing God that we saw in Chapter One – a memory of a former belief system, perhaps associated with childhood and a particular culture. This account from 1970 in the Alister Hardy Archive illustrates how hymns can be the last remaining traces of religion:

> At the age of 88 years I am practically religionless except that most days I am obsessed with Moody and Sankey hymns.[3]

Similarly Theresa May MP chose the hymn *When I survey the wondrous cross* among her *Desert Island Discs* choice, because it reminded her of the togetherness of a church congregation.[4]

Some of these people, however, would also subscribe to the aesthetic position that I am challenging that these 'great' works with religious texts will inspire a spiritual experience wherever and whenever they are played. For other people, the religious texts will have their dogmatic meanings intact; if they feel bruised or hurt by their experience of Christianity or a particular brand of it, they may find these works unpalatable. Ian Cross indicates the complexity of finding meaning in music in the intersection between cultures:

3 1970 Alister Hardy Archive.

4 *Desert Island Discs*, November 28th 2014 9 am. BBC Radio 4.

> Musics only make sense as musics if we can resonate with the histories, values, conventions, institutions and technologies that enfold them; musics can only be approached through culturally situated acts of interpretation. Such interpreted acts ... unveil a multiplicity of musical ontologies, some or most of which may be mutually irreconcilable. (Cross 2003 p. 236)

Alan Bennett, who professes no current religious faith, illustrates it by talking about a sense of belonging:

> Up the words come, unbidden. Known but never learned. Some of that weightless baggage carried down the years not from piety or belief, and more credentials than creed; a testimonial that I am one of those boys state educated in the 40s and 50s who came by the words of *Ancient and Modern*[5] through singing them day in and day out at school every morning in assembly. It's a dwindling band, old fashioned and of a certain age. You can pick us out at funerals and memorial services because we can sing the hymns without the books. 'Alleluia, alleluia, hearts to heaven and voices raise. Sing to God a hymn of triumph, sing to God a hymn of praise' ... I have never found it easy to belong. So much repels. Hymns help, they blur. And here among the tombs and tablets and vases of dead flowers and lists of the fallen, it is at least less hard to feel tacked on to church and country. (Bennett 2001 no pages)

The context of the performance may also colour responses, as a culture will decide on the appropriateness for works to various contexts; this was well illustrated by the Pussy Cat Dolls' performance in an Orthodox church. Many congregations will be happy with an organ as an accompanying instrument in a service but dislike a rock group, even if they would go to rock concerts in their life outside of the church building and vice versa. It is where the domain of Values constrains and governs the domains of Materials (which instruments are appropriate) and Expression (which expressive characters are appropriate in worship). When we get to the domain of Values we see clearly how different views of the Divine colour all the domains. There are many texts in the area of music in worship (Ingalls, Landau and Wagner 2013) and who and how the nature of the Divine

5 Monk, William and Nicholson, Sydney (1922) *Ancient and Modern*, London; Novello and Co. This hymnbook was in regular use in churches and schools for much of the twentieth century.

finds it expression in different styles of music and chant. Many faiths use communal singing as a way of creating community in worship, although Islam restricts the use of music to (a word that they do not use in relation to worship) chanting, mostly by the imam. The constraints here are also gendered, as they are in other religious traditions – again reflecting the Value systems ascribed to the Divine (Boyce-Tillman 2014).

So religion with its texts, codes and creeds sits in the domain of Values – those of the individual, the culture and the context. They also will give the spiritual experience names – Paradise, Nirvana or just bliss; in pieces using myths, other concepts will be developed like the underworld and mythical beings such as naiads and fairies. Some people would be happier listening-in-audience to these pieces than performing in them, which in their view requires a greater degree of commitment to the ideas.

Situating these religious narratives in the domain of Values and not at the heart of the experience itself may free up the domain of spirituality to be dogma free and contentless. So it seems that, however beautiful the sounds may be, for some people, a problem may be created here by:

- The beliefs of a particular faith group that generated the music or in the context which the music is performed or received
- The Materials used to make the sound, such as a rock group or organ within a particular Christian tradition
- The theology of the text
- A dislike of religion in general
- The use of inclusive or non-inclusive language

This answers some of the questions raised in the article *Goin' Down to the River to Pray: The Slippery Slope of Spirituality and Music Education* (D. Bradley 2010), which sees the spirituality as inseparable from religion in the US context – that, far from encouraging peace-making, it increases divisions of a racist kind. The view of this book – placing the religious in the domain of Values not the Spiritual – separates cultural religious concepts from the experience itself and sees them as interrelated but separate.

There is further discussion to be had in this area which is continued in Interlude Two. Plenty of people use the canonical works from the Western classical traditions, such as the Mass in B minor and the St Matthew Passion, for a spiritual experience without subscribing to the belief system themselves. Here the words seem to function more like an integral part of the music without giving it a particular meaning. Another possibility is that this usage is related to their familiarity with the Construction. The works become familiar rooms around which people can wander freely; people can use them in the same way as the familiar rituals of the church for a variety of purposes of imagining and exploring (Cook 1990 p. 242). In the area of the settings of the Requiem Mass text, my experience is that a recording of one of the popular Requiems, such as those by Mozart or Verdi, does still provide comfort for people who would not subscribe to the doctrine underpinning them; it functions for them like a religious ritual may once have done. This is broadly in the area explored by Lucy Green (1987, 1998) in her definition of delineated meanings; but it is worthy of much more detailed study than is possible here.

An Interesting Experiment

These conclusions have been drawn from an experiment I have been doing with various groups of people in various contexts and various countries. I ask them to reflect on various musical pieces and say whether it is likely to give them a spiritual experience (perhaps in a different context or in a longer excerpt). The music is played with no introduction. The first piece I play is the slow movement of Mozart's clarinet quintet. For British people of the generation born in the mid twentieth century, this is the most likely to give them a spiritual experience (as we saw in the previous chapter). One notable exception to this was a man in his twenties, for whom it had been a set work for his examination aged sixteen. This experience had meant that, far from increasing the quality of experience through increased knowledge of the Construction, he never wanted to hear it again.

The second piece I play is a Salvation Army hymn *At the Cross where I first saw the light*. This tends to divide groups. Some have rejected Christian doctrine altogether; others dislike this particular theology. Some see the Construction as naïve, while others find the bouncy feel not in tune with their mood at the time; but they acknowledge that at other times they might be emotionally in tune with it. Here reaction in the domain of Expression depends on the mood of the musicker.[6] Some find the military nature of the music reminds them of interactions with military regimes in their past. Here cultural memories intrude on the experience.

The third piece is part of an aboriginal ceremony from the Torres Strait Islands. It uses some chanting, didgeridoo and clap sticks. Here some people are fascinated by the overtones produced by the didgeridoo; but others find the instruments too unfamiliar (a problem in the domain of Materials).

The fourth piece is rock group called Spiritualise, who want to put the Spiritual back into rock music. Here again the criticism is often that the Construction is too naïve and resembling film music, whereas other people find the idiom a good route into the spiritual experience. They are familiar with the Expression of the piece as one that is often associated with the Spiritual in our culture.

The fifth piece comes from the Self Actualisation Fellowship in California. It uses a harmonium and singer. The tune is introduced first on the harmonium before a voice comes in with a text about shades and spirits. This divides people. Some people see it immediately as spiritual because of its Indian type sound. Others dislike it as soon as the voice comes in with its mix of theological ideas.

The sixth piece is Leona Lewis singing her X factor hit – *A Moment like this*. This generates a huge debate about commercialism and spirituality. This is supported by an argument that nothing can both spiritual and capitalist. I point out that Leona Lewis's style was born in the black Pentecostal traditions of London and that it would be as possible to read this song as an encounter with the Divine (as in the Hindu bhajan) as with a lover. For some people it has extrinsic memories of a rich emotional encounter.

6 This would be true of any of the pieces but this particular one has a very upbeat mood.

The seventh piece is Widor's Toccata for organ. Here again reactions vary. Some dislike the organ intensely because of its relation with Christianity and also the way it drowns singing in some churches. For others, it was played at a wedding and will always draw them into a spiritual place.

This experiment has played a significant part in the development of the model. It is interesting that, for one large group of people, one of the pieces which had no spiritual intention (the Mozart clarinet concerto) is the most likely to give them a spiritual experience. It is for them 'pure' music with no attached dogma, and also situated in a familiar idiom that enables them to enter the liminal/spiritual place easily and regularly.

The Extrapersonal and Conscientisation

In this domain the ethical dimension, that we saw in Chapter One, surfaces – the relationship that we might be able to develop with other cultures, both historical and geographical. By paying attention to this domain, we are including the notion of the musician as psychagogue, who prepares people to develop their own sense of The Right.

Drama has traditionally had a greater sense of the capacity of the arts to develop the human conscience. The supporters of this view often draw on Paulo Freire, who constantly stressed the fluid and unfinished nature of human consciousness: 'It is our awareness of being unfinished that makes us educable' (Freire 1998 p. 58). Freire outlines the human need for conscientisation:

> In truth, conscientisation is a requirement of our human condition. It is one of the roads we have to follow if we are to deepen our awareness of our world, of facts, of events, of the demands of human consciousness to develop our capacity for epistemological curiosity. (Freire 1998 p. 55)

This is often achieved by enabling participants to see a society more clearly through artworks (Willett 1978 p. 192). Brecht's concept of *Verfremdungseffekt* can help us here, through which

> the learner … is enabled to form a critical relationship with her lived experience that sets that experience within the broader discourses of both history and contemporary politics … [It] opens up the space in which critical consciousness can flourish. (Prentki 2013 p. 8)

This enables the participants to understand the 'deep structures' of the dominant culture that operate under the superficial 'surface' structures (Freire, 1972 p. 33). Freire points to how dangerous the notion of objectivity can be, critiquing education's embracing of neutrality, which denies the deeper values underpinning society (Freire 1998 pp. 89–90). Theorists such as Susan McClary and the protest song writers of the 1960s have increased cultural awareness of the Values within musicking.

Dominant and Subjugated Values

The rest of this chapter will look at the dominant values of Western culture and how these play out in music. Normativity is established by those in power by means of the exclusion of the deviant 'Other'. These subjugated ways of knowing are always in flux and cannot be defined specifically, but only in relation to the dominant value system of any particular culture at a particular time. I will illustrate this with a story of a culture whose dominant values are different from those in the West:

> I was privileged to spend some time with a native people in North America. I had been present at several sweat lodges at which a particular medicine man had been working. I had also purchased a small hand drum and he had consented to beat the bear spirit into it for me. One evening he was preparing for a sweat lodge and said that he needed a powerful woman to help him and sit alongside him. This would usually be his wife but she was unable to be there so he asked if I would help him. I was both honoured and terrified; but he said he would help me with the ritual and so I agreed to the role. The first round of prayer took place and he concluded it by saying that now June would sing a song about the eagle and the sunrise. It was here that I thought that I had met an insuperable problem. But I remembered that, in the songs I had heard, each phrase started high and then went lower in order to bring the energy of the sky to the earth. So I started each phrase high and took it lower,

> singing about the eagle and the sunrise. It was a powerful experience for me, and my voice seemed to come from a place of power deep inside me, that I had not experienced before. With the prayer round ended, we went outside to cool in the night air. 'Great song, June' said the leader of the sweat lodge. I was about to say that, of course, I had to make it up, and then I remembered, from my previous conversations with some of the women singers, that in this culture everything is given, and is not the creation of an individual. So I replied: 'The Great Spirit gave it to me when I was in the Lodge.' (Boyce-Tillman 2007b pp. 23–4)

There I was in a culture with a different dominant Value system. There the intuitive way of receiving a song was construed as coming from a connection with a spiritual source. In the West, we would probably have interpreted the process in a different way. We would have claimed the creative process for ourselves, and said that we had to make the song up on the spur of the moment. However, hidden away in Western culture, are people who would still see music in a different way, such as Noel Gallagher, who, in his *Desert Island Discs* interview, described his need to catch the songs as they fall. A similar understanding is clear in this account from a British woman in 1972:

> When I was fifty five music invaded my soul and a tremendous joy filled me for eight months ... [Then came depression] ... As the months went by, there developed within me an ability to hear the voices and music of an inner world ... I felt the voice of eternal love communicating with me through music. It seemed to me I was a seven stringed lyre, and when God played on the tautened strings I heard the music with an inner ear.[7]

Western Value Systems

There are signs that in the early twenty-first century the West is trying to heal a rift that has developed in its intensely rationalistic culture that we discussed in Chapter One. Gooch (1972) defines this rift in terms of

7 Alister Hardy Archive.

two systems of thought, both of which co-exist in the human personality. The favoured characteristics of Western culture (System A) (according to Gooch, although his analysis has been critiqued) are

- activity leading to products
- objectivity
- impersonal logic
- thinking and thought
- detachment
- discrete categories of knowledge which is based on proof and scientific evidence

The other system (System B) favours

- being
- subjectivity
- personal feeling
- emotion
- magic
- involvement
- associative ways of knowing
- belief and non-causal knowledge

I have called the ways of knowing that characterise System B subjugated ways of knowing, a term based on such theorists as Foucault (S. J. Ball 1990) and Belenky (et al 1986). This system is regularly devalued. In the UK media, for example, this can be carried out through public ridicule, or simply by ignoring those events which reflect the System B values. People who wish to embrace the Values of system B can easily be pathologised or criminalised, as the dominant culture seeks to reinforce the validity of its Type A Values. For example, intuitive people are loath to share their visionary and spiritual experiences for fear of being labelled as mad. Academic, medical, psychological and even sociological research concentrates on so-called objective methodologies, associated with scientific ways of knowing and often using numbers in some shape or form. Qualitative methodologies, such as collecting people's stories, are often regarded with suspicion because of the suspected subjectivity of the approach. So the Values of system B become hidden or repressed by Western culture.

There is a clear link between those who hold power and which ways of knowing will become subjugated. In this diagram the top section of the circle are those who control the dominant value systems in the West.

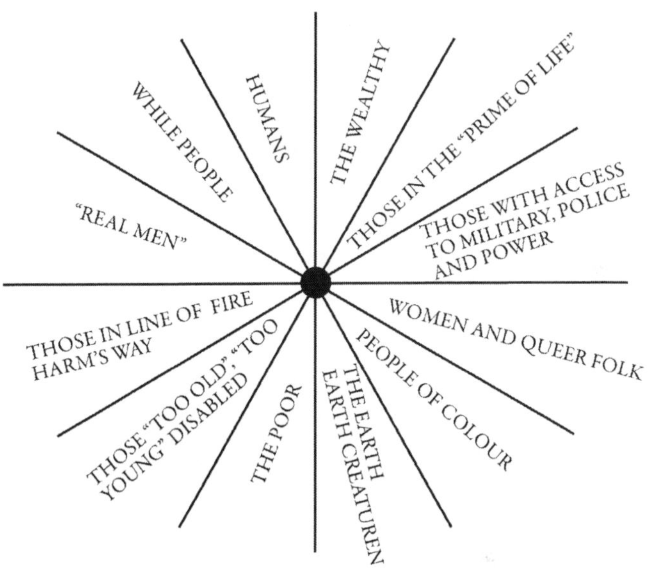

Figure Eight: Positions of Power (Carter Heyward 2003).

The following model attempts to show the dominant Values of the West, which are on the right hand side, while the subjugated Values are on the left. The thrust of this chapter is that we need to be aware of what is dominant and bring it into relationship with the subjugated, and that this can be achieved through musicking. Ideally these polarities should have a constant flow between them (Boyce-Tillman 2007b). The dominant culture will validate one of the poles more highly than the other; so effort will be required to keep the flow moving to the subjugated way of knowing and to ensure that a variety of Values are honoured and respected. We will examine the Values of various musical systems using this model.

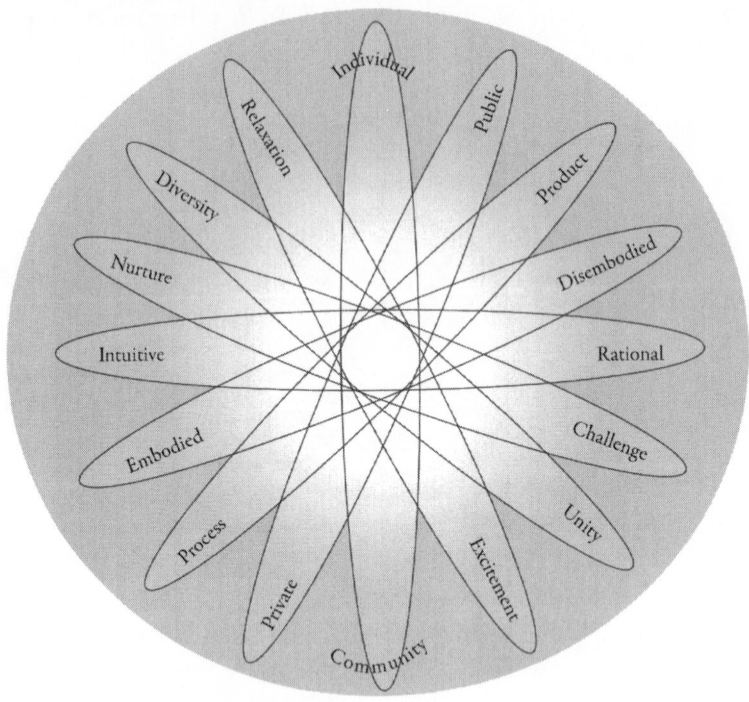

Figure Nine: Value Systems (Boyce-Tillman 2007).

Unity/Diversity

When diversity and unity are brought together, as we saw in Chapter Two, they can produce creativity. The dominant classical tradition reflects a high level of control to produce unity as we saw in Chapter Six. We saw, in the Prelude, how Western classical music was associated with the Apollonian – the ordered; Western classical music has set great store by order and control. The Cartesian view of the unified, separated self has been central to the project of Western rationalism. Bringing the orate and the literate together is a route to integrate the Apollonian and Dionysian aspects of Western culture.

The degree of tolerance for diversity is an important element in the way a community defines itself – in terms of how many groups it defines as 'Other'. This includes the communities of musicians. The tightness of the boundaries established by a particular society, is a product of the degree of threat that is seen – either from without, or, more significantly, from within. And yet it is by the admitting of diversity, that new societies and new ways of conceiving society, have emerged. When the two poles of unity and diversity are balanced in a society, it can grow and change creatively. In the West, we have placed a high value on unity; our children live in a world where normalisation is taking control, with standardised testing for all children, regardless of race, economic class or gender, and all the factors that make children various rather than the same.

At a personal level, the pursuit of the integrated self and the perception of the journey as being a straight and steady progress have resulted in a certain internal fascism, which we may describe as rigidity or, indeed, obsession. In Chapter Two, we saw the descent into darkness or chaos (diversity) as part of personal growth. The work of the philosopher, Gillian Rose (Tubbs 1998), includes the notion of working in what she calls 'the broken middle' – the diversity at the heart of the personality; this has, within it, the necessity of living with the contradictions and paradoxes that make up the diversity within the self. Music clearly has a significant part to play here, as we saw in Chapter Five.

Public/Private

The people who hold positions of power in a tradition will control who has access to the public positions within it. The Values here have had important significance for women's position in musical traditions. The binary of male = public, female = private (domestic) applies in many musical cultures. The public executants will often be paid professionals; the more private musicians will be volunteers and receive nothing. These latter have a hard time getting their experience known at all; finding a place in the construction of musical canons and histories will be difficult or impossible for this hidden musicker. The Western classical tradition has been dominated by white men, while white women have been very active in teaching roles and in the more community-based activities. Some other traditions have not allowed women in any public performances and the stereotyped positions for women in jazz and rock traditions (Green 1997, Bayton 1998) are on their way to changing in the twenty-first century. Indeed, there are moves in all the musical traditions in the West to pay some regard to issues of gender. My encounter with the medieval composer Hildegard of Bingen, in the middle of my life, transformed the hidden messages I had received from all the music curricula that had shaped me – that women do not compose or conduct.

Rational/Intuitive

We have already seen in Chapter One how post Enlightenment Western culture has valued reason and devalued intuition. The Enlightenment project, based on 'I think therefore I am', saw the answer to successful human society as the dominance of reason over human beings' unruly passions and imaginings. The intuitive aspects of the Church were suppressed in favour of theological codifications. Academe was suspicious of anything that smacked of the emotional or spiritual. Human beings were seen as being at their best when they were dispassionately objective about objects, situations and even other people. The cult of 'objectivity' played a crucial part in tyrannising groups of all kinds with notions of normality. In this culture, musicking can play a significant part if the domains of Expression and Construction are valued equally and brought together effectively. Qualitative research is becoming valued and the methodology of crystallisation that underpins this book values a variety of sources of truth.

The literate Western tradition requires a considerable degree of rationality to grasp its notational system and use it to enter the more emotional and intuitive areas of the personality. The orate traditions allow a far greater degree of intuition within their performance practices because of the greater amount of improvisation within them. In this complexity, the role of the visionary experience is being re-evaluated and its place in musical creativity rediscovered. There is increasing interest in medieval visionaries, such as Hildegard of Bingen (Boyce-Tillman 2000b), Julian of Norwich and Teresa of Avila. So the challenging of the rational leads us inevitably to the mystical. The visionary world, with its stress on imagination, has been repressed by years of heavily controlled educational enculturation. The restoration of a right relation with the intuitive area is part of musicking and leads us closer to the exploration of the liminal space.

Embodied/Disembodied

We have already seen how Western society, constructed as it was around the elements of (Greek-influenced) Christianity, had – deep in its conceptualising – a notion of the body/soul split. The Enlightenment added a third element that could be split off – the mind or rational intellect. Few other human societies have achieved such an effective split between these elements. The consequences for life in Western cultures have been considerable; and these have been inflicted on cultures to whom they were absolutely foreign. Manual labour is now split from white and blue collar labour. One uses the bodies of people as if they have no minds, the other the mind as if it has no body. It can be seen in the Western classical tradition in the relation to the control of the mind of the composer over the bodies of the performers. The ubiquity of computer technology requires most people to use a mind with minimal movements of the body, which now has to be exercised separately – almost with no mind – in activity in a gym separated from everyday living. Work is for the mind and leisure for the body, with religion for the spirit, if your cosmology includes a religious strand.

We have examined the concept of the soul in Chapter One. Within Western society it is still a basic human challenge to keep body, mind and soul together, and, as we have seen in Chapter Four, musicking offers immense possibilities here; these are being explored in the rise of the popularity of musical phenomena such as the community choir.

Individual/Community

The prevailing values of Western society might be summarised as a 'normalised individualism.' On the one hand, people are conceived as individuals in competition with one another; on the other hand, individuals are treated by simple cause-and-effect principles (in situations in health care and education), as if all of them were the same. Music transcends these limitations, however, and can offer the possibility of belonging to a group of people who listen, perform, and improvise/compose within a common tradition. Those who favour more individualised approaches may feel drawn to Western classical traditions, while those looking for more communal systems may seek out other more communal traditions. Sonia Gergis, a north London music teacher, ran a 'Music in Harmony' festival in which youngsters, who included so-called recalcitrant teenagers, could only participate as a group and not as soloists. This produced a tremendous amount of cooperation and developed skills in sensitivity. These young participants learned how to tune their music to other people, match their rhythms to each other, blend their tone colours and pitch, and, in general, support others in difficulty rather than in competition.

The relationship between the individual and the community has been expressed in different ways in different cultures that has affected what is valued in its musicking. If the role of the community is paramount, there will be often be a certain conservatism in the society maintained by the elders in the interests of the communal life of the group (Floyd 1993). In societies where individualism is most prominent, there will be a greater stress on the freedom and innovation, as we saw in Chapter Two; this is linked with the idea of the composer as journeying hero. The male hero narrative (based on *The Odyssey* and *Aeneid*) tells of one who asserts his individuality and 'finds himself' through the undertaking of a journey. This usually occurs without a permanent companion, although many temporary traveling associates (who may either be embraced or killed) are usually involved. Autonomy and independence are valued over intimacy and closeness. This Value system is alive and well in the notion of the musical genius.

Community building is not a heroic journey. It is the story of women in many cultures and of the poor in most cultures with whom the community musicking traditions often reside; it is often devalued and has few financial returns. The classical traditions have followed the dominant individualism of the heroic journey model, with solo examinations and performances occupying a paramount position. This has produced a generation of pianists who have little ability in the necessary skill of accompanying; but it is accompanying that is required for community music making. The process of coming together to sing, drum, and move to music somehow can make us psychologically, spiritually and physically more like each other. Harmonious activity having a shared pulse, such as singing and marching, can produce in us an experience of 'entrainment' (Leonard 1978) and actually make those participating more like one another. This can happen in a concert when a performer has such power that s/he can create a unity in which the audience is breathing in 'sync' with one another (Ortiz 1997 p. 318).[8]

The process of entrainment starts when the music is roughly at the common pulse of the group. This process has been used practically to

8 As we saw earlier, this power can be used for a variety of purposes. Entrainment has been used in events involving music by many dictatorships.

create a common pulse for groups of diverse individuals that require synchronised action, as with rowing boats or hauling ropes (as in sea shanties). The process of entrainment is why regular rites, rituals, and family gatherings have included music so prominently. John Blacking (1987) links music and dance together and gives them a central place in the inculcation of human values, saying: 'Human attitudes and specifically human ways of thinking about the world are the results of dance and song' (Blacking 1987 p. 60). The chief loss resulting from the decline of Judeo-Christian theology in our culture may not be the theology itself, but a spiritual loss of the whole community coming together once a week to make music. No Sunday morning do-it-yourself activity offered by a single person in an individualised dwelling can replace the community building power of a hymn or worship song. This is where the attraction of retaining the school assembly in the UK lies; it offers an opportunity for the whole school to sing together once a day. In the last fifty years the nature of song may have changed, but deep in the psyche of educational planners (although often not publicly acknowledged) is the wisdom that retains this central act of communal musicking in the school curriculum. The twentieth century saw attempts to recreate Value systems in music that stress community. Carl Orff and his associate Gunhild Keetman wrote of a music called 'elemental', which is earthy, connected with movement and dance and accessible for everyone: '[It] builds up the humus of the soul, the humus without which we face spiritual soil-erosion' (as cited in Hamel, 1978 p. 18).

The rediscovery of these values in community music has been a rediscovery of Value systems that were once part of Western traditions (Boyce-Tillman, 2000a). The Western classical music tradition up to the Renaissance included a concept of community that embraced the cosmos and, in particular, God or gods, as we saw in the Music of the Spheres. During this period, healing traditions were widely found within the creation of community. With the Post-Enlightenment, however, the heroic journey model gained prominence, and individual composers were set over and perhaps against the community, which often increased divisions between the audience and the High Art composers of Western Europe. Notions of aesthetics replaced God, and notions of healing were replaced by personal enlightenment and amelioration.

Musical groups vary in the degree of exclusivity under which they operate. The Western classical tradition has constructed itself as quite elitist, with groups of people traditionally excluded from its higher rankings on grounds of gender, race, education and class. The pursuit of excellence is closely linked with elitism but, elitism is a form of aggression which often leads to a lack of partnership between individuals. Competition is inbuilt and discourages many from even entering the classical tradition.

The classical tradition has constructed itself with a limited range of sounds that are regarded as acceptable and beautiful, and systems that promote uniformity have developed along quite authoritarian lines. The encompassing of a good unison singing sound (the sound of plainchant and choristers) has been courted. Even with choirs of different voices, singers within each line are encouraged to develop a good unified sound, where individual differences are limited in the interest of a group sound. The orchestra, similarly, is a coherent group of players with soloists in some sections (woodwinds, for example), but also with large groups of stringed instruments who are encouraged to make the most unified sound possible. Over both of these phenomena presides the figure of the conductor, the symbol of externalised imposed authority who has the power to dictate what sort of sound is acceptable and to hire and fire people whose 'sound' does not 'fit'. There are an increasing number of groups on the fringe of the classical tradition that do allow access, but in most of them admittance requires acquired notational and instrumental/vocal skills.

In general, it is in the writings of composers about their own compositional processes, rather than in writings from the annals of classical musicology, that elements of community will be found:

> I need to feel that my separate egotistical identity has been replaced by a sense of belonging to one wholesome organism, and that my function is to serve and enrich that organism ... It may seem odd that in order to be truly original one has, in some way, to deny one's individuality, but it is surely true that much of the world's most beautiful music has been created by people who are happy to remain anonymous. (Downes 1998)

Into this aggressive individualism has moved music therapy, which has always stressed the nature of music as relationship, and New Age music, which offers a community characterised by inclusivity and democracy and community music (Higgins 2012). These developments have validated a wider variety of sounds and offer, in general, more inclusive musical communities organised along non-hierarchical and more democratic lines.

Inclusivity develops structures that promote and contain diversity for individuals, minorities, and the underprivileged. Thoreau once said: 'If a man does not keep pace with his companions, perhaps it is because he hears a different drummer. Let him step to the music which he hears, however measured or far away.' The more different the drumming, the more difficult it is for others to make sense of it – and the more creativity is required to include difference within a musical structure. In our multicultural contemporary society, structures need to be created in which these different drums can fit together. If reconciliation through music-making is to be achieved, we need respect for the position in which the other person is standing. Within our communities, we need to build structures and events which allow us to cooperate musically. I started to illustrate this in the previous chapter and will continue it in Chapters Nine, Ten and Eleven.

A Pluralist Society

Community musicians are now working to bring cultures together. By engaging in musical activity together, we engage deeply with one another. If we can resolve problems musically, we may solve them in other ways as well. Conflict resolution in this area is not about establishing a unity based on a single style, but rather about the creation of musical and sociological structures that encourage the peaceful coexistence of diversity (Boyce-Tillman 1996, 2013b), as in my composition *The Call of the Ancestors* (Boyce-Tillman, 1998) described in Chapter Six. Dr Svanibor Pettan, a Croatian ethnomusicologist, set up an imaginative project to help integrate Bosnian refugees into Norwegian society. He worked with Norwegian university music students and visited Bosnian clubs to get to know their folk musicians. He encouraged the Norwegian and Bosnian musicians to work together and to learn each other's repertoire, so as to create new pieces from the fusion of the cultures. The music groups then played in the Bosnian clubs, as well as at the university. Those involved in the project felt this joint venture had aided the integration process considerably and had helped each group value its own indigenous traditions more highly. Esteem at an individual and cultural level is closely bound up with acceptance.

Courses embracing a variety of traditions are being developed (Boyce-Tillman, 1995). This is clear in papers such as Peter Douskals (2012) in *Multiple Layers of Culture and Multiple Layers of Society*, where he sets out how to organise programmes of this kind. In New York, Lois Holzman works for the revitalisation of democracy and views community as process: 'a collective, creative process of people bringing into existence a new social unit and sharing a collective commitment to its sustainability ... [with a] potential for human growth and social transformation' (Holzman 2002 p. 2). She has worked with a worldwide interdisciplinary project called *Performing the World*, a new online community[9] for people interested in performance as a human, social need. She sees these as:

> A set of semi-concentric, semi-overlapping circles, [which include] hospitals, social services agencies, schools, cultural institutions, and professional associations, inner city children and teens, theater artists, corporate executives, Wall Street financiers ... It's an unusually and radically inclusive community. (Holzman 2002)

Through performance events, she is developing ideas of self and identity as well as understandings of social therapy as a way of enabling personal growth and enhancing community. An example of this is:

> The All Stars Talent Show Network [which] is an ongoing process of creating new forms of association by and between poor (mostly Black and Latino) young people, theater artists, and middle class and wealthy (mostly white) professionals. (Holzman 2002 pp. 16–17)

Here, children of all backgrounds have a chance to contribute to the formation of a community of performing musicians.

9 <www.performingtheworld.org>

Intercultural projects showing a respect for diversity offer models for a globalisation (as we shall see in Chapter Eight) that is different from the global peddling of a normalised individualism. There is much work to be done in ways of bringing cultures together on a basis of equality and not through the colonisation that has characterised the Western classical traditions in particular.

Product/Process

Capitalism deals only in products. Those who are too old, too young, too ill or not skilled enough to produce products have no value and often little means to support themselves. This Value system validates de-humanising forms of production and requires many musicians to play too often and too long to earn their wages. We saw in Chapter One how spirituality sits more easily in process philosophies and theologies.

Western society shows a valuing of literacy over orality, as we saw in Chapter Six. Indeed systems, such as Schenkerian analysis concentrate on this domain in order to identify 'greatness' in music. In orate traditions the process has a greater value as Olu Taiwo described in the previous chapter. There is an ephemerality about orate traditions; there is less desire to retain material from particular situations which may be inappropriate for different contexts. People who prefer orality to literacy in our culture reflect this capacity to re-member material in ways appropriate to any given situation in which they find themselves. Characteristics of orate cultures are:

- The absence of a definitive form of any story
- A fluidity in formal structures which are free flowing rather than linear and analytical
- Increased subjectivity
- Transmission by face-face contact, not a book
- Open religion, rather than a fixed revelation contained in a book

Instrumental lessons in the Western classical tradition have traditionally involved the decoding of notation to realise the 'products' that make up the Western musical canon. Improvisation is less often taught, although most children starting music lessons enjoy exploring sound. Often this is discouraged and described in such terms as 'messing about'; it has been devalued in the interest of reading the dots. I had an eleven-year-old bass recorder player who said five minutes before a concert: 'I've got some bad news for you, miss. I've forgotten my music.' It was a part of which I had no second copy and did not know what we could do. 'Don't you worry, miss. I'll busk it!' he said. He was also the drummer for the local Assembly of God Church, and so regularly improvised every Sunday for over two hours. He had both skills. He had retained both because he could function in two differing traditions. He was a real example of a musician who valued both ways of knowing – the orate, based on process and the literate, based on product – equally.

Excitement/Relaxation

Music has profound effects on balancing relaxation and excitement. Our society has become increasingly excited by loud and fast popular music. However, in the twentieth century, a new philosophy of the functionality of music was developing in Europe. Edward Satie in the 1920s invented the idea of Musique d'ameublement or Furniture Music (Lanza 2007 p. 18), which was meant strictly to be nothing more than a background music with no subject matter; it was not intended to attract attention in any way. He produced pieces like *Gnossiennes*. Roderick Swanston says it arose because classical composers took themselves too seriously (Lanza 2007 p. 18). Restaurants welcomed what was sometimes called wallpaper music to cover up the sound of knives and forks and relax customers. Then came Muzak originally designed to encourage workers. It was in the 1970s, when Brian Eno invented ambient sound. Whereas conventional background music was produced by stripping away all sense of doubt and uncertainty (and thus all genuine interest) from the music, ambient music retains these qualities. And, whereas the intention of Muzak was to 'brighten' the environment, ambient music is intended to induce calm and a space to think, as in Brian Eno's 1978 *Music for Airports*. It was the beginning of music for meditation. It used a great deal of repetition; but uncertainty was there sometimes, as in *Discreet Music*, a piece consisting of repeated chord progressions not rooted in any set key (Lanza 2007 p. 210). Many of these pieces have proved very popular for meditation, peace and relaxation. Theorists have claimed that repetition is inherent in the way the mind processes the outside world, and, therefore, in the domain of Construction this may be conducive to meditative states and the experience of a different time/space dimension.

Some of the most systematic work on the use of music to control the excitement of the body in clinical settings has been carried out by the German doctor, Ralph Spintge. He is in charge of a pain clinic at which he has constructed a database of the effects of music on 90,000 patients (Robertson 1996 pp. 26–7). He makes music available to his patients through high quality sound systems all the time; his research has shown that anxieties about being in hospital are calmed by it and recovery improved. In surgical procedures, he and his team have composed pieces which are designed to put patients in the optimum condition both mentally and physically. So effective is the fifteen minutes of soothing music that lulls the patient, that only fifty percent of the recommended doses of analgesics and sedative medication usually used are required for painful surgery. Some procedures are even carried out without anaesthetic. This is followed by more invigorating music which is designed to encourage the patient's systems actively to respond to the surgical procedures (Robertson 1996 p. 27).

Robin Knowles-Wallace's survey of hymnody saw them as calming, relaxing sad and angry moods and lifting people above everyday chores. We have already seen the role of music with the dying:

> I work with dying people and often hymns are among the last things they forget … Hymn singing at the very end of life is incredibly reassuring to people of faith because

> it reminds them of their history with God in this life and the history of God over human time. (Knowles Wallace 2015 p. 8)

So the development of a very excited culture is being balanced by music designed to rebalance the self, both in the background and also more in the foreground to accompany meditative practices or the processes of dying.

Challenge/Nurture

We have already seen how Western culture is based on the myth of progress (Boyce-Tillman 2000a) which values challenge and devalues nurture. In music this is apparent in the structure of examining in the classical traditions and its stress on repeated challenges. Nurturing roles, such as those of parenting, nursing and social work, are either unpaid or poorly paid and students of music often see teaching as less attractive than a career as a soloist. We have already examined in Chapters Two and Five that the context needs to be empowering, drawing on the notion of Vygotskian scaffolding. When musical challenge and nurture are balanced effectively, people are empowered; so, The *Can't Sing* choir has enabled a man to achieve part of his goal which was to read musical notation:

> I cannot sing, but I like to sing, and always wished that I could sing with a choir. Until I read about the *Can't Sing choir* I did not have the courage to join a choir in case my voice or standard of singing was unacceptable. The *Can't Sing choir* has taught me more to enjoy my voice and singing. I have also learned more about reading music.

Finding their voice, through appropriate levels of challenge, has led many people to the 'flow' experience seen by many as spiritual.

Sarah Morgan (2013 p. 61) arrived at a model for the community choir leader that kept these two in balance drawing on the literature and her extensive experience:

← *Performance*	Ethos	*Participation* →
Conductor Musically demanding Authoritative Provides musical challenges High level of musical theory Skilled use of gesture Classical music prominent in repertoire Formal musical education Fluent sight reader Criteria for repertoire – musical excellence Task orientation	**Muse** Musically enabling Persuasive Develops musical confidence Demystifies music technicality Interpersonal skills Emotional intelligence World/folk prominent in repertoire Informal musical experience Skilled in oral/aural methods Long term relationship Criteria for repertoire- uplifting and fun Process orientation	↑ *Music* Focus
Organizer Creates order and stability Organisational focus Attention to detail Understands the 'business side' 'Backroom' role Technical knowledge Manages and promotes events Keeps up to date with legalities – tax, insurance, copyright etc Task orientation	**Catalyst** Creates change Community focus Attention to big picture Understands community/group dynamics Highly visible Balances challenge and support Inclusive approach Project based Process orientation	*Organisation/community* ↓

Figure Ten: Community Choir Leadership (Morgan 2013).

Robin Knowles Wallace's survey of hymns in everyday life sees two major functions for hymns in sustaining and nurturing. One person sees music as the closest approach to God, a prodding by the Spirit and making herself present to God (Knowles Wallace 2015 p. 3).

A Project in Musical Ecology

As a composer I wanted to explore different value systems through my own compositions. This led to the piece *The Healing of the Earth* (Boyce-Tillman 2001a and reworked as 2012 for Hampshire Music Services and

Winchester Cathedral). It has been performed in several situations but I will concentrate here on a performance with 500 children aged 6–16 for the Queen's Jubilee in Battersea Technology College, London, UK.

The starting point of the piece was in the domains of Values and Spirituality. It is a piece with an intentionally ethical system based on the valuing of diversity and connecting with the environment supported by feminist theoreticians of music (Subotnik 1996). It is based on a notion of community in which, through participatory performance, professional musicians and children work together with integrity (Sharp 1998). There are few examples in musicking traditions of the West where adults can behave as adults and children as children and they can both be included in a musical event. There are situations like the cathedral choir where children have to behave like adults to be accepted. Other situations like nursery classes ask adults to behave like children to facilitate group music making. In this work I tried to develop an inclusive structure in which experienced musicians played quite complex textures while children had sections which they themselves devised.

The Valuing of the environment is reflected in the titles of the nine movements: Wisdom, Water, Knowledge, Fire, Technology, Earth, Compassion, Air, and Communication. Many of the pieces include theological and musical ideas from Hildegard of Bingen, who has influenced so much of my work (Boyce-Tillman 2000b). The themes of the songs are ecological; but this ecology includes the recycling of ourselves and our experiences, alongside the care for the environment – it is extended to include personal and community transformation.

This pluralistic Values system is reflected in the range of cultures from which the songs are drawn. These include Native American, Urdu, Israeli, Yoruba, Muslim, and Christian sources. These fit alongside newly composed material in a more Western classical style. Diversity is put together with respect for both the differences and common elements.

The Values of the Western classical concert with its separation between the composer, performer and audience are in this work balanced by a more democratic process of creating and performing. There are devised sections in the piece; so the performers have a hand in the compositional process. The players and singers are placed around the audience who also have to sing. The notion of a musical performance as packaged by a conductor at one end of a space and propelled to the other where it is received by an audience, is now replaced by one in which each member of the audience has to construct their own listening experience; this will depend on which group of musicians are near them. So we all collaborate together – performers, composers and audience – to make things happen musically and also ecologically. Behind the piece is the notion that through such music making we affect the ecology of the planet. It was, in general, the children who found these ideas easier to accept than the adults, who were already enculturated into a culture of rationality and non-belief in magical systems. However, it was interesting to see how many of the teachers, somewhat cautiously at first, declared their belief in the notions of an ecological Spirituality.

In the domain of Construction, I chose a structure with holes for improvisation, as well as containing material from a variety of sources – both instrumental and vocal material – as well as pieces devised by the children. The development of this Construction system has been described in the previous chapter.

Summary

This analysis of various value systems has highlighted the Values that underpin various musical traditions – both orate and literate – how they do or do not interrelate. This domain has raised the difficult issues associated with the narratives that underpin the various religious traditions that are embedded in certain musics, and the Values they bring with them.

By linking the musical experience with its context we open up the possibility of The Good as being defined in relation to the intention of the musickers and the appropriateness of the musicking to its context. This area of the relationship to everyday living has been carefully explored by Tia DeNora (2013) in a book subtitled *Wellbeing through Music in Everyday Life*. This helps people reflect on the role that music plays in various contexts in their living. Constance Classen (1998) opens up the possibility of including senses which have not been traditionally included in the Western concept of the aesthetic – such as touch, taste and smell. The use of music in the context of massage – particularly the sort of music that is used which is clearly in a line developing from Brian Eno's ambient music – opens up the possibility of looking at the combination of touch, smell and hearing in the concept of the aesthetic – The Beautiful.

This domain also raises the inclusion of the Extrapersonal strand that I identified in Chapter One in the musical experience; this raises the important moral questions concerning how we view other cultures and Otherness in general. If we see the totality of the musical experience, composers, performers and music educators will be able to construct a vision of a musical culture that is really reflective of the interrelationship of music with a pluralist society – a truly musical ecology – and a reworking of The Good in music.

INTERLUDE TWO

Music and Christian Theology

I expect that many readers of this book might have expected a greater exploration of this area. However, I have set out above a situating of religion in the domain of Values; this enables the liminal/spiritual space, which we shall explore next to be either religion-full or religion-free. This interlude will examine in a little more detail how Christian theology has viewed music as spiritual experience.[1] It has been regarded as an icon and a sacrament; but Thomas and Manning see the iconic effect lying in the relationship between the music and personal taste. These authors, although acknowledging the dominance of Western classical music in the literature, open up the power of the sacred to a variety of musics (Thomas and Manning 1995). Geoffrey Moore sees the hymn as iconic because it is physical and guides our vision, thought and understanding (G. Moore 2015 p. 7).

The function of religion in relation to spirituality is to situate it within an integrated system of global meaning. Some writers see a religious frame as essential for a balanced spirituality. Miner and Dowson (2012) see philosophy and psychology as:

> an objective means of describing and analysing aspects of spiritual experiences, but not of fully expressing their ineffable qualities. On the other hand, music, literature and the arts are often used to give partial expression to spiritual traits, states and experiences. Yet, there is always a sense of incompleteness in musical, literary and

1 There is a considerable literature on music in Christian worship and liturgy from a variety of denominational positions such as Ingalls (2013), discussing such aspects as its efficacy, style and appropriateness.

> artistic expressions of the spiritual because they lack the capacity for a systematic explanation and contextualisation of the experience (Miner and Dowson 2012 p. 23).

They see some explanation (as in a Christian frame) as necessary to integrate the transcendent experience within the self. Without this they see the possibility of 'cognitive fragmentation and confusion' (Miner and Dowson 2012 p. 23). So they see a necessary link in the area of wellbeing between religion and spirituality.[2] What we see here is the paradoxical nature of the spiritual experience offered by music. Music does not offer meaning. It invites people to undertake the journey:

> [Music] does not offer meaning but triggers the effort to produce the meaning. (Voegelin 2010 p. 165)

Anne McElvoy, writing of the Promenade concerts in London, also affirms the freedom given by music to its recipients to make their own meanings:

> Works like the great Mahler symphony with its evocation of chaotic life and the finality of death allow us to remember human sacrifices without being told what to think. (McElvoy 2014 p. 15)

Brynjulf Stige (2002) emphasises how meaning is contextualised and necessarily reflects the norms, values and assumptions of a particular context. It may be that for the purposes of wellbeing, this meaning needs rooting in a more formulated system; but this is beyond the scope of this book.

Christian theology would place all the strands identified in Chapter One in the context of a world which is a manifestation of God. Christian theology of music has to some extent been regularly plagued by St Augustine's dilemma in the *Confessions* of how the sensuous nature of music might detract from the meaning of the text (*Confessions* X. 33. 9–30). However,

2 The Trance/Rave culture of the late twentieth century in the UK with its use of loud music, prolonged dancing and hallucinogens did produce spiritual experiences but unrooted in a religious tradition which was shared by participants and no guidance from elders (as would have been the case in spirit possession rituals) the experiences were often not helpful to participants' wellbeing (Boyce-Tillman 2000a).

when Augustine describes his own conversion he talks of the part music played, causing him to cry and take the truth into his heart (Confessions IX. 6). This trope appears regularly in Church history, as in the Council of Trent at which some music was criticised for delighting the ear rather than the mind and encouraging lascivious thoughts (Thomas and Manning 1995 p. 167). This is part of an ongoing struggle between the relative importance of music and text which has exercised many theologians. Although the musical style is often critiqued, it is often the text that is regarded as the real content.

However, Jeremy Begbie, in *Theology, Music and Time*, sees music's temporality as providing the theologian with:

> Conceptual tools – ways of thinking, models, frameworks, metaphors – for exploring, clarifying and re-conceiving the dynamics of God's world and his ways with the world. (Begbie 2000 p. 271)

Here he sees the centrality of the domains of Construction and Expression in illuminating Christian theology. Rowan Williams sees this as a significant aspect of music:

> If music is the most fundamentally contemplative of the arts, it is *not* because it takes us into the timeless but because *it obliges us to rethink time*. (R. Williams 1994 p. 250. Author's italics)

This links with the concept of chronos. that we shall see later.[3] Other theologians have used music as a metaphor in theological reflection. David Ford (1999) uses its transformative quality in *Self and Salvation, Being Transformed*. Richard Holloway (2000) in *Godless Morality: Keeping Religion out of Ethics* uses musical improvisation as a metaphor for moral choice – ascribing a capacity for improvisation to God. I wrote a hymn using music as a metaphor for living:

3 There is much less writing on time in the orate traditions that we discussed in Construction. The comparison of the linear construction of notated traditions and the much greater sense of the present in orate traditions would provide a very interesting new comparative study.

1. Melody of God's grace, shape us,
As we form life's curving phrase
From the essence of your loving
Flowing through each passing phase.
May our lives reflect the singing
Of the angels' endless praise.

2. Harmony of God's peace, move us
To resolve disputes with love;
So the discords drive us forward
To the joy of heaven above.
May our lives reflect the music
Of the flying Spirit-dove.

3. Counterpoint of God's grace, teach us
How to give the diff'rent respect;
So we live alongside Others
And with various musics connect,
So that ev'ry race and culture
Hear how they all intersect.

4. Rhythm of God's order, structure
Patterns of vitality;
Vibrant pulse, your strength is flowing
From hope's creativity.
May our lives reflect your priesthood
Dancing in humanity.

(Boyce-Tillman 2006c revised)

Because of the musical taste of many leading European theologians (especially Karl Barth and Hans Kung), there is a tight interface between the Western classical music tradition and the Church, which offered employment to musicians for so much of its history. Kung writes of Mozart's *Coronation Mass*:

> Herein is the strangely exciting but at the same time calming quality of his music: it evidently comes from on high, where (since everything is known there) the right and the left of existence and therefore its joy and sorrow, good and evil, life and death, are experienced in their reality but also in their limitations. (Barth cited in Kung 1992 p. 69)

It is in this thinking that the idea that some music as intrinsically spiritual lies and therefore that certain pieces will generate a spiritual experience whatever the context. However, it is clear that a person's ability to relate to this tradition is based on both enculturation and training. This thinking is often supported by considering intention as an important part in the 'sacredness' of the experience. In such experiences the theological understanding is both in the piece and in the mind of the perceiver – both implicit and explicit. This line of thought, that would limit this to Western classical 'masterpieces', is now challenged by the popularity of folk and jazz traditions and is sometimes being tempered by the embracing of a greater variety of styles in the approach to the transcendence of God (Saliers 2007), evidenced in churches by the contrasting traditions of the classical choir with organ and the music group with its guitars and drums.

This would include popular traditions, including those which challenge and question religious traditions. These can play an important part in the spiritual development of a new generation. Christo Lombaard (2015) analyses this in some detail in relation to the popular Afrikaans band Fokofpolisiekar. He identifies their formative early life influences of the Church and then their search for alternative expressions of Christianity. He traces these influences to the official 1976 Afrikaans Psalms-en-Gesangeboek, used in most Afrikaans churches until the new millennium (and still in some):

> Although it may at first glance seem that these two musical expressions, namely the Psalms-en Gesangeboek and Fokofpolisiekar's oevre, reflect very diverse contexts, these unexpected influences of the 1976 hymnal on at least some of the songs of the band show aspects of cultural continuation-in-reinterpretation. (Lombaard 2015 p. 1)

This would be part of the searching that involves the rejection of traditional dogma that was identified in the very nature of spirituality in Chapter One. Lombaard sees how their rejection of traditional Afrikaans religiosity and of aspects of faith in general makes their music extremely acceptable to contemporary South African culture. The rebellion he finds not only in the texts but also in the structure of the music.

When we turn to the hymnody in use in churches, we have another example of implicit and explicit theology, which here is sometimes called lyrical theology, because it can cause theological understanding to penetrate beyond memory and emotion deep into the believer's psyche. Thomas Troeger calls hymns 'theology in ecstasy' (Brown 2015 p. 1). Indeed the theology of the Church, especially the Protestant traditions, was taught primarily by its hymnody because of the interface between the domains – the body (Materials), the emotions (Expression), the understanding (Construction) and the community (Values). However, the issue of the conservatism of texts and their lack of inclusion or social protest in their explicit Value systems, means that even some who retain a Christian belief fail to get any sort of spiritual experience from the musicking, because they have embraced a different theological position(Boyce-Tillman 2014). Geoffrey Moore (2015) draws on Luther's view of a sacrament as a sharing in God's grace to see the hymn as sacramental, because of its transformative qualities and its ability to bring spiritual and created realities together. He then echoes Isabel Clarke's transliminal way of knowing:

> That God relates to us through sacramental exchange means that the sacraments provide a framework for thinking of knowledge *relationally* rather than merely ratio-nally, and thinking of music in this way allows us to reframe the purpose of music-making relationally. (G. Moore 2015 p. 9. Author's italics)

However, the cultural place of religious music, whether sung or listened to, means that some people who no longer subscribe to the doctrinal tenets of Christianity may still be transported by religious music. According to *Gimell* Records press release in August 2012, there has been an increase in downloads of classical sacred music and also in attendance at cathedral services involving professional choirs. At the outset of his book on *Sacred Music in Secular Society*, Jonathan Arnold (2014) describes his personal experience of sacred music in the context of a liturgy – when the listener is asked to perform certain acts that imply belief, such as kneeling and turning to face the altar – and sacred music in a concert, when such enactments of belief are not required (Arnold 2014 pp xii-xiv). The context, as we shall see in the next chapter, changes the character of the experience.

In the concert context, the theology of the words for many listeners changes from a devotional meaning to a cultural meaning, as we discussed around the Narrative strand of spirituality in Chapter One. This can be at a personal or a cultural level. I remember a self-declared atheist singing with great joy *How great thou art* because of its relationship to his Welsh cultural roots. For many older people now, hymns learned in childhood have reminiscence power, regardless of contemporary personal belief; so a hymn such as *Praise my soul the King of Heaven* was used for many services like weddings and funerals for much of the twentieth century and will recall those events for people singing it (as reminiscence discussed Chapter Five). Many members of cathedral choirs will be transported by the music without believing the words which seem to function as musical sounds rather than doctrinal manifestations (discussed Chapter Six). The interface between religion and culture makes such experiences not uncommon. The alliance of religion and music has reinforced the distinction in Western culture between the sacred and secular; in this context culturally religious music may generate a spiritual experience for the musickers regardless of their personal belief systems. The use of music with religious texts as cultural artefacts is an acceptable way of using music in educational contexts, indeed it is an excellent way to enable people to enter into the spirit of history in the same way as an old piece of jewellery or an ancient statue.

To revisit the distinctions made in the strand of Narrative in Chapter One, it is possible to encourage an expressive engagement with the text as simply a story rather than a story that demands belief through a religious interpretation of it. William Boyd[4] helpfully contributes to this debate in talking about the novel: 'You know that it's fiction; but you can believe it in a make-believe world'. The music associated with a text can act in the same way as the novel format, to enable the musicker to entry into a make-believe world; this is a temporary state and has no necessary relation with the person's actual belief systems beyond the experience itself. This is the least controversial way of treating music with religious texts in an educational context.

4 Interview on the BBC Radio 4 Today programme August 26th 2015. Boyd is famous for blurring the distinction between fact and fiction in his novel *Nat Tate: An American Artist*, a piece of fiction masquerading as non-fiction.

For believers, music can play an important part in what Miner and Dowson call 'spiritual behaviours' (Miner and Dowson (2012). Of these behaviours, prayer, reflection and surrender can be associated with music in some ways. I use meditative piano pieces in the one-woman performances exploring women mystics as ways of reflecting on the narrative. The development of repetitive chanting traditions, such as those associated with the Taizé community, has meant that Christian words are 'breathed' by congregations as music. Don Saliers goes on to connect this with the mystery of God:

> There are occasions when the singing becomes very much 'listening for' and a 'hearing of' more than words. (Saliers 2007 p. 70)

In the area of surrender, a woman, in a memorial service where the dead were remembered, described how, during Faure's *in Paradisum*, she let her husband go into the communion of saints and the mystery of God (Saliers 2007 p. 71):

> Music confers upon musical language addressed to God the appropriate silence and mystery required by prayer. Music is the language of the soul made audible especially as music is the performative mode of the prayer and ritual engagement in a community. (Saliers 2007 p. 4)

In liturgy, the combination of movement, music, speech, costume and theatre contributes to the mood of uplift that many seek in Christian worship, well-illustrated in the elaborate rituals associated with Easter. However, the effectiveness of the music depends entirely on a particular context and, transplanted, it may lack sacred power (showing the power of the Values domain). In a concert setting, Thomas and Manning refer to the 'latent iconicity' of liturgical music as opposed to the 'manifest iconicity' of the liturgical setting (Thomas and Manning 1995 p. 164). This iconicity in a concert setting will be released by the congruence of the Value systems of the music and the musicker.

Christian liturgies are often highly controlled and we saw in the previous chapter how I have attempted to relax some of this control. We have already seen above the tensions between notated and improvised traditions in terms of freedom. However, many community choirs are now looking for that same uplift outside of a Christian frame using movement and uplifting songs without explicit religious content. Even within the Christian literature there is an acknowledgement that 'secular' music can act sacramentally in giving one a sense of the divine and its attributes (Brown and Loades 1995 p. 11).

> Every real creation of art is independent, more powerful than the artist himself, and returns to the divine through its manifestation. (Scott 1934 p. 125)

James Lancelot (1995), in declaring music as a sacrament and linking it with Divine generosity, concludes that secular music can act in a sacred way, although he does go on to limit this to 'the mainstream of Western music as millions of people understand it' (Lancelot 1995 p. 183).

In summary, there are many claims for the essential relationship between spirituality and religion, in this case the Christian one. In the underpinning phenomenographic map set out in this book, these systems of meaning are located in the domain of Values and will have a significant impact upon the nature of the experience. However, these meaning systems are not essential during the experience, although they may help integrate it into life after the event.

CHAPTER EIGHT

Crossing a Threshold: Encountering the Spiritual

A Poem

I went to the garden as the sun was descending …

It was as if the great ferns had grown longer and greener
It was as if the greening power of the earth was everywhere – filling the world with love and strength
It was as if the entire world was singing

It was as if I loved everything and everything loved me
It was as if I had found the place I was really meant to be
It was as if I was in the place just right – the valley of love and delight

It was as if God had made me just for this moment
It was as if I was alive for the first time
It was as if I saw the world made new

It was as if the garden enclosed me and held me safe
It was as if everything was higher than it had ever been
It was as if everything was cool

It was as if nothing mattered but this one moment of Divine promise.
(Boyce-Tillman 2011 June 24th unpublished)

Introduction

This was an attempt to encompass in poetry one of the experiences to which I would give the name spiritual. It followed the experience of the performance of one of my pieces in Winchester Cathedral. It is related to the Metaphysical strand outlined in Chapter One. Music has the possibility of creating such a liminal space and, indeed, the perceived effectiveness of a musical experience is often situated in this domain. Insofar as a musical experience takes us out of 'everyday' consciousness with its concerns for food, clothing and practical issues and moves us into another dimension, we regard the musical experience as successful, whether we are a composer, performer or listener. Indeed some would see music as the last remaining ubiquitous spiritual experience in a secularised Western culture (Boyce-Tillman 2000c, 2006b), as the peace studies theorist, Johan Galtung writes:

> Art uproots us into virtual reality ... Time in the standard sense of *khronos* is suspended, and space is irrelevant because the viewer/listener/reader is encapsulated in the art, the virtual space provided by the artists. (Galtung 2008 p. 54. Author's italics)

Rowan Williams describes the 'aesthetic sense of inaccessibility' as 'unrestricted time' (R. Williams 2012 p. 18). Galtung goes on to describe how the various domains of the experience need to be brought together to make the performance transformative:

> Art and peace are both located in the tension between emotions and intellect. Another false dichotomy. Any good, deep intellectual construction gives a deep emotional satisfaction, and in the most emotionally touching piece of art there is architecture in the hidden plan, of the novel, the symphony, the painting, the sculpture ... And art, like peace, has to overcome such false dichotomies by speaking to the heart and to the brain, to the compassion of the heart and construction of the brain. (Galtung 2008 p. 60)

To Galtung's analysis, I would also add the body and action. This fusion in the use of music to create sacred space is found in reviews of health contexts:

> Sacred space, and its instruments – beauty, stillness, music and so on – inspires and uplifts us. (Wright and Sayre-Adams 2009 p. 13)

It 'fills us with awe, with joy, with wellbeing, that which adds meaning to our lives' (Agwin, 1998 p. 6) and so helps to deal with burn-out in healthcare contexts, for staff as well as patients. In the *Elevate* programme in Salisbury Hospital, members of the hospital staff were actively observed taking part in the artists' sessions, just by singing a song with the musicians, or improvising a little dance in the middle of the bay in the ward:

> It was also noticed that the staff would sing or hum the tune of a song in a variety of situations, for example, while they were washing a patient behind the curtains, when they were taking the blood pressure of a patient or giving them their medications. Furthermore, it became increasingly evident that some of the staff was using music to distract the patients from the procedure they were carrying out. (Preti and Boyce-Tillman 2014 no pages)

Wright and Sayre-Adams describe music as a soul food, along with art, nature and scripture (Wright and Sayer-Adams 2009 p. 29). They summarise the history of music in healing contexts:

> From the relaxation effect of soft background music, to patient participation in music making, there are many opportunities for carers to find a path for music in holding the sacred in right relationship. Music, the 'food of love' has inspired people to the heights of human achievement, and has been used in all cultures as a meditative and contemplative tool to alter states of consciousness, from the repetitive drumming of the shaman to the ragas of India and the complex and intricate qawaal songs of the Sufis. Latterly, we have witnessed some of the most ground-breaking work in the care of the dying with the application of music at the point of death in the Chalice of Repose Project led by Dr Therese Schroeder-Sheker. A whole new (some might argue, renewed) science and art is emerging of 'music thanatology' (Schroeder-Sheker, 1994) bringing prescriptive music to the dying and seriously ill, with profound beneficial and spiritual effects being reported. (Wright and Sayer-Adams 2009 p. 94)

There is an increase in the use of music in healthcare. New singing groups have arisen. Singing groups for the homeless, for the mentally ill, people with memory loss and stroke victims started to emerge, such as the Seaview singers in Kent for people with dementia (Vella-Burrows 2012 pp. 11–13) and Recovery Choirs for people with mental health problems. Within some of this thinking we have the concept of being able to hold a sacred (transformative) space by means of music:

> When you came to our church and sang, I had more energy than I have had in many months. When you and the choir sang to my mom, I felt your singing was able to hold a space open that we all fear. That 'space' could be death or just the struggle of sickness, and when it's held open like that, we are less alone in it. (Threshold Choir 2014)

The Winchester Centre for the Arts as Wellbeing has evaluated the *Elevate* programme of Artswork in Salisbury hospital, Costanza Preti (2014) writes how skillfully the artists were able to handle sensitively the implications of extrinsic musical meaning:

> The artists were not intimidated by the patients' emotional reactions; they welcomed them instead as an expression of emotional release that was perceived as beneficial and somehow therapeutic. They were observed to take immediate notice of these reactions addressing the patients asking if they wanted them to stop playing a certain song or reading a certain poem. (Preti and Boyce-Tillman 2014)

Overall, the patients were very appreciative about the opportunity to release their emotions:

> Her final choice reduced me to tears but I can only describe them as good tears. (Preti and Boyce-Tillman 2014)

Music was seen in Salisbury Hospital to work with the elderly as an extremely important way of unlocking painful memories – making the private more public so that it can be healed. Patients would request a song that they were keen to hear, such as *The White cliffs of Dover*, *It's a Long Way to Tipperary*, *Edelweiss* or *Oh What a Beautiful Morning*. The varied repertoire of the artists allowed patients to engage actively with the songs, singing along, recognising the tunes. In these cases, the transformative properties of the spiritual/liminal space are clear.

At the University of Winchester, we developed a programme giving music lessons to children diagnosed with acute anxiety (Walker and Boyce-Tillman 2002). Grenville Hancox and Stephen Clift have done cross cultural surveys on the benefits of choral singing. For the more marginalised by society, they report marked improvements in the area of a sense of well-being (Clift et al 2001). Further studies, especially those of Bailey and Davidson (2005), contain repeated descriptions of physical, psychological, and social benefits of choral singing. These include reduced stress levels, distraction from on-going concerns, enhanced positive feelings, a sense of intellectual challenge and achievement, personal friendship and social support, and a sense of group identity and belonging. Homeless men participating in a choral project attributed the positive responses from audiences as validating them as important members of society. They could imagine a better future (Bailey and Davidson 2003).

Complementary therapists have seen music as one of their tools for longer than allopathic medicine; sitting often in New Age spiritualities, they are more likely to use the word spiritual to describe its effect:

> In holistic medicine, spiritual concerns rank with those of mind and body. We are creatures who puzzle over what life means, where we come from and where we are bound. To be anxious and bewildered at times is to be human. For many of us, the past has been painful, the present insecure and the future uncertain. In the struggle to make sense of life, certain activities create a supportive framework that connects us to our inner selves, to each other and the world. These activities include art, literature, music, community, family, worship and play and they are especially important when illness presents us with the reality of vulnerability, limitations and dependency. Broadly speaking, this is the realm of spirituality. (Woodham and Peters 1998 p. 80)

Other theorists, such as Stephen Arnold, see the sacred as once residing either in the intentions of the composer or the context of the performance; but now it rests in what he calls 'the *genius* of an art form that, when perfected, appeals to those needs, desires and doubts that are experienced by all thinking and truly human individuals'(S. Arnold pp. 10–11). This includes within it, the concept, that I shall explore, of the meeting of these within the music with the needs of the musicker. We have already seen how, in Gabrielsson's descriptions of strong experiences in music, one category includes the transcendental and existential (Gabrielsson and Lindstrom 1993). They demonstrate the synergy between the aesthetic and the spiritual; for example, one person following a deep experience of a Sibelius symphony went to the woods to thank God. Hills and Argyle (1998) concluded that religious and musical were very similar, including such characteristics as giving musickers a glimpse of another world and a sense of transcending the self.

My Definition

In my model I am defining Spirituality as the ability to transport the musicker to a different time/space dimension – to move them from everyday reality to 'another world', as described in the opening poem. We have already seen in Chapter Seven and Interlude Two how, if the experiencer has a particular religious frame, they may want to use words like heaven, God or Nirvana in its description; but these are not necessary. Liminality would be another possible term, as we have seen defined by Turner (V. Turner 1969, 1974) or the 'limit experience (Tracy 1975). It represents the reintegration of the body (Materials), the emotions (Expression), the intellect (Construction) and the culture (Values). Turner focused his attention on the second stage of rites of passage – the stage of liminality, the stage when pilgrims separate from ordinary everyday life. This, he described as having a character of being or dwelling for extended periods of time in a spatial, social and spiritual threshold. In his article *Pilgrimages as Social Processes* he writes:

> A limen is, of course, literally a 'threshold.' A pilgrimage centre, from the standpoint of the believing actor, also represents a threshold, a place and moment 'in and out of time,' and such an actor – as the evidence of many pilgrims of many religions attests – hopes to have their direct experience of the sacred, invisible or supernatural order, either in the material aspect of miraculous healing or in the immaterial aspect of inward transformation of spirit or personality. (V. Turner 2004 No pages available)

The variety of encounters within the musical experience makes the possibility of transformation both likely and rich. So far in this book, I have attempted to tease out the domains within the musical experience to reveal the nature of its complexity in which lies its depths:

> Art is the highest concentration of all the biological and social processes in which the individual is involved in society, that it is a mode of finding a balance between man [sic] and the world in the most critical and responsible moments in life. (Vygotsky, 1925/1987, quoted in Jordanger 2008)

My thesis is that, if the experiencer can negotiate a relationship with all the domains, they will move to this different time/space dimension, which is potentially transformative; this dimension may or may not be linked with religion:

> In a significant number of cultures music seems to act as a form of mediation between the known and the unknown, the acceptable and the unacceptable, that which is powerful and that which is dangerous. (Shepherd 1991 p. 214)

The phenomenographic map enables the relationship with the beyond established in the musical/spiritual experience to be named or unnamed.

Latching on

Katya Mandoki sets out the notion that at the heart of this experience is one of relationship. She describes humans' relation to art as latching-on:

> I am referring to the act of *latching-on* to the nipple and thriving from it. Instead of the mystic 'contemplation' that cancels the somatic condition of the subject, I will metaphorically project to aesthetics' theoretical domain this primordial archetype of bonding between mother and child that starts at this corporeal experience of the infant *latching-on* to the mother's nipple. What makes this coupling possible is the morphological affinity between the subject and the object. This morphological, and thus formal, coupling between the mouth of a mammal and the mother's nipple permits *adhesion* ... Adhesion is the essential aesthetic operation both at an individual and at a collective level. (Mandoki 2007 p. 67 Author's emphasis)

This writing effectively links the aesthetic with the spiritual, which can now be seen, as in Chapter Five, as nourishing. There is undoubtedly a link here; but I have chosen the word spiritual, because aesthetic has come to be associated with the Western classical tradition. We see this in the engagement of the small child in this account:

> An eight-years-old child immerses herself in a piano improvisation, exploring with particular care and concentration aspects of musical ideas that emerge and develop in the moment of their occurrence. One can hear her mind at work, in the ways she uses familiar material, suddenly breaking into the unexpected, in the manner in which she responds to the unsuccessful renditions of an idea finding ways forward. There is an

> overwhelming sense of fragility in this music-making process, as well as a density of attention, a care for maintaining fluency, and a prevalent sense of adventure. There is also a sense of ease and confidence in her playing. (Kanellopoulos 2013 No pages available)

Looking forward to later discussions, some would see this as a good example of flow, and we shall see how my concept of the spiritual draws on a number of other descriptors from different disciplines.

Liminality and Transformation

However these experiences are described, there is some agreement that they are potentially transformative, as we saw in Interlude One. The notion of transformation is central to religious ritual – whether it is a Christian Eucharist or a shamanic healing rite (Driver 1998). It can be personal or communal or both. Turner drew on Van Gennep (1908/1960 quoted in Roose-Evans 1994 p. 6) who saw parallel stages in any ritual. This he entitled: 'severance, transition and return'. Severance he associated with leaving everyday life by means of ritual gestures, such as holding hands or lighting candles. In the Transitional or Liminal phase contact was made with the transpersonal; this might take the form of a change of consciousness. The Return phase signalled a coming back to everyday life and the beginning of a new life. It is possible to identify these moments in a musical piece, even when not associated with ritual, and to relate accounts of transformation through experiencing music with this concept. Turner develops it to include the notion of encounter with mind, body and spirit involved. In the world of music therapy, Anthi Agrotou (1993) links religious rituals with her music therapy work, likening it to the Christian Eucharist (Agrotou 1993, p. 191). Csikszentmihaly (1990) saw the connection with flow and religion, especially its association with the arts in its history:

> In fact, flow and religion have been intimately connected since earliest times. Many of the optimal experiences of mankind [sic] have taken place in the context of religious

> rituals. Not only art but drama, music and dance had their origins in what we would now call 'religious' settings: that is, activities aimed at connecting people with supernatural powers and entities … This connection is not surprising, because what we call religion is actually the oldest and most ambitious attempt to create order in consciousness. (Csikszentmihalyi 1990 p. 76)

Ellen Dissanayake confirms this:

> In pre-modern societies, where arts and ceremony are joined, aesthetic empathic means are invariably used to express feelings of unity. (Dissanayake, 1992 p. 4)

In rock and popular musical traditions spirituality often rested in the notion of a universal philosophy, that we explored in Chapter One; it often arose in the West's interest in Hinduism and Zen Buddhism, in particular, seen most clearly in the Beatles' *Within you and without you*, using both a sitar and Indian philosophy. These ideas permeated all the domains of the experience – affecting the Materials (in terms of instruments like the sitar), the Expression (in terms of texts and emotional colouring), Construction (in experimenting with structures from other cultures) and Values (in terms of looking beyond the financial). Steve Turner, in his study *Hungry for Heaven*, argues that the conviction that human beings are made for a transcendent world is 'essential' to the spirit of rock music, drawing on such artists as Bob Dylan, Bob Marley, Yes and U2; this is not only in the words chosen (S. Turner 1998, pp. 8–9, quoted in A. Moore 1999 p. 25), but also in the music itself. Mysticism appeared in music, either in musical content or as an intervention introduced into the process of musicking, particularly in improvising contexts, such as Stockhausen's *From the Seven Days*. Tim Hodgkinson and Ken Hyder undertook research into a method of improvising without predetermined structural constraints; they began to look at the state of mind of the performers, and this led them to investigate shamanism. The most important element they, as Westerners, were able to draw from a shamanic culture was the very close connection made between the natural environment (as we saw in Chapters One and Four) considered as sound, and the inner state of a person's being (Hodgkinson 1996 p. 59).

Understanding Different Ways of Knowing

I have developed the concept of Spirituality/liminality in the musical experience from a variety of sources. I will highlight the aspects relevant to music. We have already seen how Victor Turner drew on an analysis of ritual for the concept of liminality. He saw the liminal space as transpersonal and consciousness-changing. It included the quality of communitas – like the bond that develops between pilgrims in the liminal stages of a pilgrimage, which includes I/Thou awareness. Commmunitas transforms what might be regarded as an individualised state into a 'lostness' in a wider reality that includes the rest of the cosmos. This is often fleeting and transient:

> A moment of insight which was ... like the moment when a tightly-coiled spring begins to release its energy, and then a violent explosion of pure happiness which passed so rapidly that I became conscious of it and identified it only as something that was already fast receding and becoming forgotten. I found myself snatching at it as it slipped away, melting though my fingers. (Cupitt 1998 p. 8)

Ron Best (2014), who, as we have seen earlier, is critical of the word spirituality, sees that there is no other possible word for some experiences – that, although there are affective elements, it cannot be reduced to an emotional experience. He supports this with an experience of dancing with his four year old grand-daughter, which he describes as lacking

> the dimensions of cognition (recognition or understanding) and desire (motivation or goal-directedness) which philosophers tell us are two other components of emotions. (Best 2011 pp. 364–5)

He notes the elements of play (as we saw in Chapter Two) in this experience, describing an:

> unspoken but profound level of *trust* and a *letting-go of self* in order to allow the other to fill my world and bring a sense of wholeness. It was also a *total* experience – physical or bodily – as well as awareness and affect, and there was an element of play or *playfulness*. (Best 2014 p. 18. Author's italics)

Isabel Clarke's (2005, p. 93) notion of the transliminal way of knowing which we explored in Chapter One, has to do with our 'porous' relation to other beings and tolerating paradox. She distinguishes this from the propositional knowing of the everyday. In an echo of Victor Turner, she claims that to access the other way of knowing we cross an internal 'limen' or threshold. Returning to points made by Levinas and Derrida about the need to maintain the Self/Other difference in the encounter, the experience also becomes the discovery of this alterity within the self (Jackson 1998 p. 119). This possibility allows for a loosening of traditional social roles, as happens in carnivalesque traditions (Savery 2007). Csikszentmihaly identifies the strengths and weaknesses of this liminal state, which re-echoes the debates about music and morality in the previous chapter:

> The flow experience, like everything else, is not 'good' in an absolute sense. It is good only in that it has the potential to make life more rich, intense and meaningful; it is good because it increases the strength and complexity of the self. But whether the consequence of any particular instance of flow is good in a larger sense needs to be discussed and evaluated in terms of more inclusive social criteria. (Csikszentmihalyi 1990 p. 70)

This echoes debates in Interlude Two about the need to root the Spiritual in the religious for wellbeing.

We saw in Chapter Two how the psychologists of creativity (Csikszentmihalyi M. and Csikszentmihalyi I.S. 1988, Csikszentmihalyi, 1993, Custodero 2002, 2005a) entered this domain; but contributions to understanding it come from a variety of sources:

- ecstasy, often associated with idea of 'the holy' coming from the religious/spiritual literature (R. Otto 1923, Laski 1961). The roots of the concept lie in a society where religion had a much higher and more universal value. However, it does have a sense of these experiences being 'given' and coming from beyond in some way.
- Trance, coming from anthropological (Rouget 1987), New Age (Collin 1997, Goldman 1992, Stewart 1987) and psychotherapeutic literature

(Inglis 1990).[1] This literature again comes from cultures with a very different frame in which they see the world. However, it does suggest entering a different form of consciousness from everyday living for the purposes of healing.

- mysticism, coming from religious traditions, especially Christianity (Underhill in Rankin 2008 pp. 52–3). This comes from a literature presupposing a Christian world-frame, but it has a sense of going beyond creedal statements and moral codes to the 'heart of the matter' and also has a deep sense of embracing unknowing. This is sometimes called the apophatic experience – beyond the realm of ordinary perception into a discovery of what the divine is not.
- peak experiences (Maslow 1967), which Maslow saw as being as necessary to human beings as food and shelter and as characterised by many of the attributes already listed in Chapter Two. However, its origin lies within the human being rather than the beyond in some way.
- the religious experience (Rankin 2005), which has variously been defined and treated by a variety of writers who see it as situated within a religious frame.
- the spiritual experience of children (Hay and Nye 1998, Erricker, Erricker, Ota, Sullivan and Fletcher 1997, Hay 1982, E. Robinson 1977), where the stress is placed on identity construction and meaning-making.
- intuition (Noddings and Shore 1984).
- the Greek agora (Yeorgouli-Bourzoucos 2004), a concept based on the old Greek market place where ideas were freely exchanged and debated.
- studies in consciousness (Lancaster 2004), including Midrashic logic.
- creative imagination (Corbin 1998), which draws on Sufi sources.

1 Brian Inglis sees an evolutionary purpose in trance:
The apparent diversity ceases to be puzzling when trance is set in its evolutionary context. Animal life in general is spent in trance; but there are intimations of mind in territories, and in birds in flocks, which suggest the development of something more purposeful than simple natural selection could have been expected to provide. It is as if evolution had found a way to introduce a 'pull', enabling species to perform in more sophisticated ways than, examining their limitations, we would think possible. (Inglis 1990, pp. 267–9).

- symmetric logic (Matte Blanco set out in Bomford 2005), which embraces paradox.
- liminality or liminoid (V. Turner 1969, 1974), which is rooted in religious ritual and is be found in religionless contexts in contemporary society.[2]

Elements of all of these are to be found in what people call the spiritual experience in various cultures and religious traditions. Although they can be defined distinctively, the different terms may represent staging points along what is really a continuum, describing a state that is more or less differentiated from everyday knowing.

The Problematisation of the Metaphysical

Academic postmodernism, with its mistrust of metanarratives, attempted the marginalisation of this strand, already started by post-Enlightenment suspicion of anything concerned with magic or belief. There is a real need for academe to reconsider its position with regard to the Metaphysical. Debates about the domain of the liminal experience in the arts are facilitating this process, especially as people often require that the arts take them into this other way of knowing (Jackson 1998).

It is theorists who, in general, have had problems with the area, and composers', listeners' and performers' accounts of the musical experience regularly include it. Handel, for example, recounts experiences of angelic figures surrounding him, during the composition of *Messiah*. John Tavener talks about this domain of his own musical experience:

> I suppose, actually, thinking back to when I first heard a piece of music performed by a professional orchestra, I was aware of a dimension that was 'other worldly', and

2 Turner actually uses the terms liminal and liminoid to distinguish between the intentional creating of these spaces through acts like ritual (liminal) and places where the experience happens in marginal spaces (liminoid). In this book I have chosen to use the words liminal and liminality throughout.

> which actually surprised me. Where that 'other worldliness' comes from is a mystery. (Tavener 2005)

He rediscovers this dimension when composing:

> I'm not sure who the angel is. I'm just aware of another dimension when I'm writing music. I always say that the imagination originally was given to man [sic] in order to imagine God, and those atheists who say, you know, that God is just a product of man's imagination are actually speaking the total truth, because that is what God is a product of. We were given the imagination in order to imagine Him, and we spend our lives, some of us, imagining God. Of course, the imagination, down the years, becomes corrupted, and the imagination is used for all sorts of other less important things, but I believe primordially in the beginning, as it were, the imagination was given to us to imagine God. (Tavener 2005)

Developments that we explored in Chapter One, such as anthroposophy, became fascinated with altered states of consciousness. Mediaeval visionaries, such as Hildegard of Bingen and Julian of Norwich, have been rediscovered and there is a rethinking of mental health and the religious experience (I. Clarke 2008). Notions of the self were developed that include spiritual elements, as in Rudolf Steiner's concept of physical, etheric, mental and astral bodies. A case study on the effect of Wagner's *Valkyrie* on a young woman uses this frame to explain the spirituality:

> Before the performance began, she seemed rather listless and indifferent. The health aura showed signs of delicate health. The astral body was full of the usual colors, with signs here and there of irritation ... Her mental body was replete with thought-forms of music, [she had been studying the score before the performance] ... Before the first act was half over, a great difference in her health aura was noticed; it now glowed and scintillated with new vigor ... I noticed some streams of light protruding from her mental body like long, waving tentacles: on the end of each was a spinning thought-form similar to a vortex-like whirlpool in water, caused by suction As some familiar motif floated up from the general vibrations of the music ... these tentacles in her mental body sucked the vibrations into themselves in large proportions ... The thought-forms already there, from the previous study of music, were strengthened, until they filled the body with beautiful light. It seemed to relate her to the deep pulsations of the Law of Rhythm in all nature, and the experience made the separating walls (the vibratory difference) between the lower and higher mental bodies to disappear and the ego was able to approach nearer to the personality and

> to impress it with loftiest ideas ... What was the effect on the astral body? ... It was not very long ere it was great boiling mass of beautiful color – a mighty many-hued bird beating its wings against a cramped cage to escape ... It found its way of least resistance and rushed through that – into tears ... The young girl wept violently for a while, until some of the pressure of it was exhausted, then she grew calm and for the rest of the evening was benefited – in fact, she was a 'new being' when she left the hall. (Heline 1964 pp. 136–7)

The use of such frames did not find a ready acceptance in academic circles; but these ideas lived on in some areas of psychoanalytical thought. Robert Assagioli, founder of psychosynthesis, in describing the bringing together of areas of the personality used the language of transcendence:

> Because of the multiplicity of human nature, of the existence in us of various and often conflicting subpersonalities, joy at some level can coexist with suffering at other levels ... The realisation of the self, or more of *being a self* ... gives a sense of freedom, of power, of mastery, which is profoundly joyous. The mystics of all times and places have realised and expressed the joy and bliss which are inherent in the union of the individual will and the Universal Will. (Assagioli 1974'94 p. 201. Author's italics)

Here we see how powerful intrapersonal interactions can trigger the spiritual experience.

The Nature of the Experience

We have already identified various strands in the spiritual in Chapter One. The spiritual experience can be contentless and only given content either by the musicker after the event, as in the opening poem. It may be in a religious context but have no religious content, as in this account of an experience in 'a ramshackle building with a cross on top':

> Somehow the singing wore down all the boundaries and distinctions that kept me so isolated. Sitting there, standing with them to sing, sometimes so shaky ... that I felt like I might tip over. I felt bigger than myself, like I was being taken care of, tricked into coming back to life. (Lamont 1999 pp. 47–8)

It can also be distinct from the religionful narratives in the domain of Values.[3] John Sloboda (2000) looks at a variety of responses to music. He refers to several of the domains we have already examined, including the personal associations of the music and the analytical approach, recognising musical patterns. He asks people to be aware of the community being created through the music and the musicker's part in it. He sets at the pinnacle what he calls 'non-judgemental contemplation', which means responding on a moment to moment basis to the unfolding music – a real process approach. He prizes this above the other ways; but what I am saying here is that these experiences of the other domain are strands that will lead to this spiritual place. They are part of the whole experience.

The phenomenographic map of the domains enable us to examine a musical experience through different lenses; the focus of the experiencer at any given point may vary:

> If a particular way of experiencing a phenomenon is seen in relation to particular features of awareness, then the varying ways of experiencing that phenomenon should be seen in relation to the particular features of diverse awarenesses ... This is a shift from individual awareness that varies as to focus and simultaneous awareness of aspects of a phenomenon to a collective awareness in which all such variations can be seen. (Marton and Booth 1997 pp. 108–9)

What accounts by a variety of musickers – composers, listeners and performers – show is how the domains interact within the experience:

> The variation between different ways of experiencing something, then, derives from the fact that different aspects of different parts of the whole may or may not be discerned and be objects of focal awareness simultaneously ... The unit of phenomenographic research ... is an internal relationship between the experiencer and the experienced. (Marton and Booth 1997 pp. 112–13)

But it can start or be concentrated in one of the domains. This can happen gradually as this account of a listener's first experience of sitar music shows:

3 In the history of the visionary experiences of the Virgin Mary, the initial encounter is with a flash of blue or a beautiful female figure; it is only later shaped by the authorities into the Virgin Mary as a religious narrative is overlaid onto the mystical experience.

> For the first twenty-five minutes I was totally unaware of any subtlety ... whilst wondering what, if anything, was supposed to happen during the recital. What did happen was magic! After some time, insidiously the music began to reach me. Little by little, my mind all my senses it seemed- were becoming transfixed. Once held by these soft but powerful sounds, I was irresistibly drawn into a new world of musical shapes and colours. It almost felt as if the musicians were playing me rather than their instruments, and soon, I, too, was clapping and gasping with everyone else ... I was unaware of time, unaware of anything other than the music. Then it was over. But it was, I am sure, the beginning of a profound admiration that I shall always have for an art form that has been until recently totally alien to me. (Dunmore 1983 pp. 20–1)

We see here how the Materials of the sound and the 'shapes' of the Construction gradually begin to be integrated into his/her own being so that the experiencer and the experienced become fused. The model I have developed attempts to portray this, bearing in mind the fact that any model can only contain some aspects of truth.

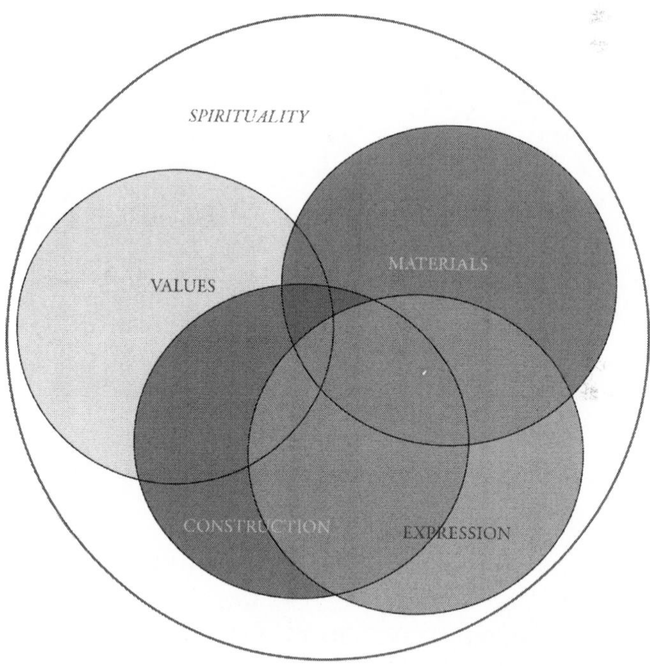

Figure Eleven: The Spiritual Experience in Music (Boyce-Tillman 2006a and c).

The converse of this is that where there is too much dissatisfaction with one domain, or between two domains, that means there is no spiritual experience at all. For example, while in Greece, I encountered a group of Greek Orthodox worshippers who were deeply racist and homophobic. When I turned on the television on the Sunday morning, there was Greek Orthodox chanting. I had, in the past, found this a wonderful experience; but now the domain of Values had been disrupted and the music could no longer transport me to the Other World, because it was now associated with Values to which I could not subscribe.

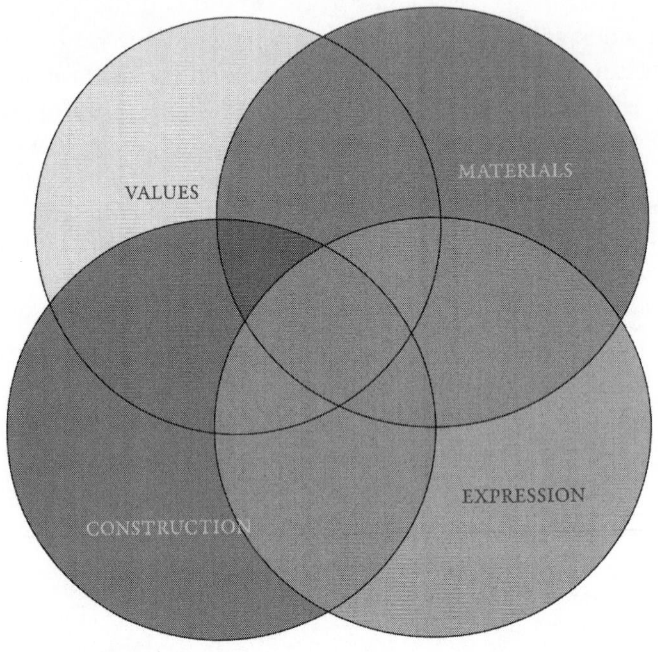

Figure Twelve: The Absence of the Spiritual Experience (Boyce-Tillman 2005).

In this account, we encounter the role meta-awareness plays in the quality of the experience. So this meta-awareness, or reflection, which expands our knowledge about the music, can disrupt a piece that previously could be relied upon to produce a spiritual experience. It makes the case for musical experiences unmediated by words (Blake 1997) which is virtually impossible in a world filled with such phenomena as programme notes, tweets and blogs. On the other hand, there is in the meta-awareness of the social/cultural/life-history dimension the possibility of the expansion of our wider meta-awareness, as we saw in the description above of the encounter with the sitar piece. It will enable us to see when we meet a new piece of music what is 'other' to us – where the problematic domains for us lie. So, for example, we may have to work at the nasal timbres associated with the singing style of Beijing opera in order to enter into it more fully, or accustom ourselves to the volume levels associated with some popular musics (both the dilemmas sitting in the domain of Materials).

The area of the effectiveness of the domain of Values is at least partly dependent on the context of the musicking experience which will set up various associational processes that resonate with all the domains of the experience. Further reflective processes will make these links stronger so that a certain set of associational patterns will be linked with that piece or the style of that piece. They can similarly be reinforced by these associations as in the case of a feminist's relationship to pieces by women. If these relational associations are benign to the experiencer then the level of absorption into the experience will be increased.

Differing Intensities

The model can also show us how the different intensities within the experience arise. The experience may well start with a close relationship between two of the domains. The more the domains resonate together within the experiencer, the more intense the experience is likely to be. Dewey suggests that it is in the intensity that the spirituality lies, he describe an experience that is 'so intense that it is justly termed religious' (1929 p. 188). Other examples show how the degree of intensity might be affected by the way the various domains interact within an experience. Here is an example which might be a parent watching a child playing their first piece. The grasp of Materials on the part of the child may be minimal, but the powerful interaction between the domain of Values and the other domains initiates the entrance into the Spiritual domain, which may include their hopes and dreams for their child:

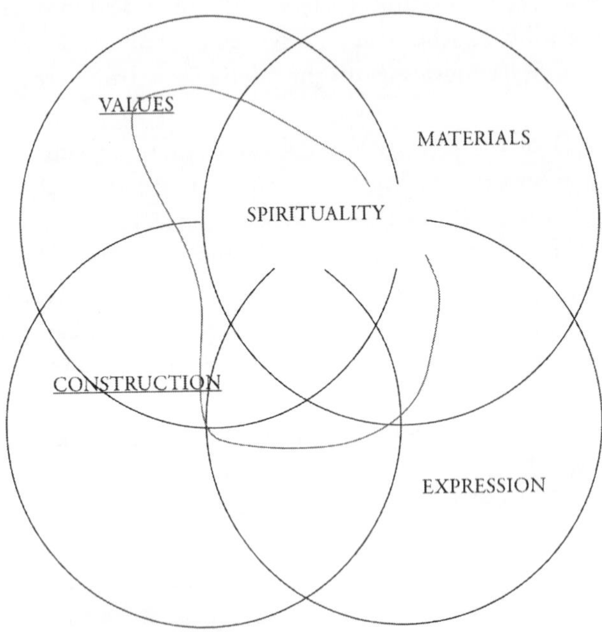

Figure Thirteen: A Child's Concert (Boyce-Tillman 2005).

Here is an example of 'they are playing our tune' where a tune with powerful emotional value is being experienced. Expression and Values come together powerfully even though the domain of Construction may be simple.

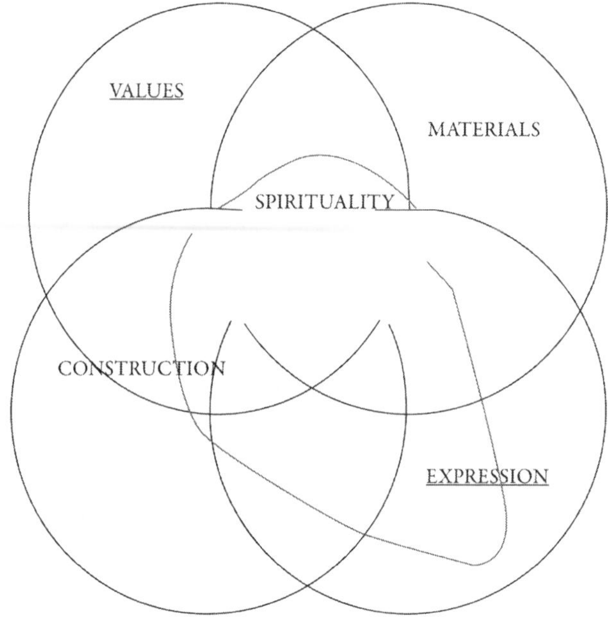

Figure Fourteen: 'They are playing our tune' (Boyce-Tillman 2005).

Figure Fifteen is an example of pattern created by a piece from the Classical tradition, such as Beethoven or Mozart where the domain of Construction interacts powerfully with Expression and the experiencer is able to rest peacefully in a familiar landscape.

Figure Sixteen is an example of a piece where the experiencer is taken up with the technical prowess of the performer which gradually comes together with the other domains.

The Spiritual domain of the experience can be entered through the three activities central to music making:

- Performing/improvising (Gonski 1999)
- Composing/improvising (Paterson and Odam 2000, Downes 1998)
- Listening in audience (Moody 1999)

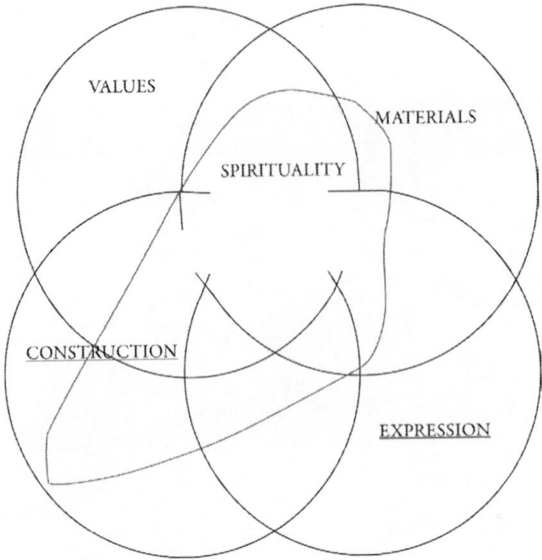

Figure Fifteen: A Classical Concert (Boyce-Tillman 2005).

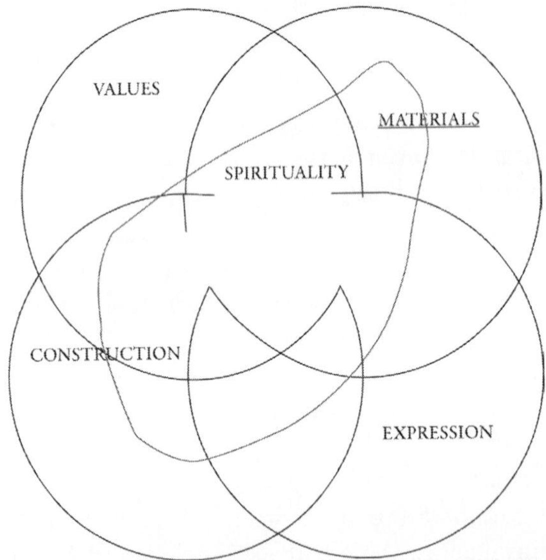

Figure Sixteen: A Virtuoso Performance (Boyce-Tillman 2005).

The starting point of the experience may tend to be different in the three different activities, because the process of the experiencer is different. So a performer may be acutely aware of the domains of Materials and Expression, whereas the composer those of Construction and Expression and the listener-in-audience may be taken up with Expression and Values. The other domains will necessarily come into play later.

In the Prelude, I showed how I followed up one performance of *The Healing of the Earth* (Boyce-Tillman 2001c) by semi-structured interviews with children, teachers and parents. The focus of various people was in different domains. For some, it lay in the Values domain, as we saw in the Prelude with the boy who likened it to peace on earth. For a head teacher, it was a combination of Value and Expression, as she concentrated on the Interpersonal strand:

> It improved the children's co-operative skills. I saw them supporting one another and encouraging other schools in their work. This is unusual for our children whose poverty often makes them quite self-centred.

Teachers often commented the improvement on their pupils' ability to use music for expressive purposes, concentrating on the Intrapersonal:

> It encouraged me to encourage children to make their own music and value their pieces.

Also in the domain of Expression is the Intrapersonal notion of the development of personal qualities. Parents often concentrated on their children's confidence and self-esteem (bearing in mind many of the schools in the project were in geographical areas regarded as deprived):

> It improved my child's self-confidence and assurance. She is always singing the songs around the house.

A ten-year-old girl commented on the Spiritual domain:

> There was this power there. I don't know what it was. It was simply a power.

So here we can see how the attention of the experiencer may circulate around the domains during the experience, which in the end fuse.

Characteristics of the Experience

So we can see how the elements that we identified in Chapter One appear here in relation to the music experience:

METAPHYSICAL – Encountering a mystery that is beyond

NARRATIVE – The inclusion within it of religious stories, often coloured by a particular culture

INTRAPERSONAL – A sense of empowerment, bliss or realisation, which may be fleeting and evanescent and frees up the intuitive faculties, so that everything feels charged with meaning and a sense of seeing/understanding, which is transformative of the deepest level of being

INTERPERSONAL – A profound empathy with other human beings who may not actually be present at the performance itself – but may be separated geographically or historically – which can transform antagonisms into a desire to care or bless

INTERGAIAN – A sense of oneness and deep relationship with the other-than-human world

EXTRAPERSONAL – A profound communitas – profound unity with other beings, people and the cosmos which leads to a desire for peaceful relationship and a healing of fragmentation at a global level

Music and Mindfulness: A Case Study in Spirituality

We have already seen that one of the strategies that people today are using in their search for spirituality is a practice called mindfulness; it has great popularity today with its sense of a non-judgemental resting in the present.[4] It is often defined as 'paying attention on purpose moment by moment without judging' (Kabat-Zinn 1990). Some descriptions of the musical experience bear remarkable similarities to the claims of mindfulness:

> Contemporary culture increasingly suffers from problems of attention, over-stimulation, and stress, and a variety of personal and social discontents generated by deceptive body images. This book [Shusterman's Body Consciousness] argues that improved body consciousness can relieve these problems and enhance one's knowledge, performance, and pleasure.[5]

We have already seen how in the aesthetic of Dewey and his successors, Beauty is related to everyday beauty like the archer hitting the mark. This makes art an active phenomenon:

> [Experience] signifies active and alert commerce with the world; at its height it signifies complete interpenetration of self and the world of objects and events. (Dewey 1987 p. 25)

So experience is not merely an individualised psychological experience but rather involves active participation in the world instead of being concerned simply with private feelings and sensations confined in an inner world. Therefore art can become transformative and the basis for new possibilities for engaging with the everyday world.

We have seen how all music consists of organisations of concrete Materials drawn both from the environment and the human body. Kimberley Powell in an ethnographic study of Japanese American taiko drumming describes how somaesthetic training occurs and is connected to aesthetic/transformative experience, ethics and politics (Powell 2004, 2005):

> As I strike the drum in front of me [a colleague Fuong] – a former wine barrel with its two ends replaced by animal skins and large tacks, arms aching from nearly an hour of repetitive strikes, adjusting the hand and wrist, elbow and shoulder. I have worked

4 <http://www.cbt-partnership.org/mindfulness/> accessed June 11 2012.

5 <http://www.cambridge.org/gb/knowledge/isbn/item1162720/?site_locale=en_GB> Accessed June 1st 2012.

> muscle and bone through countless sit-ups, crunches, and a timed run required of us in the first hour of our rehearsal, and indeed before all of our rehearsals.' Becoming 'strong and embodied'- by which I now interpret [her] to mean a powerful physical presence, filling space with movement – exudes a presence larger than corporeality. I try to move beyond the physical pain by envisioning myself as fluid, moving beyond my own flesh and encompassing the drum. (Powell 2010 no pages)

Such an experience is part of a performer's experience of musicking and has powerful similarities with mindfulness. It is also approached mindfully with a focus totally on the instrument and its relationship with the body and the context. She links this with social justice:

> It is worth considering the transformative power of musical experience and its ability to create alternative realities and facilitate social justice ... As the disciplined somatic training required of a practice becomes part of one's skills and knowledge base, these practices may inspire new ideas for ways to make such practices more authentic to the expression of identity. (Powell 2010 no pages)

Accounts in the Alister Hardy Archive (RERC) link meditation with the concentration of the concert pianist:

> I think I should say that some time before this first [spiritual] experience my wife and I had belonged to the Ramakrishna Vedanta Centre in London. We each had a mantra for meditation and although, in my case, I am sure that meditated badly and with mixed motives (I was certainly seeking 'an experience'). I think that the hours of meditation combined with another sort of concentrated meditation in my own work as a concert pianist may have produced an experience which I was certainly not mature enough to receive and use.[6]

In the domain of the Spiritual, mindfulness develops the ability to pay deliberate attention to experience from moment to moment, tuning into the mind's activity, which has echoes of the descriptions of time in the orate traditions that we saw in Chapter Six. The sensitive interplay of an improvising group where expressive musical motifs are explored between performers, can draw others into their world. A solo improviser may also

6 1970 from the RERC.

draw people into that world by meditating on his or her own pieces.[7] There are, on the market, a number of recordings designed for use in meditation, which often contain a great of repetition and have an improvisatory character. The spiritual experience in music in its process has much in common with notions in mindfulness; some people can get close to the state of mindfulness by means of music, particularly music involving some degree of repetition in its Construction, and where its texture is thin enough to allow for the thoughts of the experiencer.

Summary

I have suggested that there is a potential domain of spirituality/liminality within the experience of music. This happens when all the domains come together, so that the experienced and experienced become fused. I have suggested that:

- It can be approached through all music-making activities
- The domain, in which the experience is initially triggered, may vary
- It can be related to a universal spiritual frame, but is often linked with a particular traditions culturally
- The aesthetic may be a secular term for this domain of the musical experience.
- Its social nature causes it to be identified as closely linked to all the strands in spirituality outlined in Chapter One, such as ethics, identity, personal and social development

7 I am grateful to Malcolm Floyd for this insight. It also links to my very simple pieces designed for meditation. These pieces are often very simple in texture in particular to allow for this process of mindfulness.

- The unitive nature of the experience leads to feeling connected with something beyond and outside the self – the wider community of human beings and/or the natural world and/or spiritual beings
- The spiritual experience is born of a working relationship between the experiencer and the experienced

So the spiritual experience involves the move from everyday or propositional knowing into a different time/space dimension, where everything is connected and paradox embraced. In relation to the model set out in this book, this involves the experiencer establishing a relationship with all the domains in the music. It is an experience that can vary in intensity and start and move around the various domains. It is a complex experience that brings together mind, body, spirit and heart, thereby counterbalancing the fragmented nature of the contemporary world. It therefore has significant potential for transformation within and beyond the person, and in relationships with the environment, mystery and other cultures.

CHAPTER NINE

The Extrapersonal Dimension: The Use of the Musical Liminality as a Space for Peace and Justice Making

Introduction

As we saw in Chapter One, one of the central purposes of music is community building. In general that has been done within a cultural frame – such as Western classical music – or even within a particular subculture such as religious traditions or folk clubs. By reading authors like Levinas and Derrida I became taken up with how our culture handles encounters with the Other and how the standard reaction is to make the Other like us. This is, of course, particularly true of those religions with an internal drive to conversion like Islam and Christianity. The chief rabbi's book *The Dignity of Difference* (J. Sacks 2002) affirmed my desire to develop frames in which difference was honoured and celebrated. I saw the possibilities in music for this. If the terrorist attacks epitomised by the Twin Towers disaster have taught the secularised view of liberal democracy anything, it is that religion is an intense driver of human action. Since 9/11 there has been a renewed interest in the urgency of interfaith dialogue for the establishment of world peace. This requires the acceptance of the validity of anOther's point of view in the area of faith, an area particularly problematic for those faiths that lay claim to a monopoly of absolute truth. Religion cannot be left out of debates concerning, what Huntington (1996) called, the clash of civilisations. It needs to be included in the analysis of the problem so that it can be included in the strategies for the solution. The questions for this chapter are: can the spiritual possibilities of the musical experience operate across cultures? How might it do this to create peace between cultures? This chapter will examine a series of case studies examining various attempts at this; it uses the model developed in this book to analyse them, concentrating particularly on the interface of the domain of Values with the other domains of the experience.

The History

Experiments in cultural mixing were occurring regularly in the twentieth century and worked at every level. In the domain of Materials, instruments had already been regularly imported from other cultures into the Western classical tradition, such as the use of Turkish percussion in the Classical period and Debussy's entrancement with the gamelan. Expression from other cultures was often used, as 'exotic' stories and poetry were used by Western composers like Gustav Holst in his opera *Savitri*. Structural fusions in the domain of Construction were less often attempted and little attention was given to Value systems because, as we saw above, these were not regarded as relevant to music. Spiritually they often drew on a notion of a universal philosophy expressed in music – the common core examined in Chapter One.

Case Study One: The Meeting of Christianity with Indigenous Traditions

The notion of establishing a better relationship with indigenous traditions was explored by Christian traditions, from the mid twentieth century onwards. Christianity embarked on a deliberate cross-cultural approach in its work, in what was once called 'The Mission field'. It started to become aware of how, along with its belief system, it had exported Western culture. The first efforts to right this aspect of colonialism were in the area of music and resulted in such popular works as *Missa Criolla* and *Missa Luba*. These attempted to use the vernacular of the indigenous traditions within Christian worship.

It was a deliberate attempt at peace making with the indigenous culture. If we analyse the way it was done, in terms of Materials these pieces often used instruments from the indigenous tradition. Expressively they represented a merger of the expressive character of the indigenous style and the Christian Mass. The forms used in the Construction were often taken from the indigenous culture and orate techniques were brought in association with texts that had been set in notated forms for much of their history. These pieces had sufficient value in the West to support tours by groups and successful recordings; but because of the texts, they reflected the Value systems of Christianity. They represented a pagan and a Christian culture fused; many claims were made that these fusions were spiritual but not necessarily 'religious'. Such claims were based on the peace-making, cross cultural intentions of their originators.

Case Study Two: The Use of Recorded Material in Western Composition

This case study is an extension of the Christian fusions identified above. African Sanctus was the work of the composer/explorer David Fanshawe, who was given a Winston Churchill scholarship in 1972 to collect the tapes that form the African elements in the piece. It too had the intention of merging Western with African traditions and is regarded by many as a deeply spiritual experience, often because of this intention:

> *African Sanctus* attempts to fuse different peoples and their music into a tightly knit unit of energy and praise. It reflects the changing moods of music today and I hope moves with the times, for we are all living and sharing life together on a very small planet. (Fanshawe 1963 Sleeve notes)

In the domain of Materials the work uses tapes of African singers and players alongside rock and classical instruments from the West. The Expression mixes the characters of the various African traditions, the Christian Mass with that of opera and commercial music. The Construction reflects the interplay of the African tapes with the Western forms of David Fanshawe's own tradition. They are fitted into Western shapes and structures. Although initially I was excited by the possibilities of the piece, meta-awareness in the domain of Values intruded on the experience. The recipient of the royalties was David Fanshawe. Although it is clear from his book (Fanshawe 1975) that the African performers gave permission for their pieces to be used and that he treated them with respect and friendship, there is no record of any of the royalties being given to them. This is in marked contrast to systems being developed by ethnomusicologists, especially those associated with the Smithsonian in the US. Indeed Western notions of ownership of music are in direct conflict with the collective ownership that characterises such notions in the societies from which he collected the material. There is a notion of Spirituality in the composer's intentions, which relate to praise of the 'One God'. This is very much within the frame of monotheistic religions, which would have shaped Fanshawe's own thinking, also drawing on the notion of the common core, that we explored in Chapter One.

The work clearly fits into a longstanding Western colonial tradition; but the use of tape for such borrowings from orate traditions is a new phenomenon and different from the integration into one's personal style of elements of other cultures. For many audiences and performers, however, Fanshawe's work has represented a valid fusing of various traditions in the interests of world peace. Whether, however, in the domain of Values it represents a valuing of both traditions equally is highly debatable and this presents considerable ethical problems. The capacity to collect the Material on tape sets it apart from *Missa Luba* which required a live tour for the performers or Debussy's use of the gamelan tradition which was integrated into the tradition by means of the use of the scales that underpinned the tradition. Although the intentions of the composer have led many into the Spiritual domain, there are considerable ethical problems in the domain of Values.

Case Study Three: An Intercultural Festival and Beyond

This is a personal account of my first foray into the area of interfaith dialogue which is given much more detail in *Stories of the Great Turning* (Boyce-Tillman 2013b). One day in 1986 everything was in place for a celebration of diversity on South London. A huge diversity of people and cultures were involved including tap dancers, Ruposhi Bangla, the local Indian jeweller, carnival costumes from the Commonwealth Institute, the harpsichordist with his Baroque recital and the marching Scout band. But what could be done on the Sunday to celebrate the spiritual dimension of the neighbourhood? We had many Christian places of worship, embryonic mosques were established in several houses, and the representation of many other faiths was also growing.

And so my interfaith vision was born. Some Christians had encountered the essentially Hindu practices of Transcendental Meditation or yoga. But interfaith dialogue was largely limited to hearing what different traditions had to say about death, suffering or partnerships. The notion that a multi-faith group might celebrate together with all their differences – but also some similarities – was seldom considered. Most interfaith dialogue at that time was not between ordinary people but just the leaders – the Dalai Lama meeting the Archbishop of Canterbury in the highly ceremonial environment of Westminster Abbey. My vision was different – that people of different traditions living near one another could offer a spiritual dimension to a neighbourhood festival.

We trod uneasily on an unknown landscape – aware of sensitive images of crusading armies. Some chose not to join. It was the beginning of a long journey of giving dignity to difference. My interfaith dialogue began at the school gate, with the mothers whom I met there each day – Muslims, Hindus, Sikhs and Christians of various denominations. I started my journey by visiting the various faiths in their places of worship.

Gradually, a diverse and informal group gathered together and took responsibility for planning an interfaith event. We decided that peace was an appropriate theme for our first attempt at a sharing since this was at the heart our motivations for embarking on this journey. The sharing took place in the Anglican Church in which I was deeply involved and included children from the local primary school in which I taught. Piano, organ and guitar were used to accompany the sharing. Later in the story of the interfaith event there were many debates about using the organ, which was regarded by some as a Christian instrument, showing how each tradition has defined itself by the musical instruments it defines as sacred. In the end we chose to sing unaccompanied.

We planned the event with separate sections for each faith, sharing little except some songs familiar to the school children, such as *When I needed a neighbour* and the Jewish round *Shalom* (which has remained in every sharing since). All these shared songs were carefully discussed in the group; but I was aware that they were all from Western traditions. The Christian contribution included a Bible reading and a wonderful tambourine dance from the Salvation Army; the Quakers read the peace declaration. The Jews chose to bring with them one of their very precious scrolls, which was ceremoniously and movingly opened – a risky and generous act. The Hindus kindled the sacred fire – the *arti* – with ceremonial purifying of the space before the event and covering it with clean cloths. The Sikhs sang a hymn about unity between the faiths, accompanied by harmonium and tabla. The Buddhist offered something of Zen meditation. The Muslims offered girls singing a song about being a light in the world and the boys explained the call to prayer. The sectional layout meant that the event took some time; but it held people's attention, because much of it was colourful and involved movement and singing. The arts proved a valuable way of dialogue. We trod gently, aware of how close we were to people's hearts and core identities. It was a first encounter; and for many present what was offered was strange and exotic. It was an example of Fraternal Dialogue (Pire 1967), in which different faiths worked together for a shared end discussing what they did or did not share along the way.

Over the years we encountered challenges that needed careful exploration, often in the area of the arts. From the Sikh *gurdwara* came young women doing harvest dances. Were these a religious or a cultural tradition? In some of the faith traditions the culture and the religion were inextricably entwined, especially when there were influxes of migrant groups. The places of worship were becoming important centres for the sharing of the artistic cultures of the lands they had left. This led us to discuss issues of women's bodies and what they are allowed to do artistically and religiously. Some traditions found dance in our interfaith act of sharing inappropriate. Some found the costumes they wore unacceptable. Sometimes the objections were between faiths. What one faith found acceptable, another one did not. It led to issues around how the faiths each saw the body in their spirituality. The area of women's spiritual authority followed quite quickly here. This was interesting, as many of the group were women. It became clear that the women in the faiths did not always share the views of their male leaders. We came to no conclusions; but the issues were well aired. The interaction of faith, culture and the arts was a continual backdrop to our creation of an interfaith event, which many have said have taken them into that liminal space – where paradoxes are held together and communitas between people of different backgrounds is established, often expressed by singing and holding ribbons joining them all together.

Case Study Four: Light the Candles and the European Intercultural Project

The first interfaith sharing enabled me to develop the anthology I was developing for schools entitled *Light the Candles* (Tillman 1987a). This was the sixth of a series of anthologies I produced for schools; but I also had the notion that it would be a useful collection for interfaith celebrations. I had contact with a number of people who were collecting material in culturally diverse communities around the UK and I drew on my knowledge of Christian material from my own religious experience and pagan songs from my knowledge of the folk tradition. It was a bold venture and I was in an area where I was inexperienced. There were many associated problems like transcriptions from different languages by different people but most of all was the problem of crossing cultural boundaries that had once been crossed by imperialist ventures. 'Are you going to take our music like you took our land?' said one of my most helpful participants. Suddenly I was confronted with the Value systems of imperial ventures like ethnomusicology. Although all the songs were contextualised and contributors acknowledged, the question still haunts me.

A further project in this area was one initiated by the European Union, collecting material from migrant workers; it was based at the London University Institute of Education. This was exciting, as it was done orally on cassette tape with associated descriptions. This was intended for use in schools, but interestingly we never found a format for effective dissemination. Both of these projects gave me insight into the dilemmas of cross cultural work and also a source of material, that I was to use in later pieces.

These two projects showed how the domain of Materials is handled in dissemination differently in orate and notated traditions – notated book and recorded material. The literate book was restricted in the way in which Materials could be represented, as many essentially orate traditions had to be accommodated within the demands of Western classical notation. Again Expression was much more apparent in orate form than on a flat notated page, although in my descriptions I tried to indicate the character of the original source. Texts from different languages again are better represented in orate form and the dilemma of transcription is not present in orate versions. Issues of Construction were problematic in the notated form, when pieces and sections of pieces were often repeated in their orate form, often as their context demanded. We have already seen the dilemmas in the domain of Values, when putting music together from other cultures under a single editorship. As such, the issues raised by *African Sanctus* in the domain of Values rear their heads again.

Case Study Five: Paul Simon and Graceland

In the area of popular musics the fusions have sometimes been linked with a deliberate concern for justice. Paul Simon, in his recording *Graceland*, in the more folk/popular tradition had the explicit intention of justice within the context of apartheid in South Africa. Here again African performers were used alongside the resources of Western popular music. The texts were newly constructed and they had more of the character of Western commercial traditions which within themselves have elements of the African traditions that passed via jazz into Western popular music. The fusion in the domain of Construction is therefore not so complex as in Western classical works whose roots are more from the classical Graeco-Roman traditions. Paul Simon describes how working with the African musicians affected the structure of his songs:

> In the process of working, I discovered ways of turning the form around, from constantly listening to the way African guitarists and the bass players were altering what they were playing from verse to verse. (Simon 1994 p. 11)

Some of the royalties were channelled back to the South African Musicians Alliance so the understanding of Values was shared. The recording certainly helped the valuing in the West of the lesser-known traditions of South Africa.

Case Study Six: The Meeting of Orality and Literacy

In Figure Nine showing subjugated value systems, we saw how Western societies value products above process (often using unethical processes in the interest of cheaper products). Indigenous traditions are often orate (with no notation systems). This led to different structural systems. The discovery of the evolving nature of the musical structure of traditional musics has been an important contribution that traditional musics have made to Western classical and popular music. Judith Vander, working on the songs of the Shoshone Indians, saw the songs as characterised by inexact repetition (Vander 1986). Terry Riley, father of minimalism, describes his meeting with more improvisatory musical structures, which he found through his contact with Eastern musics:

> In the last ten years I have given up the traditional role of the composer in favour of self-interpretative improvisation. (Riley 1978 p. 144)

The Construction of his music in this way has led to many people being drawn into a meditative mood by his work. His work *Morning River* for Francis Silkstone's (1977) multicultural ensemble *Sounds Bazaar* illustrates this structure clearly (Riley 1999). At the level of Materials it uses voice with a singer who often uses vocalisation of various kinds, cello, keyboard and surbahar. The form unfolds freely and meditatively which is the intention of much of Riley's work. Small motifs unfold slowly in a notated form that resembles improvisation. It uses scales from other traditions particularly on the surbahar. Notions of a universal spirituality underpin much of Riley's thinking, and the texts are deliberately about questions concerning meaning, rather than the giving of definitive answers. This case study shows a genuine attempt at fusing Value systems, which leads to changes in systems of Construction and has drawn musickers into the domain of the Spiritual.

Case Study Seven – The Development of WOMAD

One high-profile example of intercultural work in music is Peter Gabriel's development of the Realworld Music label and the WOMAD (World of Music, Arts and dance) organisation specifically to bring musicians from all over the world together. Started in 1980, it had its first festival in 1982:

> We aim to excite, to inform, and to create awareness of the worth and potential of a multicultural society. (Gabriel 2000)

By bringing so many different musicians together, exciting fusion pieces occurred. These were released on the Realworld label and issues of Value are carefully addressed. The work of Peter Gabriel and WOMAD represents a real attempt at methods of fusion that reflect ethical Value systems. This is achieved by doing it with live representatives of the various cultures and remunerating them for their work. The WOMAD festival has become a regular event for many justice seekers who are drawn into a liminal space by the variety musicking at the festival. It has inspired their own work in the area of reconciliation and peace-making.

Case Study Eight: World Musics at King Alfred's – An Experiment in Course Design[1]

The Field of World Musics at King Alfred's College, Winchester (now the University of Winchester) was initiated in 1993 and ended in 1999. The field was developed in response to reflection on the Value systems that

1 Based on Boyce-Tillman and Floyd (2003)

have underpinned the academic study of music; it was concerned with reconsidering relationships between culture and hierarchies, including power relationships within and between cultures and breaking distinctions between 'high' and 'low' culture. It was based on theorists, some of which have already been discussed:

- The deconstruction of the musical canon (Goehr 1992)
- Work on the gendered nature of the European tradition (Green 1997, McClary 1991, Belenky 1986)
- A rebalancing of traditional musicological concentration on the more abstract aspects of the musical experience (Langer 1953, Meyer 1956, 1967)
- A reconsideration of the role of popular musics (Middleton 1990)
- An examination of the relation of music to the surrounding society (Blacking 1976, Myers 1992, Shepherd 1991, Shepherd and Wicke 1997)
- The development of a concern for pluralism in the context of globalisation (Braidotti 1994)

The starting point for the course team was that study of the music of a culture can be a valuable route into knowledge and understanding of that culture as a whole, and a powerful antidote to prejudice and stereotyping; in Norway, Kjell Skyllstad set up the Resonant Community Project in schools with similar aims:

> Multicultural music education bases itself on the ability of music to cross boundaries and communicate between cultures. This crossing of boundaries means that we finally begin to accept the artistic expressions of other cultures to be of equal value with our own heritage. (Skyllstad 2008 p. 182)

The course was also linked with developments in the British school music curriculum which wanted to widen the curriculum to include a greater variety of musics; but these musics were grafted onto a core curriculum founded on the Western classical music tradition. The adaptation of the curriculum followed the two models identified by Julia Hess. One she entitles tokenistic and as reinforcing dominant power structures by including musics seen as Other and inferior to the dominant tradition. The second she calls 'musician-as-tourist' (Hess 2015 p. 339) or the 'add world music and stir' (Morton 1994) model, which leaves Western classical music as central to the curriculum, with various excursions into the exotic often in a decontextualised form like 'African drumming'. The model we used was what Hess calls the Comparative Musics model, which:

> emphasises the interconnectedness between the musics and the contexts of the musics ... Such a course will bring the intersections of race, class, gender, dis/ability, and nation to the forefront and focus on the way that these fluid categories intersect with each other and also the subject matter. (Hess 2015 p. 341)

Our course was deliberately inclusive, in reaching out to groups of people who had not traditionally been in Higher Education, like rock and pop musicians and retired people with experience of musicking. The general description for the Field (as part of a combined honours programme) considered the field of World Music to be essentially a practical course designed to enrich students' understanding of a variety of traditions through practical experience. This was to be achieved through a balance of listening-in-audience, performing and composing/improvising. Various traditions were examined in depth – the Caribbean steel orchestra, jazz, the European classical style and the Thai piphat. While still including elements of the European classical tradition, the intention was to explore the relationship between this and other traditions (including popular musics in Europe). The analytical work in the area of listening-in-audience would attempt to set up a non-Eurocentric model for examining a variety of cultures in a way that differed from most existing music degrees at that time, which grafted other cultures onto Eurocentric models. In this way it was not a narrowly academic course, although it was underpinned by a sound academic thinking.

The emphasis in the course also included personal narratives and students were encouraged to develop their own styles and methods in composing, performing and criticality in relation to personal and negotiated agendas. It was based on the tree model explored in Chapter Three (Boyce-Tillman 1995). This saw a model of musical cultures in the form of a tree sharing a common trunk of Expression. In the domain of Values it embraced pluralism:

> Our sense of crisis stems largely from the pluralism of our society; but this unease is related to the expectation that society should, in fact, be linear and non-pluralistic.

> Pluralism does not produce conflict unless the expectation is for unity. (Steinecker 1976 p. 7)

The course sought to resolve some of the dualisms that Dewey had identified as plaguing education:

1. Academic versus artistic study
2. Process versus product
3. Specialised versus comprehensive musicianship
4. Music for the talented versus music for every child
5. Fine arts versus practical arts
6. Cognitive versus the affective domain.
   (Drawn from Steinecker 1976)

It used a model that David Elliott (1989) called dynamic multiculturalism. It opened up the possibility of the generation of unfamiliar values, procedures and behaviours in the interest of understanding or 'knowing' musics of a variety of cultures. It attempted to preserve the integrity of musical traditions from the past, but also to allow students to develop ideas about music that will counterbalance unconscious prejudice either academic or social (Elliott 1989 p. 817). It attempted to set up a scaffolded space (Holzman 2008) for the transformative meeting of people from a variety of musical traditions, that would result in a transformation in the area of respect for difference:

> The combination of the widest range of world musics and a world view of musical concepts separates the dynamic curriculum model from all the rest. Thus, in addition to developing students' abilities to discriminate and appreciate the differences and similarities among musical cultures, a dynamic curriculum has the potential to achieve two fundamental expressive objectives or ways of being musical: 'bimusicality' at least, and 'multimusicality' at most. (D. Elliott 1989 p. 18)

Our thinking was supplemented by Elliott's later work on musical thinking. He identifies four kinds of musical knowing, all of which can be taught and learned (D. Elliott 1994):

- Formal musical knowledge (or verbal information)
- Informal musical knowledge (or practical experience)

- Impressionistic musical knowledge (or musical intuition)
- Supervisory musical knowledge (musical metacognition)

Also influential in our thinking was Catherine Ellis's book *Aboriginal Music – Education for living* which includes a Transcendent Level (Ellis 1985 p. 198). I saw this in the first lecture with one group, when a young woman brought up in the Western classical tradition through the Associated Board Examination system met a rock musician who looked and embraced a totally different tradition. The expression on her face when she said 'Music is his life as it is mine' showed that moment of profound illumination, as her perception of music transcended the limitations of the culture within which she had been enculturated.

The first year of the course saw the introduction of the intercultural tree model on which the criteria for performance were based:

GRADE LINKED CRITERIA

Third Class:	There is a degree of technical competence which is not related to expressive or structural grasp in either performance or the accompanying notes.
Lower Second Class:	The technical grasp is sufficient to make a certain degree of expressive character possible. The general principles of the style are grasped and identifiable.
Upper Second Class:	Technical, expressive and structural elements are fused into a grasp of a particular idiom.
First Class:	Real musical communication is achieved in a performance that fuses technical, expressive and structural domains. It is an impressive, coherent and original musical statement made with commitment.

These were developed as the course progressed. Composing assignments also used the model as the basis for assessment. Students were encouraged to develop their own personal style, as well as being taught a variety of techniques from differing traditions e.g. Bach chorales and Nigerian high-life. These were the questions they were encouraged to ask of their work:

1. How far the writing is suitable for the instrument or voices chosen.
2. How far the intended atmosphere was created.

3. How far the musical construction hangs together.
4. How far the style is coherent – whether the composer has worked within the context of a particular historical or geographical or developed their own individual style.
5. How far there is evidence of the composer's own individuality.
6. How far the composer is able to reflect on and be articulate about his/her processes of composing in the accompanying verbal description.

All performances were contextualised in various ways and composing and performing were assessed in contexts in the surrounding community; these included the back room of a public house and a beautiful medieval hall. It was a bold course breaking new ground. One module was on the Spirituality of Music which produced striking startling assignments – like a pagan sunrise ritual on a local hill performed at dawn and followed by a memorable picnic. This produced a liminal experience for all present and lives on vibrantly in their memories.

Case Study Nine: Foundation Music at the University of Winchester

The University of Winchester is an Anglican Foundation endeavouring to find what this might mean in the contemporary world. As a member of the university's Foundation Committee – charged with examining what this might mean. I examined how Music had and might contribute to the Christian Foundation of the University. I identified from the history of higher education in the UK (which was based in Christianity with universities like Oxford and Cambridge) three aims:

- Love of Knowledge (Amor scientiae)
- Formation in a strong community of learners
- Usefulness to society

A literature was developing in the late twentieth century supporting the significant place for extra-curricular activities in the context of higher education. In the area of student formation in a collegial community, in

Student Learning outside the Classroom: Transcending Artificial Boundaries, Kuh and his associates claim that:

> the authors note that out-of-classroom experiences have a more lasting and defining impact on students than do the classroom experiences. (Kuh et al. 1994 p. xi)

It seemed to me that by offering a musical experience to all students at the university, we would provide them with an experience that would enrich their humanity by developing a broader awareness, expand their horizons and help them construct meaning for themselves.

Kuh and his associates saw this process as better done outside the curriculum than in the carefully crafted modules of learning, where they had to run on paths to pre-set learning outcomes that they had not had a hand in setting:

> Students take responsibility for their own learning when they participate in out-of-class activities and events that enrich the educational experience (e.g., orientation, guest lectures and internships), develop a portfolio of out-of-class learning experiences and associated benefits, and discuss with others their academic progress and how what they are learning in classes applies to other aspects of their life. (Kuh, et al. 1994 p. xi)

So, in 1998, Foundation Music was born. Its aims were:

a. To enrich the student experience at the university, by providing a variety of musical ensemble experiences (embracing cultural diversity and including student led and student initiated ensembles), and creating a smaller musical community within the wider university community
b. To forge links with the local and national community through high-profile performance events involving local community groups, such as schools and choirs
c. To represent the Christian ethical principles of the Anglican foundation of the university by serving the needs of the local community, through such events as raising money for local charities and performing in venues involving marginalised groups, such as Winchester Community Prison
d. To support the liturgical life of the university and beyond, including the Church Colleges and Universities Choirs festival, Winchester Cathedral and places of worship in the wider community

The plan was to initiate a raft of musical activities across the whole university reflecting a wide variety of musical styles and cultures – diversity in terms of gender, ethnicity, cultural origin, orality and literacy. I set up what Charles Handy (1995) called a 'shamrock' structure, in which each ensemble was self-contained and related directly to the centre; this was a Foundation Music Working Group, consisting of the leaders of all the ensembles, the Director of Foundation Music, an administrator and one external member from the wider community. It grew very quickly, and now includes about 300 students across the whole university, in such ensembles as a flute choir, a music theatre choir, a guitar/ukulele ensemble, steel pans, a gospel choir, a string orchestra and a classical choir. Some are taught orally and some use notation. These ensembles fulfil a number of local engagements including concerts in local care homes, weddings, charity events and evensongs in the cathedral. It is a space where students can initiate their own learning paths – they can play safely and negotiate success and failure. As such, it is a place where Wisdom can be engendered; for Wisdom has the characteristics of creativity and involves the ability to make choices and use discretion. Many students have found these activities as giving them a real experience of liminality that has transformed their university experience.

Case Study Ten: Between

In 2008, I was asked to write a piece for an interfaith event at Roehampton University. I drew on a poem that expressed my developing feeling about intercultural dialogue. I saw rebirth not being in the coherent centres of society but in the cracks between them:

BETWEEN
Between the God and the Goddess
And the mosque and the synagogue

The bullet holes in the tumbled statues
The grass blades on the landfill,

The shaman and the cleric
The hysteric and choleric

The slaying and the praying
And the coping and the hoping

In the fractured rapture
In the hole in the soul

At the crack
The lack

Might
Bite

The Contradiction of 'both'
Meets

The Paradox of 'and'
Rebirth.

I decided the piece would have a cruciform shape with four choirs at North, South, East and West. I drew on my existing experience of interfaith dialogue. I decided to use various elements that reflected my thinking on interfaith dialogue. I used four choirs with a string quintet in the middle of the space representing eternity. So the initial pairs of lines in the poem were divided up across the four choirs with a continuous string quintet sound in the middle. As the central theme was mystery and questioning, at any time one choir was humming, one whispering and the other constructing repeated tunes from a given set of notes. I wrote two chants in which the audience could join and incorporated them into the piece:

1. *At the heart of the cosmos there lies a deep mystery we can know and not know.*
2. *As the water with the rock and the air with the sun*
   So we are drawing nearer with love and respect.

The words 'At the crack, the lack might bite' are difficult words, as the path to mutual respect is difficult and fraught with problems, complexities, misunderstandings and setbacks. The quintet plays a march like theme, while the four choirs move in, saying one of the words on each step (which they take at their own choice); they also have two stones to knock together showing the 'crack'. Paradox and contradiction was portrayed when the choirs are together, by having major and minor tunes conflicting with each other. This apparent confusion continues until they all sing the same tune in octaves. Gradually the notion of rebirth emerges on the upper voices from this. Robert Kaggwa, the Roman Catholic chaplain, wrote of his experience of this music:

> We look at the world through analytical lenses. We see everything as this or that; either/or; on or off, positive or negative; in or out; black or white. We fragment reality in an endless series of 'either/or'. In short, we think the world apart. Of course, this has given human beings a great power over nature, a lot of success, many gifts of modern science and technology. But we can say that we have also lost the sense of mystery. This dualism of 'either/or' thinking has also given us a fragmented sense of reality that destroys the wholeness and wonder of life. It misleads and betrays us when applied to the perennial problems of being human in this world. Therefore, we need to move away from an 'either/or' attitude to a 'both/and' attitude. In certain circumstances, truth is a paradoxical joining of apparent opposites, and if we want to know that truth we must learn to embrace those opposites as one. Obviously in the empirical world there are choices to be made: an apple tree cannot be both an oak tree and an apple tree. But there is another realm of knowing and here binary logic ('either/or') misleads us. This is the realm of profound truth. (Kaggwa 2008)

He has a lovely vision of how we build up truth as divine sparks scattered among us join with one another:

> According to the sixteenth century Cabbalist, Rabbi Isaac Luria, the world was created in a divine catastrophe. In the beginning, everything was God. But God was lonely, and in order to create partners. He needed to contract Himself in order to make it possible for there to be others. During the process of creation, however, something went terribly wrong; the vessels by which God was transformed into the something other than divinity burst, scattering fragments of holiness throughout an aborted and incomplete creation. The task of human existence, according to Luria, is to locate and reunite these holy sparks – he called them 'hidden lights' – which came to rest in each living soul, so that the primordial calamity of existence can be corrected and the process of creation completed. (Kaggwa 2008)

This experience as a composer showed me how Value systems colour decisions in all the other domains, and that meta-awareness in that domain enabled the piece to take others into the Spiritual domain, in which they were able to develop their own meanings.

Summary

This chapter has set out the possibilites of the Spiritual/liminal experience in the area of the Extrapersonal in establishing relationships between cultures that honour and respect difference. It has outlined the ethical problems that might intrude on this and how these may be born out of previous colonial enterprises and value systems that are heirarchical. It has shown how intercultural musical projects need to address issues in the domain of Values to approach the domain of Spirituality/liminality. It has illustrated this in a variety of contexts and in a variety of musicking activities.

CHAPTER TEN

Radical Musical Inclusion: An Ecclesiology of Music

A Story

I attended a performance of John Adams's opera *The Gospel according to the other Mary*:[1]

> Can the theatre do the job of the Church? Can it, in fact, do it better? A bishop once observed mournfully how much larger were Handel's audiences than his own. 'Yes, Sir: because we are in earnest,' the composer replied. The stage and the sanctuary share a common theme. Love is the central preoccupation of the composer, the librettist, the playwright, the performer, and of their audience too. Erotic love, whether doomed or fruitful is guaranteed to inspire and appeal. But Love is just as much at the heart of the liturgical drama, as the handful of those who still go to church attest. In the hands of Peter Sellars and John Adams, the triumphs and tragedies of this kind of love – humane, expansive, costly – are made every bit as compelling as the adventures of an Isolde, a Violetta or an Anna Nicole. (Marshall 2014 p. 30)

Audience reactions varied. One person said she only came because it was religious and the music was not 'her thing'. A man asked his companion whether perhaps she had enjoyed it just a little. I did not hear her reply.

1 Performance at the London Coliseum, English National Opera, November 27th 2014.

Introduction

This story opens up a further dialogue between the arts and religion and its use of religious subjects which recalls debates in the domain of Values about how the subject might be acceptable to the musicker; but the style of the Construction may preclude any spiritual experience. More fundamental is the claim of the cleric writing in the programme that both the arts and religion are about love.

This chapter continues the theme of love being extended by developing new forms that include greater diversity. It sets out the possibility of events that that bring music-making groups from a variety of traditions effectively into a single event, charting the challenges and strategies. This is based on a vision of radical inclusion/belonging through the processes of musicking (Small 1998). As previous chapters have shown, I draw on the fields of philosophy, spirituality, ecclesiology and social psychology to construct a potential theory of inclusive musical events.

It has also been influenced by the development of the field of interfaith dialogue using music. Ruth Illman, after describing the ground-breaking work of the Spanish musician Jordi Savall in bringing people of different faiths together, concludes that 'music can assist the delicate balance of identification and integrity' (Illman 2010a p. 192). She concludes:

> The world is really changed, and Savall's project really is an artistic way of showing the importance of combining notions of plurality and peace. (Illman 2010a p. 193)

This chapter strives towards re-imagining the global community through musicking:

> It is not enough to imagine the global community; new and wider forms of political association and different types of cultural community will first have to emerge ... it is likely to be piecemeal, disjointed and largely unplanned. (Smith 1991 p. 160)

Ruth Illman shares with the author (Boyce-Tillman 2011a) a belief that 'the plurality of self and other is peace' (Levinas 1969 p. 203) and that music can play a significant part in this process. Joshua Heschel claims that 'To meet a human being is a major challenge in mind and heart' (Heschel 2000 p. 312). Illman sees the need, therefore, for tools that are:

> more than just intellectual tools. We need to see the other, hear him/her call, and answer to him/her in a concrete way. (Illman 2009 p. 168)

In her thinking, she questions the notion of a shared identity (on which much Western classical music is based), concentrating on social and personal complexity:

> A fixed and stable identity – uniting us with some who share it and separating us from others who do not – is fiction. The human way to survive is [...], to accept the complexity of our interpersonal world ... the goal of finding oneself and finding a deeper meaning in life seemed central as the focus shifted from theories, institutions and collectives to emotional experiences, creative combinations and personal choices. (Illman 2010b p. 241)

The sacred space is created by the dialogue of difference:

> in the meeting of art and dialogue. Consequently, spirituality can be envisioned both as a 'dialogue of souls' and as an 'incarnating encounter.' (Illman 2012 p. 60)

It is on this encounter with difference that my vision of musical inclusion is based.

Music and the Dignity of Difference:[2] The Problem of Utopia

The ability to embrace difference within musical events has been my challenge, generated by the inherent dangers in totalitarianism. We have seen this desire developing in various aspects of the Western classical music tradition. Milan Kundera shows how totalitarianism leads to the breakdown and the need for advocacy for certain groups:

2 I am indebted to Jonathan Sacks (2002) for this title.

> Totalitarianism is not only hell, but all the dreams of paradise – the age-old dream of a world where everybody would live in harmony, united by a single common will and faith, without secrets from one another. Andre Breton, too, dreamed of this paradise when he talked about the glass house in which he longed to live. If totalitarianism did not exploit these archetypes, which are deep inside us all and rooted deep in all religions, it could never attract so many people, especially during the early phases of its existence. Once the dream of paradise starts to turn into reality, however, here and there people begin to crop up who stand in its way, and so the rulers of paradise must build a little gulag on the side of Eden. In the course of time this gulag grows even bigger and more perfect, while the adjoining paradise gets even smaller and poorer. (Kundera 1991 pages unavailable)

There have been many theories of utopia, not least coming from the Frankfurt School, in particular that of Ernst Bloch in *The Principle of Hope* (1986, first published 1938–47). From this thinking, I have distilled the idea of looking towards the future rather than the past. The shaping of a future that values diversity and can bring it into relationship without enforcing a normalising unity is my underpinning philosophy. This idea owes a great deal to the process philosophers, which I have drawn on so heavily in Chapter One:

> There is urgency in coming to see the world as a web of interrelated processes of which we are integral parts. (Mesle 2009 p. 9)

Whitehead saw creativity and freedom as part of establishing this essential interrelationship and encouraged human beings to make choices that would enable these connections. Whitehead saw freedom as existing within the limits of a culture (Cobb 1977 p. 52) but encouraged people to make informed creative choices.

The Problems of Western Culture

Many theorists have analysed the present crisis in Western culture as related to power concentrated in the hands of a limited group of people. This has led to the devastation of the Other in various forms including the natural world, different cultures, women, the poor and the different (Levinas 1969). As the powerful of Western society limit the range of what is considered normality, more people are pushed to the margins as being 'different' or 'Other'; in the UK, more prisons and more psychiatric treatments are being developed in order to normalise – but often simply to marginalise – the Other. There is an increasing imperative to look at a more inclusive agenda in the wider society, so that diversity is valued. The failure to do this is dangerous from both a personal and cultural perspective:

> The mental space in which people dream and act is largely occupied today by Western imagery. The vast furrows of cultural monoculture left behind are, as in all monocultures, both barren and dangerous. (W. Sachs 1992 p. 4)

The tendency, and indeed intention, of any monoculture is to obliterate difference. As it is the juxtaposition of difference that produces contrast or surprise, in a monoculture safety tends to replace risk and excitement. This reduces the possibility for creativity and cultural evolution. So the central problem for an encroaching monoculture is the limitation of the imagination which becomes increasingly programmed to run along pre-set and prescribed lines. The Brandt Report of 1980 clearly signalled the urgent necessity of changing from a culture of growth to one of respect and reciprocity; but little has been done to take up its recommendations.

Even in our schools, children's imaginations are stifled by controlled curricula which tend to teach these pre-set lines prescribed by the dominant hierarchy. Rabindranath Tagore described his school curriculum as 'branded bales of marketable result' (Tagore and Elmshirst 1961 p. 3). This tendency has increased over the last fifty years. Children's dreams are now formed primarily, not by their own imaginations but by the world of celebrity and advertising. These are designed to create a uniform society of consumers of a limited range of products:

> As children's expectations lose contact with reality, they are torn between their inner lives of fame and fortune and the humdrum reality their minds no longer inhabit ... An economy driven by dissatisfaction, could scarcely fail to cultivate mental illness. (Monbiot 2006)

The suggestion here is that children need to be given in the process of education the tools to re-imagine the world in order to claim their own power.

How do we as arts educators awaken the imagination so that children can think 'outside the box' of the monoculture (Boyce-Tillman 2007b)? There is a need for the arts to help re-envision the domain of Values – the nature of The Good – for the wider society. This requires artists of all kinds to ask themselves about the domain of Values. This requires first perception and understanding, and then, perhaps, courage to abandon treasured values upon which they have relied for much of their artistic lives (Diamond 2005 pp. 522–3).

I have shown throughout this book how I have been increasingly concerned with how difference can be given dignity. As Levinas suggests, one dilemma for our society is forming a relationship with the different 'Other' without attempting to make the Other the same as ourselves. This is what Sacks (J. Sacks 2000) calls 'the dignity of difference'. The Brazilian pedagogue Paulo Freire identified how the 'oppressed' have to reclaim their ability to 'name the world' and not accept the labels put upon it by the rich and powerful:

> This is not a matter of conventional revolution and counter-revolution in the struggle to control the master-narrative but rather the search for an alternative to the power games of yester year. (Prentki date unknown p. 5)

To summarise, an aggressive monoculture driven by economics is in the process of obliterating differences and imposing limitations on our imaginations' capacity to think outside the established boxes which have been established by those in power. The suggestion here is that in the arts we can find effective strategies of resistance and sites for the development of new imaginings (Boyce-Tillman 2007b).

The Arts as Cultural Intervention

The arts have always potentially been tools for cultural intervention. Our colleagues in drama have long been engaged in the use of drama to empower the disempowered, inspired by the work of Augusto Boal:

> Performance as cultural intervention [which] takes many forms ... Performance can be offered *to* a community by professional artists and students, can be created *with* the community, or may be produced *by* the community with or without external facilitation. Whatever the politics and poetics of these performances, they are bound by the Freirean concept of co-intentionality. (Prentki date unknown p. 5)

The carnival is an older community event, cited by the Russian theorist Mikhail Bakhtin as cultural intervention (Bakhtin 1993). Although some theorists have seen it as a way of controlling the dissenting voices in a society, he saw the freedom of the carnival event as a place for negotiating new identities through its embracing of multiplicities of identity. He talks of the carnival's antithesis to authoritative discourse such as religious dogma; he looks at how the hybridity of meanings present in the carnival offers the possibility of transformation. Commedia dell' Arte is similarly described by Rudlin (1994 p. 133); he also saw how, when these ideas were brought into the twentieth century, it involved a shift of power: 'the re-empowering of the actor would entail the disempowering of the director' (Rudlin 1994 p. 177). He uses Breughel's painting *Carnival and Lent* to inform his argument; he regards it as a battle 'between asceticism and artistic licence, censorship [supported by the Church] and freedom of expression [present in carnival]' (Rudlin 1994 p. 32). I have sought to bring the two traditions together – fusing the Apollonian and the Dionysian, as set out in the Prelude – and seeing this fusion as a way of re-accessing the Spiritual through musicking.

Embracing Paradox

Hybridity in the area of meaning was embraced by the poets as the twentieth century went on; they were requiring more of the reader in terms of the construction of meaning. They embraced ambiguity, improvisation and multiplicity in the area of meaning. Apollinaire, his contemporaries and their aesthetic heirs, abandoned the idea of delivering coherent prepackaged units of poetry. They played with creative disorientations and disjunctions. 'Fragment is the unit; juxtaposition is the method; collage is the result' (Hoagland 2010). These poets set up a 'heteroglossaic space' by their inclusion of a multiplicity of voices. The term originated with Bakhtin in his analysis of the novel. It is seen as potentially transformative because of the reader's power to construct their own meaning; he contrasts this with the 'authoritative discourse' of religious dogma which requires only assimilation of the author's intention. I have already explored this in the distinction between religion and spirituality in Chapter One, and have seen the Spiritual space as embracing paradox and contradictions, rather than resolving them in the way that religious dogma may be seen as doing.

So other art forms developed ways of embracing paradox by juxtaposition and paradox and so challenging a normative culture. I have been exploring how music can embrace contradictions.

An Ecclesiology of Music

The vision of ecclesiology was a Church that was inclusive but over its history this vision has been lost in a normalisation based on the mistaking of uniformity for unity. I have based the Values of my musical events on a reworking of an ecclesiological frame. The four pillars of the traditional church were:

- Unity
- Holiness
- Catholicity
- Apostolicity

Drawing on the work of Elisabeth Schüssler Fiorenza (2000) and Robert Goss (2002), Tiffany Steinwert reworked these in order to produce a truly inclusive model of church. Unity, she suggests, needs to be transformed from doctrinal uniformity (expressed traditionally in creedal statements) to solidarity, a concept central to the thinking of liberation theologians. In my musical thinking this has become the inclusion of a variety of styles (orate and literate) in the same piece to produce a unity that is not based on uniformity; this has transformed my role as the composer into a frame-builder (see below), both rooted in the past and also alive to new possibilities, often suggested by my interaction with the participants through the process of co-creation. Pat and Kathie Debenham describe a dance project bringing deaf and hearing people together, co-creating an interdisciplinary performance entitled *Beyond Words* which:

> engendered ways to build respect for difference, compassion, understanding and a sense of being connected to the greater themes of life. (Debenham and Debenham 2008 p. 52)

Holiness in Steinwert's model ceases to be individualised piety and becomes justice-seeking. Many of my musical events are concerned with justice, such as The *Great Turning* (2014) – with its concern for respect for the earth and ecology – and the restoring of respect for traditions and styles that have been downplayed and not honoured. Catholicity, which is traditionally worked out in a form close to Roman imperialism – both in the so-called Roman Catholic Church and the Protestant traditions, especially in their colonial enterprises – needs to be about radical inclusion and the accepting of difference. My musical policy has been one of including everyone and trying to find the place where they fit. Apostolicity has to cease to be about a male lineage, but about working out of what it means to be an apostle – in other words, committed action (Steinwert 2003). In musical terms, this is reflected in the immense stress on wellbeing and commitment through musicking which is available to everyone. The principles underpinning my work are thus a reworking of these pillars of the Church – unity, holiness, catholicity and apostolicity (Boyce-Tillman 2007b) through the medium of musicking – a reworked ecclesiology, expressed through musicking.

Case Study One: Dialogue in Music

Following the reflections on the case studies in Chapters Six and Nine, including the act of celebration which I had started in the 1980s, I started to create and explore musical structures that might enable dialogue through the arts, that will take everyone into the Spiritual/liminal domain. The first was a larger interfaith event called *Space for Peace* that uses Winchester Cathedral as a resonant meditative space, able to contain and merge diversity, accepting it without obliterating it.

The main strands that coloured the project's development were the notion of shared power in the areas of composing, performing and listening by challenging traditional hierarchies. Elements of carnival were present in the relaxation of central control of event and the presence of improvisatory elements. I used collage approaches to Construction and the event was designed to promote the experience of Spirituality/liminality.

For the events entitled *Space for Peace* (which we have carried out at the time of writing ten times in various contexts) I assemble together local choral groups from a variety of sources – such as community choirs, school choirs from church and state schools, the university, the cathedral choristers, a rabbi, a Jewish cantor, a Muslim imam, a singer in the Hindu/Sikh tradition, a Bahai singer and Buddhist chanters. There are some solo singers and a saxophone and flute who wander around freely improvising on some Hildegard chants. Some groups use notation; some have no grasp of it and learn everything orally; some are older and singing for fun; others are skilled musicians; the age range is often 7–85.

It starts with the assembled choirs and soloists on the chancel steps in the nave singing seven shared peace chants, which are sung by all the choirs together with the congregation joining in some of the chants. These work together in the form of the English quodlibet where tunes fit together to create an effective contrapuntal texture. It is very approachable for less experienced groups as each group is singing a tune rather than a part. After the chants the choirs start to process one by one to the place they will occupy for the middle section. Each choir sings one piece of the ones they have chosen to sing for peace before they came to the event. As the choirs move away the sound gradually disappears into the depth of the cathedral mixing gently, as the sound of the distant choir is joined by the next one leaving the nave.

In the middle section, each choir has to sing one of the opening group of chants every twenty minutes; so the chants provide some common themes which thread their way through the complex texture binding the diversity together. This middle section is created by the participants on the basis of choice. The groups are situated around the cathedral in various chapels and transepts singing the pieces they have chosen in advance – pieces that for them are about peace. The musical material includes motets, hymns, worship songs, chants and chanting. Each group not only chooses when to sing and when to be silent in relation to the whole texture but can also be invited by the congregation to sing. The congregation has not a programme but a map showing where all the musicians are placed. The congregation and the performers move around the building, lighting candles, praying, being quiet, as they choose, but also participating in creating the musical sound. People become very sensitive to their surroundings and to one another. Some of the soundscapes are very complex as a number of pieces are performed simultaneously in various areas of the cathedral and sometimes they are quite simple. At the end of this section or movement candles are lit and long processions fill the cathedral singing shalom, salaam and ohm-shanti on a single note while the instruments and soloists improvise over this pedal note, placed high in the organ loft. The piece ends with a reprise of the opening peace chant quodlibet.

The Value underpinning the work/event is the valuing of difference, which can be seen as a new model of peace-making – from the bottom up rather than the top down; in the model being used here, we all do what we want to do; but then we have the responsibility of working out how far what we are doing fits with what other people want to do. Everyone present had a part in the creation of beauty and togetherness; they experience intuitive ways of relating to and co-operating with others.

Developing Musical Construction that Value Diversity

Various elements characterise *Space for Peace*. The first area to be explored is that of shared power. We have seen above how one of the issues for Western culture is the concentration of power in a limited group of people who control many lives, such as politicians, media moguls and controllers of industry; many theorists see the possibilities of structures which include shared power – democratisation. We have also seen how the hierarchies of Western classical musical traditions developed from a male Christian God. These concentrated power in the hands of a privileged few people and disempowered others; notions of value became associated with difficulty and complexity rather than intention; this has led to the favouring of the notated, literate traditions over the orate traditions (Ong 1992), as we have already seen in Chapter Six.

This has made it difficult for people of varying degrees of expertise and experience of differing traditions to co-operate in a single work. The challenge then is to create pieces where adults and children can participate together each using their own level of skill and experience. The same gulf can be seen between the developing community choir movement in the UK, which is primarily an orate tradition (Ong 1992), and the Western classical choirs, which are primarily literate. As a composer, I have already shown how I have been working towards structures that embrace dominant and subjugated Value systems – the orate with the literate, the process with the product, diversity with unity within a single event. I started this with pieces containing 'windows', such as The *Call of the Ancestors* (Boyce-Tillman 1998) described earlier. The composer becomes a kind of frame-builder where others can achieve empowerment through musicking. The composer constructs a frame in which musical weaving can take place. This type of musical Construction is intended to embody the dignity of difference.

Space for Peace moves the notion of carnival into the cathedral space so bringing together the figures of Lent and Carnival in the Breughel picture used in the work of Mikhail Bakhtin. The middle section of *Space for Peace* was described as a 'musical sweet shop' by one member of the audience because he could go round and sample a variety of delights. As we have seen, the Church has traditionally been very controlling, not only in its dogma, but also in its liturgies with their fixed literate form. The central free improvisatory section has the sounds merging in and out with one another; this is like a carnival procession, although situated in an enclosed space. In this sense, it reflects the structure of Charles Ives' *Fourth of July*; but here it is not controlled by the composer but by the performers and the audience.

Many comments following *Space for Peace* showed that a heteroglossaic space had been created, as in the opening poem of Chapter Four. The hybridity of voices was a source of delight to many participants:

> I particularly enjoyed the counterpoints produced by the solo singer and Rabbi Mark Solomon as we were singing in our spaces. (Unpublished comment 2009)

The cathedral proved a space that was well suited to mixing difference and containing differing voices effectively:

> It was an incredibly brave and innovative venture which worked brilliantly ... Your inspired idea of removing the pews and placing individual choirs in different areas and having them sing spontaneously meant every nook, cranny and nave was filled with the most incredible music. I loved the fact that you could walk around, sampling different styles and interpretations and, along the way, enjoy the surprise of a lone voice suddenly appearing from a balcony or behind a pillar. (Unpublished comment 2009)

The opening of the event was more conventional and led those present gently into the idea of carnival:

> To a selection of pieces selected for the occasion by each of the choral groups was added a shared corpus of chants, including chants of forgiveness, and those honouring diversity and the earth, by Boyce-Tillman herself, plus the overarching anthem of *Shalom my friends*. From the chancel steps, where massed voices conducted by the composer delivered these melodies in unison, the performers processed to specific locations within the cathedral. There, as the audience moved around the building, free to join in, pray or listen, the singers were likewise at liberty to choose among their material, answering the music of neighbouring groups or responding spontaneously. From the Lady Chapel, a children's choir made fascinating duets with Just Sing It, a London-based peace group. In the nave, cleared medieval-style of all chairs, and maybe some of our preconceptions, the effects were especially rewarding. Amid echoes of Sydney Carter, English folksong and the *Missa di angelis* from beyond the chancel, of Taizé chant and South African Alleluias from the west door, and of Tallis from the aisle, the cantor sang from the pulpit. At one point he paused to listen to the rich motet harmonies, before resuming his cantillation from Leviticus – a sweet moment. (N. Williams 2009)

The event sees diversity held in a unity that is not a uniformity. It is a shift from the authoritative discourse of the Church with its regular stress on doctrinal uniformity and liturgical control linked as it is with the classically notated tradition, to the creativity of a diverse group of people given freedom to exercise their own choices. It reflects a democratisation of liturgy/concert which frees up a space to give the possibility of greater freedom and celebration of diversity.

The celebratory improvisational approach enables performers to explore the possibilities of their own chosen style and work out their relation to other styles. The work is about process which is now merged with project (as in other performing arts developments such as *Shout*). It is this that enabled the rabbi to approach the imam near the end of the piece and sing with him a shared verse. Kathleen McGill sees improvisatory techniques originating in the Commedia dell'Arte as drawing on female oral and collaborative culture:

> What many women in the arts desire is not the passive-active poles of the oppositional model but an alternative definition of the process entirely, one which chooses a field rather than a chain of being and conversation in preference to dialectic. (McGill 1991 p. 69)

She links this with women's desire for forms that enable social co-operation. They favour forms that do not 'enact difference in oppositional terms'; instead, she sees women as favouring forms where difference becomes 'multiple, inclusive and highly adaptive' (McGill 1991 pp. 68–9). *Space for Peace* enacts this characteristic of social collaboration; it is a democratic project designed to foster co-operation (not least between the university and the local community).

I drew on the poetics of juxtaposition, fragmentation and collage, we have already seen in the poets of the twentieth century. This results in hybrid forms, which have the characteristics of 'fruitful chaos', resulting from the freeing up of the 'dialectical imagination' (Hoagland 2010). This links with the ideas of Buber, Levinas and Derrida on encounter, where they stress the energy flowing between the difference of the encounterer and the encountered. Many people talk about a powerful energy generated during *Space for Peace*. Because the Construction is in the hands of all present rather than a single author they are able to experience fully the spaces between them. I concentrated, in the Construction of the frame, on the space between the fragments and the creative possibilities of chaos. The interconnections in the central section are intense and, as the piece moves forward, participants become more skilled at creating complex interrelationships.

The Construction uses improvised collage which allows surprising things to happen that were not in the original planning. A Jewish participant asked the rabbi to sing Kaddish for a relative for whom it had not been sung. Some members of the audience formed an impromptu choir in an empty chapel. A liturgical dancer danced for quarter of an hour in the north transept. A singer, who was experienced in the Greek Orthodox chant, joined the rabbi in a duet. The freeing up of the space liberated the creativity of all present.[3] Certainly the sum of the whole of the pieces chosen by the choirs was far greater than the individual parts making it up. For example, a performing artist punctuated one event with a dramatic intervention from a gallery that consisted of chanting 'Can you hear me? Can you hear me above the sounds of war?'; this would have been meaningless on its own, and yet was regarded as striking by participants. The composer no longer controls what happens; this enables a dynamic complexity that can produce non-obvious consequences.

Throughout the piece the energy was felt to build with the stones creating echoing loops from the complex soundscape (Boyce-Tillman 2010). These are the elements of communitas described as a central part of Turner's liminality and these are clearly present in the behaviour of the participants. People embrace one another as they meet in their explorations. Many of the accounts reveal that participants entering a liminal space during the event that becomes transformative for them:

> *Space for Peace* was one of the high points of my life ... The cathedral was cleared of chairs which was wonderful – one great echoing space. It was all about peace – calls for peace constantly mingling and changing ... I was able to sit and meditate on the stone floor in the middle of the North Transept, one of the most beautiful parts. It came to me that 'peace is possible'. (Unpublished comment 2009)

3 This is similar to the characteristics identified by the theorists of complexity theory.

Children caught the spirit of prayerfulness.

> As the whole event drew to a close I noticed a child near me sitting on the floor in the classic Eastern meditation position. (Unpublished comment 2009)

Others linked it with notions of heaven:

> My favourite part was at around 8.25pm sitting in the (then empty) choir whilst the sounds and performances washed in and out. It reminded me of the 'offstage' singing of 'Praise to the Holiest' in *Gerontius* – I think that is what Heaven must be like! (Unpublished comment 2009)

Space for Peace shows the development of a Construction that will embrace difference with respect. All the strands of the analysis of Spirituality in Chapter One were drawn together in a musical event involving children, adults, a variety of cultures (orate and literate) and a variety of ages and styles. This opens up a liminal space that offers the possibility of personal and cultural transformation, by encouraging people to think and experience 'outside of the box' of Western culture.

Case Study Two: Choral Singing and Community

Traditionally the Church used singing to create community. The Gallery Choir was popular c1700–1850; and the continuing church choir traditions, particularly in country communities, often struggled to include all – young and old, rich and poor, experienced and inexperienced, literate and orate, folk and classical:

> Mr Annett's [church choir conductor] patience snapped suddenly. He rattled his baton on the reading desk and flashed his eyes … We were off. Behind me the voices rose and fell, Mrs Pringle's concentrated lowing vying with Mrs Willet's nasal soprano. Mrs Willet clings to her notes so cloyingly that she is usually half a bar behind the rest. Her voice has that penetrating and lugubrious quality found in female singers' renderings of 'Abide with Me' outside public houses on Saturday nights. She has a tendency to over-emphasize the final consonants and draw out the vowels to such

> excruciating lengths, and all this executed with such devilish shrillness, that every nerve is set jangling. (Read 1955 pp. 47–8)

The decline of organised religion, that we saw in Chapter One, and hence regular attendance at a place of worship in which singing would have played a prominent part – once a week – has created a need for this ecclesiology. It is in essence a philosophy of inclusive community – expressed in a new way. So in this context, community choirs grew up in the mid to late twentieth century. Significant in this development was Frankie Armstrong and the Natural Voice Network (1988):

> Natural Voice is about celebrating the voice you were born with, rather than trying to train it to an ideal of perfection. It's about building accepting, non-judgmental communities that sing together. It's about welcoming all voices into a group without audition and working from there to make a group sound. It's about making learning by ear accessible to the whole group so that nobody needs to be able to read music. (Natural Voice 2014)

This network challenged the prevailing classically based traditions of choral singing.

Cultural Perceptions of 'Choir'

For a considerable time the classical music model has dominated the concept of 'choir'. This has been based on the pursuit of artistic perfection, often rated in relation to a printed score, the ability to realise it with accuracy and produce a tone that is acceptable to the group as a whole. All of these were checked by the process of auditioning which meant the exclusion of many who could not achieve in all these areas. They usually would accept the negative musical identity imparted by this process:

> Those involved in less formal music making (often identified as music making 'just for fun'), will say 'I'm not really a musician', regardless of how significant a part music plays in their lives. (Turino 2008 p. 25)

These processes can happen as early as aged five. Well documented now is the effect of this exclusion upon the well-being of the excluded. Sarah Morgan sees the rise of community choirs as a counterbalance to this model of choir:

> The tremendous popularity of community choirs may well indicate the large numbers of 'musically disenfranchised' people whose desire to give voice has not found a welcome in our previously existing choirs and choral societies. That is not to decry music excellence and technical skill, nor to underrate the cultural richness provided by our history of choral singing. The community choir model simply provides something different – not 'better than', but certainly not 'the same as'. (Morgan 2013 p. 54)

The very different ways of recruiting and maintaining these groups have caused some people not to use the title choir but revert to new descriptors, such as singing group. But the problem for community music has been the Value system embraced by the Academy, which have dominated the thinking about singing for some time, as we saw in Chapter Six. This resulted in a hierarchical view of singing groups and traditions:

> The worth and status of oral, improvised, informal or amateur music making can be eroded both explicitly ... and in more subtle ways, by the use of terminology such as high or low culture, amateur and professional musician, national, or local performer, and so on. (Morgan 2013 p. 26)

So in the early twenty-first century there are two choral aesthetics alive in our UK society:

- A classical perspective emphasising performance, perfection and virtuosity – the standard or 'taproot' aesthetic that has been recognized in music education since its inception in the mid-1800s.
- The second is an aesthetic for singing which stresses community building, diversity, group collaboration and relationship. (Pascale 2005)

The development of this second aesthetic has opened up new horizons for the use of music in social and personal wellbeing:

> [It may] involve learning new skills and expanding the meaning of concepts, often 'unlearning' what was formerly believed to be true ... Through performance, communities are finding ways of seeking truth and also recognizing its multiple faces. (C. Cohen 2008 p. 31)

It is into this general aesthetic landscape that the radically inclusive choir appeared. The post-modern challenge to monolithic value systems in the Academy enabled a revisiting of their Value systems. Sarah Morgan calls for the establishment of a multiplicity of Value systems:

> Convenient though it may be to assume a binary opposition between the supposedly objective, analytic, fixed and exact literate approach and the 'warmly human' participatory oral approach, I do not believe this opposition to be entirely helpful, any more than I find it helpful to privilege learning by ear over singing from written music at all costs. Many singers and musicians make use of both systems of music learning. (Morgan 2013 p. 24)

The Benefits of Singing

As early as 1939, music was recommended as a prescription to be given by a doctor (Podolsky 1939). With this amount of activity since the middle of the twentieth century in various contexts has resulted in an increasing literature researching the benefits of singing:

- Increased life-expectancy (Bygren, Konlaan and Johansson 1996)
- Social, emotional, physical (Clift and Hancox 2001)
- Improved life-satisfaction (VanderArk, Newman and Bell 1983)
- Improvement in well-being, social benefits, lifestyle and functional ability and improvements in breathing, breath control and physical health for people with chronic obstructive pulmonary disorder (COPD) (Clift et al 2013)
- Improvement in wellbeing, communication, cognition and understanding, relations with others, organisation and structure, skills and physical ability for people with Parkinson's (Vella-Burrows and Hancox 2012)

The revaluing of the orate meant a considerable growth in new choirs. Here are a few of the many examples. The Seaview singers in Kent and the Winchester Singing for Wellbeing choir include people with dementia and their carers (Vella-Burrows 2012 pp. 11–13). Recovery choirs enable people to be rehabilitated after hospitalisation for mental health issues (Wellbeing Community Choir 2014). The Raucous Caucus Recovery Chorus is made up of people in active recovery from drug and alcohol addiction. Threshold choirs support the process of dying through bringing ease and comfort to clients, family and caregivers. The Amies project choir works with trafficked women.

Bringing it together: Musical Inclusion

Now we have recovered the notion that everyone can sing, and my question is:

> Can these various groups be brought together?

In my own composing I have already shown how I have developed strategies for the Materials, Expression and Construction of these pieces reflecting a different Value system. *The Great Turning*, on ecological themes in 2014, saw the number and range of community choirs increased. *From Conflict to chorus: A Intermezzo for Peace* (Boyce-Tillman 2015) included the Singing for Wellbeing Choir as well as a school for young people with profound and multiple learning difficulties, community choirs and notated choral and orchestral parts. The inclusion of a young man who is visually impaired and has learning difficulties singing his own solo involved careful scoring of the accompaniment. The problem for a scored piece with children with severe cognitive impairment and people in the later stages of dementia are the random sounds which they create. These were built into the events by having a composer working with their sounds and integrating them into the pre-composed parts of the piece. It is a choral/orchestral event that included whoever wishes to be involved. This provides a model of a truly inclusive society where the organiser (previously composer) is a frame builder. Composing becomes the building of a scaffold (Holzman 2008) in which everyone can realise their full potential rather than the imprinting of one person's ideas on a group of people.

There are a number of challenges in the development of inclusive musical events, which can be summarised as:

- The presence of a variety of bodies and culturally constructed sounds
- A concern for the expressive elements in music including extrinsic meaning which will be important for groups like those with mental health issues for example
- The inclusion of musical forms that are orate in origin as well as musical scores that are notated and musical structures that embrace both
- The embracing of inclusive Value systems, valuing diversity and different cultural forms of singing as well as nurturing leadership styles
- The embracing of a variety of criteria for success, both accuracy and/or uplift

Strategies related to particular impairments have been well summarised in a useful article in the International Journal for Music Education (Yinger 2014), including visual impairment, haptic impairment, hearing problems and cognitive-memory impairment and visual attention and spatial cognition.

Summary

The last half of the twentieth century has seen an opening up of the concept of 'choir'. Community choirs have developed all over the UK in a variety of contexts and a variety of purposes. My aim to create an inclusive ecclesiology using music has resulted in the building of two musical frames that can encompass diversity. One is concerned with the mingling of various faith traditions; the other is a more structured event which can encapsulate as wide a diversity of people as possible. By concentrating on the experiencing of music and the processes involved in creating events rather than musical products, music has been seen as a way of enabling people to encounter and respect difference in order to create a unity based on encompassing diversity. It has seen this as potentially replacing the community singing that characterised worship in a parish church. Based on philosophies of interrelationship and interconnectedness in a fragmented society, my vision is of a radically inclusive musical event where it is possible to bring all sorts and conditions of people together in a single event in which all are valued. In terms of spirituality these groups are replacing the communitas which was once created by the local church. The question is: how far are these new communities ecclesial?

I am still on this journey; my vocation is to create artistic frames in which differences and similarities can be shared, expressed and experienced – where people are free to be different, but can yet share a place at an artistic table. I am working for a world where my six-year-old granddaughter can flourish. My hope is that this work in music will contribute to a sustainable life for the planet in which all are valued in their infinite diversity. This is an aim that would once have been located within the theologies of religions. Here it is located in the much less specific Spiritual/liminal space.

POSTLUDE

Orpheus Rediscovered: The Way Forward

A Story

> The rabbi goes to the woods to celebrate his ritual. He finds the place, lights the fire, and sings the service. God says: 'It is enough.'
> The rabbi goes to the woods to celebrate the service. He finds the place but has forgotten how to light the fire. God says: 'It is enough.'
> The rabbi can no longer find the wood but he sings the service. God says: 'It is enough.'
> The rabbi can no longer remember the words of the service. But he sings the tune. God says: 'It is enough.'[1]

Introduction

The Jewish story here describes the origins of the Nigun, the wordless Jewish song tradition. It represents the move from a time when music was inextricably bound up with religious ritual to a freestanding music – independent of the ceremony. And yet, in this story, this now wordless song is still conceived of as a religious experience. This book has asked the basic questions underpinning the story:

- Is all music potentially a sacred experience?
- Is there actually a secular music?

1 I am grateful to Irith Shillor for this story.

- Is the aesthetic a contemporary version of spirituality?
- Can spirituality be freed from a particular religious tradition?

In the Prelude we saw the possibility of the restoration of a spiritual dimension to music to produce transformative situations. The opening of the domain of the Spiritual releases the healing possibilities of music – personal, cultural and environmental; this was also true of the father of European Music – Orpheus. John Tavener encapsulates this in his philosophy:

> If I stopped [composing] then it would be a state of great happiness that one would stop. It wouldn't be in a state of misery, but for me not to compose at the moment is Hell. Only in composing do I enter this sense of what the ancients called 'the great happiness'. Rather than what I say, I'd rather quote what they say, because you've asked me about the whole problem of suffering. The original intention of music, according to the ancients – all of them, is that it gives heart's ease, and I think that is the one thing. If I'm able to give one inch of heart's ease, that would make my life – my work – worth doing and living. (Tavener 2005)

In another interview, he sees music as the transubstantiation of pain. Richard Harries sees music as encompassing dark and light and capable of transfiguring them, taking the negative up into the positive (Harries 1993 pp. 145–6). Michael Tippett, who embraces no conventional belief system, saw the potential of music to make human beings whole again (Tippett 1974 pp. 16–18). I am aware that for many of the readers of this book the spiritual will be related to the Western classical tradition. However, a new raft of songs is taking the place of hymns; they seem to provide the hope and comfort, once provided by hymnody. These include songs such as Whitney Houston's *The Greatest Love of all*, Carole King's *You've got a friend*, and Leonard Cohen's *Hallelujah*. I have already discussed in Interlude Two how hymns can been treated in a variety of ways – as story, devotion or cultural artefact.

This Postlude will set out the transformative possibilities of the creation of Spiritual/liminal space by means of musicking, seen through the lens of the phenomenographic map set out in the Prelude. It will show how, by drawing together strands from a variety of disciplines – musicology, music therapy, ethnomusicology and community music – the holistic nature of the experience will be revealed:

> The structuralist orientation of traditional music analysis and the psychology of music has meant that both disciplines have tended to confine themselves to a consideration of the immediate sources that lie either within an individual work or a generic style ... The ecological approach challenges the idea of representation in perception and resists ordering phenomena hierarchically ... The mutualism of perceiver and environment means that different perceivers will be attuned to different invariants and at different times. We all have the potential to hear different things in the same music ... listening must be considered in relation to the needs and capacities of *particular* listeners rather than in general and abstracted terms. (E. Clarke 2005, pp. 190–2. Author's italics)

Here Eric Clarke, the Heather Professor of Music at Oxford University, calls for a move towards an ecological way of approaching listening, drawing on many disciplines in the way I have set out in this book.

The Transformative Possibilities of the Liminal Space in Music

In the Prelude I examined the potential role of the psychagogue. This blurs the boundaries between music therapy and musicking in general by seeing the musicking process as transformative. It means rethinking music education to include within it the totality of the experience:

> Rescuing the healing and transformative dimensions of education should not be regarded as turning education into a therapeutic process. The main goal of integral education is not personal healing or group binding (although these may naturally occur and any genuine integral process should welcome and even foster these possibilities) but *multidimensional inquiry* and the *collaborative construction of knowledge* ... in the context of integral education, transformative healing opens the doors of human multidimensional cognition. (Ferrer, Romero, Albareda 2005 p. 17. Authors' italics)

To examine the elements discussed in this book, I return to the themes already outlined in the Prelude and in more detail in the Interlude One, where they are related to the magical wood in Shakespeare's *A Midsummer Night's Dream*.

Relationship to the Everyday

The space of liminality/spirituality is not unconnected with the world of everyday reality. Ideally the experience colours the viewing of the everyday world of propositional thinking. Participants bring into their musicking their own background and circumstances and, in the end, will return to the everyday world in the same way as participants in a religious ritual will return to everyday life transformed and re-empowered (Driver 1998 p. 82). Accounts from music therapy reveal numerous examples of active lifestyle change; and we have seen how musicking is increasingly becoming part of the tools of peace making (Urbain 2007). But it is the removal from everyday or propositional knowing that is central to the Spiritual domain, the entry into a transitional space, as described by Winnicott and Klein (Bouwen et al 2008 p. 2). Here imagination is nurtured; Mary Warnock describes the role of imagination in the linking of the two worlds:

> It is my view that it requires imagination to perform the trick of connecting the momentary and ephemeral with the permanent, the particular with the universal. (Warnock 1999 p. 2)

So the liminal/Spiritual experience is transformative in that it is related to the everyday world. We come into the experience with situations that may be problematic; we leave it with those situations changed because of the imaginative possibilities of entering this other time/space dimension.

Boundary Loss in a Boundaried Space

As we have seen, Turner developed the notion of *communitas* from the bond that develops between pilgrims in the liminal stages of the pilgrimage. He concentrates on a sense of intimacy and I-Thou awareness. The liminal/spiritual musical experience includes a unitive element that resembles that of the ecstasy of religious mystics. This often takes the form of a feeling of being united with the universe, other beings and the natural world. Nicholas Cook (1990 p. 242) develops the idea through the domain of Construction by seeing the formal structure of the music as a container in which the imagination of the listener can flow free; but he emphasises the links with the cultural presuppositions of the listener (Cook 1990 p. 242). This links music closely with traditional rituals. A musical piece, especially one that is familiar to us, can become a place of reflection and meditation. Many of the familiar pieces of the Western classical canon serve this purpose, particularly for people of particular educational backgrounds. The security of the space provided by the musical event enables normal boundaries to be porous. This opens up new possibilities of elaborate and innovative fusions between the alterities within the self and also with others who are different from us.

A Place of Intuition

We have looked at Isabel Clarke's (2005 p. 93) notion of the transliminal way of knowing with its characteristics of porous reality and the tolerance of paradox unlike rationality. The important aspect here is that difference co-exists easily here. This can be linked to childhood playing and its joining of joy and seriousness. Brian Lancaster's work postulates a link between this and Jewish Midrashic logic, the property of the newly born baby. Western culture has devalued intuition; in its most extreme form, this has resulted in its pathologisation. The literature on spirituality and creativity asks us to restore the place of the spiritual in our understanding of human beings. This opens up the way for the discovery of alterities within the self where the Other is accepted and celebrated, as in the practice of mindfulness. The hold of traditional social roles is loosened, as in carnivalesque traditions (Savery 2007). The most powerful and life-transforming experiences of musicking take place where there are at first differences; these are overcome by the persistence of the experiencer in the face of a very different Other and the two join with a bisociative click (Koestler 1964). This is particularly important in the face of different cultures. The musical spiritual experience accesses the less conscious parts of the human being, where Wisdom for the whole group resides, untapped by rationality. In this area there is a tolerance of apparent paradox and contradiction which makes it differ from rational thinking. So, the new logic of the liminal is a both/and logic not the either/or logic of the everyday world. This enables paradox and contradiction to co-exist easily – so difference-in-relationship can be enabled, as expressed by Robert Kaggwa in Chapter Nine.

Encounter

Encounter has been an essential part of the thinking in this book, based on Levinas, Derrida and Buber. It is encounter that links the strands of spirituality with the domains of the musicking experience. The accessing of intuitive processes enables easy encounter. In music we encounter the same range of domains as the various groups in the Shakespearian wood. The domain of Materials is equivalent to the wood and its plants, the domain of Expression to the range of emotions encountered by the players, the domain of Construction to a new discourse – in the wood it is the way of the fairies – and in the domain of Values to a release from patriarchy. Some would see the whole experience as an encounter with the spiritual when the limen is crossed, at the magical time of the solstice:

> As I listened to a Bach fugue, I became aware of a hovering presence. I felt that I was in some kind of trance and my friend had to nudge me hard when the music stopped. At the same time, she said 'Why are you looking so yonderly?' I found it difficult to explain to her that I had been conscious of a presence greater than myself.[2]

In the liminal/spiritual musical space we are brought into encounters with a huge range of possibilities. This means that the interaction between these various encounters – with the other-than human world, the volatile expressive world, new discourses and new cultures –contain the possibility of new patterns and ways of knowing.

2 RERC.

Loss of Responsibility

The link with the Divine – however this is perceived or described – takes the responsibility out of the hands of the musicker. The link between God/ Goddess and music in Western culture is deep, as we saw in mystics like Hildegard of Bingen (Van der Weyer 1997 p. 79). In Renaissance thinking, we see the shift from the Christian view of music to more humanistic views by a rediscovery of Graeco-Roman ideas. In the hands of the philosophers of the Enlightenment, the link between music and the Spiritual became weakened and the search for the Spiritual – which had characterised the musical tradition of Europe for hundreds of years – became an essentially human search. Words like truth started to reappear in philosophers, such as Heidegger (1886–1976). The notion of the connection with the Divine now reappeared in the human sphere and music and the aesthetic came to be about the highest expression of human achievement. The spirits, that once characterised the outer world of the beyond, can now be identified as human personality traits and emotions.

We have seen how the peak experience became associated with notions of self-fulfilment in Maslow's hierarchy of human needs (Maslow 1967 pp. 40–55), in which he includes the aesthetic – the need for beauty, order, symmetry. This is placed immediately below his pinnacle of self-actualisation – realising one's full potential. These experiences include an intense experience of the present, concentration, self-forgetfulness, a lessening of defences and inhibitions, empowerment, trust, spontaneity, and a fusion of person with the world, which is close to Csikszentmihalyi's concept of 'flow' (M. Csikszentmihalyi and I.S. Csikszentmihalyi 1988, M. Csikszentmihalyi, 1993) and to experiences in psychosynthesis set out by Assagioli (1974/94).

When we experience a power beyond our normal consciousness and surrender to it, we become free to play. Vegar Jordanger, in a project in the Caucasus, describes the entry into this freedom in the area of improvisation:

> In the context of the mixed groups in Rostov, there was no time to mentally prepare for improvisation. The music was improvised on the spot. Once the musicians started playing on their instruments, we saw mental concentration and playfulness in their

> faces. In other words, once the musicians started playing they instantly entered the zone of risk and uncertainty – this is the zone of dialogue par excellence (Jordanger 2008 p. 13)

This opens up the possibility of the discovery of deep joy (Robbins 1993, pp. 15–16). Freed of responsibility in the liminal space, we are able to play and take risks without fear of consequence. This can engender real joy.

Empathy with Others

Music can take the listener on the same journey as the composer. Anthony Rooley, for example, gives an account of the cathartic effect of performances of John Dowland's *The Songs of Mourning* (Rooley 1990) for people who have suffered a bereavement. We have already seen the power in Rik Palieri's song healing the abusive relationship with his father. Hildegard writes of the complexity within the experience:

> In music, you can hear the sound of burning passion in a virgin's breast. You can hear a twig coming into bud. You can hear the brightness of the spiritual light shining from heaven. You can hear the depth of thought of the prophets. You can hear the wisdom of the apostles spreading across the world. You can hear the blood pouring from the wounds of the martyrs. You can hear the innermost movements of a heart steeped in holiness. You can hear a young girl's joy at the beauty of God's earth. (Van der Weyer 1997 p. 79)

So music is able to handle the paradoxes set up by feeling mixed and contradictory emotions which are embedded in its structure (Langer 1953). Vegar Jordanger, in his work in Crimea, uses this notion to interrogate the complexity of emotional tensions:

> Rather we will explore in depth a particular case in Crimea, during which Guided Imagery and Music (GIM) was introduced at a critical phase of a dialogue with Chechen, North Ossetian and Russian participants ... We want to demonstrate the transformation of group emotional tensions into a flowing 'moment' called 'collective vulnerability' by Neimeyer and Tschudi (2003). (Jordanger 2007 p. 129)

He describes the difficulties of the journey:

> In the Crimea music journey case, there are no attempts to downplay, avoid deliberately addressing, or 'erase' social distinctions or differences. Rather, the group processes initiated touched directly and involved very deeply the affective layers of the participants. A reconfiguration of human relations resulted. (Jordanger 2008, p. 144)

The complexity of the emotional world of music in the liminal space can facilitate individual and group vulnerability; this can lead them to a place of empathy (Laurence 2008). This can bring about new qualities of understanding of the complexity of inner emotional life and enable relationship.

Trying out a New Persona

Through this empathy within group vulnerability, people are free to discover new parts of themselves:

> Therapy should facilitate peak experiences, those sublime moments wherein one is able to transcend and integrate splits within the person, within the world. Since the arts facilitate the occurrences of peak experiences, aesthetic endeavors are seen to be a central aspect of life and therefore of therapy. (Bruscia 1987 p. 33)

An example of this happened in the *Family Grooves* (Cortis and Price 2005) project – a project aimed at disadvantaged people living in an area of South London. Here a nine-month-old baby was condemned as naughty by his parents. Having finally persuaded his parents to place him in the middle of collection of musical instruments, he shows obvious delight; his obvious pleasure influenced his depressed parents to join him, leading the family into an experience of real joy. Looked-after children in a project in Hampshire UK, through the medium of music, encountered another way of being in the Spiritual/liminal space of the music session, which affected their relationships beyond the music group. The Spiritual/liminal space enables us to try out new personas based on the experience of others and to have a greater variety of behaviour strategies in real life.

New Discourses

In the domain of Construction, there is an encounter with the way discourse works in another culture whether these are separated historically or geographically. Here we encounter the complexity of encountering the relationship between religion and music in our own culture that we explored in the domain of Values. It is in this area that debates about the universality of the language of music centre. Martha Nussbaum highlights that effort is necessary to cross cultural boundaries:

> Music may be universal in the sense that people widely separated by language and culture can learn to love the same music. It is not universal in the sense that this response is automatic or without effort. (Nussbaum 2003 p. 263)

Through musical encounter we can learn to acknowledge that truth is multiple. The possibilities of this in the area of multicultural education are highlighted by a number of projects (Boyce-Tillman 2007c). In musicking we encounter new ways of discussing and debating and this gives us insight into the ways of other cultures. This can enrich our own ways of processing and interrogating other knowledges. It may well take considerable effort to learn these discourses but having learned them in music the understanding can be applied to other areas in unfamiliar cultures.

Agency

Many writers see the liminal experience as a source of empowerment. Cynthia Cohen sees the need for agency as an antidote to violence:

> By 'agency' we mean the ability to imagine circumstances beyond the constraints of the present situation, and to make choices and take action based on one's own thoughts and feelings and/or the sensibilities and interest of one's community. (C. Cohen 2008b, p. 2)

Many of the interviews following my music projects highlight personal empowerment. 'I feel braver than before – braver in real life' (Boyce-Tillman 2007d). Within the Spiritual/liminal space, we can imagine new worlds for ourselves and others and generate hope for ourselves and our culture. This is because we are outside the real life situation. This enables us to re-enter that situation with ideas of strategies for resisting or surviving situations of oppression.

The Opening Myths

The opening Prelude was based on three Greek myths – those of Psyche, Hermes and Orpheus. This book has established a place for Psyche that reunites her with Eros. The Materials domain of the experience with its concentration on instrumental and vocal technique and the grasp of notational systems has been expanded to include the domains of Expression, Construction and Values to open up a place for Psyche to dwell in the experience. It has suggested that this requires a multi- and inter-disciplinary approach. It certainly means bringing together the areas traditionally covered by Musicology, Music Therapy and Ethnomusicology.

I have set out the possible reintegration of The Good, The True and The Beautiful, once integrated within the figure of Psyche, through musicking. We can reinstate into the musical experience the domain of The Good (by reinstating Values as a domain of the musical experience) and The True (by reinstating the domain of Expression within the musical experience). This means that the area of The Beautiful (traditionally central to musicological study) – Aesthetics – can be redefined as not only in the domain of Construction but in the interrelationship between these domains. In reintegrating these elements within the musical experience, the fragmented Psyche of Western culture stands a chance of being reunited.

In the myth of Hermes the messenger of the gods the dilemma of the narratives has been encountered. Do we – as some religions claim – need particular narratives to make meaning from the spiritual experience? How do these play out in a pluralist world? Within the development of the idea of the spiritual, the centrality of the narratives to the spiritual dimension of faith has been challenged by a greater stress on relationship and the validation of the possibility of a multiplicity of narratives. This has enabled the multidimensional musical experience to play an important part in a view of spirituality as primarily encounter. The combination of this with Turner's idea of liminality has set out a model of spirituality within a secularised society; so musickers can take on the role of the psychagogue to enrich their lives and that of the wider cosmos.

The Orpheus myth, founded as it is in the notion of an anima mundi that enlivens the whole universe or Gaia, enables us to embrace a widening view of musicking that encompasses both experiencer and experienced and includes the natural and the metaphysical world within its embrace. It also includes orate traditions, which often have a greater degree of improvisational characteristics than notated traditions. The inclusion of these includes more Dionysian elements within Western concepts of musicking which at the time of Nietzsche was associated with Apollonian order. In restoring some unity to a fragmented world it challenges dominant paradigms and offers possibilities of integration.

Summary

In this book, I have set out a phenomenological model of musicking as a complex series of encounters, in an attempt to understand the spiritual experience involving music. I have described the fusion in the experience of the musicker to produce a liminal space and linked this with the spiritual and the soul. I have illustrated this with reference to Shakespeare's play *A Midsummer Night's Dream*. Music can generate multiple meanings and engage all the faculties of the musickers – the spiritual, intellectual, emotional and sensory. This makes it an ideal tool for constructing meaning by asking questions, for re-membering the past and setting up fresh imaginings of the future. I have illustrated these from a variety of musicking events, showing the transformative possibilities of music in a variety of contexts and linking these with the spiritual. It has been possible to analyse these events by including the domains of the Materials of sound, the Expressive qualities of sound, the mode of discourse and debate used by the sounds (Construction) and the Values contained within and around the sounds in the frame.

If we embrace the complexity and richness of the musical experience, we may rediscover the soul of Western culture and reunite it with the material world– re-incarnate it – not as separate from the tangible world but as the anima mundi flowing through it and animating it. I have discussed how these can be understood using the dogma and doctrines of established faiths, particularly Christianity; but I have also postulated how the model can be used to make sense of religionless spirituality.

I hope that this map/model will enable readers to see music as a real tool for negotiating the complexity of the contemporary world – strategies for resistance and survival (to use Foucauldian terms) and meaning-making; for the musical experience is not isolated from everyday life. At the end of the Shakespeare play, it is the Amazon queen Hyppolyta – the incomer to the civilised Athenian world – who sees what has happened most clearly. She notes the permanence of the changes achieved in this magical liminal space:

> But all the story of the night told over,
> And all our minds transfigured so together
> More witnesseth than fancy's images,
> And grows to something of great constancy;
> But howsoever, strange and admirable. (Bate 2008)

No model could contain the strange and admirable musical experience; but I have attempted to unpick the domains and link them with strands of spirituality; I hope that people will find it helpful to enrich their use of music to nurture their lives.

A Final story

> Four rabbis went up to heaven and there beheld the face of God. When they returned to earth one said that it was nothing – simply an aberration of the brain. One spent the rest of his life wandering in the desert foaming at the mouth and going mad. One

> turned it into a dogmatic system and bored everyone with his sermons. One was a singer of songs and a teller of tales and transformed the world. (Pinkola Estes 1992)

This story encapsulates many aspects of the spiritual in Western society. The first rabbi represents the secularists denying the presence of the experience. The second one represents the reaction of a society to an intuitive experience that has been pathologised in a culture that degrades the intuitive. The third rabbi shows the limiting power of the development of a product based approach by trapping it in creeds and dogmatic statements; religion can free up the spiritual but also limit its scope. The role of the fourth rabbi has often been overlooked but it contains within it the vocation to be a psychagogue – to lead people from a limited way of knowing into a wider vision. I hope that this book will enable you to find a way of musicking the spiritual with the intention of finding the deepest wellbeing within yourselves and the wider cosmos.

Bibliography

Abrams, David (1996), *The Spell of the Sensuous*, New York: Pantheon Books.

Adamek, Karl, trans Ruff, A. (1996), *Singen als Lebenshilfe. Zur Empirie und Theorie von Alltagsbewaeltigan. Plaedoyer fuer eine 'Erneute Kultur des Singens'* (Singing as Self-Help. Empirical Data and Theory of Coping with daily Life. Appeal for a 'Renewed Culture as singing'), Münster: Waxmann-Verlag.

Addison, Richard (1975), Children (even musical ones) make Music, *Music in Education*, Vol. 39, No. 372, pp. 60–3.

Adorno, Theodore, trans Hullor-Kentor, R. (1997, first published 1970), *Aesthetic Theory*, Minneapolis: University of Minnesota Press.

Agrotou, Anthi (1993), Spontaneous Ritualised Play in Music therapy: A Technical and Theoretical Analysis. In Heal, Margaret and Wigram, Tony (eds) (1993), *Music therapy in Health and Education*, London: Jessica Kingsley, pp. 175–91.

Aldridge, David (1996), *Music Therapy Research and Practice in Medicine – From Out of the Silence*, London: Jessica Kingsley.

Alexander, H.A. and McLaughlin, T.H. (2003), Education in Religion and Spirituality. In Blake N., Smeyers, J. and Standish P. (2003), *The Blackwell Guide to the Philosophy of Education*, Oxford: Blackwell, pp. 356–73.

Allsup, Randall (2013), Music Teacher Quality and Expertise, Paper at the *Ninth International Symposium on the Philosophy of Music Education*, Teachers College, Columbia University, New York, USA, June 5th–8th.

Amies choir <http://www.pan-arts.net/pages/support-our-work.html> Accessed June 2014.

Anderson, Benedict R. (1991), *Imagined communities: Reflections on the origin and spread of nationalism*, London: Verso.

Agwin, R. (1998), Creating sacred space, *Positive Health*, Dec/Jan, pp. 6–7.

Argyle, Michael (1997), *The Psychological perspective of Religious Experience* (2nd Series Occasional Paper 8) University of Wales Lampeter: Alister Hardy Religious Experience Research Centre.

Aristotle, (trans Butcher, S.H.) (1922), *The Poetics of Aristotle*, London: Macmillan and Co.

Arnold, Stephen (2014), *Sacred Music in Secular Society*, Farnborough: Ashgate.

Arnott, P.D. (1991), *Public and Performance in the Greek theatre*, London: Routledge.

Assagioli, Robert (1994 first published 1974), *The Act of Will*, London: Aquarian/Thorsons.

Augustine, trans Pine-Coffin, R.S. (1961), *Confessions*, New York: Penguin Classics.

Bacon, Francis ed by G.W. Kitchin (1973), *The Advancement of Learning*, London: J.M. Dent and Sons.

Bailey, B and Davidson, Jane W. (2003), Amateur Group Singing as a Therapeutic Instrument, *Nordic Journal of Music Therapy*, 12, pp. 18–32.

Bailey, B and Davidson, Jane W. (2005), Effects of group singing and performance for marginalised and middle-class singers, *Psychology of Music*, 33, 3, pp. 269–303.

Baird, Joseph and Ehrman, Radd (translators) (1994), *Letters of Hildegard of Bingen*, Oxford: Oxford University Press.

Bakhtin, Mikhail, trans Iswolsky, Hélène (1993), *Rabelais and His World*, Bloomington: Indiana University Press.

Bakhtin, Mikhail (1996), *Speech Genres and other late Essays*, Austin: University of Texas Press.

Ball (ed.) (1938), *The Basic Writings of Sigmund Freud*, New York: Random House.

Ball, S.J. (ed.) (1990), *Foucault and Education: Disciplines and Knowledge*, London: Routledge.

Badham, Paul (2012), Researching Religious Experience from a Comparative Perspective: The Alister Hardy Global Project, *Interreligious Insight* Vol. 10 no. 2, December, pp. 18–27.

Barron, Frank (1963), Creative Vision and Imagination. In Frazier (ed.) (1963), *New insights and the Curriculum Year Book 1963*, Washington D.C., Association of Supervision in Curriculum Development, pp. 285–305.

Bate, Jonathan (2008), Seems when everything is double. Article in Programme for *A Midsummer Night's Dream*, Stratford upon Avon: Royal Shakespeare Company (no page numbers).

Bateson, Gregory (1972), *Steps to an ecology of mind*, New York: Ballantine.

Batzoglou, Antonia (2011), *Towards a theatre of psychagogia: an experimental application of the Sesame approach into psychophysical actor training*, Unpublished PhD thesis submitted at the Central School of Speech and Drama, University of London.

Bauer, Joachim and Blanchard, Tsvi (2010), In my flesh I see God: A Neurobiological perspective on being human, *Tikkun*, January/February, pp. 43–5, 72–3.

Bayton, Mavis (1998), *Frock Rock: Women performing popular music*, Oxford: Oxford University Press.

Beattie, Tina (2007), *The New Atheists: The Twilight of Reason and the War on Religion*, London: Darton, Longman and Todd.

Begbie, Jeremy (2000), *Theology, Music and Time*, Cambridge: Cambridge University Press.

Belenky, Mary Field, McVicker Clinchy, Blythe, Rule Goldberger, Nancy, Mattuck Tarule, Jill (1986), *Women's Ways of Knowing: The Development of Self, Voice, and Mind*, New York: Basic Books.

Bell, Judith and Bell, Tim (2012), Nurturing Students in School Music programme after a Natural Disaster. Paper given at *the International Society for Music Education Conference*, Thessaloniki, Greece, July, pp. 59–64.

Bender, Courtney (2010), *The New Metaphysicals: Spirituality and the American Religious Imagination*, Chicago: The University of Chicago Press.

Bennett, Alan (2001), Hymn. Radio 4 22nd December.

Berliner, P. (1997), Give and Take: The Collective conversation of Jazz Performance. In R.K. Sawyer (ed.) *Creativity in Performance*, CT: Ablex, pp. 9–41.

Bernard, Rhoda (2009), Music making, transcendence, flow, and music education, *International Journal of Education and the Arts* 10, no. 14 <http://www.ijea.org/v10n14/v10n14.pdf>.

Best, Ron (2004), Spirituality, Faith and Education: Some Reflections from a UK Perspective. In Watson, Jacqueline, De Souza Marian and Trousdale, Ann (eds) (2004), *Global perspectives on Spirituality and Education*, Abingdon: Routledge, pp. 5–20.

Best, Ron (2011), Emotion, Spiritual Experience and Education: A Reflection, *International Journal of Children's Spirituality* 13 (4), pp. 361–8.

Beyer, Anders (ed.) (1996), *The Music of Per Norgard: Fourteen Interpretative Essays,* Aldershot: Scolar Press.

Blacking, John (1976), *How Musical is Man?* London: Faber and Faber.

Blacking, John (1977), *The Anthropology of the Body*, London: Academic.

Blacking, John (1987), *A Commonsense View of all Music,* Cambridge: Cambridge University Press.

Blackmore, Susan (1999), *The Meme Machine,* Oxford: Oxford University Press.

Blake, Andrew (1997), *The Land without Music: Music Culture and Society in Twentieth Century Britain*, Manchester: Manchester University Press.

Bogdan, Deanne (2013), Musical Spirituality in Listening, Learning and Performance, Panel presentation at the *Ninth International Symposium on the Philosophy of Music Education*, Teachers College, Columbia University, New York, US, June 5th–8th.

Bohlman, Philip V. (2003), Music and Culture: Historiographies of Disjuncture. In Clayton Martin., Herbert Trevor and Middleton Richard (eds) *The Cultural Study of Music: A Critical Introduction*, Oxford: Routledge, pp. 45–56.

Bomford, Rodney (2005), Ignacio Matte Blanco and the Logic of God. In Clarke, Chris (ed.) (2005), *Ways of Knowing: Science and Mysticism today*, Exeter: Imprint Academic, pp. 127–42.

Bonenfant, Yvon (2014), The Uluzuzulalia Project. <http://www.yvonbonenfant.com/uluzuzulalia/> Accessed December 2015.

Bourgeault, Cynthia (2008), *The Wisdom Jesus*, Boston and London: Shambhala.

Bouwen Rene, Jacques Haers, Elias Lopez Perez, Stephan Parmentier, Luc Reychler (2008), Transitional Spaces: Transforming Conflict Borders into Frontiers of Peace, Lessons learnt from the Advanced master's programme in Conflict and Sustainable Peace. Paper delivered at *International Peace Research Association Conference*, Leuven University, Belgium, July 2008.

Bowman, Wayne (2012), Music as ethical Practice: The Contemporary Significance of Ancient Greek Insights. Keynote for *Musical Paedia, International Society for Music Education Conference*, Thessaloniki Greece, July.

Bowie, Fiona (1998), Trespassing Sacred Domains: A Feminist Anthropological Approach to Theology and Religious Studies, *Journal of Feminist Studies in Religion*, Vol. 14 No. 1, pp. 40–62.

Boyce-Tillman, June (1991a), Towards a Model of Development of Children's Musical Creativity, *Canadian Music Educator*, Vol. 30/2, pp. 169–74.

Boyce-Tillman, June (1991b), Children's Musical Development, *Portuguese Journal of Music Education*, March, pp. 16–28.

Boyce-Tillman, June (1993), Women's Ways of Knowing, *British Journal of Music Education* 10, pp. 153–61.

Boyce-Tillman, June (1994), The Role of Women in the passing on of Tradition and its Implications for the School Music Curriculum. In *Musical Connections/ Traditions and Change*, Proceedings of *Twenty-first World Conference International Society for Music Education*, Tampa, Florida, USA.

Boyce-Tillman, June (1996), A Framework for Intercultural Dialogue in Music. In Floyd, Malcolm (ed.) (1996), *World Musics in Education*, Farnborough: Scolar Books, pp. 43–94.

Boyce-Tillman, June (1998), *The Call of the Ancestors*, London: The Hildegard Press.

Boyce-Tillman, J.B. (2000a), *Constructing Musical Healing: The Wounds that Sing*, London: Jessica Kingsley.

Boyce-Tillman, June (2000b), *The Creative Spirit- Harmonious Living with Hildegard of Bingen*, Norwich: Canterbury Press.

Boyce-Tillman, June (2000c), Promoting Well-being through Music Education, *Philosophy of Music Education Review*, vol 6, no 2, Fall pp. 89–98.

Boyce-Tillman, June (2001a), Sounding the Sacred: Music as Sacred Site. In Ralls-MacLeod, Karen and Harvey, Graham (eds) *Indigenous Religious Musics*, Farnborough: Scolar, pp. 136–66.

Boyce-Tillman, June (2001c), *The Healing of the Earth*, reworked 2012 for Winchester Cathedral, London: The Hildegard Press.

Boyce-Tillman, June (2002a), Subjugated Ways of Knowing, *The Journal of Critical Psychology, Counselling and Psychotherapy*, Vol. 2 No. 4 Winter, pp. 208–13.

Boyce-Tillman, June (2002b), Sound Balance – Music and Well-being with Young Children, *Early Childhood Connections – Journal of Music- and Movement-based learning*, Vol. 8 No. 2 Spring – *The Healing Power of Music*, pp. 29–37.

Boyce-Tillman, June (2002c), Promoting Well Being through Music Education with young children, *Early Childhood Connections*, pp. 29–37.

Boyce-Tillman, June (2003), Assessing Diversity, *The Journal of the Arts and Humanities in Higher Education*, pp. 23–62.

Boyce-Tillman, June (2004), Towards an Ecology of Music Education, *Philosophy of Music Education Review*, Vol. 12 No. 2 Fall, pp. 102–25.

Boyce-Tillman, June (2005a), *Ways of Knowing*. In Clarke, Chris (ed.) (2005), *Ways of Knowing, Science and Mysticism today*, Exeter: Imprint Academic, pp. 8–33.

Boyce-Tillman, June (2005b), *PeaceSong*, London: The Hildegard Press.

Boyce-Tillman, June (2006a), Music as Spiritual Experience, *Modern Believing: Church and Society*, Vol. 47 No. 3, July, pp. 20–31.

Boyce-Tillman, June and White, Victoria (2006b), *An Evaluation* of *Music with Looked After Children*, University of Winchester, <http://www3.hants.gov.uk/education/hms/hms-listen2me.htm>.

Boyce-Tillman, June (2006c), *A Rainbow to Heaven*, London: Stainer and Bell.

Boyce-Tillman, June (2007a), The Spirituality of Music Education. In Bresler, Liora (ed.) (2007), *The International Handbook of Research in Arts Education*, Amsterdam: Springer, pp. 1405–21.

Boyce-Tillman, June (2007b), *Unconventional Wisdom*, London: Equinox.

Boyce-Tillman, June (2007c), Music and Value in Cross-cultural work. In Urbain, Olivier (2007), *Music and Conflict transformation: Harmonies and Dissonances in Geopolitics*, London: I.B. Tauris, pp. 40–52.

Boyce-Tillman, June (2007d), Peace Making in Educational contexts. In Urbain, Olivier (2007), *Music and Conflict transformation: Harmonies and Dissonances in Geopolitics*, London: I.B. Tauris, pp. 212–28.

Boyce-Tillman, June (2007e), The Wounds that Sing: Music as Transformation. In Baxter, Jonathan (ed.) (2007), *Wounds that Heal: Theology, Imagination and Health*, London: SPCK, pp. 229–50.

Boyce-Tillman, June (2007f), *Ecological Celebration*, London: Hildegard Press.

Boyce-Tillman, June (2007g), Spirituality in Early Childhood Music Education. In Smithrim, Katharine and Upitis, Rena (eds) (2007), *Listen to their Voices: Research and Practice in Early Childhood Music Education*, Waterloo, Canada Music Educators' Association as Volume 3 of the Biennial series *Research to Practice* (Lee R. Bartel, series editor), Waterloo, Canada, pp. 102–25.

Boyce-Tillman, June (2007h), *Step into the Picture*, Choral and orchestral work performed in the Anvil Concert Hall, Basingstoke, UK.

Boyce-Tillman, June (2009a), The Transformative Qualities of a liminal Space created by musicking, *Philosophy of Music Education Review*, Vol. 17 No. 2 Fall, pp. 184–202.

Boyce-Tillman, June (2009b), *Space for Peace* <http://www.spaceforpeace.8k.com/>.

Boyce-Tillman, June (2010), Even the stones cry out: Music Theology and the Earth. In Isherwood, Lisa and Bellchambers, Elaine (ed.) (2010) *Through us, with us, in us: Relational Theologies in the Twenty-first Century*, London: SCM Press pp. 153–78.

Boyce-Tillman, June (2011a), Making Musical Space for Peace. In Laurence, Felicity and Urbain, Olivier (2011), *Peace and Policy Dialogue of Civilization for Global Citizenship*, Vol. 15, *Music and Solidarity: Questions of Universality, Consciousness and Connection*, New Brunswick and London: Transaction Publishers, pp. 185–201.

Boyce-Tillman, June (2012a), Music and the Dignity of Difference, *Philosophy of Music Education Review*, Vol. 20 No. 1 Spring, pp. 25–44.

Boyce-Tillman, June (2012b), And still I wander: Deconstructing Music Education through Greek Mythology, Keynote Panel at *Musical Paedia, International Society for Music Education Conference*, Thessaloniki Greece, July.

Boyce-Tillman, June, Bonenfant, Yvon, Bryden, Inga, Taiwo, Olu, de Faria, Tiago, Brown, Rohan (2012c) *PaR for the Course: Issues involved in the Development of Practice-based doctorates in the Performing Arts* <http://www.heacademy.ac.uk/resources/detail/disciplines/dance-drama-music/Boyce-Tillman_2012>.

Boyce-Tillman, June (2013a), 'And still I wander ... A Look at Western Music Education through Greek Mythology.' *Music Educators Journal*, Vol. 99 No. 3 March, pp. 29–33 <www.namfe.org>.

Boyce-Tillman, June (2013b), The Dignity of Difference. In Reason, Peter and Newman, Melanie (eds) (2013), *Stories of the Great Turning*, Bristol: Vala Publishing, pp. 169–77.

Boyce-Tillman, June (2013c), Embodied Cognition, *Work based Learning e-journal international* Vol. 3, 1, May, <http://wblearning-ejournal.com/currentissue.php>.

Boyce-Tillman, June (2013d), A Box full of Darkness, *Feminist Theology* Vol. 21, No. 3, May, pp. 326–42.

Boyce-Tillman, June (2014), *In Tune with Heaven or Not: Women in Christian Liturgical Music*, Oxford: Peter Lang.

Boyce-Tillman, June (2015) *From Conflict to chorus: A Intermezzo for Peace*, London: Hildegard Press.

Boyce-Tillman, June and Floyd, Malcolm (2003), *Encompassing Diversity – An Experiment in Music Course', Intercultural Music* Vol. 5, pp. 247–302.

Brabazon, J. (1981), *Dorothy L. Sayers – The Life of a Courageous Woman*, London: Victor Gollancz.

Bradley, Deborah (2010), Goin' Down to the River to Pray: The Slippery Slope of Spirituality and Music Education. Paper presented at *The Eighth International Society for the Philosophy of Music Education Symposium*, Helsinki Finland, June 9–13.

Bradley, Ian (1993), *The Celtic Way*, London: Darton, Longman and Todd.

Braidotti, Rosi (1994), *Nomadic Subjects*, New York: Columbia University Press.

Braidotti, Rosi (1995), The Body as Metaphor: Seduced and Abandoned: The Body in the virtual world' (1995), Videotape quoted in Ruth Mantin, *Thealogies in Process: The Role of Goddess-talk in Feminist Spirituality*, Unpublished PhD Thesis, May 2002, Southampton University.

Bridges, Robert (1932), Poems. In Parrott, Thomas Marc and Thorpe, Willard (1932) *Poetry of the Transition (1850–1914)*, New York: Oxford University Press, pp. 454–69.

Bright, Ruth (1993), Cultural Aspects of Music Therapy. In Heal, Margaret and Wigram, Tony (eds) (1993), *Music Therapy in Health and Education*, London: Jessica Kingsley, pp. 196–225.

Briskman, L. (1981), Creative Products and Creative Process in Science and Art. In Dutton, D. and Krausz, M. (eds) (1981), *The Concept in Creativity in Science and Art*, Boston: Martinus Nijhoff Publications, pp. 129–55.

Brown, Rosalind (2015), Singing Theology: the contribution of hymns to the liturgy. Keynote presentation at *Hymns in Liturgy and Life, International Conference of Hymn Societies*, Cambridge, UK, 26th July–1st August.

Brown, David and Loades, Ann (1995), *The Sense of the Sacramental: Movement and Measure in Art and Music, Place and Time*, London: SPCK.

Bruscia, Kenneth E. (1987), *Improvisational Models of Music Therapy*, Springfield Ill: Charles Thomas.

Bruner, Jerome (1966), *The Process of Education: Towards a theory of instruction*, Cambridge MA: Belknap Press.

Buber, Martin, trans Kaufmann, Walter (1970), *I and Thou*, New York: Charles Scribner's Sons.

Bunt, Leslie (1994), *Music Therapy – An Art beyond words*, London: Routledge.

Busoni, Ferruccio, trans Ley, Rosemary (1957/65), *The Essence of Music and other Papers*, New York: Dover Publications.

Bygren, L.O., Konlaan, B.B. and Johansson S. (1996), Attendance at cultural events, reading books or periodicals and making music or singing in a choir as determinants for survival. Swedish interview survey of living conditions, *British Medical Journal*, 313, pp. 1577–80.

Cage, John (1978), Silence, quoted in Ross, M. (1978), *The Creative Arts*, London: Heinemann.

Cage, John (1980), The Future of Music. In Cage, John (1980), *Empty Words: Writings '73–'78 by John Cage*, London: Marion Boyars.

Cameron, Julia (1997), Unlocking your creativity. In Toms, Michael (ed.) (1997), *The Well of Creativity*, Carlsbad CA: Hay House, pages not available.

Carr, David (2010), The Philosophy of Education and Educational Theory. In Bailey, Richard, Barrow, Robin, Carr, David, McCarthy, Christine (eds) (2010), *The SAGE Handbook of the Philosophy of Education*, London: Sage, pp. 37–54.

Carrette, Jeremy and King, Richard (2005), *Selling Spirituality: The Silent Takeover of Religion*, London: Routledge.

Carson, Ciaran (1986), *Irish Traditional Music*, Belfast: Appletree Press.

Charlesworth, Max (1988), *Religious experience. Unit A. Study guide 2* (Deakin University) <http://en.wikipedia.org/wiki/Religious_experience> accessed June 4th 2012.

Chazan, Saralea (2002), *The Profiles of Play*, London: Hamish Hamilton.

Chisholm, Roderick (1966), *Theory of Knowledge*, Englewood Cliffs NJ: Prentice Hall.

Chittister, Joan (1991), *Wisdom distilled from the Daily: Living the Rule of St Benedict today*, New York: HarperCollins.

Christ, Carol P. (1997), *Rebirth of the Goddess: Finding meaning in Feminist Spirituality*, Reading, Massachusetts: Addison Wesley.

Christ, Carol P. (2003), *She who changes: re-imagining the Divine in the World*, New York and Basingstoke: Macmillan Palgrave.

Chua, D. (199), *Absolute Music and the Construction of Meaning*, Cambridge: Cambridge University Press.

Clack, Beverley (2012), Keynote address at the *Anniversary conference of the Britain and Ireland School of Feminist Theology*, July, University of Winchester, UK.

Clarke, Chris (2002), *Living in Connection: Theory and Practice of the New Worldview*, Warminster: Creation Spirituality Books.

Clarke, Chris (ed.) (2005) *Ways of Knowing: Science and Mysticism today*, London: Imprint.

Clarke, Eric (2005), *Ways of Listening*, Oxford: Oxford University Press.

Clarke, Isabel (2005), There is a crack in everything, that's how the light gets in. In.

Clarke, Chris (ed.) (2005), *Ways of Knowing: Science and Mysticism today*, London: Imprint, pp. 90–102.

Clarke, Isabel (2008), *Madness, Mystery and the Survival of God*, Ropley: O Books.

Classen, Constance (1998), *The Color of Angels: Cosmology, Gender and the Aesthetic*, London and New York: Routledge.

Claus, D.B. (1981), *Toward the Soul: An Inquiry into the Meaning of Psyche before Plato*, London: Yale University Press.

Claxton, Guy (2002), *Mind Expanding: Scientific and spiritual foundations for the schools we need.* Public lecture, University of Bristol, 21st October.

Claxton, Guy, Lucas, Bill and Webster, Rob (2010), *Bodies of knowledge, How the learning sciences could transform Practical and Vocational Education*, London: Edge Foundation.

Clift, Stephen, Hancox, Grenville, Morrison, Ian, Hess, Bärbel, Stewart, Don and Kreutz, Gunter (2001), *Choral Singing, Wellbeing and Health: Summary of Findings from a Cross-national Survey*. <http://www.canterbury.ac.uk/centres/sidney-de-haan-research/docs/report_6.pdf> Accessed January 2010.

Clift, Stephen and Hancox, Grenville (2001), The Perceived Benefits of Singing: Findings from preliminary surveys of a university choral society, *Journal of the Royal Society for the Promotion of Health*, 121, pp. 248–56.

Cobb, Edith (1977), *The Ecology of Imagination in Childhood*, New York: Columbia University Press.

Cochereau, Pierre (1994/6), Notes to the recording *Pierre Cochereau l'organiste de Notre-Dame* SOCD 94/96.

Cohen, Alan (2003), *Expressions of the Soul*, <www.expressionsofsoul.com/id27.html2> Accessed March 20th 2003.

Cohen, Cynthia (2008a), Acting Together on the World Stage: Performance and Peacebuilding in Global Perspective. Paper delivered at *International Peace Research Association Conference*, Leuven University, Belgium, July 2008.

Cohen, Cynthia (2008b), Music: A Universal Language? In Urbain, Olivier (ed.) (2008), *Music and Conflict transformation: Harmonies and Dissonances in Geopolitics*, London: I.B. Tauris, pp. 26–39.

Cohen, Leonard (1985) <http://www.azlyrics.com/lyrics/leonardcohen/anthem.html> Accessed August 21st 2012.

Collin, Matthew (1997), *Altered State: The Story of Ecstasy Culture and Acid House*, London: Serpent's Tail.

Collingwood, R.G. (1938), *The Principles of Art*, Oxford: Clarendon Press.

Cook, Nicholas (1990), *Music, Imagination and Culture*, Oxford: Clarendon Press.

Cook, Nicholas (1998), *Music: A very short Introduction*, Oxford: Oxford University Press.

Corbin, Henry, trans Manheim, Ralph (1998), *Alone with the Alone: Creative Imagination in the Sūfism of Ibn 'Arabī*, Princeton: Princeton University Press.

Coroniti, Joseph (1992), *Poetry as Text in Twentieth-Century Vocal Music: From Stravinsky to Reich*, Lampeter, Wales: Edwin Mellin Press.

Cortis, Ray and Price, Hilary (2005), *Evaluation Report on the Family Grooves Project*, Unpublished paper.

Costen, Melva Wilson (1993), *African American Christian Worship*, Nashville: Abingdon Press.

Cottle, T.J. (1973), A Simple Change in Creativity, *Journal of Creative Behaviour*, Vol. 7 No. 3 (3rd quarter), pp. 161–4.

Cross, Ian (2003), Music and biocultural evolution. In Clayton, Martin, Herbert, Trevor and Middleton, Richard (eds) (2003), *The Cultural Study of Music: A Critical Introduction*, Oxford: Routledge, pp. 19–30.

Crossan, John Dominic, 1992 [1973], *In Parables: The Challenge of the Historical Jesus*, Sonoma, California: Polebridge Press.

Crowe, B. (2004), *Music and Soul Making: Toward a New Theory of Music Therapy*, Oxford: Scarecrow Press.

Csikszentmihalyi, M. and Csikszentmihalyi, I.S. (1988), Optimal experience, *Psychological Studies of Flow in Consciousness*, Cambridge: Cambridge University Press.

Csikszentmihalyi, Mihaly (1990), *Flow – The Psychology of Optimal Experience*, New York: HarperPerennial.

Csikszentmihalyi, Mihaly (1993), *The Evolving Self*, New York: Harper and Row.

Cumming, Naomi (1997), The subjectivities of 'Erbarme mich', *Music Analysis*, 16, pp. 5–44.

Cupitt, Don (1998), *The Revelation of Being*, London: SCM.

Custodero, Lori (2002), Seeking challenge, finding skill: Flow experience in music education, *Arts Education and Policy Review*, 103 (3), pp. 3–9.

Custodero, Lori A. (2005a), Observable indicators of flow experience: A developmental perspective of musical engagement in young children from infancy to school age, *Music Education Research*, 7 (2), pp. 185–209.

Custodero, Lori (2005b), 'Being with': The resonant Legacy of Childhood's Creative Aesthetic, *The Journal of Aesthetic Education* Vol. 39, No. 2, Summer, pp. 50–4.

Dahlhaus, C., trans Bradford Robinson, J. (1989), *Nineteenth Century Music*, Berkeley: University of California Press.

Daly, Mary (1973), *Beyond God the Father: Toward a Philosophy of Women's Liberation*, Boston: The Beacon Press.

Damasio, Antonio (1994), *Descartes' Error: Emotion, Reason and the Human Brain*, New York: Avon Book.

Damasio, Antonio (1999), *The Feeling of What Happens: Body, Emotion and the Making of Consciousness*, Heinemann: London.

Davie, Grace (2002), *Europe; The Exceptional Case*, London: Darton, Longman and Todd.

Davies, James (2013), *Cracked: Why Psychiatry is doing more harm than good*, London: Icon.

Dawkins, Richard (2012), Interview on BBC Radio 4, 9am Sept 4th.

De Backer, J. (1993), Containment in Music Therapy. In Wigram, T. and Heal, M. (eds) (1993) *Music Therapy in Health and Education*, London: Jessica Kingsley, pp. 30–41.

De Botton, Alain (2012), *Religion for Atheists: A Non-believer's Guide to the Uses of Religion*, London and New York: Hamish Hamilton,.

De Quincy, Christian (2002), *Radical Nature: Rediscovering the Soul of Matter*, Montpelier VT: Invisible Cities Press.

de Saint Exupery, Antoine (1950), *Letter to a Hostage*, London: William Heinemann.

Debenham, Pat and Debenham Kathie (2008), Experiencing the Sacred in Dance Education: Wonder, Compassion, Wisdom and Wholeness in the Classroom, *Journal of Dance Education*, 8: 2, pp. 44–5.

Denk, Jeremy (2011), Taking on Taruskin. First published in Oct 16th 2011. <http://jeremydenk.net/blog/2011/10/16/taking-on-taruskin-2/> Accessed March 6th 2015.

DeNora, Tia (2013), *Music Asylums: Wellbeing through Music in Everyday Life*, Farnham and Burlington, VT: Ashgate.

Department for Education and Employment (2001), *Curriculum Guidelines*, London: Department for Education and Employment.

Department for Education and Skills (2002) *Transforming Youth Work – resourcing excellent youth services*, London: Department for Education and Skills/Connexions.

Derrida, Jacques (1972), *Margins of Philosophy*, Chicago: University of Chicago Press.

Derrida, J. and Psyche: Invention of the Other. Kamuf, P. (1991), In *A Derrida Reader: Between the Blinds*, New York: Columbia University Press, pp. 200–20.

Dewey, John (1910), *How we think*, New York: Heath and Co.

Dewey, John (1929), *The Quest for Certainty*, New York: G.P. Putnam's Sons.

Dewey, John (1934), *Art as Experience*, New York: Minton Balch and Co.

Dewey, John (1987), Art as Experience. In Dewey, John Boydston, Jo Ann (ed.) (1987), *The Later Works, 1925–1953, vol. 10: 1934*, Carbondale, IL: Southern Illinois University Press.

Diamond, Jared (2005), *Collapse: How Societies Choose to Fail or Survive*, London: Allen Lane.

Dissanayake, Ellen (1992), *Homo Aestheticus: Where Art comes from and why*, New York: The Free Press.

Dolan, Jill (2005), *Utopia in Performance: Finding Hope at the Theater*, Michigan: University of Michigan Press.

Dollinger, Stephen J. (1993), Research Note: Personality and Music Preference: Extraversion and Excitement Seeking or Openness to Experience?, *Psychology of Music*, January Vol. 21 no. 1, pp. 73–7.

Douskals, Peter (2012), Multiple Layers of Culture and multiple layers of society. Paper given at *Musical Paedia, International Society for Music Education Conference*, Thessaloniki Greece, July, pp. 89–99.

Downes, Andrew (1998), *Meditation: Its value to composers and other musicians?* Unpublished paper.

Dresser, Horatio (1919), *A History of the New Thought Movement*, New York: Thomas Y. Crowell Co.

Drinker, S. (first published 1948, reissued 1995), *Music and Women, The Story of Women in their relation to Music*, City University of New York: The Feminist Press.

Driver, Tom F. (1998), *Liberating Rites: Understanding the Transformative Power of Ritual*, Boulder, CO: Westview.

Duarte, Eduardo (2013), Music as Philosophical Education, Keynote lecture at the *Ninth International Symposium on the Philosophy of Music Education* at Teachers College, Columbia University, New York, US, June 5th–8th.

Dudek, S.Z. (1974), Creativity in Young Children – Attitude or Ability, *Journal of Creative Behaviour* Vol. 8, No. 4 (4th quarter), pp. 95–9.

Dunmore, Ian (1983), Sitar Magic, *Nadaposana One*, London: Editions Poetry.

Dupre, Louis (1990), *World Spirituality: An Encyclopaedic History of Religious Quest*, New York: Crossroad Publishing Co.

Dweck, Carol (1999), *Self-theories: Their Role in Motivation, Personality and Development*, Psychology Press: Philadelphia.

Eames, Penny (1999), *The ART and health partnership*, Wellington: Arts Access Aotearoa.

Easterling, P. and Hall, E. (eds) (2002), *Greek and Roman Actors: Aspects of an Ancient Profession*, Cambridge: Cambridge University Press.

Ellingson, L. (2008) *Introduction to Crystallization* <http://www.sagepub.com/upm-data/23241_Chapter_1.pdf> Accessed May 12th 2013.

Ellingson, L. (2009), *Engaging Crystallization in Qualitative Research: An Introduction*, London: Sage.

Elliott, David (1989), Key concepts in multi-cultural music education, *International Journal of Music Education* 13, pp. 11–33.

Elliott, David (1994), Music, Education and Musical Values, *Musical Connections: Tradition and Change*, ISME Proceedings Tampa Florida, US, pp. 8–24.

Elliott, R.K. (1971), Versions of Creativity, *Proceedings of Philosophy of Education Society of Great Britain*, Vol. 5, No. 2, pp. 139–52.

Ellis, Catherine J. (1985), *Aboriginal Music – Education for living*, Queensland: University of Queensland Press.

Emerson, Ralph. Waldo (1842), *Defining Transcendentalism: In the words of Ralph Waldo Emerson*. <http://www.transcendentalists.com/terminology.html> Accessed June 4th 2012.

Erikson, E.H. (1963), *Childhood and Society*, New York: W.W. Norton and Co.

Erricker, Clive, Erricker, Jane, Ota, Cathy, Sullivan D. and Fletcher, M. (1997), *The Education of the Whole Child*, London: Cassell.

Erricker, Clive and Erricker Jane (eds) (2001), *Meditation in Schools*, London: Continuum.

Escot, Pozzi (1999), *The Poetics of Simple Mathematics in Music*, Cambridge, MA: Contact International.

Evans, K. (1971), *Creative Singing*, London: Oxford University Press.

Fanshawe, David (1963), *African Sanctus*, Sleeve notes 6558 001 Philips label.

Fanshawe, David (1975), *African Sanctus*, London: Collins.

Feki, Soufiane (2011), Universals in music: Music as a communicational space. In Laurence, Felicity and Urbain, Olivier (2011), *Peace and Policy Dialogue of Civilization for Global Citizenship*, Vol. 15, *Music and Solidarity: Questions of Universality, Consciousness and Connection*, New Brunswick and London: Transaction Publishers,

Peace and Policy Vol. 15, pp. 45–63.

Ferrer, Jorge N., Romero, Marino T., Albareda, Ramon V. (2005), Integral Transformative Education: A Participatory Proposal, *Journal of Transformative Education, Vol. 3 No. 4, October* pp. 306–30 <http://nextstepintegral.org/wp-content/uploads/2011/04/Integral-Transformative-Education-Ferrer-Romero-Albareda.pdf>.

Fiorenza, Elisabeth Schussler (2000), *Jesus and the Politics of Interpretation*, New York and London: Continuum.

Floyd, Malcolm (1993), *The Trouble with Old Men*. Paper given at a research seminar at King Alfred's College, Winchester, UK.

Floyd, Malcolm (ed.) (1996), *World Musics in Education*, Aldershot: Scolar Books.

Floyd, Malcolm (2001), Individual: Community: Nation; A Case Study in Maasai Music and Kenyan Education, *International Journal of Music Education*, 38, pp. 13–38.

Ford, David (1999), *Self and Salvation, Being Transformed*, Cambridge: Cambridge University Press.

Fordham, M. (1986), *Jungian Psychotherapy*, London: Maresfield.

Foucault, Michel/Gordon, Colin ed. (1980), *Power Knowledge: Selected Interviews and Other writings 1972–77*, Hemel Hempstead: Harvester Wheatsheaf.

Foucault, Michel, trans Sheridan, Alan ([1963] 1973), *The Birth of a Clinic*, London: Penguin.

Fowler, Jennifer (1985), My own ears, *NMA4*, Victorian Ministry for the Arts, pp. 3–6.

Fox, Christopher, Brougham, Henrietta and Pace, Ian (eds) (1997), *Uncommon Ground: The Music of Michael Finnissy*, Aldershot: Ashgate.

Freire, P. (1972), *Cultural Action for Freedom*, Harmondsworth: Penguin Books.

Freire, P. (1998), *Pedagogy of Freedom*, Lanham: Rowman and Littlefield.

Freud, Sigmund (1949), *The Unconscious*, Collected papers No. 4, London: The Hogarth Press.

Freud, Sigmund (1970), Creative Writers and Daydreaming (1908). In Vernon P.E. (ed.), *Creativity*, Harmondsworth, Penguin, pp. 126–35.

Froebel, F., trans Barnard, H.H. (1879) *Papers on Froebel's Kindergarten with suggestions of Principles and Methods of Child Culture*, Syracuse: C.W. Bardeen.

Frost, Anthony and Yarrow, Ralph (1990), *Improvisation in Drama*, Basingstoke: Palgrave Macmillan.

Frowen-Williams, Gareth (1997), *Between Earth and Sky: Explorations on the Shamanic Path*. Unpublished Dissertation for MA in Ethnomusicology, University of Central England.

Fuller, Robert (2001), *Spiritual but not Religious: Understanding Unchurched America*, Oxford: Oxford University Press.

Gabriel, Peter (2000), <http://realworld.on.net> Accessed November 2000.

Gabrielsson, Alf, trans Bradbury Rod (2011), *Strong Experiences with Music: Music is much more than just music*, Oxford: Oxford University Press.

Gabrielsson, Alf and Lindstrom S. (1993), On strong experiences of Music, *Musik, psychologie, Jahrbuch der Deutschen Gesellschaft fur Musikpsychologie*, 10, pp. 118–39.

Gadamer, Hans-George, R. Bemasconi (ed.), trans Walker, N. (1986), *The Relevance of the Beautiful and Other Essays*, Cambridge: Cambridge University Press.

Gadamer, Hans-George, trans Smith, P. Christopher (1988), *The Idea of the Good in Platonic-Aristotelian Philosophy*, New Haven, CT: Yale University Press.

Gaertner, Mae (1998), The Sound of Music in the dimming, anguished world of Alzheimer's disease, *Music in Health and Special Education Seminar of the International Society for Music Education*, South Africa, July 1998 (no pages).

Gaita, Raimond (1999), *A Common Humanity*, Melbourne: Text Publishing.

Galtung, Johan (2008), Peace, Music and the Arts: In Search of Interconnections. In Urbain, Olivier (ed.) (2008), *Music and Conflict transformation: Harmonies and Dissonances in Geopolitics*, London: I.B. Tauris pp. 53–60.

Gardner, Howard (1983/1993), *Frames of Mind: The Theory of Multiple Intelligences*, New York: Basic Books.

Gardner, Howard. (1999), *Intelligence Reframed: Multiple Intelligences for the 21st Century*, New York: Basic Books.

Gardner, Kay (1990), *Sounding the Inner landscape: Music as medicine*, Rockport Mass and Shaftesbury, Dorset: Element Books.

Gass, Robert and Brehony, Kathleen A. (2000), *Chanting: Discovering Spirit in Sound*, London: Broadway.

Geertz, Clifford (1971), Religion as a cultural system. In Banton M. (ed.) (1971) *Anthropological Approaches to the Study of Religion*, ASA Monograph 3, London: Tavistock Publications, pp. 1–46.

Geertz, Clifford (1973), *The Interpretation of Cultures: Selected Essays*. New York: Basic.

Ghiselin, B. (ed.) (1952), Introduction to Ghiselin. B. (ed.) (1952), *The Creative Process*, New York: Mentor Books, pp. 11–13.

Ghiselin, B. (1956), The Creative Process and its Relation to the Identification of Creative Talent. In Taylor, C.W. (ed.) *The 1955 University of Utah Research Conference on the Identification of Creative Talent*, Salt Lake City: University of Utah Press, pp. 95–203.

Giddens, Anthony (1999), *Tradition*, Third Reith Lecture.

Godwin, Joscelyn (1979), *Robert Fludd: Hermetic Philosopher and Surveyor of Two Worlds*, London: Thames and Hudson.

Godwin, Joscelyn (1987), *Music, Magic and Mysticism: A Sourcebook*, London: Arkana.

Goehr, Lydia (1992), *The Imaginary Museum of Musical Works: An Essay in the Philosophy of Music*, Oxford: Clarendon Press.

Golann, S.E. (1963), Psychological Study of Creativity, *Psychological Bulletin*, Vol. 60, No. 6, pp. 548–65.

Goldman, Jonathan (1992), *Healing Sounds – The Power of Harmonics*, Shaftesbury: Element Books.

Gonski, Richard (1999), Symphonic Mind: States of Consciousness in Orchestral Performance. In Steer, Maxwell (ed.) (1999) *Contemporary Music Review: Music and Mysticism* (I), Vol. 14 Parts 3–4, pp. 55–64.

Gooch, Stan (1972), *Total man: Towards an Evolutionary Theory of Personality*, London: Allen Lane, Penguin Press.

Goss, Robert E. (2002), *Queering Christ: Beyond Jesus acted up*, Chicago: The Pilgrim Press.

Gowan, J.C. (1967) What makes a gifted child creative? Four Theories. In Gowan, J.C., Demos, C.D., Torrance, P.E. (eds) (1967), *Creativity: Its Educational Implications*, New York, London: Wiley, pp. 9–15.

Grainger, Roger (1995), *Drama and Healing: The Roots of Drama Therapy*, London: Jessica Kingsley.

Grainger, Roger (2004), Theatre and Encounter, *Dramatherapy*, 26 (1), pp. 4–9.

Green, Lucy (1988), *Music on Deaf Ears: Musical Meaning, Ideology and Education*, Manchester and New York: Manchester University Press.

Green, Lucy (1997), *Music, Gender, Education*. Cambridge: Cambridge University Press.

Grey, Mary C. (1989), *Redeeming the Dream: Feminism, Redemption and Christian tradition*, London: SPCK.

Grey, Mary (1993), *The Wisdom of Fools: Seeking Revelation for Today*, London: SPCK.

Grey, Mary (delivered originally in 1995), Till we have faces. Chapter in Atkinson-Carter, Gloria (ed.) (2001), In Being: The Winton Lectures 1979-2000, Winchester: King Alfred's, Winchester, pp. 61–8

Grey, Mary (2007), Ecomysticism: a contemporary path of Christian healing. In Jonathan Baxter (ed.) *Wounds that heal: Theology, Imagination and Health*, London: SPCK, pp. 36–56.

Gross, Richard (2012), *Being Human: Psychological and Philosophical Perspectives*, Abingdon: Routledge.

Guilford, J.P. (1962), Creativity. Its Measurement and Development. In Parnes, S.J. and Harding, H.F. (eds) (1962), *A Source Book of Creative Thinking*, New York: Charles Scribners Sons, pp. 156–67.

Gutman, H (1967), The Biological Roots of Creativity. In Mooney R.L. and Razik T.A. (eds) (1967) *Explorations in Creativity*, New York: Harper and Row, pp. 29–30.

Habel, Norman C., O'Donoghue Michael T. and Maddox, Marion (1993), *Myth, Ritual and the Sacred: Introducing the Phenomena of Religion*, Adelaide: Texts in Humanities, University of South Australia.

Habermas, Jürgen (2008), Secularism's Crisis of Faith: Notes on Post-Secular Society, *New Perspectives Quarterly*. vol. 25 p. 17-29

Hall, G. Stanley (1907), *Aspects of Childhood and Education*, Boston: Ginn and Co.

Hamel, Peter, trans Lemesurier, Peter (1978), *Through Music to the Self – How to appreciate and experience music anew*, Tisbury: Compton Press (first published in German in Vienna 1976).

Hamilton, Paul (1998), *Old Harry's Game*, Radio play broadcast on BBC Radio Four, April 23rd.

Handy, Charles (1995), *The Age of Unreason – New Thinking for a New World*, London: Arrow.

Hanslick, Eduard, trans Payzant, G. (1986), *On the Musically Beautiful*, Indianapolis: Hacket.

Haraway, Donna (1988), Situated Knowledges: The Science Question in Feminism and the Privilege of Partial Perspective, *Feminist Studies* Vol. 14 No. 3 Autumn, pp. 575–99.

Harries, Richard (1993), *Art and the Beauty of God: A Christian Understanding*, London: Mowbrays.

Hartigan, K.V. (2009), *Performance and Cure: Drama and Healing in Ancient Greece and Contemporary America*, London: Gerald Duckworth and Co Ltd.

Harvey, Jonathan (1996), Introduction in Steer, Maxwell (ed.) (1999) *Contemporary Music Review: Music and Mysticism* (I), Vol. 14 Parts 3–4, pp. 7–9.

Harvey, Jonathan (1999), *Music and Inspiration*, London: Faber and Faber.

Hauerwas, Stanley (2004), The Church and the Mentally Handicapped: A continuing challenge to the imagination. In Swinton, John (ed) (2004) *Critical Reflections on Stanley Hauerwas' Theology of disability: Disabling society, Enabling Theology*, Binghampton, NY: Haworth Press, pp. 53–62.

Hay, David and Nye, Rebecca (1998), *The Spirit of The Child*, London: Fount.

Hay, David (1982), *Exploring Inner Space*, Harmondsworth: Penguin.

Hay, David (1990), *Religious Experience Today*, London: Mowbray.

Heal, M. and Wigram, Tony (eds) (1993), *Music Therapy in Health and Education*, London: Jessica Kingsley Publishers.

Heelas, Paul and Woodhead, Linda (2005), *The Spiritual Revolution: why religion is giving way to spirituality*, Oxford: Blackwell Publishing.

Heidegger, Martin, trans Stambaugh, Joan (2002), *On Time and Being*, Chicago: University of Chicago Press.

Heline. Corinne (1964), *Color and Music in the New Age*, Marina del Rey, CA: De Vorss.

Herrick, James A. (2003), *The Making of the New Spirituality: The Eclipse of the Western Religious Tradition*, Westmont, IL: InterVarsity Press.

Hess, Julia (2015), Decolonizing Music Education: Moving beyond Tokenism, *The International Journal of Music Education*, Vol. 33 No. 3 August, pp. 336–47.

Heyward, Carter (2003), Seminar on Christology, Episcopal Divinity School, Cambridge, Mass., US.

Heymel, Michael, trans Luff, A. (2012), *Das Gesangbuch als Lebensegleiter (The Hymnal as Companion)*, Gütersloh: Gütersloher Verlagshaus.

Higgins, Lee (2012), *Community Music in Theory and Practice*, Oxford: Oxford University Press.

Hills, Peter and Argyle, Michael (1998), Musical and Religious Experiences and their Relationship to happiness, *Personality and Individual Differences*, 25, pp. 91–102.

Hills, Peter and Argyle, Michael (2000), *Psychology and Religion*, London and New York: Routledge.

Hindemith, Paul (1952), *A Composer's World*, New York: Doubleday and Co.

Hoagland, Tony <http://www.cortlandreview.com/issue/33/hoagland_e.html> Accessed January 3rd 2010.

Hodgkinson, Tim (1999), Siberian Shamanism and Improvised Music. In Steer, Maxwell (ed.) (1999) *Contemporary Music Review: Music and Mysticism* (I), Vol. 14 Parts 3–4, pp. 59–65.

Holloway, Richard (2000), *Godless Morality: Keeping Religion out of Ethics*, Edinburgh: Canongate.

Holzman, Lois (2002), Practicing a psychology that builds community. Keynote Address, *APA Division 27: Society for Community Research and Action (SCRA) Conference,* Boston. East Side Institute for Short Term Psychotherapy, March, New York <www.eastsideinstitute.org> Accessed March 10th 2005.

Holzman, Lois (2008), *Vygotsky at Work and Play*, London and New York: Taylor and Francis.

Huizinga, J. (1955), *Homo Ludens*, Boston: The Beacon Press.

Hull, Kenneth (2015), Do we become what we sing? The Role of the Music of Congregational Song in Congregational Spiritual Formation. Keynote presentation at *Hymns in Liturgy and Life, International Conference of Hymn Societies*, Cambridge 26th July–1st August.

Huls, Jos (2011), SPIRIN Encyclopaedia as an exposition of the field of spirituality. In Hense Elisabeth and Maas, Frank (eds) (2011), *Towards a Theory of Spirituality*, Leuven, Paris, Walpole MA: Peeters, pp. 141–54.

Huntington, Samuel P. (1996), *The Clash of Civilizations and the Remaking of World Order*, New York: Simon and Schuster.

Huskinson, L. (2004), *Nietzsche and Jung: The Whole Self in the Union of Opposites*, Hove and New York: Brunner-Routledge.

Hutchinson, E.D. (1949), *How to think Creatively*, New York: Abingdon Cokesbury.

Huxley, Aldous (1945), *The Perennial Philosophy*, New York: Harper and Brothers. <http://en.wikipedia.org/wiki/Perennial_philosophy#Aldous_Huxley> Accessed June 4th 2012.

Hyers, Conrad (2007), *The Spirituality of Comedy*, New Brunswick and London: Transaction Publishers.

Illman, Ruth (2009), Momo and Ibrahim – 'Thus-and-otherwise' A Dialogical Approach to Religious Difference, *Journal of Contemporary Religion*, Vol. 24, No. 2, May, pp. 157–70.

Illman, Ruth (2010a), Plurality and Peace: Interreligious Dialogue in a Creative Perspective, *International Journal of Public Theology* 4, pp. 175–92.

Illman, Ruth (2010b), Embracing Complexity – The Post-secular pilgrimage of Eric-Emmanuel Schmitt. In Ahlback, Tore(ed.) (2010), *Pilgrimages Today*, Scripta Instituti Donneriani Aboensis Vol. 22, pp. 228–43.

Illman, Ruth (2012), Incarnating Encounters, In Giordan, Giuseppe and Pace, Enzo (eds) (2012), *Mapping Religion and Spirituality in a Postsecular World*, Leiden and Boston: Brill, pp. 43–62.

Ingalls, Monique, Landau, Carolyn and Wagner, Tom (eds) (2013), *Christian Congregational Music, Performance, Identity and Experience*, Farnborough: Ashgate.

Inglis, Brian (1990), *Trance: A Natural History of Altered States of Mind*, London: Paladin, Grafton Books.

Isherwood, Lisa (ed.) (2000), *The Good News of the Body: Sexuality and Feminism*, Sheffield: Sheffield Academic Press.

Jackson, Philip W. (1998), *John Dewey and the Lessons of Art*, New Haven and London: Yale University Press.

James, Jamie (1995), *The Music of the Spheres: Music, Science and the Natural Order of the Universe*, London: Abacus.

James, William (originally published 1902, this edition 1997), *The Varieties of Religious Experience*, New York: Simon and Schuster.

Janacek, Leos (2008), BBC Radio 3 April 26th. Interview on *The Glagolitic Mass.*

Jarrett, Keith (1997), The Creative Power of the Moment. In Toms, Michael (ed.) (1997), *The Well of Creativity*, Carlsbad CA: Hay House.

Jaspers, Karl, trans Mannheim, Ralph (1951, 2nd edition. 2003), *Way to Wisdom: An Introduction to Philosophy*, New Haven, CT: Yale University Press.

Jaspers, Karl, trans Bullock, Michael (1953), *The Origin and Goal of History*, New Haven, CT: Yale University Press.

Johnson, J.H. (1995), *Listening in Paris: A Cultural History*, New York: Henry Holt and Co.

Jordaan, Gerrit (2015), Improvisation in a spiritual context of a religious community, Paper at *Spirituality of Music Education Conference*, North West University, Potchefstroom, South Africa March.

Jordanger, Vegar (2007), Healing Cultural Violence: 'Collective Vulnerability' through Guided Imagery with Music. In Urbain, Olivier (ed.) (2007), *Music and Conflict Transformation: Harmonies and Dissonances in Geopolitics*, London: I.B. Tauris, pp. 128–46.

Jordanger, Vegar (2008) Verbal and musical dialogues in the North-Caucasus – creating transnational citizenship through art, Paper delivered at *International Peace Research Association Conference*, Leuven University, Belgium, July.

Jorgensen, Estelle J. (1987), Percy Scholes on Music Appreciation: Another view, *British Journal of Music Education*, Vol. 4, Issue 02, July, pp. 139–56.

Jorgensen, Estelle J. (2008), *The Art of Teaching Music*, Bloomington and Indianapolis: Indiana University Press.

Jung, Carl G., trans Hull, R.F.C. (1991 [1946]), *On the Nature of the Psyche*, London: Ark Paperbacks, Routledge.

Jung, Carl G. (1964), *Man and His Symbols*, London: Aldus Books.

Jung, C.G. (2004 [1957]), *The Undiscovered Self*, London and New York: Routledge.

Kabat-Zinn, J. (1990), *Full Catastrophe Living: Using the Wisdom of Your Body and Mind to Face Stress, Pain, and Illness*, New York: Bantam Dell.

Kaldor, Sue and Miner, Maureen (2012), Spirituality and Community Flourishing – A case of circular causality. In Miner, Maureen, Dowson. Martin and Devenish Stuart (eds) (2012), *Beyond Well-being – Spirituality and Human Flourishing*, Charlotte, NC: Information Age Publishing, pp. 183–98.

Kanellopoulos, Panos (2013), Response to Boyce-Tillman's paper Spirited Education – Religionless Spirituality at the *Ninth International Symposium on the Philosophy of Music Education*, Teachers College, Columbia University, New York, June 5th–8th no pages.

Keen, Sam (2010), *In the Absence of God, Dwelling in the Presence of the Sacred*, New York: Harmony Books.

Keller, Catherine and Daniell, Anne (2002), *Process and Difference: Between Cosmological and Poststructuralist Postmodernisms*, New York: Suny.

Keller, Catherine and Schneider, Laurel (eds) (2010), *Polydoxy: Theology of Multiplicity and Relation*, London and New York: Routledge.

Keller, Catherine (2011), *'And Truth – so Manifold!' – Transfeminist Entanglements*, Antoinette Brown Lecture.

Kershaw, Baz (2010), Paper given at a seminar on Interdisciplinarity at The Central School of Speech and Drama.

King, Ursula (2009), *The Search for Spirituality – Our global quest for meaning and fulfillment*, Norwich: Canterbury Press.

King James Bible <http://www.kingjamesbibleonline.org/Genesis-Chapter-1/> Accessed November 14th 2010.

Kivy, Peter (2002), *Introduction to a Philosophy of Music*, New York: Oxford University Press.

Klass, Morton (1995), *Ordered Universes: Approaches to the anthropology of religion*, Boulder, Colorado: Westview Press.

Klessmann, Michael, trans Ruff, A. (2003), Kirchenmusikahs Seelsorge (Church Music as Pastoral Care). In Fermor, Gotthard and Scroete-Wittke, Harald (eds) (2003), *Kirchenmusik als religioese Praxis (Church Music as Religious Praxis)*, Leipzig: Evangelische Verlagsanstalt, pp. 230–4.

Knowles-Wallace, Robin (2015), Congregational Singing and Everyday life. Keynote presentation at *Hymns in Liturgy and Life, International Conference of Hymn Societies*, Cambridge, UK, 26th July–1st August.

Koestler, A. (1964), *The Act of Creation*, London: Hutchinson.

Koestler, A. (1981), The Three Domains of Creativity. In Dutton, D. and Krausz M. (eds) (1981), *The Concept of Creativity in Science and Art*, Boston: Martinus Nijhoff Publications, pp. 1–17.

Kortegaard, H.M. (1993), Music Therapy in the Psychodynamic Treatment of Schizophrenia. In Heal, Margaret and Wigram, Tony (eds) (1993), *Music Therapy in Health and Education*, London: Jessica Kingsley, pp. 55–63.

Kris, E. (1952), *Psychoanalytic Explorations in Art*, New York: International Universities Press.

Kris, E. (1953), Psychoanalysis and the Study of Creative Imagination, *Bulletin of the New York Academy of Medicine*, pp. 334–51.

Kris, E. (1965), On Inspiration. In Ruitenbeck, H.W. (ed.) (1965), *The Creative Imagination: Psychoanalysis and the Genius of Inspiration*, Chicago: Quadrangle Books, pp. 23–46.

Kwok, Pui Lan (2002), Spiritual and also religious? *The Brown Papers*, Vol. IV No. 3, January/February, Pages not available.

Kubie, L.S. (1958), *Neurotic Distortions of the Creative Process*, Lawrence: Kansas University Press.

Kubler Ross, Dr Elizabeth (1983), A broadcast talk in *The Listener*, 19th September, Vol. 110, No. 2828.

Kundera, Milan, trans Kussi, Peter (1991), *Immortality*, New York: Grove Press.

Kuh, George D. et al. (1994), *Student Learning Outside the Classroom: Transcending Artificial Boundaries, ASHE*-ERIC Higher Education Report No. 8. Washington: The George Washington University.

Kung, Hans (1992), *Mozart: Traces of Transcendence*, London: SCM.

Lafferty, Megan (2013), John Dewey on the Rhythmic ordering of experiencing, Keynote lecture at the *Ninth International Symposium on the Philosophy of Music Education*, Teachers College, Columbia University, New York. US, June 5th–8th.

Lamont, Anne (1999), *Travelling Mercies: Some Thoughts on Faith*, New York: Pantheon Books.

Lancaster, Brian L. (2004), *Approaches to Consciousness: The Marriage of Science and Mysticism*, London: Palgrave Macmillan.

Lancelot, James (1995), Music as Sacrament. In Brown, David and Loades Ann (eds) (1995), *The Sense of the Sacramental: Movement and Measure in Art and Music, Place and Time*, London: SPCK, pp. 179–85.

Langer, Suzanne (1942), *Philosophy in a New Key*, Cambridge: Harvard University Press.

Langer, Suzanne (1953), *Feeling and Form: A Theory of Art*, London: Routledge and Kegan Paul.

Lanza, Joseph (2007), *Elevator Music; A surreal history of Muzak, Easy listening and Other Moodsong*, Ann Arbor: University of Michigan Press.

Laski, Marghanita (1961), *Ecstasy: A Study of some Secular and Religious Experiences*, London: Cresset Press.

Laub-Novak, Karen (1976), Creativity and children, *Momentum*, Vol. 7, No. 1, pp. 13–19.

Laurence, Felicity (2008), Music and Empathy. In Urbain, Oliver (ed.) (2008) *Music and Conflict Transformation: Harmonies and Dissonances in Geopolitics*, London: I.B.Tauris, pp. 13–25.

Lawson, Dominic (2013), There's no morality in music – so happy birthday to Hitler's favourite composer, *The Independent* May 14th, pp. 12–13.

Le Huray, Peter and Day, James (eds) (1981), *Music and Aesthetics in the Eighteenth and Early-nineteenth Centuries*, Cambridge: Cambridge University Press.

Leech, Kenneth (1995), *True Prayer: An Invitation to Christian Spirituality*, Harrisburg, PA: Morehouse Publishing.

Leonard, George (1978), *The Silent Pulse*, New York: E.P. Dutton.

Levinas, Emmanuel, trans Lingis, Alphonso (1969), *Totality and Infinity: An Essay on Exteriority*, Pittsburgh: Duquesne University Press.

Levi-Strauss, Claude, trans Weightman, John and Doreen (1970), *The Raw and the Cooked: Introduction to a Science of Mythology*, 1, London: Jonathan Cape.

Lewis, I.M. (1971), *Ecstatic Religion: An Anthropological Study of Spirit Possession and Shamanism*, Baltimore, MD: Penguin Books.

Lewis, C.S. (1980 first published 1956), *Till we have faces – A Novel of Cupid and Psyche*, Boston: Houghton Mifflin Harcourt.

Lieberman, J.N. (1977), *Playfulness: Its Relation To Imagination and Creativity*, New York: Harcourt, Brace, Jovanovich.

Linzey, Andrew (1994), *Animal Theology*, London: SCM.

Lindley, Margaret (1995), Competing Trinities: The Great Mother and the Formation of the Christian Trinity. In Barton Julie S. and Mews, Constant (eds) (1995), *Hildegard of Bingen and Gendered Theology in Judaeo – Christian Tradition*, Monash: Monash University: Centre for Studies in Religion and Theology, pp. 29–40.

Loane, B. (1984), Thinking about Children's Compositions, *British Journal of Music Education*, Vol. 3, November, pp. 205–31.

Lombaard, Christo (2015), Sing unto the LORD a new song' (Ps. 98: 1): a selection from the Afrikaans punk-rock group Fokofpolisiekar's songs as rearticulated aspects from the 1976 Afrikaans Psalms- en Gesangeboek, Paper at *Spirituality of Music Education Conference*, North West University, Potchefstroom, South Africa, March.

Lorenz, K. (1972), The Enmity between Generations and its Probable Ethologic Causes. In Piers, M.W. (ed.) (1972), *Play and Development – A Symposium*, New York: W.W. Noughton and Co, pp. 50–72.

Love, Andrew (2001), *Musical Improvisation as the Place where Being Speaks: Heidegger, Language and Sources of Christian Hope*, Unpublished Thesis.

Love, Andrew (2003), *Musical Improvisation, Heidegger and the Liturgy – a Journey to the Heart of Hope (Studies in Art and Religious Interpretation)*, New York: Edwin Mellen Press.

Lucciano, Anna M (1999), *Jan Christou: The works and Temperament of a Greek Composer of our Time*, Belfast: Harwood Academic Press.

Luchte, J. (2004), *Kant, Bataille and the Sacred*, <http://www.ferrum.edu/philosophy/kant2.htm> Accessed 7th October 2009.

McClary, Susan (1991), *Feminine Endings*, Minneapolis: University of Minnesota Press.

McClary, Susan (2001), *Conventional Wisdom*, Berkeley: University of California Press.

McCoy, Marin (2007), *Plato on the Rhetoric of Philosophers and Sophists*, Cambridge: Cambridge University Press. <http://dx.doi.org/10.1017/CBO9780511497827.007> Accessed April 10th 2012.

Macdonald, Margaret Y. (1996), *Early Christian Women and Pagan Opinion: The Power of Hysterical Women*, Cambridge: Cambridge University Press.

McElvoy, Anne (2014), Music minus affectation: The Joy of the Proms, *Evening Standard* Aug 6th <http://www.standard.co.uk/comment/anne-mcelvoy-music-minus-affectation--the-joy-of-the-proms-9651090.html> Accessed July 4th 2015.

McGill, Kathleen (1991), Women and Performance: The Development of Improvisation by the Sixteenth-Century Commedia dell'Arte, *Theatre Journal* 43, pp. 59–69.

McLaren Brian D. (2010), *Naked Spirituality*, London: Hodder and Stoughton.

McLaughlin, T.H. (2003), Education, Spirituality and the Common School. In Carr D. and Haldane J. (eds) (2003), *Spirituality, Philosophy and Education*, London: RoutledgeFalmer, pp. 185–99.

Macmillan, James (2000), Creation and the Composer. In Astley, Jeff, Hone, Timothy and Savage, Mark (2000), *Creative Chords: Studies in Music, Theology and Christian Formation*, Leominster: Gracewing, pp. 3–19.

Mandoki, Katya (2007), *Everyday Aesthetics: Prosaics, the Play of Culture and Social Identities*, Farnborough: Ashgate.

Mantin, Ruth (2002), *Thealogies in Process: the Role of Goddess-talk in Feminist Spirituality*. Unpublished PhD Thesis, May 2002, Southampton University.

Marcuse, Herbert (1978), *The Aesthetic Dimension: Toward a Critique of Marxist Aesthetics*, Boston: Beacon.

Marjanen, Antti (1996), *The woman Jesus Loved: Mary Magdalene in the Nag Hammadi library and related documents*, Netherlands: E J. Brill.

Marples, Roger (2006), Against (the use of the term) Spiritual Education, *International Journal of Children's Spirituality*, 11 (2), pp. 293–306.

Marton, Ference and Booth, Shirley (1997), *Learning and Awareness*, Mahwah NJ: Lawrence Erlbaum Associates.

Marshall, Melanie (2014), Love in Action. Programme Note for *The Gospel According to the other Mary*, The Coliseum, London, UK, pp. 30–1.

Martin, David (1997), *Does Christianity cause War?* Oxford: Regent College Publishing.

Maslow, A.H. (1958), *Creativity in Self-actualising People*, Lecture for *Creativity Symposium*, Michigan State University, East Lansing, February 28th.

Maslow, Abraham H. (1962), *Towards a Psychology of Being*, Princeton: D. van Nostrand Company.

Maslow, Abraham. H. (1967), The Creative Attitude. In Mooney R.L. and Razik T.A. (eds) (1967) *Explorations in Creativity*, New York: Harper and Row, pp. 40–55.

Melanson, Peggy (2003) <www.findingcourage.com> Accessed March 20th 2003.

Mesle, C. Robert (2009), *Process-Relational Philosophy: An Introduction to Alfred North Whitehead*, West Conshohocken: Templeton Foundation.

Metzger, Deena (1997), Writing: the Gateway to the Inner World. In Toms, Michael (ed.) (1997), *The Well of Creativity*, Carlsbad: Hay House. Pages not available.

Meyer, Leonard (1956), *Emotion and Meaning in Music*, Chicago: Chicago University Press.

Meyer, Leonard (1967), *Music – The Arts and Ideas*, Chicago: University of Chicago Press.

Mezirow, J. and associates (2000), *Learning as Transformation: Critical Perspectives on a Theory in Process*, San Francisco: Jossey-Bass.

Middleton, R. (1990), *Studying Popular Music*, Milton Keynes: Open University Press.

Milbank, John (1997), *The Word made Strange*, Oxford: Blackwell.

Miller, Alice (1987), *For your own good – The Roots of Violence in Child-rearing*, London: Virago.

Mindfulness <www.mindfulnesspractice.co.uk> Accessed March 17th 2011.

Miner, Maureen and Dowson, Martin (2012), Spirituality as a Key Resource for Human Flourishing. In Miner, Maureen, Dowson. Martin and Devenish Stuart (eds) (2012), *Beyond Well-being – Spirituality and Human Flourishing*, Charlotte, NC: Information Age Publishing pp. 5–31.

Monbiot, George (2006), *The Guardian*, Tuesday, June 27th

Moody, Ivan (1999), *The Mind and the Heart*. In Steer, Maxwell (ed.) (1999) *Contemporary Music Review: Music and Mysticism* (I), Vol. 14 Parts 3–4, pp. 65–79.

Mooney, R.L. (1962), A Conceptual Model for Integrating Four Approaches to the Identification of Creative Talent. In Parnes, S.J., and Harding H.F. (eds) (1962), *A Source Book of Creative Thinking*, New York, Charles Scribners Sons, pp. 74–84.

Moore, Allan (1999), Signifying the Spiritual in the Music of Yes. In Steer, Maxwell (ed.) (1999), *Contemporary Music Review: Music and Mysticism* (II), Vol. 14 Parts 3–4, pp. 25–33.

Moore, Geoffrey (2015), Hymning the Kingdom: Originating, Resonating, Consummating. Keynote presentation at *Hymns in Liturgy and Life, International Conference of Hymn Societies*, Cambridge, UK, 26th July–1st August.

Moore, Basil and Habel, Norman (1982), *When Religion goes to School*, Adelaide: South Australia College of Advanced Education.

Morgan, Sarah (2013), *Community Choirs – A Musical Transformation*, Unpublished DProf Context Statement, University of Winchester, UK.

Monk, William and Nicholson, Sydney (eds) (1922), *Ancient and Modern*, London: Novello and Co.

Morton, C. (1994), Feminist Theory and the Displaced Music Curriculum: Beyond the 'add and stir' projects, *The Philosophy of Music Education Review*, 2 (2), pp. 106–21.

Muir, D.P.E. (2000), Friendship in Education and the Desire for the Good: an interpretation of Plato's Phaedrus, *Educational Philosophy and Theory*, 32 (2), pp. 233–47.

Muir, Edwin (1963), *Collected Poems*, London: Faber and Faber.

Murray, H.A. (1958), The Vicissitudes of Creativity. In Anderson, H. (ed.) (1958), *Creativity and its Cultivation*, New York, Harper Row, pp. 96–118.

Myers and Torrance (1965), *Can you Imagine?* Boston: Ginn and Co.

Myers, Helen (1992), *Ethnomusicology: An Introduction*, London, Macmillan.

Nachmanovitch, Stephen (1990), *Free Play: Improvisation in Life and Art*, New York: Penguin Putnam.

Natural Voice Network (2014), <http://www.naturalvoice.net/> Accessed May 11th 2014.

Navone, John (1974), *The Theology of Failure*, New York: Paulist Press.

Nietzsche, F. ed. W. Kaufmann (1954, reprinted 1976), *The Portable Nietzsche*, New York: Penguin.

Nelson, Marcia (2005), *The Gospel According to Oprah*, Louisville: Westminster John Knox Press.

Nettl, Bruno (1972), *Music in Primitive Culture*, Cambridge, MA: Harvard University Press.

Niebuhr, H. Richard (1941), *The Meaning of Revelation*, New York: Macmillan.

Noddings, Nel (2003), *Happiness and Education*, Cambridge: Cambridge University Press.

Noddings, Nel and Shore, Paul J. (1984), *Awakening the Inner Eye: Intuition in Education*, New York: Teachers College Press.

Nussbaum, Martha (2003), *Upheavals of thought: The Intelligence of Emotions*, Cambridge: Cambridge University Press.

O'Driscoll, Dennis (2002), *Exemplary Damages*, London: Anvil Press Poetry, Cited in *The Guardian* 07.12.02.

Oldfield, A. (1993), A Study of the Way Music Therapists Analyse their Work, *Journal of British Music Therapy*, Vol. 7 No. 1, pp. 14–22.

Oliveros, Pauline (1989), *Deep Listening*, CD.

Ong, Walter (1982), *Orality and Literacy: The Technologizing of the Word*, London and New York: Methuen.

Ortiz, John M. (1997), *The Tao of Music: Sound Psychology*, Dublin: New Leaf.

Otto, Rudolf (1923), *The Idea of the Holy: An inquiry into the non-rational factor in the idea of the Divine and its relation to the Rational*, Oxford: Oxford University Press.

Otto, W.F. (1955), *The Homeric Gods: The Spiritual Significance of Greek Religion*, London: Thames and Hudson.

Palieri, Rik (2008), Working in the Trenches: Surviving Conflicts through Folk Music and Tales. In Urbain, Olivier (ed.) (2008), *Music and Conflict Transformation: Harmonies and Dissonances in Geopolitics*, London: I.B. Tauris, pp. 187–200.

Palmer, Anthony (2000), Consciousness studies and a Philosophy of Music Education, *Philosophy of Music Education Review* Vol. 8 No. 2 Fall, pp. 99–109.

Pascale, L.M. (2005), Dispelling the Myth of the Non-Singer: Embracing Two Aesthetics for Singing, *Philosophy of Music Education Review*, 13, pp. 165–75.

Paterson, Anise and Odam, George (2000), *Composing in the Classroom: The Creative Dream*, Bath: National Association of Music Educators.

Patrick, C. (1935), Creative Thought in Poets, *Archives of Psychology* Vol. 26, pp. 1–74.

Patrick, C. (1937), Creative Thought in Artists, *Journal of Psychology* LV, pp. 35–73.

Patrick, C. (1949), How Creative Thought is Related to Thinking, *American Psychologist, IV*, pp. 260–69.

Paynter, John and Aston, Peter (1970), *Sound and Silence*, London: Cambridge University Press.

Paynter, John (1977), The Role of Creativity in the School Music Curriculum. In Burnett, M (ed.) (1977), *Music Education Review I*, London: Chappell, pp. 3–26.

Perennial Philosophy <http://en.wikipedia.org/wiki/Perennial_philosophy #Traditionalist_School> Accessed 4th June 2012.

Perry, Michael (ed.) (1987), *Deliverance: Psychic Disturbances and Occult Involvement*, London: SPCK.

Piaget, Jean (1951), *Play, Dreams and Imitation in Childhood*, London: Routledge and Kegan Paul.

Pinkola Estes, Clarissa (1992), *Women who run with the Wolves*, London: Rider.

Pire, Dominique Georges, trans Ogg, Graeme M. (1967), *Building Peace*, London: Transworld.

Plummeridge, Charles (1980), Creativity: The Need for Further Classification, *Psychology of Music*, Vol. 8, No. 1, pp. 34–9.

Podolsky, E. (1939), *The Doctor prescribes Music: The Influence of Music on Health and Personality*, New York: Frederick A. Stokes Company.

Popper, Karl (1950), Indeterminism in Quantum Physics and Classical Physics, *British Journal for the Philosophy of Science* quoted in Briskman (1981).

Powell, Kimberley (2004), The Apprenticeship of Embodied Knowledge in a Taiko drumming ensemble. In L. Bresler (ed.) (2004), *Knowing bodies, moving minds: Embodied knowledge in Education*, Dordrecht: Kluwer Press, pp. 183–95.

Powell, Kimberley (2005), The Ensemble Art of the Solo: The social and cultural construction of artistic practice and identity in a Japanese American Taiko Ensemble, *Journal of Art and Learning Research*, 21 (1), pp. 273–95.

Powell, Kimberley (2010), Somaesthetic training, aesthetics, ethics, and the politics of difference in Richard Shusterman's 'Body Consciousness'. Action, Criticism, and Theory for Music Education Vol. 9 No. 1, 1–18. <http://act.maydaygroup.org/articles/Powell9_1.pdf> Accessed June 2011.

Pratt, Douglas (2012), The Persistence and Problem of Religion: Exclusivist Boundaries and Extremist Transgressions, Keynote address at the *Conference of the British Association for the Study of Religions*, University of Winchester, UK, Sept 6th.

Prentki, Tim (Date unknown), Unpublished inaugural address for the opening of the Centre for Development Studies at Liverpool Hope University, UK.

Prentki, Tim (2013), A Dog's Obeyed in Office: beyond the Boalian Binary, Paper presented at the *Research and Knowledge Exchange Symposium*, University of Winchester, UK, May 29th 2013.

Preti, Costanza and Boyce-Tillman, June (2014), *Elevate, Using the Arts to uplift people in hospital*, Research Report, University of Winchester, UK. http://www.winchester.ac.uk/research/attheuniversity/Education_Health_Social%20Care/artsaswellbeing/projects-and-research/Pages/Projects-and-Research.aspx

Price, Kingsley (2000), How can music be merry?, *Philosophy of Music Education Review* Vol. 8, No. 2, Fall, pp. 59–66.

Primavesi, Anne (2008), *Gaia and Climate Change: A Theology of Gift Events*, Sydney and Canberra: Boomerang Books.

Purce, Jill (1998), Publicity leaflet for *The Healing Voice*.

Pullman, Philip (2000), *The Amber Spyglass*, London: Scholastic/David Fickling Books.

Rahn, John (1994), What is valuable in art, and can music still achieve it? In John Rahn (ed.) (1994) *Perspectives in Musical Aesthetics*, New York: Norton, pp. 54–65.

Rahner, Hugo, trans Battershaw and Quinn (1965), *Man at Play*, London: Burns and Oates.

Rankin, Marianne (2008), *An Introduction to Religious Experience*, Lampeter, Wales: Religious Experience Research Centre.

Raucous Recovery Choir <http://naturalvoice-net.greenstrata.com/choir_profile/779/Raucous%20Caucus%20Recovery%20Chorus> Accessed Oct 1st 2014.

Read, Miss (1955), *Village School*, London: Michael Joseph.

Reason, Peter and Newman, Melanie (eds) (2013), *Stories of the Great Turning*, Bristol: Vala Publishing.

Regelski, T. and Gates, J.T. (eds) (2010), *Music Education for Changing Times*, New York: Springer.

Rehding, Alexander (2009), *Commemoration and Wonderment in Nineteenth Century Germany*, Oxford: Oxford University Press.

Reinke, Stephan, trans Ruff, A. (2015), A 'Hymn at Journey's End'? Hymns as Companions. Keynote presentation at *Hymns in Liturgy and Life, International Conference of Hymn Societies*, Cambridge, UK, 26th July–1st August.

Reimer, Bennett (1970), *A Philosophy of Music Education*, Englewood Cliffs, NJ: Prentice Hall.

RERC – Religious Experience Research Centre accounts of Religious Experience, held at Trinity St David's University under the Alister Hardy Trust.

Ribot, Theodore (1906), *Essay on the Creative Imagination*, Chicago: Open Court Publishing Company.

Richard, Lucien (2000), *Living the Hospitality of God*, Mahwah, NJ: Paulist Press.

Richardson, L. (2000), Writing: A method of enquiry. In N.K. Denzin and Y.S. Lincoln (eds) (2000), *Handbook of Qualitative Research*, Thousand Oaks CA: Sage, pp. 923–43.

Richerme, Lauren, Kapalka (2013), Who are the musickers? Paper at the *Ninth International Symposium on the Philosophy of Music Education*, Teachers College, Columbia University, New York, US, June 5th–8th.

Ricoeur, Paul (1994), Appropriation. In Thompson, John (ed) (1994), *Hermeneutics and Human Sciences*, Cambridge: Cambridge University Press.

Ridley, Aaron (2004), *The Philosophy of Music: Theme and Variations*, Edinburgh: Edinburgh University Press.

Riley, Terry quoted in Hamel, Peter, trans Lemusurier, Peter (1978), *Through Music to the Self – How to appreciate and experience music anew*, Tisbury: Compton Press.

Riley, Terry (1999), *Morning River*, Unpublished Score.

Robbins, Clive (1993), The Creative Processes are Universal. In Heal, Margaret and Wigram, Tony (eds) (1993), *Music therapy in Health and Education*, London: Jessica Kingsley, pp. 7–25.

Robertson, Paul (1996), *Music and the Mind*, Series of programmes for BBC Channel 4.

Robertson, Paul (2015), <http://www.musicmindspirit.org/new_paul2.html> Accessed August 19th 2015.

Robinson, E. (1977), *The Original Vision: A Study of the Religious Experience of Childhood*, Oxford: Religious Experience Research Centre.

Robinson, Ken (2001), *Out of our minds: Learning to be Creative*, Oxford: Capstone.

Robinson, Ken (ed. for National Advisory Committee for Creative and Cultural Education) (1999), *All Our Futures: Creativity, Culture and Education*, London: Department for Education and Employment.

Rogers, Carl (1970), Towards a Theory of Creativity. In Vernon P.E. (ed.) (1970), *Creativity*, Harmondsworth: Penguin, pp. 137–51.

Rogers, Carl (1976), *On Becoming a Person*, London: Constable.

Roof, Ward Clark (1993), A *Generation of Seekers: The Spiritual Journeys of the Baby Boomer generation*, New York: HarperSanFrancisco.

Roof, Ward Clark and Carroll, Jackson W. (1995), *The Post-war Generation and Establishment Religion: Cross-cultural Perspectives*, Boulder: Westview Press.

Roof, Ward Clark (1999), *Spiritual Marketplace: Baby Boomers and the Remaking of American Religion*, Princeton: Princeton University Press.

Rooley, Anthony (1990), *Performance: Revealing the Orpheus Within*, Shaftesbury: Element Books.

Roose-Evans, James (1994), *Passages of the Soul*, Shaftesbury: Element Books.

Rorem, Ned (1970), *Critical Affairs: A Composer's Journal*, New York: Braziller.

Ross, Malcolm (1978), *The Creative Arts*, London: Heinemann.

Rossman, J. (1931), *The Psychology of the Inventor: A Study of the Patentee*, Washington DC: Inventors Publishing Company.

Rouget, Gilbert, trans Biebuyck, Brunhilde (1987), *Music and Trance: A Theory of the relations between Music and Possession*, Chicago and London; University of Chicago Press.

Roth, Gabrielle (1992), *Sweating my Prayers: An interview with Alex Fisher.*

Rowson, Jonathan (2013), The Brains behind Spirituality, *RSA Journal* Summer, pp. 40–3.

Rudlin, John (1994), *Commedia dell'arte: An actor's handbook*, London and New York: Routledge.

Sachs, Hanns (1947), *The Creative Unconscious*, Cambridge, MA: Sci-Art.

Sachs, Wolfgang (1992), *The Development Dictionary*, London: Zed Books.

Sacks, Jonathan (2002), *The Dignity of Difference – How to avoid the Clash of Civilisations*, London: Continuum.

Sacks, Oliver (1985), *The Man who mistook his Wife for a Hat*, New York: Summit Books.

Sacks, Oliver (2011 first published 2007), *Musicophilia: Tales of Music and the Brain*, London: Picador.

Sadgrove, Michael (2000), Foreword. In Astley, Jeff, Hone Timothy and Savage, Mark (eds) (2000), *Creative Chords: Studies in Music, Theology and Christian Formation*, Leominster: Gracewing, pp. xi–xix.

Salazar, Ryan and Randles, Clint (2015), Connecting ideas to practice: The Development of an Undergraduate Student's Philosophy of Music Education, *The International Journal of Music Education*, Vol. 33 No. 3, August, pp. 278–89.

Saliers, Don E. (2007), *Music and Theology*, Nashville TEN; Abingdon.

Samples, Mark and Wallmark, Zach(2015), *The Taruskin Challenge* <https://taruskinchallenge.wordpress.com/>. Accessed March 6th 2015.

Sartre, Jean-Paul P., trans Freckman, Bernard (1947), *Existentialism*, New York: A Philosophical Library.

Savery, Donna (2007), Liminal Spaces: Absence and Presence in Drama. Paper given at conference on *Liminality*, Buckingham Chilterns University College, April.

Sayers, Dorothy (1941/47), *The Mind of the Maker*, London: Methuen.

Schechner Richard (2003) *Performance Theory*, London and NY: Routledge.

Schmidt, Leigh Eric (2005), *Restless Souls: The Making of American Spirituality*, New York: HarperSanFrancisco.

Scholes, Percy A. (1938), *The Oxford Companion to Music*, Oxford: Oxford University Press,.

Schroeder-Sheker, Therese (1994), Music for the dying: a Personal account of the new field of Music Thanatology, *Journal of Holistic Nursing* 12 (1), pp. 56–64.

Scott, M.M. (1934), *Beethoven*, London: Dent.

Schumacher, E.F. (1977), *A Guide for the Perplexed*, London: Jonathan Cape.

Schucman, Helen and Thetford, William (eds) (1992), *A Course in Miracles*, Mill Valley, CA: Foundation for Inner Peace.

Sessions, R. (1955), The Composer and his Message. In Ghiselin, B. (ed.) (1956), *The Creative Process*, New York, The New American Library, pp. 45–9.

Sebold, Alice (2002), *Lovely Bones*, London: Picador.

Shapiro, Svi (2011), *Educating for Peace*, <http://www.tikkun.org/nextgen/educating-for-peace> accessed March 20th 2011.

Sharkey, John (1975), *Celtic Mysteries – The Ancient Religion*, London: Thames and Hudson.

Sharp, Ian (2000), *Classical Music's Evocation of Childhood: Studies in the History and Interpretation of Music* Vol. 78, New York: The Edwin Mellen Press.

Sheldrake, Philip (1995), *Living Between Worlds: Place and Journey in Celtic Spirituality*, Cambridge, MA: Cowley Publications.

Sheldrake, Philip (1998), *Spirituality and Theology*, London: Darton, Longman and Todd.

Shepherd, John (1991), *Music as Social Text*, Cambridge: Polity Press.

Shepherd, John and Wicke, Peter (1997), *Music and Cultural Theory*, Cambridge: Polity Press.

Shusterman, Richard (1995), Popular Art and Education, *Studies in Philosophy and Education*, 13, Pages unavailable.

Shusterman, Richard (2007), Somaesthetics and the Revival of Aesthetics, *Filozofski Vestnik*, vol. XXVIII, no. 2, Pages unavailable.

Shusterman, Richard (2008), *Body Consciousness: A Philosophy of Mindfulness and Somaesthetics*, Cambridge: Cambridge University Press.

Shusterman, Richard (2012), *Somaesthetics and its Implications for CHI*, Invited Lecture Ballroom C, Florida Atlantic University, USA, May 7th <http://chi2012.acm.org/program/desktop/Session14.html#sp105> Accessed June 1st, 2012.

Silkstone, Francis (1997), The more you play it, the more it comes out differently improvisation and composition in Thai tradition, *Resonance, Structure and Freedom* Vol. 6 No. 1, pp. 35–7.

Simon, Paul (1994) quoted in White, Timothy *Lasers in the jungle: the Conception and Maturity of a Musical Masterpiece* CD 9 46430-2 Warner Brothers.

Sinnott, E.W. (1970), The Creativeness of Life. In Vernon P.E. (ed.) (1970), *Creativity*, Harmondsworth: Penguin, pp. 107–15.

Skyllstad, Kjell (2008), Managing Conflicts through Music: Educational Perspectives. In Urbain, Oliver (ed.) (2008), *Music and Conflict transformation: Harmonies and Dissonances in Geopolitics*, London: I.B. Tauris pp. 172–83.

Sloboda, John (2000), Music and Worship: a Psychologist's Perspective. In Astley, Jeff, Hone, Timothy and Savage, Mark (eds) (2000), *Creative Chords: Studies in Music, Theology and Christian Formation*, Leominster: Gracewing, pp. 111–23.

Small, Christopher (1998), *Musicking: The Meanings of Performing and Listening*, Middletown, CT: Wesleyan University Press.

Small, Christopher (2010), Prologue: Misunderstanding and Reunderstanding, *Peace and Policy Dialogue of Civilizations for Global Citizenship* Vol. 15, pp. 1–8.

Smart, Ninian (1984), *The Religious Experience of Mankind*, New York: Charles Scribner's Sons.

Smeijsters, Henk and van den Hurk, Jose (1993), Research in practice in the Music Therapeutic Treatment of a client with symptoms of anorexia nervosa. In Heal, M and Wigram Tony (eds) (1993), *Music Therapy in Health and education*, London: Jessica Kingsley, pp. 250–62.

Smite and Kasha, M (2013), Somatic, Feelingful and Cognitive Engagement. Paper at the *Ninth International Symposium on the Philosophy of Music Education*, Teachers' College, Columbia University, New York, US, June 5th–8th.

Smith, Anthony D. (1991), *National Identity*. London: Penguin.

Sondheim, Stephen and Lapine, James (1987), *Into the Woods*, <http://theatre-musical.com/intothewoods/libretto.html> Accessed October 20th 2013.

Sparshott, F.E. (1981), Every horse has a mouth: A Personal Poetics. In Dutton D. and Krausz, M. (eds) (1981), *The Concept of Creativity in Science and Art*, Boston: Martinus Nijhoff Publications, pp. 45–54.

Stanczak, Gregory C. (2006), *Engaged Spirituality: Social Change and American Religion*, New Brunswick, NJ: Rutgers University Press.

Stein, Maurice. A. (1962), Creativity as an Intra-personal and Inter-personal Process. In Parnes, S.J. and Harding, H.F. (eds) (196) *A Source Book of Creative Thinking*, New York: Charles Scribners, pp. 85–92.

Stein, Maurice A. (1967), Creativity and Culture. In Mooney R.L. and Razik T.A. (eds) (1967) *Explorations in Creativity*, New York: Harper Row, pp. 101–20.

Steinecker, John Leonard (1976), *John Dewey's Empirical Pluralism: Implications for Music Education*, Doctoral Thesis at Temple University.

Steiner, Rudolf, trans Parsons Whittaker, Nancy (1996), *The Foundations of Human Experience. Foundations of Waldorf Education Vol. 1*, Allgemeine Menschenkunde als Grundlage der Pedagogik, Pedagogischer Grundkurs, 14 Lectures, Stuttgart, 1919, Hudson, NY: Anthroposophic Press, pp. 136–40.

Steinwert, Tiffany (2003), Paper given in Carter Heyward's class on Queer Theology at the Episcopal Divinity School, Cambridge, Massachusetts, US, April 28th.

Sternberg, R.J. (2003), *Wisdom, Intelligence and Creativity Synthesized*, Cambridge: Cambridge University Press.

Stewart, R.J. (1987), *Music and the Elemental Psyche: A Practical Guide to Music and Changing Consciousness*, Wellingborough: The Aquarian Press.

Stige, B. (2002), *Culture-Centered Music Therapy*. Gilsum, NH: Barcelona Publishers.

Storr, Anthony (1972), *The Dynamics of Creation*, London: Seiber and Warburg.

Storr, Anthony (1993), *Music and the Mind*, London: HarperCollins.

Stravinsky, Igor (1936), *An Autobiography*, New York: W.W. Norton & Company.

Suanda, Endo (2012), Cultural Education (seen from a Cultural Studies Perspective) in the Application of its activities in the form of Nusantara Art Education, Paper given, *Festival of Ocean Mountain Arts* Borobudur Temple, Indonesia.

Subotnik, Rose Rosengard (1996), *Deconstructive Variations: Music and Reason in Western Society*, Minneapolis: University of Minnesota Press.

Sullivan, Lawrence E (1997), *Enchanting Powers: Music in the World's Religions*, Cambridge MA: Harvard University Press.

Swanwick, Keith, and Tillman, June B. (1986), The Sequence of Musical Development, *British Journal of Music Education*, Vol. 3. No. 3, November, pp. 305–37.

Swinburne, Richard (1981), *Faith and Reason*, Oxford: Clarendon Paperbacks.

Sypher, Wylie (ed) (1956), *Comedy*, New York: Doubleday.

Tabaczynski, Tom (2009) Somaesthetics: pragmatic or critical on *Mooklish*, <http://mooklish.com/2009/09/20/pragmatic-and-critical-somaesthetics/> Accessed March 2013.

Tagore, R. and Elmhirst, L.K (1961), *Rabindranath Tagore. Pioneer in Education. Essays and Exchanges between Rabindranath Tagore and L.K. Elmhirst*, London: John Murray.

Taiwo, Olu (1998), *The Return Beat*, Unpublished PhD thesis, University of Winchester, UK.

Taiwo, Olu (2012), Unpublished email.

Taruskin, Richard (2005, 2009), *The Oxford History of Western Music*, 6 volumes, Oxford: Oxford University Press.

Taskin, Richard (1992) in Buhle, Mari Jo, Buhle, Paul and Georgakas, Dan (1992), *Encyclopaedia of the American Left*, Urbana and Chicago: University of Illinois Press.

Tavener, John (2005), Interview on *The Mystery of Faith* with June Boyce-Tillman, Winchester Theatre Royal, March 11th.

Taylor, Charles (2007), *A Secular Age*, Cambridge, MA and London: Belknap Press of Harvard University.

Taylor, Millie (2013), *Humanity, Community and Excess: 'Feel the flow' in musical theatre performance*. Inaugural lecture as Professor of Music Theatre, University of Winchester, UK.

Tchaikovsky, Peter (1878) Letter. In Vernon P.E. (ed.) (1970) *Creativity*, Harmondsworth: Penguin pp. 57–60.

Thalbourne, M.A., Bartemucci L, Delin P.S., Fox B. and Nofi O. (1997), Transliminality, its nature and correlates, *The Journal of the American Society for Psychical Research* 91, pp. 305–31.

Thatcher, Adrian (1999), Theology, Spirituality and the Curriculum – An Overview. In Thatcher Adrian (ed.) (1999), *Spirituality and the Curriculum*, London: Cassell, pp. 1–11.

Thomas, Terence and Manning Elizabeth (1995), The iconic function of music. In Brown, David and Loades Ann (eds) (1995), *The Sense of the Sacramental: Movement and Measure in Art and Music, Place and Time*, London: SPCK pp. 159–71.

Thompson, Kevin (2003), Forms of Resistance: Foucault on Tactical Reversal and Self-formation, *Continental Philosophy Review* 36, pp. 113–38.

Threshold choirs <http://thresholdchoir.org/> Accessed June 30th 2014.

Tillich, Paul (1964), *Theology of Culture*, New York: Oxford University Press.

Tillman, June B. (1976), *Exploring Sound*, London, Stainer and Bell.

Tillman, June B. (1983), *Forty Music Games to make and play*, Basingstoke: Macmillan.

Tillman, June B. (1987a), *Light the Candles*, Cambridge: Cambridge University Press.

Tillman, June B. (1987b) *The Christmas Search*, Cambridge: Cambridge University press.

Tillman, June B. (1987c) *Towards a model of the development of musical creativity: A Study of the Compositions of Children aged 3–11*. Unpublished PhD Thesis, University of London Institute of Education.

Tinker, George E. (2004), The Stones Shall Cry Out: Consciousness, Rocks, and Indians, *Wicazo Sa Review* 19.2 (Fall), pp. 105–25.

Tippett, Michael (1974), *Moving into Aquarius*, London: Aquarius.

Tisdell, E. (2007), In the new millennium: The role of spirituality and the cultural imagination in dealing with diversity and equity in the Higher Education Classroom, *Teachers College Record*, 109, pp. 531–60.

Tolstoy, Leo (1930), *What Is Art?* London: Oxford University Press.

Trevarthen, Colwyn (1979), Communication and cooperation in early infancy. A description of primary intersubjectivity. In Bullowa, M. (ed.) (1979) *Before Speech: The Beginning of Human Communication*, London: Cambridge University Press, pp. 321–47.

Tomkins, Silvan S. (1962), *Affect, imagery, consciousness: Vol. I. The positive affects*, Oxford: Springer.

Toms, Michael (ed.) (1997), *The Well of Creativity*, Carlsbad CA: Hay House.

Tournemire, Charles (1936), *Precis d'execution, de registration et d'improvisation a l'orgue*, Paris: Max Eschig.

Tracy, D. (1975), *Blessed Rage for Order: The New Pluralism in Theology*, Chicago: University of Chicago Press.

Transcendental Meditation (2012) <http://en.wikipedia.org/wiki/Transcendental_Meditation_technique> accessed June 4th 2012.

Tremayne, Peter (1997), *The Spider's Web: A Celtic Mystery*, London: Headline.

Trotter, Yorke, *Principles of Musicianship*, London: Bosworth and Co Ltd, Published at the beginning of the twentieth century.

Tschudi, Finn (2005) *Accepting vulnerability – necessary for a good society?* Revised draft of paper for Telemark symposium August 18–21 2005 <http://www.humiliationstudies.org/documents/TschudiAcceptingVulnerability.pdf> Accessed 12, 28 August 3rd 2008.

Tubbs, Nigel (1998), What is Love's Work? *Women: A Cultural review Vol. 9, No. 1* October pp. 34–46.

Turino, Thomas (1999), Signs of Imagination, Identity, and Experience: A Peircian Semiotic Theory for Music, *Ethnomusicology* 43, 2, pp. 221–55.

Turner, Steve (1988), *Hungry for Heaven*, London: Virgin Books.

Turner, David H. (2001), *From here into eternity: Power and Transcendence in Australian Aboriginal Music*. In Ralls-MacLeod, Karen and Harvey, Graham. (eds) (2001), *Indigenous Religious Musics*, Farnborough: Scolar, pp. 35–55.

Turner, Victor (1969, 1974), *The Ritual process: Structure and Anti-structure*, Baltimore: Penguin Books.

Turner, Victor (1982), *From Ritual to Theatre: The Human Seriousness of Play*, New York: PAJ Publications.

Turner, Victor (2004) <http://www.creativeresistance.ca/communitas/defining-liminality-and-communitas-with-excerpts-by-victor-turner.htm> Accessed June 25th 2004 Unpublished paper.

Urbain, Olivier (ed.) (2008), *Music and Conflict Transformation: Harmonies and Dissonances in Geopolitics*, London: I.B. Tauris.

VanderArk, S., Newman, I, and Bell S. (1983), The effects of music participation on quality of life of the elderly, *Music Therapy, 3*, pp. 71–81.

Van Gennep, Arnold ([1909] 1960), *The Rites of Passage*, London: Routledge & Kegan Paul.

Van der Weyer, Robert (ed.) (1997), *Hildegard in a Nutshell*, London: Hodder and Stoughton.

Vella-Burrows, Trish (2012), *Singing with people with dementia*, Canterbury: Canterbury Christchurch University.

Vella-Burrows, Trish and Hancox, Grenville (2012), *Singing and People with Parkinson's*, Canterbury: Canterbury Christchurch University.

Vernon, P.E. (ed.) (1970), *Creativity*, Harmondsworth: Penguin.

Vinacke, William Edgar (1952), Creative thinking. In Vinacke W.E. (ed.) (1952) *The Psychology of Thinking*, New York: McGraw-Hill, pp. 238–61.

Vitz, Paul (1979), *Psychology as Religion: The Cult of Self Worship*, London: Lion.

Voegelin, Salome (2010), *Listening to Noise and Silence: Toward a Philosophy of Sound Art*, New York and London: Continuum.

Vygotsky, L.S. (1925/1987), Psikhologiya Iskusstva (The Psychology of Art), Moscow: Pedagogica pp. 330–31 quoted in Jordanger, Vegar (2008) Verbal and musical dialogues in the North-Caucasus – creating transnational citizenship through art, Paper delivered at *International Peace Research Association Conference*, Leuven University, Belgium, July.

Walker, Jan and Boyce-Tillman, June (2002), Music Lessons on prescription? The impact of music lessons for children with chronic anxiety problems, *Health Education – The Arts and Health*, Vol. 102, No. 4, pp. 172–9.

Walker, Wyatt Tee (1979), *'Somebody's calling my name': Black Sacred Music*, Valley Forge: Judson Press.

Wallas, Carl. (1926), The Art of thought. In Vernon P.E. (ed.) (1970) *Creativity*, Harmondsworth: Penguin pp. 91–7.

Ward, Hannah and Wild, Jennifer (1995), *Guard the Chaos: Finding Meaning in Change*, London: Darton, Longman and Todd.

Warnock, Mary (1999), *Music and Imagination*, Lecture given to the Bernarr Rainbow Society, London University Institute of Education.

Waterman, Fanny (2010), Interview on *Desert Island Discs*, Programme broadcast on BBC Radio 4 July 9th.

Wellbeing Community Choir <http://www.ukrw2013.co.uk/wellbeingcommunitychoir>. Accessed Oct 1st 2014.

Westerlund, Heidi (2002), *Bridging Experience, Action, and Culture in Music Education*, Studia Musica 16, Helsinki: Sibelius Academy.

Westheimer, Dr Ruth (2003), *Musically Speaking: A Life through Song*, Philadelphia: University of Pennsylvania Press.

Wheeler, B.L. (1985), The Relationship of Personal Characteristics to Mood and Enjoyment after hearing live and recorded music and to musical taste, *Psychology of Music* 13, pp. 81–92.

White, Dominic (2015), *The Lost Knowledge of Christ*, Collegeville, Minnesota: Liturgical Press.

Whitehead, Alfred North (1929), *Process and Reality. An Essay in Cosmology. Gifford Lectures Delivered in the University of Edinburgh During the Session 1927–1928*, Macmillan: New York, Cambridge: Cambridge University Press.

Whitehead, Alfred North (1975), *A Philosopher Looks at Science*, London: Harper Collins.

Wigglesworth, Cindy (2012), *SQ21: The Twenty-one skills of Spiritual Intelligence*, New York: Select Books.

Wilber, Ken (1997), *The Eye of the Spirit: An integral Vision for a World gone slightly mad*, Boston, Mass: Shambhala Publications.

Wilber, Ken (2000), *Integral Psychology: Consciousness, Spirit, Psychology, Therapy*, Boston: Shambhala Publications.

Wilcock, Liz (1997), Unpublished interview.

Willett, J. (1978), *Brecht on Theatre*, London: Eyre Methuen.

Williams, Nicholas (2009), Review *in the Church Times* Feb 27th.

Williams, Rowan (1994), Keeping Time. In Williams, Rowan (ed.) (1994), *Open to Judgement*, London: Darton, Longman and Todd, pp. 247–50.

Williams, Rowan (2012), *Faith in the Public Square*, London: Bloomsbury.

Wilson, Ken (2009), *Mystically Wired: Exploring New Realms in Prayer*, Nashville: Thomas Nelson.

Winnicott, D. (1971), *Playing and Reality*, London: Tavistock.

Witkin, Robert (1974), *The Intelligence of Feeling*, London: Heinemann.

Woodham, A. and Peters D. (1998), *Encyclopaedia of Complementary Medicine*, Edinburgh: Churchill Livingstone.

Woodworth, R.S. (1934), *Psychology*, New York: Henry Holt.

Wolffe, John (1994), *God and Greater Britain*, London: Routledge.

Wright, Stephen G. and Sayre-Adams, Jean (2009 first published 2000), *Sacred Space – Right Relationship and Spirituality in Healthcare*, Cumbria: Sacred Space Publications.

Wuthnow, Robert (1998), *After Heaven: Spirituality in America since the 1950s*, Berkeley and Los Angeles: University of California Press.

Wuthnow, Robert (2005), *America and the Challenges of Religious Diversity*, Princeton: Princeton University Press.

Yalom, I.D. (1985), *The Theory and Practice of Group Psychotherapy*, London: Basic Books.

Yaran, Cafer (2007), *The Varieties of Religious Experience of Muslims in Turkey*, Paper presented at the Conference of the British Association for the Study of Religions, University of Edinburgh 3rd–6th Sept.

Yeorgouli-Bourzoucos, Styliani (2004), *Improvisation in the Curriculum of the Special Music Schools in Hellas*, Unpublished PhD thesis, University College, Winchester, UK.

Yinger, Olivia Swedberg (2014), Adapting choral singing experiences for older adults: The implications of sensory, perceptual and cognitive changes, *International Journal of Music Education*, Vol. 32 No. 2 May pp. 203–12.

Yob, Iris (2001), Cognitive Emotions and Emotional Cognitions in Religious Studies, *Religion and Education*, Vol. 28, No. 1, Spring, pp. 95–14.

Zaehner, Robert Charles (1957), *Mysticism: Sacred and Profane*, Oxford: Clarendon Press.

Zinnbauer, Brian J., Pargament, Kenneth I., Cola, Brenda, Rye, Mark S., Butter, Eric M., Belavich, Timothy G., Hipp, Kathleen M., Scott, Allie, B. and Kadar, Jill L. (1997), Religion and Spirituality: Unfuzzying the Fuzzy, *Journal for the Scientific Study of Religion*, Vol. 36, No. 4 (Dec.), pp. 549–64.

Zohar, D. and Marshall, I. (2004), *Spiritual Capital: The Wealth We Can Live By,* San Francisco: Berrett Koehler.

Index

Music and Spirituality

Edited by

JUNE BOYCE-TILLMAN

Music and Spirituality explores the relationships between spirituality and music in a variety of traditions and contexts including those in which human beings have performed music with spiritual intention or effect. It will address the plurality of modern society in the areas of musical style and philosophical and religious beliefs, and give respect to different positions regarding the place of music both in worship and in the wider society. It will include historical, anthropological, musicological, ethnomusicological, theological and philosophical dimensions and encourage multi-disciplinary and cross-disciplinary contributions.

It looks for well-researched studies with new and open approaches to spirituality and music and will encourage interesting innovative case-studies. Books within the series are subject to peer review and will include single and co-authored monographs as well as edited collections including conference proceedings. It will consider the use of musical material in either written or recorded form as part of submissions.

The Series Editor

The Rev Professor June Boyce-Tillman MBE is Professor of Applied Music at the University of Winchester, where she runs the Centre for the Arts as Well-being. She has wide experience in education, spirituality and music and has published widely in these areas. She is a self-supporting ordained Anglican Priest and received an MBE for her contribution to music and education.

Proposal submissions should be sent to oxford@peterlang.com

Vol. 1 June Boyce-Tillman
In Tune With Heaven Or Not: Women in Christian Liturgical Music. 2014. ISBN 978-3-0343-1777-1

Vol. 2 June Boyce-Tillman
Experiencing Music – Restoring the Spiritual: Music as Well-being. 2016. ISBN 978-3-0343-1952-2

Praise for *Experiencing Music –Restoring the Spiritual*

'Music surrounds us on a daily basis, but do we have any real understanding of it? In a society that increasingly prizes visual stimulus and instant gratification, music can easily seem peripheral and little more than ornamental. Within the western art tradition, current comparisons of minor differences in the interpretation of art music and an obsession with the aesthetically pleasing can only mean that the position of music in our lives is in danger of being reduced to a sadly primitive stage. To the old patrician assumption that *classical* music is the only truly valuable part of our activity, this revolutionary book is the perfect antidote. Drawing upon a global range of sources and disciplines, June Boyce-Tillman displays immense flair, imagination and intelligence as she invokes an altogether broader concept of musical experience. In her own inimitable way she contrives to weave together philosophy, theology, musics, poetry and musical practice in the course of her spiritual journey, which effectively portrays truth as a crystal whose different facets act as lenses to reveal different aspects of itself. This transformational book extends way beyond musical agendas to explore and celebrate the very question of what it is to be human.'

— PROFESSOR COLIN LAWSON,
Director, Royal College of Music